PRIVATIZATION
Critical Perspectives on the World Economy

PRIVATIZATION
Critical Perspectives on the World Economy

Edited by George Yarrow and Piotr Jasiński

VOLUME IV

Routledge
Taylor & Francis Group
LONDON AND NEW YORK

First published 1996 by Routledge

2 Park Square, Milton Park, Abingdon, Oxfordshire OX14 4RN
52 Vanderbilt Avenue, New York, NY 10017

Routledge is an imprint of the Taylor & Francis Group, an informa business

First issued in hardback 2019

Typeset in 10pt Times by Solidus (Bristol) Ltd

British Library Cataloguing in Publication Data
A catalogue record for this book is available from the British Library

Library of Congress Cataloguing in Publication Data
A catalogue record for this book has been requested

ISBN 978-0-415-12124-8 (set)
ISBN 978-0-415-14324-0 (vol. 1)
ISBN 978-0-415-14325-7 (vol. 2)
ISBN 978-0-415-14326-4 (vol. 3)
ISBN 978-0-415-14327-1 (vol. 4) (hbk)

Contents

VOLUME IV

Part XIII Transformational Privatization: The Design

Part XIV Associated Issues

PART XIII: Transformational Privatization: The Design

68

Property Reform as a Basis for Social and Economic Reform

Janusz Lewandowski and Jan Szomburg

Source: *Communist Economies*, 1(3), 1989, pp. 257–68.

Assumptions

The passage of time spent discussing and testing a variety of half-measures stimulates an increasingly bold quest for economically efficient solutions, free from any doctrinal prejudice. This economic pragmatism, however, must take account of the real balance of forces, the power of the administration, widespread passivity and general disbelief in any potential improvement. Along with market disequilibrium, inflation, decapitalisation and foreign debt, these are fundamental features of the current situation and must be included in any potential scenario of changes.

As there is general agreement about the course and achievements of economic reform in Poland hitherto, our preliminary diagnosis can be brief. The main failures of the economic reforms carried out so far are as follows:

- the lack of a breakthrough in the economic performance of companies. Instead of the entrepreneurship and innovative behaviour which had been expected in the production of real goods and services, ingenuity and resourcefulness have been directed to regulation and the accompanying tax pathology and sharp accounting practices;
- inadequate care for productive assets and the lack of objective asset pricing;
- the lack of what, back in 1981, was called 'conversion of productive assets' and is now referred to as 'restructuring'. Instead of a mechanism which would ensure an efficient allocation of resources, we still have the rivalries of various industrial lobbies, which contribute to the perpetuation of our distorted production and investment structures;
- the lack of potential risk-takers, i.e. the lack of initiatives which could shake up the monopolised core of our economy;

- the lack of hard budget constraints and natural selection of the better and more efficient firms.

These ills, which have so far proved incurable, form a specific 'langour syndrome', showing that economic reform failed to strike at the sources of the economic inadequacy of 'real socialism'. This obviously leads to doubts about the sense and sincerity of reform efforts confined to the streamlining of management, which evade the possibility of political changes or a serious approach to the question of ownership. The present-day diagnosis reaches deeply into property relations and has gone far beyond the mental threshold of the early 1980s, and beyond the horizons of Kornai's analysis of the 'economy of shortage'.

The division of property rights between the founding organ, employees' self-management and the director, which was a direct consequence of the political compromise of 1981, ushered new nominal 'co-owners' onto the economic scene; new holders of state property, apart from the administration which had always been the state's traditional trustee. It can hardly be viewed as a step towards the establishment of economic responsibility, and still less towards financial responsibility.

The present system can enforce production quotas and extract revenue or taxes from companies, or ensure the observance of specific directive indices, but it cannot enforce responsibility for their property. There is still no one to lose anything from the decapitalisation of state property. We do not even recognise economic obsolescence, nor have we escaped from the book-keeping approach to asset pricing which ignores the assets' profitability.

Moving along the existing axis of economic reform brings us no nearer to an economy where property interests are represented, ushering new logic into the economic system, to replace the outgoing logic of administrative management. No 'tuning' of the system, be it the managerial or self-management variant, can produce miracles with respect to attitudes and motivation, just as changes in the formal position regarding the protection of state assets cannot introduce an economic approach to the pricing of the means of production. Property rights must be exclusive and transferable to ensure that the right to dispose of productive assets could take the form of control over capital rather than over the physical assets.

All the above is conventional wisdom nowadays, repeated in concert by all economists. A breakthrough reform must therefore satisfy the following criteria:

- to bring new actors into the centre, not merely the periphery of the economic scene. These actors would have to represent the interests of ownership, that is, to exercise the full range of property rights in order to maximise long-term income from capital;
- to create a mechanism of capital allocation, which would be set in motion

by the interests of ownership and would ensure the market pricing of assets.

These are the criteria which should be used in the evaluation of concepts, and we shall base our reasoning on them in the remainder of this paper.

Choice of Solution

Stimulated by the diagnosis outlined above and the already recognised need for the transformation of property relations, reform thought offers a number of concepts which are evidence of the dynamically developing discussion and the shattering of many doctrinal barriers in the countries of 'real socialism'.

We devote least attention to proposals insisting on investing still more time and effort into the streamlining of state ownership, even though they are likely to be implemented, given that they reflect the economic philosophy of the current ruling elite, and some time will still be spent on testing their illusory value.

The concept of boards of directors has been resuscitated, though to a limited extent. In the years 1980–81 this was an alternative to the self-management philosophy and postulated as a way to socialise control over state companies, through broad representation of the interests of the 'remaining owners' (e.g. consumer, ecological and local interests). It is obvious that this points in exactly the opposite direction to the idea of exclusive and transferable property rights, and the responsibility the latter involve. The decision-making system offered by a coalitionist board of directors is inadequate for the competitive environment of the non-state sector, but can be very useful as an instrument of reform in public utilities, and that is the role it will play in our model.[1]

The concept of leasing state property to groups of people or simply entrepreneurs, already in practice in some CMEA countries, is more promising. Under these arrangements the State Treasury remains the legal owner of the property and receives interest on the capital. This model offers certain opportunities for the legal 'fine tuning' of decision-making rights and responsibility for day-to-day running, but clearly fails to meet our criteria for the fullest possible articulation of ownership interests and for ensuring efficient resource allocation. In other words, this model focuses on day-to-day operation, while we need solutions which would take care of assets and investment in the long term, which in addition would offer better chances to liberate companies from negative administrative control and informal pressures. The legal innovations of 1988 and the guidelines of the 'consolidation plan' seem to herald the official version: the transformation of state companies into partnerships of the State Treasury and other institutional shareholders (banks, local self-governments), or even with a dash of employees' shareholdings, plus some germs of a capital market, in the form of bonds. Extrapolating this trend, we end up with a vision of a *quasi-capital game played by state and mixed partnerships*, with a prospective stock exchange, the right to issue bonds and to buy out other companies.[2] This project for the reorganisation of the state sector seems to take account of the need to graft some elements of the capital market onto our economy and to increase the adaptability of economic organisations. However, just like the other proposals concerning changes in control over state property, it commits one mortal sin: it promises more than the formula of state property as such can deliver.

There is ample evidence to be drawn from the experience of West European countries to demonstrate that there are certain impassable limits to the rationalisation of state property, which in these countries is only an element of an exacting, competitive and 'tough' economic environment and of a different work culture. First there were attempts to 'commercialise' the public sector, then to 'deregulate' it; and eventually, they decided on privatisation. It can be assumed beforehand, therefore, that the level of rationalisation of state companies in Poland will be considerably lower—and we might as well reject any illusions about it. There can be no convergence of the market behaviour of state and private companies, and the logic of administrative supervision will always differ from that of private shareholders. The administration will always represent bureaucratic logic and will not adopt the logic of the capital 'game'.

With an 'un-democratised' political structure there are additional features reinforcing the thesis that the projected partnerships with the State Treasury, as the dominant future company type, are only an illusory step forward in comparison with the model of the company negotiated in the 1980–81 period. The elimination of employees' self-management, which occasionally confirmed its merits as a defence against administrative high-handedness, increases rather than diminishes the danger of politicisation of the economy.

Rejecting projects which involve the streamlining of state ownership, which we regard as a continuation of the present strategy of 'pacing around, doing nothing', we see three reform options which can stand up in the face of the conceptual and practical challenges confronting the countries which are trying to grapple with post-Stalinist economic and political structures:

(A) a laissez-faire programme of lifting all barriers to the growth of the private sector, in the hope of a spontaneous healing of the economy;
(B) the quest for an original model of a non-state and non-private economy;
(C) the scenarios of active privatisation and attempts to bring the economy as near as possible to the private capitalist model of economic efficiency.

The first option (A) is a bet on the spontaneous effects of equal rights for all sectors and on the liberation of human resourcefulness. As an act of faith in self-reliance and the virtues of economic freedom, which are essential after years of contrary propaganda and the perpetuation of passive attitudes, it offers important benefits in terms of changing attitudes. However, this programme of economic revival through the cessation of administering and clearing the field for social enterprise is insufficient, even if complemented with the necessary government measures aimed at economic demonopolisation and deconcentration. The state-owned industrial core of the economy is too important just to wait for it to wither.[3] The decline of state ownership in capital-intensive areas would be too slow.

It is not only the pace of spontaneous privatisation which would be a problem. There are important fears about the prospective synergy effect between the theoretically doomed state-owned sector and the rising wave of new entrepreneurship. These effects can be anticipated already, by watching state companies take advantage of their recently expanded margin of freedom in the organisational sphere and the role of partnerships in this process.

Observations from the coastal region of Gdansk are both rich and instructive in this respect. The pace of development of new entrepreneurship is quite astounding, while the sociological aspect of the phenomenon is interesting insofar as it was partly the result of numerous former 'Solidarity' activists looking for a new, independent way of living, as a specific alternative to emigration. First, in 1982, the revision of the law on co-operatives had stimulated the creation of quite a number, while partnerships have become the vogue since 1985, that is, since the new law on partnerships was enacted. In 1985 there were only 25 partnerships, while there are 1300 now and others are waiting for registration. It is largely the product of an autonomous and healthy economic drive amongst young engineers, architects, data processing specialists, artists, lawyers or leisure time organisers. Facing ruthless taxation, however, these initiatives fail to generate enough capital for further expansion.[4] The relaxation of tax policies, however, can be expected to enable them to cross a certain capital threshold, while additional legal and political guarantees will permit the tapping for productive purposes of the resources of *Gastarbeiter*, which are hard to estimate.

However, one should not overrate the scale of this phenomenon. Proportions are the key element, because since 1987 there has been an increasing number of state companies which set up partnerships. The wage and tax motives behind this sudden interest in partnerships are quite clear and generally known. Dockers work in ports, shipbuilders in the shipyards, with fixed assets and materials which belong to state companies; however, they are better paid via partnerships, state firms' directors or their relatives find their way to lucrative positions on partnerships' boards and become private shareholders in these endeavours, while the continuity of production is ensured. One could say this leads to a better and more efficient use of human and material resources.

Doubts arise, however, when we look at this phenomenon from the point of view of the hypothetical owner of these assets, interested in their preservation and replacement. It then turns out to be a case of legalised parasitism. The point is that the interests of ownership are not represented. Other doubts arise when we look at the symbiosis of state companies and partnerships from the viewpoint of market structure and competition: what we are witnessing is the creation of closed circuits, inaccessible to outsiders: cheaper does not necessarily mean better. The capital barrier, often encountered by new partnerships, is easily overcome in these cases.

Such reactions, which can be observed between the private and state sector already, inspire scepticism with regard to the prospect of rivalry and victory of the 'new' forces of entrepreneurship over the 'old' state sector. Instead of the rivalry we might expect, we may well witness a durable compromise, a pathological symbiosis of the 'new' with the 'old', which will reproduce the sick tissues of the state-owned economy. The natural withering of state ownership would be too lengthy a process, contaminating the whole environment. This is why economic euthanasia is required.

What should be the objective of conscious remodelling of property relations in 'real socialism'? Is the choice of the 'third way' as a target model dictated by current economic considerations, is it a manifested social preference, or is it a consciously sub-optimal choice, an *Ersatz* as it were, adopted for tactical reasons only?

The 'third way,' between a state-owned economy and a private one, would consist in the transformation of state property into *group property*, which would link employment in a firm with a title to its property. The concept of collective ownership by the employees is a natural extension of the idea of employees' self-management, discussed in 1980–81 mostly in connection with decision-making rights, with some timid hinting at the issues of ownership and responsibility. (The Network of Leading Organisations of the Independent Trade Union 'Solidarity' withdrew its concept in the face of widespread criticism). The legislative solutions in Poland followed the line of 'joint management without joint material responsibility', while Yugoslavia has a rather artificial model in which the attributes of ownership are divided between the employees and society as a whole, and the statutory capital is not the responsibility of the employees.

Theoretically, there are several variants of group ownership which can be considered. First come the collective variant (the employees as a collective holder of property) and the individualised variant (employees' shareholdings).[5] However, since we are discussing functional solutions for large and medium companies, the collective variant must be dropped as artificial and impracticable. Nowadays, only employees' shareholdings are a real alternative to state ownership. It would no doubt be a step forward, towards the liberation of economic life from administrative control and the *nomenklatura*. There are opinion poll results showing that the concept of employees' shareholdings is gaining support in the community of industrial workers and might well be the free choice of company employees if such a choice were offered.

Yugoslav experience shows that delegating decision-making rights downwards, to the level of the so-called basic units of collective work, can trigger off disintegration processes, that is, self-propelled processes leading to the decentralisation and dismantling of large economic organisations. Both the Yugoslav model and Western experiments with employees' shareholdings are the subject of a broad technical literature, which relieves us from the obligation to discuss their drawbacks and merits here.

Coming back to the mainstream of our deliberations, we must observe that the concept of employees' shareholdings, while creating the problem of share purchasing rights, which is common to all concepts of privatisation from above, fails to satisfy our criteria fully. The logic of this solution creates a system of exclusive but non-transferable property rights. Control over shares is to be directly tied to employment. Leaving a company would have to mean the loss of property rights, unless we assume that what we want is a formula leading through an employee-ownership stage to a system of shares accessible to all and freely transferable. The ideal model of group property creates no premises for the development of a capital market, nor does it favour grassroot-level restructuring processes. By linking the whole of employees' incomes—both wages and dividends—with a particular company, it makes resource allocation even less flexible. Hence, it is a highly unsatisfactory solution from the point of view of the requirements of restructuring, and introduces one more rigid element into the system which is already highly adept at reproducing a distorted production structure.

Checking reform options (A) and (B) against the criteria adopted earlier, we find that they fail to guarantee efficiency. Neither the administration, concerned with the material effects and the day-to-day operation, nor the employees, interested mostly in their current incomes, are able to act as real owners and take part in the capital game. The interests of ownership cannot be simulated by some artificial body, nor can such nominal owners operate in the capital market. There is no way to make the nominal owners behave as if they were really taking the risks. The game must be played between the real property interests of well-defined subjects, exercising their exclusive property rights to maximise their rewards. Once we make this observation we pass the third threshold of naivety in reform thinking, if we take Lange's illusions as the first, and our own illusions—that the 1980–81 model companies ('independent, self-managing, self-financing'), being legally separated parts of state property, can promise any improvement in economic performance—as the second. The third threshold is the illusion that one can simulate the operation of a capital market, thereby obtaining true pricing indications and efficient capital allocation. We already know it is impossible and can admire the perspicacity of Ludwig von Mises, who had ridiculed such illusions as long ago as the 1920s.

This, therefore, is the end to illusions that we can found our economic development and the progress of our civilisation on economic mechanisms fundamentally different from those which have proved their efficiency elsewhere. Thus, while we generally support the pluralism of forms and free choice of solutions, we see the reform of property relations as the main link in the further transformation of the society of 'real socialism' towards a system promising better economic performance.

Strategy of Property Reform

The core of our proposal is a real and radical transfer of property rights from the state administration to the broad masses of society. We postulate that amorphous state ownership be transformed by an act of the authorities into a system of individual and transferable property rights to the existing productive assets.

Such an operation could be called the expropriation of the state or privatisation, but it is essentially a *socialisation of ownership through reprivatisation*; an actual transfer of real property rights to those who are the nominal owners by virtue of the constitution. Dispersed ownership or generalised private ownership are a more real form of socialisation than formal declarations which differ blatantly from reality. This was how Wilhelm Roepke understood the essence of his programme of 'deproletarisation' (*Entproletarisierung*) and that is also the core of the motto '*redemptio proletatorium*' drawn from the social teachings of the Church.[6] In any case, it is not the words that count, but the way the operation is carried out, its economic and social sense, and its potential impact.

The country's situation determines the kind of strategy required; it must be a real, radical denationalisation of the economy and not merely formal. Second, the operation will have to be carried out in a poor country. Thus, we come to the issue of capital scarcity among the population, which is often raised as a barrier to reprivatisation. The need to denationalise the economy radically and rapidly dictates the position we take on the controversial issue of 'sale vs. free distribution'. The sale of state property, leading to a society of shareholders, is not a feasible task, although it may supplement free distribution, to the extent that it is possible given the ratio of the population's resources to the value of state property.

We are familiar with the arguments in favour of sale. It can generate additional funds for the budget (restoring its balance) and can be a deflationary operation (a way to restore equilibrium in the consumer market). These are no doubt valid arguments, but they must give way to simple necessity. The optimists estimate the time horizon of reprivatisation at 15 to 20 years, the pessimists put it at 100 years plus. The social response to the prospect of economic transformation at this pace is obvious. No programme involving such a distant perspective can stimulate minds, overcome apathy and lack of faith, or cure 'emigration sickness'. The economy and society need a sharp turnaround, an awakening from lethargy, a breakthrough in the real and the psychological spheres—of the kind the West German population experienced in 1948 and Poland did back in the time of the Grabski reform. Poland has been drifting without hope for a number of years already, as the substantial emigration of young people demonstrates; the reform must be considered as a shock therapy, not a process stretching over 15 or 20 years.

The act of distribution of state property, so that every Polish household had some property rights, which could be potentially tested in a stock market, might well have a certain mobilising impact.

Parallel to that, however, as a second element of stimulation, society must be made aware of the economic imperatives that the elimination of the 'protective umbrella' of the state entails. Loss-making companies should have to start fighting for survival in their current or other organisational forms, as happened in the Gdansk Shipyard and in its environment after the sudden decision to close it down in October 1988. While the first element can be called positive motivation ('the carrot' is offered), the second one is a negative incentive ('the stick' is threatened).

The third element of the breakthrough should consist of lifting all barriers which choke human enterprise. We are also aware of the social dimension of this issue, as it would initiate the process of transformation of a society of hired hands into one of shareholders, entrepreneurs and rentiers. The depth of this social transformation and its pace, and the potential benefits in the elimination of passive attitudes and the potential risks it may bring, remain unknown. Nevertheless, the sociological dimension of the reprivatisation of the public sector has been very strongly emphasised in all countries where this operation was designed to create a broad class of small shareholders—mostly in the UK and other rich countries, but also in Brazil and Chile. It was a conscious operation designed to turn savings into capital and thereby create the broad stratum of risk-taking individuals required to revive the economies. This aspect of property reform is also very important to Poland.

Technique of Property Reform

Making the transition from the existing form of state ownership to the new model of property relations would involve crossing a certain threshold, which we shall call the property reform threshold, and which should create the premises for further unrestricted evolution of the ownership structure, with the use of the capital market as a regulator of subsequent changes. The preliminary operation, initiated by the Property Reform Act, would have to implement simultaneously objectives which are not easily reconciled:

- to overcome the scarcity of capital among the population, through the free

distribution of property rights (property certificates) and the parallel holding of sales of shares by tender in order to value company assets and initiate capital flow to the most attractive industries;
- to liberate companies from administrative control and subject them to control by the shareholders and, at the same time, satisfy the self-management aspirations of employees;
- to eliminate inflationary threats through temporary restrictions on share trading (sale), paralleled by the creation of the conditions required for the proper operation of the capital market and its barometer—the stock exchange.

As for the implementation of these principles, we actually have more questions than ready answers. The fundamental ones are: 'Who are to be given property rights?' and 'What is to be privatised?'

Our conception of who are to be given property rights is that all Polish citizens aged 18 plus would receive property certificates of equal face value, worth about 1 million zlotys per person. The Property Reform Act would thus embrace about 24 million persons. The face value of these property certificates would be calculated as the quotient of the book value of state property subject to expropriation (less the estimated resources of the population and of the non-state sector) and of the number of people covered by the Act. Property certificates would be registered in holders' names and could not be sold, but used only to acquire shares through the stock exchange.

Expropriation would embrace all existing state companies in the competitive sector, which would first be converted into joint stock companies, with the following exceptions and restrictions:

- a clearly delimited area of the infrastructure and public utilities would remain state property;
- state companies which become communal property controlled by local self-governments shall be exempted from expropriation;
- the State Treasury shall retain 49% of the shares in a specified number of companies in key industries;
- the assets of the economically weakest companies shall be distributed without the intermediary of the stock exchange. The right to buy-out such companies with the help of state credits would be offered first to their employees and management, then to other private legal and physical persons, domestic and foreign, and lastly, to state-owned institutions.

A schedule setting out the dates on which trading in particular shares would begin on the regional stock exchanges would be officially announced. The holders of property certificates would at their own discretion decide when to go to the exchange to buy shares, or would entrust their certificates to stock exchange brokers. It is further assumed that specialised consultancy would be available.

Apart from the free distribution of shares through property certificates, any physical person could buy an unlimited number of shares. The issues of transferable shares should be designed to match the estimated resources held by the population and private legal entities. Apart from the issues of ordinary stock, companies would issue privileged shares intended for their employees. Property certificate holders employed in reprivatised companies could choose between two courses of action; they could either acquire the ordinary shares of other companies, at their current stock exchange price, or they could acquire privileged shares in the company they work for, receiving a fixed discount of, say, 25% of the stock market price. Shares for employees should have privileged voting rights and could be an exception to the 1 vote per share rule. To some extent, this would help to meet self-management aspirations under the new conditions, as well as solving the problem of effective supervision over reprivatised companies.

The elimination of the present founding organs would create a vacuum, which theoretically should be filled by the shareholders. This, however, should not take place under conditions of total chaos, nor should the first shareholders' meeting, which will elect the board, be held in such conditions. We believe that the employees should have a decisive vote, at least in the first round, and therefore have the right to nominate the management (organising the contest for the post of chief executive).[7] We opt for such a beginning even though we realise that this is a factor which will make resource allocation less flexible. The employees can increase their leverage by buying ordinary shares, on top of the privileged stock. The opposite situation, where the employees have no interest in the shares of their company, may also arise. We leave the problem of control over such companies in the transition period without an answer, as we do the issue of the necessary restrictions on free share trading in the transition period (and later). We shall only point out the need to set up safeguards against:

- the preponderance of institutions, especially state-owned institutions, over the population in terms of disposable purchasing power, which entails the risk of recurring renationalisation;
- the risk of inflation in the event that the preference for liquidity should prove too strong (the sale of stock bought for property certificates should be prohibited during the first year, until the first dividends are paid).

What could be considered is a pilot share issue and a preliminary auction designed to establish share prices, attended only by property certificate holders and private buyers, in order to guarantee them an appropriate share in reprivatised companies.

Supplementary Issues

It is obvious that property reform must be assisted by a number of ancillary operations and calls for some prerequisites to be met. We shall mention only the most important ones. Demonopolisation and deconcentration of the existing economic structures are fundamental conditions for the introduction of market regulation in Poland. Economic freedom in various directions, such as an open economy and movement towards currency convertibility, are inseparable elements in our reasoning. The internal convertibility of local currency is a prerequisite for the tapping of domestic hard-currency savings for the purposes of production. External convertibility and an open economy would make the policy of demonopolisation more realistic in Polish conditions and would also rationalise the price structure, aligning it with world patterns, thereby extending the scope of cost/benefit analysis and efficient allocation. Furthermore, it is required to stimulate investment of foreign capital.

We believe the participation of foreign capital is absolutely indispensable in the revival of the economy, both in joint ventures and in the sale by tender of privatised state companies. However, the doors should be opened to foreign capital only after the introduction of the new actors into our economic game, that is, after the property reform, so that foreign investors would be dealing with partners, customers or competitors who will be more or less similar to themselves in terms of goals and aggressiveness. Exploitation by foreign capital is a possible risk only if Polish companies fail to show an equally market-oriented approach, which can be said of the present-day state companies. The confrontation of partners so unequal in their commercial determination could presage the same pathology that we have today on the interface between the state and private sectors.

The infrastructure of the capital market must be built from scratch. A total lack of institutional patterns to follow, and of any experience whatsoever in this respect, produce a situation where even Third World reprivatisations may be said to have been carried out under comfortable conditions, in comparison with those under which ownership transformation has to start in Poland. We will not discuss stock exchanges, securities and other obvious elements of the infrastructure of the capital market here. We would like, however, to stress the need for the establishment of new institutional investors in our economy, taking care of small savings, investing them in securities and paying income thus earned to their clients.

The above would also call for a realignment of the tax system so as to mobilise small savings for production purposes and to stimulate reinvestment of profit. There are a number of good foreign patterns to follow in this respect, like the French *Loi Monory* of 1978, to name just one.

The considerably curtailed state property would have to undergo a major reorganisation. The State Treasury would have to become a legal entity, represented by the Finance Minister. It would take over the property rights to state-owned utilities from their existing founding organs. These socialised utility companies should be managed by boards of directors. Moreover, the State Treasury would take over state shareholdings in companies in the competitive sector. We also suggest an intermediate link between the State Treasury and the corporations partly owned by the state, in the form of a holding company. The management of such a holding company, responsible for state shareholdings in the corporations, would be accountable for and remunerated depending on the economic results of its activities. We feel this would be a way to depoliticise state control and make it more flexible.[8] Here we merely point out these issues, but for some time already they have been the object of animated discussions in the specialised press.

Guarantees and Questions

Reform concepts which assume the setting up of capital markets and the operation of exchanges with the broad participation of various social strata inevitably lead to the question of guarantees. The implementation of these concepts is hardly conceivable without some confidence in the stability of the rules of the game, failing which society will opt for liquidity and foreign capital will not invest. Hence, we come to the problem of credible guarantees, and a political compromise worked out in Poland alone would not appear to be a satisfactory solution to the problem. We concur with Andrzej Kozminski, that such an internal compromise would have to be endorsed by our main economic partners and foreign creditors. It would therefore be a multilaterally negotiated programme, which would have to provide, among other things, for a conditional rescheduling of our foreign debt.[9]

The problem of adequate guarantees is also only one of the questions. Questions and doubts can be raised in connection with almost any element of the programme we have presented here. If the most important ones concern the safeguards against renationalisation, others concern the behaviour of the population, the impact of the proposed operation on monetary and budget equilibrium and the appropriate set of instruments for financial and credit policies.

Notes and References

1. The decision-making system in a coalitionist board of directors was analysed by S. Kawalec in *Model samorządowy a inne koncepcje organizacyjne gospodarki zdominowanej przez nieprywatne przedsiębiorstwa* (Warsaw, 1985).
2. Among others, this includes the concepts presented by M. Swiecicki and A. Wroblewski.
3. M. Dabrowski, *Wlasnośc grupowa jako jedna z drog przekształcenia wlasności panstwowej* (Warsaw, 1988).

4. Here we draw on an unpublished article by K. Bielecki, 'Byk czy Torreador. O spólkach prawa handlowego w Polsce'. (Sopot, 1988).

5. The classification of the forms of collective property is presented, among other authors, by L. Balcerowicz, M. Dabrowski and Z. Laski.

6. W. Roepke, *Civitas Humana. A Human Order of Society* (London, 1948).

7. A practice introduced after 1981, whereby various bodies within a company, e.g. self-management, trade unions, etc., could hold a contest for the post of chief executive. Anyone meeting the requirements, from within the company or without, could enter the contest. This was meant as an alternative to appointments from the *nomenklatura*.

8. M. Swiecicki advocates holding companies as a form of control over state shareholdings.

9. A.K. Kozminski, 'Czas Negocjacji', *Przegląd Tygodniowy*, 1988, No. 45 (6 November 1988).

69

Privatisation of the Polish Economy

Stefan Kawalec

Source: *Communist Economies*, 1(3), 1989, pp. 241–56.

1. Introduction

Privatisation of the Polish economy is intended to achieve three objectives:

(1) transform the Polish economy into an open, market-type economy, dominated by private firms and having a convertible currency;
(2) create a broad stratum of shareholders to serve as the political base of the new economic system and ensure its political stability;
(3) minimise the social costs of the economic transformation, make these changes beneficial for the majority of the population and ensure that the benefits outweigh the losses, both in the long and short term.

Privatisation would follow a 'twin-tracked' policy:

(1) lifting those barriers which restrict the operation of the market and all current limitations imposed on the functioning of private firms, thereby creating the conditions for 'privatisation from below' through the development of existing and new private firms;
(2) launching a multi-stage 'privatisation from above' by selling shares in state enterprises so as to create as broad a group of private shareholders as possible and incidentally generate important revenue for the state budget.

In this paper I concentrate on 'privatisation from above'. I attempt to show how such privatisation can be carried out and what benefits can be achieved. I argue that such privatisation can facilitate the financing of a radical, market-oriented reform with voluntary savings of the population and that it offers the best guarantee of the durability of the economic freedoms thus introduced. In the final section I discuss the changes proposed in the ownership structure of the Polish economy and the operation of free markets that will make the country prosper.

2. Main Elements of the Programme

I believe that what is required is the introduction of institutional and tax regulations which would create a framework of unrestrained business activity and for the operation of free markets, creating the conditions for 'privatisation from below' to prosper. Parallel to that, the shares of a number of state companies should be put up for sale and a schedule for the privatisation of further companies should be announced.

The conditions necessary for unrestrained business activity are, in particular:

- freedom to set up private firms having different forms of ownership, such as single proprietorship, various forms of partnership, joint-stock companies (private and public);
- free entry into practically all areas of the economy for private firms (including foreign trade, banking and other financial services);
- no legal restrictions on the size of private firms;
- a tax system which would not curb the growth of private firms;[1].
- freedom of contract and freedom to set prices (except for limitations under anti-trust legislation);
- convertibility of domestic currency (at a floating exchange rate).

Sudden introduction of these regulations, the lifting of various non-market barriers which prevent companies from increasing their prices, and the introduction of currency convertibility in particular, could produce a very strong inflationary stimulus.[2] Selling shares in state companies could offset this inflationary pressure.

Firms selected for privatisation should be profitable, to make sure their shares find buyers, and the first group of privatised companies should be big enough significantly to reduce excess stocks of money held by the population and to create conditions under which a stock market could be set up and operated.

I believe the following principles should be respected with regard to privatisation:

- the pricing of shares in state companies selected for privatisation should make their purchase a very profitable investment for the prospective buyers, but, on the other hand, the revenue generated by the sale of a firm must not be too low in comparison with its future market value;
- shares should be sold so as to ensure the widest possible distribution;
- the employees of privatised companies should be granted the right to buy a certain number of shares at preferential prices.

Procedures for privatising a company could follow the following pattern.

Shares with the nominal value of say 100 zl. would be issued up to the nominal book value of company assets. A certain proportion of the shares, e.g.

20%, would be sold at an auction in which individual Polish citizens, domestic private firms and foreign investors could take part, to determine the clearing price for the bulk of the shares. All participants would put in bids for a definite number of shares (from the lot intended for sale by auction) at a specified tender price. Also, all participants would have to deposit performance bonds equal to, say, 5% of the value of their bids in a selected bank. When the bids are opened, it is possible to establish the clearing price, P_1, for all the shares to be sold by auction. P_1 would be the highest price at which available bids would permit the sale of all shares intended for the auction. All bidders offering prices higher than P_1 would be able to buy, at P_1, the number of shares specified in their bids. The number of shares which would be sold to those originally bidding at P_1 might have to be reduced to ensure that the total number of shares allotted equals the number of shares to be sold at the auction.

The analysis of the bids would indicate the approximate future equilibrium price for the company's shares on the stock market.[3] This, in turn, would be helpful in determining the price, P_2, at which the bulk, e.g. 70%, of all the shares of the company would be sold. The latter price should ensure that when the shares are traded on the stock exchange after the flotation their market value will be higher than P_2 or, in other words, that their purchasers will have a profitable deal.

Once price P_2 had been fixed, any Polish citizen would be able to place a bid for the desired number of shares. Foreigners would be debarred from buying shares at this stage in the process, as large capital gains are likely. If price P_2 had been correctly determined (i.e. in line with the above intentions) then demand should outstrip the number of shares available for sale at this price. In such a case, an analysis would be necessary to establish the maximum number of shares sold to a single person. All bids for no more than the maximum would be fully met, while those for more would be automatically trimmed to the maximum. If price P_2 had been overestimated and there were too few bids to cover all shares intended for sale at that price, then all bids should be satisfied in full, while the remaining shares of this lot should be cancelled, decreasing the nominal share capital of the firm.

The remainder of the shares, for instance 10%, should be distributed to the management and workforce, each of whom should receive a given number of shares for free or for a nominal fee.[4]

The distribution of the shares of a company being completed, trading in these shares would start on the stock market. The number of shares that a single Polish citizen would be allowed to purchase would then be unlimited. In general, foreign citizens and companies would be allowed to buy shares on the stock market, although some restrictions might be necessary. Setting price P_2 at the right level is essential to the success of the whole operation, since it would be the sale price for the bulk of the shares and also the reference price for the preferential price, P_3, for employees. The correct determination of P_2

will be made easier by the earlier pilot sale of a part of the stock by auction. However, there remains the risk that major mistakes can be made in the evaluation of the future market price of the shares. Setting P_2 too high should be the first mistake to be avoided. If the prices of the shares of a large proportion of privatised companies were initially set too high and found too few buyers or, still worse, their buyers should suffer losses (when the market price fell below the price originally paid to the state), then the whole programme could collapse owing to lack of demand for the shares of other firms.

Setting the price too low would mean the loss of a part of prospective budget income and would give large profits to those who had bought shares, especially the employees of privatised companies. This however would not jeapardise the whole privatisation programme. The observation of the (already operating) stock market in subsequent stages of privatisation would afford the opportunity to rectify mistakes made in share pricing in the early stages of privatisation. Budget losses incurred in the first stage of privatisation would not be all that important as a proportion of total budget income generated through privatisation.

It would be desirable to introduce uniform conditions of purchase for employees and management as soon as possible (e.g. shortly after the sale of the first group of companies and the beginning of stock market trading in their shares), so that both these groups (in enterprises to be privatised in the future) would strive to ensure the highest possible market value of their firms, with a view to the coming privatisation.[5]

3. Benefits from 'Privatisation from Above'

I believe that 'privatisation from above' could provide the following benefits if it were properly carried out:

- better economic performance in privatised companies and also in those expecting privatisation;
- more competition in the economy;
- important additional budget income, providing opportunities to combat inflation and to finance public expenditure;
- creation of a relatively broad base of individual shareholders, offering political guarantees of the durability of the newly introduced market principles and economic freedoms.

I now enumerate these potential benefits, trying to show why they can be expected to occur, and discuss their individual importance.

Privatised companies can be expected to improve their performance as a result of the exclusive dependence of company management on their shareholders. An average shareholder follows only his financial interests and cares little about what his company produces, where it has its plants, where it secures its supplies and to whom it sells its products, as long as it generates the expected income. Thus, monitoring by shareholders has two important advantages. First, it is likely to be efficient at forcing management to operate the company profitably. Second, as long as the company generates adequate earnings, the managers are free to act as they deem fit, and nobody interferes with their decisions. What is important for the monitoring of management in companies by shareholders is the fact that their stock is freely traded on the stock exchange. The less profit a company makes, the lower its stock will trade and the more likely it is to become a takeover target for someone seeking to acquire the company's assets cheaply. A controlling block of shares may be bought by persons or firms other than the currently dominant shareholders, which would typically lead to the replacement of a large proportion of the board of directors and senior management. Hence, the managers of a joint-stock company, wishing to retain their positions, must care about adequate earnings, so as to ensure a sufficiently high price of the stock in the market.[6]

The experience of capitalist countries shows that private companies tend to perform better in a competitive environment than state-owned companies operating under comparable conditions.[7]

After many years spent on seeking ways to improve the performance of state-owned companies, many democratic capitalist countries have arrived at the conclusion, now widely accepted, that the simplest solution to the problem consisted in turning them over to private owners.[8]

This pragmatic approach has produced a situation where not only right-wing governments, but also social-democratic governments of such countries as Spain, New Zealand or Greece are implementing or contemplating privatisation.[9]

Better performance can be expected not only in the already privatised companies, but also in those singled out for future privatisation.

If the privatisation of a company has been decided upon and its employees and management have the guarantee that they can buy a part of the shares on preferential terms (fixed at the time of announcement of the privatisation of the company), then they will be interested in improved performance, counting on a higher market value of their stock at the time of privatisation. The higher the market value of the stock after privatisation, the higher will be the real financial value of the privileges they have been granted.

A decision about future privatisation can also affect the attitude of state agencies which supervise companies. Once it becomes known that in view of the impending privatisation the government will lose the chance to influence a company directly, its agencies may become very interested in the market value of the company at the time it is privatised, i.e. for how much it can be sold. During the period when the Thatcher government privatised a number of state companies, Great Britain witnessed a clear improvement in the economic performance of companies which remained in the state sector.[10]

There is general agreement that the performance of a company depends more on its environment and the degree of competitive threat to it than on its ownership alone.[11] Increasing competition calls for the removal of institutional barriers which restrict free enterprise and cut off the economy from world markets. Privatisation implemented simultaneously with the above measures can often contribute considerably to increased competition between domestic firms. Privatised companies will probably tend to be more interested in increasing their market shares at the expense of others.

In planning an aggressive marketing campaign designed to increase the market share of a company, the managers of a private firm will not be likely to concern themselves with the potential losses that competitors may suffer. The situation may not be the same in a state-owned firm, if the nomination and dismissal of the chief executive depends on some external agencies, directly or indirectly dependent on governmental authorities. The chief executive of such a firm will take account of the fact that if the operation of his company proves detrimental to another state-owned firm and contributes to its bankruptcy, he may create serious problems for his principals and fall foul of them.

There are other factors which can check the drive towards increasing market share if the chief executive is chosen and dismissed by the employees. A company where power is held by the employees will tend to have a lower propensity to invest than a private company under comparable conditions.[12] Leaving the propensity to invest aside, one must remember that if the expansion of such a firm is connected with increased employment (e.g. the creation of subsidiaries or takeover of other firms along with their employees) it may be much less beneficial to the employees than it would have been for a privately owned firm.[13] The privatisation of a group of companies in a given area of the economy can seriously increase the competitive threat to other, non-privatised firms.

The second potential benefit—budget income from the sale of privatised companies—is also of vital importance. The purchase of shares at prices lower than their expected market value will be very profitable for the citizens. Thus, 'privatisation from above' as proposed here should lead to an increase in voluntary savings and their earmarking for the purchase of shares from the state. What is important here is that unlike fixed-interest bonds, shares are a store of value which are by their very nature resistant to inflation. Hence, fears of inflation should not bear adversely on the population's propensity to buy shares. Actually, it should have quite the opposite effect and could reinforce the population's efforts to convert their stock of zlotys into shares rapidly.

Thus, privatising an appropriately selected group of companies could help to limit inflation at the very time non-market barriers which prevent companies from raising prices are lifted and currency convertibility is introduced. Income generated by the sale of state-owned firms will be helpful in averting a budget deficit, which fuels inflation, and should permit the financing of various endeavours designed to attenuate the consequences of sudden economic transformations (severance pay for people laid off following the reorganisation of companies and agencies, unemployment benefits, professional training programmes, benefits for the poor, etc.).

One must note that draining considerable sums from the population, through profitably priced shares of privatised companies, might also have an adverse impact on the economy, since it is tantamount to the collection of funds by the budget, a part of which might have otherwise gone into productive investment in the private sector. Looking at the issue in the narrow aspect of economic efficiency, radical cutbacks in budget expenditure leading to a budget surplus would have been the best method to curb inflation. If such radical cutbacks in budget spending are impossible, then the sale of shares is a lesser evil, as it is by far preferable to such alternative methods of deficit financing as heavier taxation or additional printing of money and it also appears to involve less risk than foreign or domestic debt.

In a favourable political climate, 'privatisation from above' with its powerful deflationary effect, could offer a solution to the squaring of the circle of Polish (and Yugoslav!) economic policy, that is of achieving market equilibrium without producing a dramatic decline in real wages. It can be assumed that on the most optimistic scenario a radical market-oriented reform leading to economic equilibrium could be implemented without suffering for the whole mass of the population (especially the economically weakest groups), but would be financed through the voluntary savings of prospective shareholders looking for profit.

The last of the potential benefits of 'privatisation from above', the creation of a broad base of individual shareholders, is also very important since it is necessary to secure the political stability of the new economic order. The experience of the privatisation carried out by the Thatcher government in the UK can be very instructive in this respect. In similar operations carried out by earlier Conservative governments the shares of privatised companies were turned over to other private firms or they found their way to a small group of persons, who were often the original owners. Hence, there was only a small proportion of the population interested in defending these companies against renationalisation when the Labour Party was returned to power. Thus, the whole cycle, nationalisation–reprivatisation, was repeated all over again. The Thatcher government carried out privatisation so as to avert another wave of nationalisation. It was to this aim that the shares of some of the privatised companies were distributed among as wide a group as possible of the population and pricing was designed to ensure high profitability for the buyers. Persons whose interests could suffer in the wake of privatisation—the management and employees of privatised firms and the buyers of earlier subsidised services of these companies—were offered particularly attractive terms. When Mrs Thatcher came to power in 1979, the number of individual shareholders in Great Britain was about 2 million, i.e. some 5% of the adult population. This figure increased dramatically, mostly through the privatisation of three big companies, British Telecom (December 1984), the Trustee Savings Bank (October 1986) and British Gas (December 1986). At the end of 1984 (before the privatisation of British Telecom) individual shareholders were estimated at 2.1 million,[14] while the figure in January 1987 was put at 9.2 million. In 1987 75–80% of the British public, irrespective of their attitudes towards other political issues and to Mrs Thatcher's government, approved of privatisation. The situation was similar in France after the government of Prime Minister J. Chirac carried out a very extensive privatisation programme which drew heavily on the British experience. Facing widespread public support for privatisation, both the British Labour Party and the French Socialist Party have conspicuously de-emphasised their long-standing commitment to renationalisation.[15] 'Privatisation from above', with the share pricing and distribution proposed here, ensures that all citizens will be able to buy a certain amount of shares on terms that nearly guarantee purchase to be profitable. This should induce purchases by many people who would not otherwise have bought them, fearing the risk involved in buying shares on the stock exchange. One must take account of the fact that there may soon be a fair proportion of profit-taking by buyers profitably disposing of their shares. Checking this trend in the first years might call for bonuses for abstention from sale. Such bonuses, in the form of additional shares or vouchers for company services, were introduced for several years after the privatisation of several big British companies.[16]

Profits from resale are also likely to be reinvested in the purchase of further shares in privatised companies. If no 'privatisation from above' were carried out and the whole process of privatisation were left to 'privatisation from below', the number of individual shareholders in private firms (except family farms) would probably remain well below one million for a long time to come. It is highly doubtful whether such a small group of private investors would suffice to make the new economic freedoms irreversible. This is because, apart from the desirable effects described above, a radical market-oriented reform and the abolition of restrictions on private business which would accompany it, would no doubt produce effects which a large part of the population would find most unpleasant. Inequality of income would become increasingly visible, and the situation of certain groups could deteriorate even in absolute terms. Inflation, which would be hard to contain without the additional resources generated by the sale of state property through 'privatisation from above', might prove very troublesome as a result of the liberalisation of price controls. Conflicts between the state and private sectors, including corruption at their interface, would be inevitable. Such corruption results from differences in property rights in the two sectors. In state-owned companies there are no persons who would have full property rights to the firm's capital and would thereby be interested in the proper monitoring of its managers. The officers of state-owned companies have limited rights to use company profit and without effective supervision may be tempted, by various material benefits, to make decisions resulting in concealed profit or property transfers out of their company to private companies.

Demands for governmental intervention and for the curtailment of excessive profits generated by private firms might well gain popular support in such a situation. This, in turn, could lead to tax increases aimed at private firms and to the introduction of various forms of administrative interference with free enterprise. Such restrictions will not eliminate the negative phenomena which they were designed to counter. On the contrary, they will limit competition and will improve profit-making opportunities for those private firms which manage to secure administrative decisions favouring them. Thus, there will be more opportunities for bribing politicians and officials in exchange for favourable decisions.

If the prospective investors came to fear such a course of events, this would no doubt have an adverse impact on the volume of domestic and foreign capital invested and, moreover, capital would be invested in areas offering the chances of fastest withdrawal. Eventually, all positive changes in the economy would be much shallower and slower, while the pathological effects would be much stronger than if 'privatisation from below' were taking place in conditions leaving no doubts as to the stability of economic freedom. It appears, however, that such stable conditions cannot be ensured without 'privatisation from above'.

No legislation, be it even constitutional, can guarantee the stability of any freedom, since it can always be changed. Only the existence of a social group directly interested in preserving this freedom and capable of defending it does constitute such a guarantee. This is why the introduction and consistent implementation of 'privatisation from above', leading to the rapid growth of the class of private shareholders, is the best method to convince domestic and foreign investors that economic freedom will last.

4. Pace of Implementation of the Programme

It would be advisable very promptly to establish a normal market with equilibrium prices and convertible local currency (within a few months or a year), taking advantage of the 'anti-inflationary' shield offered by the sale of profit-making state companies on advantageous terms. This would immediately change the situation of all enterprises and would probably initiate the adaptive processes desirable. The privatisation of other state companies would continue, contributing to the economic and political stabilisation of the new economic system. I think it sensible to assume that the pace of 'privatisation from above' should be such that at least two-thirds of the assets of the presently operating state-owned companies should become private over a period of 15 to 25 years.

At the end of this time GNP, company profits, personal incomes and normal budget revenue should have increased to a point where it would be possible to cope without additional funds from the sale of state property.

Spreading privatisation over such a period who enable a broad group of the population to benefit from the purchase of shares. It has been earlier assumed that the purchasing terms for shares in privatised companies would be very advantageous. Thus, even those who have no savings or property today could save and, systematically, profitably buy over the years the shares of privatised firms, eventually amassing considerable capital, provided that they are convinced such investment is profitable.

A more precise idea of thc possible and desirable timing of 'privatisation from above' would be available only some time after the sale of the first group of companies and the setting up of the stock exchange. Anyhow, spreading privatisation over 15 to 25 years in the initial stage would allow society a certain measure of control over the operation and a chance to regulate its pace depending on its results. Given such a pace of 'privatisation from above', there remains a fundamental problem to be solved: 'What to do with the companies which remain state property?' What should be their legal and organisational forms, and the rules of financing, to make them truly independent from the state administration and to make their managers interested in improving company performance and growth? If privatisation is carried out from above, this problem can be attenuated because, as mentioned earlier, the very prospect of privatisation may have a beneficial impact on the performance of state companies, be they self-governed or corporations supervised by agencies (e.g. state holdings) subordinated to the state treasury. Another solution is to accelerate the rate at which effective control of enterprises can be transferred to private owners in the following way: in some enterprises some of the shares (say one third) would be sold, as described above, to the public. The remaining shares, which would stay in the hands of the state treasury, would become non-voting stock. They would allow the state to benefit from dividends in exactly the same way as the privatised voting stock, but would not allow any influence of the state on the company's policy. When these non-voting shares would be sold to the public they would recover full voting rights. Thanks to this mechanism there would be a kind of 'gearing-up of privatisation', due to which the control of state assets could be transferred to the private sector far faster (in our example three times as fast) than their sale.

It is worth commenting here on one issue raised by Zdzislaw Fedorowicz and Pawel Glikman.[17] Fedorowicz points out that all funds at the disposal of the population and private firms at the end of 1986 accounted for less than 1% of the book value of the productive assets in the socialised sector. Hence, he estimates that the complete purchase of these assets by the population would take over a hundred years, although he admits that this period could be shorter, if we assume that share-capital could be used to finance half of company property, while the rest could be financed with bank credits or bond issues. Estimates by Glikman based on the same kind of reasoning suggest that the purchase of these assets by employees would take several hundred years. In this context it is worth considering two questions. First, whether these estimates based on the available data on bank deposits truly reflect the volume of funds that the population could use to buy shares in privatised companies. Second, and even more important, whether we should worry about the book value of the assets of privatised companies.

As regards the first question, it is sensible to assume that, if the opportunity were offered to buy shares profitably, the population could invest much more than would appear from the data concerning the population's savings in the banks. After all, the population holds convertible currencies (in bank accounts or at home), gold, jewellery, easily marketable consumer durables, cars, plots of land, flats and houses which are not used. If they came to believe a good deal was to be made, they might sell off a part of these resources for zlotys and buy shares.

Andrzei Topinski has drawn my attention to the fact that the population could also convert other elements of their property into shares and not only their zlotys and hard-currency savings. Efforts made by a part of the population to change certain resources into zlotys to buy shares would be an important and desirable deflationary effect of privatisation. If however, this deflationary effect should prove too strong (i.e. stronger than required to offset the inflationary factors) then it could be weakened or balanced through such measures as:

- state credits granted for the purchase of shares (as proposed by Topinski);
- certificates for certain amounts of zlotys, distributed to all adult citizens, with which they could pay for shares bought from the state;[18]
- increased budget spending (e.g. pay rises in the health service, infrastructural improvements, etc.);
- reduced taxation.

If attractive investment opportunities were offered, one could conceivably expect large-scale hard-currency transfers from families abroad, while many Poles might return in person to purchase shares. It is very likely that in the years following privatisation there would be a rapid growth in the funds that the population might devote to the purchase of shares. First, following the lifting of restrictions on private business, we might witness a very dynamic grassroot-level development of private firms accompanied by growing incomes of people associated with these companies. Second, those who bought shares early would be receiving additional incomes in the form of dividends. Third, growing confidence in the durability of economic freedom might induce more Poles living abroad to return to Poland, along with their money. It cannot therefore be excluded that if investment in shares proved very profitable, then, assuming the pace and extent of privatisation I propose, the population might well be able to generate and invest funds comparable to the book value of state property sold over that period.

At the end of 1986 the book value of the productive assets of the non-private sector stood at 30.3 trillion zlotys. Total money resources in bank accounts at the disposal of the population and the private sector were then 3.2 trillion zlotys, whereof 1.7 trillion was made up by savings deposits. If we assume that the value of the part of their property that the population could convert into shares without provoking major disturbances in the operation of their households amounts to at least three times their bank savings, we come to a figure in excess of 5 trillion. It is therefore conceivable that in the first year of 'privatisation from above' the population could allocate half a trillion 1986 zlotys to share purchases (which represents a mere US$700 million at the erstwhile black-market rate and 2.5 billion at the official exchange rate). If we imagine that amounts earmarked for share purchases over the next 25 years would grow at the rate of 9% annually, while the book value of companies initially owned by the state would increase by 3% annually, and that the population would buy these assets at prices corresponding to the average current book value, then after 25 years, two-thirds of these assets (at the current book value) should be in private hands. This calculation is only a simplified illustration and should not be treated as a forecast of the most likely course of events.

Let us now turn to the second question mentioned above, namely, 'does the sale of state property below its book value imply a loss for society?' Is it possible to determine some other, minimal amount which must be obtained from the sale of a company, to make sure the sale does not imply a loss to society? Speaking of potential losses or profits for society resulting from privatisation, I have in mind the losses and benefits from the point of view of those citizens who do not buy shares.

We must consider what is the real value of the property rights that society would lose as a group once a company was privatised. One must remember that the passing of a company into private hands would not imply that its operation no longer benefits society. A private firm would pay taxes, and its employees and shareholders would also be taxed. After privatisation, the company would keep on producing products and services for which there was demand. Let us, however, confine ourselves to consideration of the direct consequences of privatisation on the state budget.

Budget incomes can decline after privatisation when state-owned companies are taxed more heavily than private firms, or when they have to transfer a part of their funds to the state because of the state ownership of their capital (e.g. a part of depreciation funds or dividends from state-controlled corporations).

If, following privatisation, a company chose to lay off a considerable number of employees, then the state might incur heavy expenditure for severance pay and unemployment benefits for persons who could not find other work. On the other hand, shortly after privatisation, companies might considerably increase their profits, so that tax receipts from the companies and their owners might soon outweigh the charges that would have been paid to the state had they remained state property (a kind of privatisation Laffer effect).

One must also bear in mind that the state would no longer have to contribute to financing the investment of privatised companies. Thus extraction of substantial funds from the state-owned companies, as is now the case in Poland, is possible because these companies receive important investment funds in the form of subsidies or credits, either systematically or from time to time, which are subsequently forgiven or at least bear a negative real interest rate.

To answer the question whether or not the privatisation of a given company would be detrimental to state finances, one would have to draw up a balance sheet including all the benefits for the budget (including the proceeds from the sale of shares) and the losses it might incur; potential losses and benefits should be discounted at an interest rate at least equal to the projected GNP growth rate. Drawing up such balance sheets, even if they are rather approximate, might be difficult in the initial stage of 'privatisation from above', since it is hard to predict how privatisation would affect the economic performance of companies. However, I believe that after some time there would be more data for predicting the potential effects of the privatisation of particular enterprises on budget receipts and expenditure. When the sale of a company involved the risk of being detrimental to the state budget, then the announcement of the preliminary auction could include a minimum bidding price per share. Such an auction could be annulled failing sufficient bids. Indeed, if we decided to tax state and private companies at the same rate (which I do not advocate), and the state did not impose any additional charges on state-owned companies e.g. for capital ownership, then the privatisation of a company would be beneficial to state finances even if the shares were given away free. After privatisation, the company would be more interested in profit and it is likely that the increase in tax receipts would be higher than the potential expenditure on compensation and unemployment benefits for dismissed employees.

5. Potential Strengths of the Polish Economy and some Prerequisites for their Exploitation.

I have so far tried to show, among other things, that 'privatisation from above', if properly implemented, could benefit the majority of the population while changing the property structure of the economy. However, budget revenue generated by selling off state property at 'cut-price' will eventually disappear when there are no more state assets to sell. This might lead to certain fundamental doubts. What would happen then? Can we be sure that private property and a free market would ensure prosperity in Poland? After all, there are many countries where capitalism failed to ensure economic prosperity. Independent Poland in the years 1918–39 is one such example. Would the free market and privatisation solve such key problems of the Polish economy as its inefficient structure and the obsolescence of its productive assets, its huge foreign debt and the lack of capital?

There are three factors which can make Poland very profitable for domestic and foreign investors, provided sufficient economic freedom is granted. Under-development in many areas of the economy is the first factor, which would make it easy for investors, especially in the initial stage, to find areas where sales would be easy and profits high. Cheap labour combined with relatively high skills is the second element. If the zloty were to become convertible, then even a company paying high wages by Polish standards would still pay at least several times less for the same kind of work than in the rich countries of Western Europe. The average hourly wage in industry in 12 selected capitalist countries in 1987 ranged from under $6 in Spain to over $12 in Switzerland. In between there were the rates of the USA, Japan and the main West European countries. This means that the average monthly pay in industry, assuming 170 hours per month, varies from about US$1000 to over US$2000 (and more with more working hours).[19] Figures published by the Polish Central Office of Statistics[20] show that the average monthly pay in the so-called 'socialised' sector, which includes state-owned and co-operative firms, at the end of the three month period ending on 31 January 1989 stood at 92,000 zl. At the black-market exchange rate (approximately 3400 zl/US$ at the end of January 1989) this was about US$27 and about US$180 at the official exchange rate of about 500 zl/US$. If these firms were deprived of the opportunity to buy dollars at the absurdly low official exchange rate and if a uniform equilibrium exchange rate were introduced, then it would probably establish itself somewhere between the present official and black-market rates, giving average wages between $27 and $180 per month.

Co-operation with Polish firms or the construction in Poland of plants manufacturing labour-intensive parts, sub-assemblies or finished goods might become profitable for many Western producers. It may be that, thanks to cheap labour, the majority of plants in the traditional branches of heavy industry, which according to widespread opinion are doomed in Poland (e.g. steelmaking or shipbuilding) may successfully compete in the international market after some streamlining and trimming excessive employment. In many cases it may be profitable for Western companies to finance the modernisation of some plant in Polish factories and to move their labour-intensive operations there. Western companies may also be interested in purchasing certain plants in Polish factories and setting up their subsidiaries there.

The nearness of the West European market is one of Poland's most important advantages over, for instance, the Asian countries which based their export expansion on cheap labour. In many cases, transport costs and time can be an important element in the choice of a partner or location for industrial cooperation. Austria, without producing practically any passenger cars, has a positive trade balance with West Germany in this product group. The explanation is that West German vehicle producers take advantage of Austria's somewhat lower labour costs and import a large number of sub-assemblies. One important advantage that Austria has over its potential competitors from e.g. South Korea, is its nearness, which permits the inclusion of plants located there into a sophisticated system of just-in-time deliveries.[21]

One factor which would no doubt make operation in Poland more difficult for Western firms is the backwardness or even total lack, in some areas, of the business infrastructure in its broad sense, that is, transport, communications, hotels, banks and other specialised services. This could cause technical problems, for example the impossibility of reaching someone on the telephone or of obtaining or sending computer data by telephone, and in general it would increase costs. It would nonetheless appear that if economic freedom were introduced, most of the shortcomings of the business infra-structure could be cured promptly, as these areas would be very profitable to operate in. An appropriate state policy in this respect would also be required. On the one had, it should consist of deregulation, permitting competition in transport, mail, telecommunications and financial services and, on the other, allowing foreign capital some access to these areas. Devoting some of the means obtained from privatisation to the modernisation and development of state railways and telecommunications would also be worthwhile. Poland could thus offer important potential advantages to foreign investors which have remained almost untapped hitherto but might well become the driving force behind economic growth if economic freedom were introduced.

To take full advantage of these opportunities, Poland needs to avoid various threats which could produce a situation where the dominance of private firms in the economy would fail to turn economic growth into prosperity. Political instability, for instance, would be a disincentive to investment and might lead to capital flight. Control and 'market steering' by the state administration, leading to a situation where companies focused on their bureaucratic environment, would be another barrier to successful growth. This phenomenon can be observed in many capitalist or 'semi-capitalist' Third World countries, where the success of a company is determined not so much by its performance, adaptability to customers' requirements, low costs and ability to modernise and improve product quality to keep abreast of the competition, but rather by the right connections with various officials, who can grant permits, concessions, import licences and preferential credits and impose customs duties which effectively eliminate foreign competition.[22]

Being cut off from the most important export markets would be another major threat. Poland's experience from the period between the two World Wars is very instructive in this respect. Before World War I Polish territories were very closely tied to the empires which had partitioned Poland. After independence, Poland was largely cut off from its former markets, owing to customs frontiers and strained political relations with the states born in the place of former empires. Thus the average annual value of Polish exports to Germany between 1925 and 1928 amounted to about 45% of the mean annual value of sales from the Polish territory under Prussian rule to Germany in the 1911–13 period. Also, between 1925 and 1928 Polish exports to the Soviet Union, Lithuania, Latvia and Estonia represented less than 8% of sales from the Polish territory under Russian rule alone to Russia in the year 1910.[23] It would appear that this was one of the main causes of Poland's economic failures between the two world wars.[24]

If developments were to take such an unfavourable course, then difficult access to export markets might very seriously endanger the future of the Polish economy. There is a real risk that in the first period after the introduction of a radical, market-oriented reform, Poland might find itself cut off from today's CMEA markets. Apart from appropriate foreign policy measures, it might also be necessary to introduce institutional arrangements which would permit extensive trade with countries with inconvertible currencies and where foreign trade is highly centralised. It is worth considering in this context the potential usefulness of specific institutional arrangements which Finland had in its trade with the Soviet Union. Trade with the USSR accounted for about 26% of Finland's trade turnover in 1983. It is estimated that this trade provided important benefits to both partners.[25]

Access to Western markets might become more of a problem if export production were to develop rapidly in Poland, taking advantage of cheap labour. Cheap Polish goods coming into these countries might lead to calls for protective barriers, such as special customs duties or import quotas. Such restrictions, especially if they were introduced in the crucial EC market, might seriously harm the growth of the Polish economy and prevent it from fully exploiting its potential advantages.

Poland will nonetheless have every possibility of preserving free access to the EC market. In its efforts to maintain this access, the country can use a number of valid economic and political arguments. It is likely that a fair proportion of Poland's deliveries to the EC would be sub-contracted supplies for Western producers or the exports of Western companies' Polish subsidiaries. Moreover, apart from being a provider of cheap labour, Poland would be an attractive market for a number of Western products and industrial technologies, owing to its underdevelopment in many areas. Companies working with Poland in the framework of industrial co-operation or those which have Polish subsidiaries, as well as those exporting to Poland, would be interested in countering protective measures against trade with Poland that might be contemplated by their governments. All the above notwithstanding, there may be the need for political measures to be taken, both now and in the future, to emphasise that Poland is a part of Europe and should have a place reserved for it in the European Community, to make its future access to the Community and the gradual lifting of customs barriers possible when economic and political reforms had reached a sufficient extent.

Notes and References

This article is a slightly revised version of the paper 'Zarys programu prywatyzacji polskiej gospodarki', prepared for the seminar 'Propozycje przekształcen polskiej gospodarki', held in the Central School of Planning and Statistics in Warsaw, 17–18 November 1988.

1. I believe that private firms should pay a uniform profit tax at the rate of about 50%. The turnover tax should be abolished (with certain exceptions such as tobacco and liquor, or petrol) and replaced with a uniform value added tax. It would be desirable that the value added tax rate be set between 14% and 20%, as recommended by the EC for its member states. See N. Colchester, 'A survey of Europe's internal market—1992,' *The Economist*, 9 August 1988. The incomes of physical persons should be progressively taxed, the maximum rate being about 50%.

2. Adam Lipowski considers inflation as one of the major obstacles capable of hindering or even preventing the transformation of the Polish economy into a market economy. See A. Lipowski, *Mechanizm rynkowy w gospodarce polskiej. Podstawy teoretyczne, perspektywy, dylematy* (Warsaw, PWN, 1988), pp. 252–64. See also: A. Topinski, *Inflacja a system funkcjonowania gospodarki polskiej* (Warsaw, PTE, Oddzial Warszawski, 1986).

3. It is worth noting that bids submitted by the participants in the auction might add up to many times the number of shares on offer.

4. The percentage of shares distributed among employees would not be identical for all companies. See note 5.

5. For instance on privatisation of the enterprise each employee would have the right to a free (or almost free) allocation of shares whose par value would be given by the formula: $w = x \cdot (k/k_0)$, where x is a value in zlotys which is uniform for all enterprises in the given industrial sector, k is the book value of the enterprises capital at the moment of privatisation, and k_0 is the book value of the firm when the privatisation programme was started. In other words the more the book value of the firm has increased since the beginning of the privatisation programme, the greater the benefit to its employees.

6. M. Belka and R. Milewski discuss the role of the stock market in the monitoring of company management: 'Wymuszone fuzje w gospodarce amerykanskiej', *Ekonomista*, 2, 1987, pp. 391–414. See also: *The Annual Report of the Council of Economic Advisers*, Chapter 6; 'The Market for Corporate Control' in *The Economic Report of the President* (Washington, DC, United States Government Printing Office, 1985), pp. 187–216.

7. Empirical studies by many authors who compare the performance of private and public firms are discussed in the following publications: S. Domberger & J. Piggott, 'Privatization policies and public enterprise: a survey', *The Economic*

Record, 1986 (June), pp. 145–62: G. Yarrow, 'Privatization in theory and practice', *Economic Policy*, 1986, v 1, 2, pp. 323–77.

8. J. Vickers and G. Yarrow discuss various forms of public ownership used in Great Britain since the early 1950s, in the quest for better performance by state-owned enterprises in *Privatization: An Economic Analysis* (Cambridge, MA and London, MIT Press, 1988), pp. 123–54.

9. See *The Economist*, 12 December 1985, p. 83, 6 August 1988, pp. 47–48 and 27 August 1988, p. 65. Also, pragmatic rather than ideological motives often tempt the governments of many Third World countries, where the share of the state sector in production is considerably greater than in the advanced capitalist countries, into privatisation, See J. Aylen, 'Privatization in Developing Countries', *Lloyds Bank Review*, 1987 (January), pp. 15–30.

10. Citing other data on this subject, *The Economist*, 19 December 1987, pp. 25–26, observed that the only state-owned company which lavishly increased employment between 1984 and 1987 was the Post Office, which the Prime Minister had promised not to sell. The example of the British Steel Corporation is particularly vivid. Its losses in 1980 amounted to £660 million. Also in 1980, Ian MacGregor, its new Chairman, started a reorganisation. By 1986 British Steel was out of the red for the first time. In the financial year ending in March 1988, its pre-tax profit was already £410 million and to the great surprise of observers, British Steel has become the most profitable steelmaking company in the world, with the lowest unit costs. It was successfully privatised in 1988. See *The Economist*, 2 July 1988, pp. 57–58, 6 August 1988, p. 26, 10 September 1988, p. 77.

11. See Domberger & Piggott; and Yarrow.

12. See S. Pejovich, 'The firm, monetary policy and property rights in a planned economy', *Western Economic Journal*, 1969 (September), pp. 193–200: M. Dabrowski, *Ekonomiczne konsekwencje samorzadności pracowniczej* (Wroclaw, Ossolineum, 1986), pp. 65–79; S Kawalec, *Mechanizm przekształcen strukturalnych w gospodarce samorzadowej* (Typescript), (Warsaw, Instytut Rozwoju Gospodarczego SGPiS, Part I, 1986, Part II, 1987), pp. 60–105.

13. See K. von Delhaes, 'Implications of residual factor-remuneration for the dynamics of market processes', paper read at a symposium in Poznan, October 1982; Kawalec, pp. 119–46, 160–65 and 177–80; S. Kawalec, 'Some aspects of economic efficiency in a labour-controlled market economy', paper for the International Conference on Microeconomic Analysis, 'Micromodels 1989', organised by the Institute of Economics of the Czechoslovak Academy of Sciences, Liblice, 20–24 March 1989.

14. *The Economist*, 21 December 1985, p. 82.

15. S.H. Hanke, 'Privatization: a people's capitalism', *Economic Impact*, 2, 1988; Vickers & Yarrow; T. Jenkinson & C. Mayer, 'The privatisation process in France and the UK', *European Economic Review*, 2/3, 1988, pp. 482–90.

16. Vickers & Yarrow, pp. 189–90. What counts in the long run is that tax regulations should not discriminate against investment in shares versus other forms of savings. See Vickers & Yarrow, pp. 190–92.

17. See Z. Fedorowicz, 'Obiektywne uwarunkowania czy chciejstwo?' *Zycie Gospodarcze*, 10, 1988; P. Glikman, 'Mity i fakty', *Zycie Gospodarcze*, 19, 1988.

18. J. Lewandowski & J. Szomburg, 'Uwlaszczenie jako fundament reformy spolecznogospodarczej', paper for the seminar 'Propozycje przeksztalcen polskiej gospodarki', Central School of Planning and Statistics, Warsaw, 17–18 November, 1988); published in English in slightly revised form as 'Property reform as a basis for social and economic reform', *Communist Economies*, 1, 3, pp. 257–68.

19. *The Economist*, 6 August 1988, p. 83.

20. *Zycie Gospodarcze*, 9, 1989.
21. *The Economist*, 20 August 1988, p. 61.
22. Brazil and India are the typical examples. See *The Economist*, 4 July 1987, pp. 74–75 and 10 September 1988, p. 84.
23. W. Roszkowski, 'Polska miedzywojenna—kraj stagnacji gospodarczej?, *Przeglad Powszechny*, 5, 1982, pp. 230–45.
24. By some estimates, Poland's industrial output between World War I and World War II never caught up with the 1913 level and by others—this level was slightly exceeded only in 1939. See Roszkowski.
25. G. Oblath & P. Pete, *The Development, Mechanism and Institutional System of the Finnish–Soviet Economic Relations* (Vienna, The Vienna Institute for Comparative Studies, 1986).

Ownership and Incentives in a Transition Economy

Jean Tirole

Source: Institut D'Economie Industrielle, Toulouse, Working Paper No. 10, January 1992, pp. 1–67.

1. Introduction

As was predicted by most economists, the transition of economic incentives and institutions in the so-called reforming socialist economies is by and large progressing slowly and inflicting substantial costs on the populations. At a time when the transition path of these countries is still uncertain and even larger scale experiments are in sight, it is important to reflect on techniques of privatization that will perform decently in such environments. This paper analyzes the economic aspects of the transition of large scale industrial firms to private property.

After a brief description of some current privatization plans (Section 2), we point at some incentive and market structure features that matter greatly in western economies (Sections 3 and 4) and at some essential differences between the transition economies and ours (Section 5). These differences are important because they condition our assessment of which of the western features can carry over to the environment of a transition economy. Section 6 contrasts the case of Eastern Germany (EG) with those of Eastern and Central European (EE) countries. We then discuss the relative merits of various scenarios in the light of these differences. Roughly, we can envision seven main scenarios for the first five or ten years of a transition towards a capitalist economy:

- *Scenario 1*: Public ownership. Firms are owned and run by the State either as administrations (parts of ministries) or as full-fledged public enterprises.
- *Scenario 2*: Employee management under absentee state ownership. The managers and/or workers run the firms free of government control.[1]
- *Scenario 3*: Entrepreneurship. Firms are owned and run by entrepreneurs.

- *Scenario 4*: Diffuse private ownership. Firms are widely held.
- *Scenario 5*: Hands-on domestic private ownership. The firms are predominantly owned, tightly monitored and controlled by large private institutions such as banks or holding companies. These intermediaries are in turn widely held by the public.
- *Scenario 6*: Hands-on foreign ownership. The firms are purchased by foreign firms or institutions which similarly exert tight monitoring and control.
- *Scenario 7*: Scrappage. Under either of the above governance structures, large industrial enterprises are phased out and the countries' economic development relies entirely on domestic start-ups and newly implanted subsidiaries of foreign firms.

Needless to say, there are other variants; furthermore, one will observe convex combinations (across firms and time) of these rough scenarios.

Section 7 points at desirable economic properties of the transition process. Section 8 analyzes whether the scenario of hands-on domestic private ownership can be refined to fulfill some of these properties. Section 9 studies the alternative of hands-on foreign ownership. Section 10 summarizes some conclusions.

2. Some Current Privatization Plans

• *Poland.*[2] Issued shortly after the creation of the first non-communist government by Mazowiecki, the Balcerowicz program (October 1989) offered to transform firms into joint stock commercial properties initially owned by the State Treasury, then by a variety of owners (including the government) and finally held in majority privately.

The final proposal of the Mazowiecki government was to offer shares to the general public on the open market. The law on privatization of state enterprises, voted on July 13, 1990, foresaw that employees would be able to buy up to 20 percent of shares at reduced prices, and foreigners up to 10 percent (actually, up to 100 percent after approval from the government).

The exact share distribution isn't still completely determined. According to Lutz [1991] (quoted in Williamson [1991], a good indication of what is ahead is: 10 percent of the shares to workers, 30 percent to citizens by means of voucher schemes, 20 percent to pension funds, 10 percent to commercial banks and 30 percent to be retained by the government. The treasury share is meant to be kept for a while and later sold to a big, active investor. The voucher schemes are designed to let the citizens bid on the firms. There are several variants on this. For instance, the voucher books, which would resemble checkbooks with a number of fictitious units of account and would be used in the public offerings, could be sold (at a low price) rather than given, in order to reduce the number of bidders slightly. Also, in some recent Polish proposals, vouchers are meant to be used up in the purchase of mutual investment funds which in turn will buy shares in the firms. The Mazowiecki government also meant to start with the most successful firms to encourage investors to buy industrial property.

Lewandowski (minister in the Bielecki government that succeeded the Mazowiecki government) prepared a new program based on some reservations about public offerings. Public offerings involve large transaction costs and mainly take a long time to set up. Despite the help of several western consulting firms, there are lively debates about prices to be set. Public offerings are also limited by the extent of domestic savings, as well as the absence of a well-structured secondary market (currently organized by banks) that would enable investors to resell easily. Lewandowski has thus offered to look for alternative routes such as sales to foreigners or to employees, in order to speed up and economize on the privatization process.

• *Hungary.*[3] Hungary had a long history of experiments with private ownership during the communist period. The laws of interest to us start with the January 1, 1989 permission for state-owned enterprises to transform themselves into mixed or fully private corporations. This gave rise to spontaneous privatizations with managers arranging sweet deals with buyers, or selling the assets to themselves, and to very little bidding on the firms. A privatization agency, the State Property Agency, was created in March 1990 to oversee the privatization process. Since then, Hungary has experimented and is considering several routes for privatization. The first privatization program consisted in selecting 20 successful firms for sale to appropriate foreign buyers, with the expectation that the foreign firms would bring expertise and be financially sound. The initial idea of the agency was to give managers of the firms an active role. But to speed up the privatization process, it was decided on January 1, 1991 that investors (mainly foreigners) could initiate a privatization without the management's consent. The second privatization program (March 1991) set up an agenda for putting state holding companies for sale.

• *Czechoslovakia.* In Czechoslovakia, The Federal Assembly voted on February 26, 1991 the Transformation Law. This law opens the route for direct sales to domestic or foreign investors, as well as for the firms' incorporation followed by the sale of shares to the public. Some of the plans are quite similar to the Polish one of splitting ownership among government, workers, pension funds, and citizens. There is much interest there for voucher schemes. For instance the project director of the voucher privatization, Dusan Triska, suggests that the government play the role of a Walrasian auctioner. The citizens would buy (at a low cost) voucher books and then bid in investment points on the firms. The prices of the firm are revised depending on the exceed demand realizations. The citizens could also entrust their vouchers to private investment funds which would bid for them (Triska [1991]).

• *Foreign purchases.* An important parameter of the privatization process is the extent to which foreigners will be allowed (and willing) to purchase shares of the firms. In Poland, a majority of ministers of the Mazowiecki government were in favor of encouraging foreign investment, while some influential people warned against selling the country to foreigners. As mentioned above, the law on the privatization of state enterprises formally allocates only a small fraction to foreigners, with discretion for the government to substantially increase this share. The Czech republic plans to sell over 50 percent of larger firms to foreigners.

• *Antimonopoly laws.* The three countries have enacted antitrust laws (on February 24, 1990 for Poland, November 20, 1990 for Hungary, and January 30, 1991 for Czechoslovakia) that are similar to those of the European Community.[4] These laws differ on some aspects such as the treatment of vertical restraints. But all prohibit horizontal agreements.[5]

• *Eastern Germany.* Privatization is progressing faster in Eastern Germany than in the other countries.[6] The privatization agency, the Treuhandanstalt, was given its privatization mandate in June 1990 by a democratically elected government. Besides small businesses that have almost all been sold off, 3,000 industrial firms (out of 10,000) had been sold by end-July 1991. The Treuhandanstalt's mission is not to retain a minority holding. Except for some MBOs, sales are usually to a single owner. The Treuhandanstalt negotiates with the potential buyers about an overall package:

"The determination of a fair purchasing price is an indispensable necessity, but not the only principle governing the takeover negotiations. The following aspects are of equal importance in the context of the overall objectives:

- Acquiring a competent management team offering the company a future;
- ensuring as many viable jobs and
- as high an investment volume as possible."

(Treuhandanstalt brochure).

And indeed, investment pledges and job guarantees, enforced through contractual penalties, are important in practice. The Treuhandanstalt conducts informal, multidimensional auctions and tries in each deal to fulfill macroeconomic objectives rather than selling to the highest bidder.

With the caveat attached to these contractual constraints on nonprice dimensions, the German approach illustrates hands-on foreign ownership. That is, each firm is sold to a private investor from outside the economic area. The buyers are mostly West German firms. In fact some allegations of cronism have surfaced on the ground that the top managers of the Treuhandanstalt (who are West Germans) favor their West German friends over non-German buyers. The Treuhandanstalt denies the charges and tries to attract non-German buyers (see its brochure). The relevance of the allegations is hard to assess in view of the subjectivity of some nonprice dimensions of the auctions.

Through supervisory boards composed of westerners, the Treuhandanstalt also runs those firms that are not yet privatized, although there are signals that it does not have full control over the firms (for instance, the Treuhandanstalt was unhappy about wage and severance pay agreements between the firms and their workers). Even with a staff of 3,000 (compared to the 200 employees of the Polish privatization agency), it is difficult for the Treuhandanstalt to restructure the firms, make investment decisions, control managers and sustain employment, while bargaining with potential investors.

Two other features of the transition in Eastern Germany worth noting are the extensive use of investment subsidies; and that of policies aimed at preserving employment (Treuhandanstalt keeping firms afloat, "liquidity guarantees" to prevent bankruptcies, and payments to support employment in the firms).

3. The Wheels of Western Economies: Institutions and Incentives

Our economies are extremely complex institutions. It would be presumptuous to describe them in a few pages. But it is useful to recall some of their main features.[7]

3.1 Insiders' Incentives

The separation of ownership and control requires specific incentives for the alignment of managers' and shareholders' interests. Because of the large scope for waste, much attention has been paid to the design of managerial incentive schemes. Several imperfect mechanisms combined together keep managers under some control.

- *Earning-based incentives.* Managers generally receive bonuses based on accounting data (income, profit, output). Bonuses are more effective in fairly noiseless environments, as they then reflect managerial inputs accurately.
- *Stock market monitoring.* Accounting data do not measure increases in the value of assets (and, if they react to investments, they do so negatively when investments are incurred). Stock market analysts acquire information about the value of the firms' assets and the stock price conveys information about managerial investments beyond that revealed by the realized stream of future profits (because the stock price is an expectation of future profits and therefore yields a picture of the firm not yet garbled by future uncertainty). Stock prices can be used explicitly or implicitly for managerial control. A substantial fraction of managerial compensation in large US corporations is in the form of stocks and stock options. Like bonuses, stocks and stock options work better if the measure is not polluted by large exogenous uncertainty about the firm's cost and demand. Stock prices can be used for managerial control implicitly as well. Indeed the managers of large German and Japanese

corporations receive little stock based compensation relative to their US counterparts, but the board of directors or banks may condition the managers' tenure or discretion on how well their firm's stock performs. We come back shortly to the role of stock markets as most proposals have advocated their use in the transition economies.

• *Relative performance evaluation.* The informational value of accounting and stock data can be improved by comparing the performances of managers of firms facing similar environments.[8] Relative performance evaluation (also called yardstick competition) filters out some of the noise on managerial performance measures.

• *Board of directors monitoring.* The firm's directors are meant to check on managers and have fiduciary duty to shareholders. There have been doubts about their ability to intervene other than by firing managers; about their incentives and ability to obtain information about the firm; and about their independence relative to management.[9] Recent developments in the US seem to have created more incentives for supervision, but boards of directors are still very imperfect monitors.

• *Takeovers.* Takeovers have been an important element of the corporate picture of the US in the eighties. Their role has been less important both historically and in countries like Germany and Japan.[10] Takeovers are meant to discipline managers by replacing them if they are incompetent or else if they shirk (build empires, etc....). Managers may care about retaining their jobs because they derive private benefits from running the firm or because dismissal imposes humiliation, relocation costs and endangers future job prospects. Raiders are meant to substitute for boards of directors that either do not monitor the firm closely or else collude with top management. The limits of takeovers are well known, both in terms of managerial incentives (they induce managerial myopia) and in terms of the difficulty for raiders to prevent free riding by current shareholders.[11]

• *Bankruptcy and debt.* Like the threat of takeovers, the threat of bankruptcy may make managers worry about losing control or their job. Also, in less dramatic circumstances, debt may still lower the managers' discretion by preventing them from using retained earnings to finance new investments and forcing them to go back to the capital market instead.

• *Labor market monitoring: career concerns.* Managers have reputations and want to convince the labor market that they are efficient.[12] Outside job offers usually increase their salary whether they accept these offers or stay in the firm. Career concerns thus induce managers to behave better. Such concerns are stronger for young managers, although top managers may still hope for future appointments to boards of directors. They also are stronger for managers who frequently interact with outsiders, because external learning about managerial talent is what puts pressure on the managers' internal compensation.

3.2. What Do Stock Markets Do?

The stock market is alleged to fulfill several functions.

• *Risk sharing.* A risk-averse entrepreneur may want other economic agents to bear some of the risk associated with a risky project. Issuing stock is one way to do so. The risk sharing explanation for stock markets, however, only goes so far, as there are other methods to spread risk (e.g., through insurance markets or through claims closely held by a well-diversified financial institution).

• *Guiding investment.* Another well-known motivation for a stock market is that the firm's and the aggregate stock prices convey information about the firm's future profitability and thus help select the right amount of investment. This motivation is not very convincing. Managers are likely to possess at least as much information about investment opportunities as the firm's outsiders, and when one further accounts for the noise in the stock price, it becomes doubtful that managers would learn much about the profitability of their investment from looking at their firm's stock price. The informational content of aggregate stock indices also seems limited in an economy where agents can learn about aggregate activity from national income and investment data, interest rates, bond prices, etc.

In our view, the specificity of the stock market is its role in collecting information about firms and in acting on this information.[13] This view underlies much of the later analysis of the relevance of stock markets in reforming socialist economies.

• *Measurement of the value of assets.* We noted earlier that it is difficult to measure asset value and to give managers explicit or implicit incentives to invest in the absence of a stock market. Stock market analysts collect "speculative information," that is, information that helps predict future profits of the firm. This information does not alter future profits, but it helps measure managerial activity and is useful for incentive purposes.

• *Increase in the value of assets.* Stock market participants may also collect "strategic information," that is, information that brings new ideas for management (or about the desirability of removing the existing one) or unveils synergies with other firms. In other words, strategic information is information that, if acted upon, increases the firm's value. It differs from speculative information also in that it is useless to its proprietors unless it is acted upon by the firm, while speculative information can benefit its proprietors independently of a change in management or control.

3.3. Incentives of Stock Market Participants

We just argued that the stock market supplies information that helps discipline management and increase profit opportunities. This information does not come for free. Besides the costs of transacting and those of regulating the participants' behavior, stock markets make heavy use of highly qualified and well-paid analysts. Ultimately these costs must be borne by the firms' owners. The stock market institution implies that the participants are rewarded by trading shares. [We should warn the reader that what follows is a very orthodox or "rational" view of the stock market. This view seems warranted because we will later argue for gradualism in the introduction of such a market. It is therefore appropriate to build the best case for stock markets.]

The major obstacle to analysts' taking advantage of their acquired information is the so-called "no trade theorem": rational traders, who are risk neutral and value realized profits equally, ought not to trade simply on the basis of differences in information. In such "zero-sum game" markets, any gain by one is a loss for the other, and all traders cannot rationally expect to gain by trading. Hence trade should not occur if traders can hold on to their share. Another version of this extreme implication of the 'lemons' problem is the celebrated free-rider problem. Suppose that a raider envisions an improvement in the way the firm is operated and wants to take over the firm to implement this change. To make money she must buy at a price below the firm's value after the improvement is made. Realizing this, current owners are better off holding on to their shares, so that the raider may be unable to take over the firm.

In practice, we observe both day-to-day trading as well as occasional takeovers. Economic theory has suggested explanations for both. Holders of speculative information make money because of the existence of liquidity traders, i.e., individuals who enter the stock market or exit when buying a house or facing a medical emergency, or institutions which follow rules or legal requirements for diversification. These liquidity traders lose money on average over their trades with the speculators.

To explain the acquisition of strategic information and takeovers, theory has suggested first, that the raider can dilute the firm's assets somewhat, and, second, that even in the absence of dilution big shareholders have an incentive to search for strategic information because they at least enjoy the increase in value of the shares they hold before the takeover (or the proxy fight).

Because we will later discuss ownership structures, we ought to mention the relationship between ownership concentration and the stock market incentives to acquire speculative and strategic information. Participants have many incentives to acquire information about the firms' prospects in a "liquid market," that is a market with dispersed, liquidity traders. (Note that there is no presumption that it is socially optimal to create liquidity by "offering liquidity traders as sacrifices." But this is an easy way to create liquidity.) In contrast, stock market participants have little incentive to acquire speculative information when facing large and stable owners. On the other hand, concentrated ownership may favor the acquisition of strategic information, as the raider derives more gains from bargaining with a single owner, say, than from facing dispersed, free-riding owners.

It is important to emphasize the role of large participants in collecting the two kinds of information. As was recognized long ago, people's capitalism with direct control of small shareholders over firms is an illusion. The costs of obtaining detailed information about a firm or industry vastly exceed the gains most citizens can expect from it. People's capitalism can at best exist through large institutions (mutual funds, pension funds, insurance companies, banks . . .) holding their savings and being given adequate incentives to use them properly.

Last, we should note that acquisitions also serve to allocate productive units to their best use. Like for any economic good, wrong prices may induce misallocation of ownership rights. For instance, a firm may take socially suboptimal control of another firm if the former has information that the latter is undervalued by the market. This adds to the general point that stock markets are likely to function better when the firm is not subject to large exogenous uncertainty.

4. Some Market Structure Issues in Western Economies

4.1. Mergers and Divestitures

It is well known that concentrated ownership in an industry has the potential to raise consumer prices and reduce welfare. And, although the net effects may be smaller, vertical integration may also have anticompetitive implications by foreclosing access of buyers to suppliers or of sellers to outlets.[14]

There are two (complementary) ways of preventing excessive horizontal and vertical integration. First, the antitrust statutes often require an acquirer to report a prospective or actual merger to a merger commission who can then challenge it.[15] Alternatively, the government (or private parties) can challenge integrated firms ex post and ask for divestiture.

The evidence is that it is easier to prevent mergers than to break up firms. Several cases of divestitures (such as the AT&T 1984 settlement) have involved long and costly processes. [A current case of horizontal and vertical divestiture is that of the British Electricity system (see Vickers–Yarrow [1990b]). Interestingly enough, the break up is taking place before privatization.] Investigating the asymmetry between ex ante and ex post government intervention into market structures is outside the scope of this paper. Part of the asymmetry may result from the merged firms mixing up their activities to make future breakups more difficult. Whether such behaviors have taken place in environments lacking merger laws is unknown to us. We take the asymmetry for granted and point at its consequence for transition economies: any privatization before competition-oriented restructuring is likely to have a long term impact on market structure in those industries that are not obviously competitive and will be somewhat protected from foreign competition.

4.2. Regulation[16]

Because regulation or public ownership is likely to prevail temporarily in some industries and more permanently for natural monopolies (e.g., gas, electricity, postal service, railroads and perhaps telecommunications), it is worth discussing a few key features of regulation that will be relevant in reforming socialist economies. We will not review here the various regimes regulating pricing and incentives (such as cost-of-service regulation, profit and cost sharing schemes, and price caps); we content ourselves with pointing out the general considerations in the choice of power of regulatory incentive schemes. The power of an incentive scheme is the fraction of (marginal) cost savings or profit increases retained by the firm. Regulation exhibits a basic tradeoff between rent extraction and incentives. Incentives for cost reduction or innovation are best provided by high-powered incentive schemes, in which the firm's compensation is sensitive to its performance (an extreme example of such a scheme – the fixed-price contract – has the firm be paid a fixed amount and be residual claimant for its cost savings and profits). High-powered incentive schemes however leave substantial rents to the regulated firm. For instance, under a fixed price contract, any exogenous (technological) decrease in costs goes to the firm. Such rents are economically costly because they must be made up by distortionary taxation (if the government subsidizes the firm) or by distortionary prices or premia charged to consumers (if the firm is required to balance its budget). Furthermore popular pressure makes it politically difficult to sustain such rents. Very uncertain environments make it more difficult to extract rents and therefore require low-powered incentive schemes (such as cost-plus contracts in procurement or cost-of-service regulation).

The choice of power of regulatory incentive schemes also impacts on the possibility of regulatory capture. Low-powered incentive schemes leave little discretion to regulators; for instance, the cost-plus contract "reimburse the firm's realized cost" does not make much use of their information. In contrast, high-powered schemes require substantial use of the regulator's information (for instance, to locate the socially optimal price to be paid to the firm in a fixed-price contract). They are are thus subject to capture by interest groups, in particular the industry. Therefore countries where the threat of regulatory capture is particularly high should adopt low-powered incentive schemes for their regulated firms and public enterprises.

5. The Eastern European Environment

To understand how incentive structures must be tailored to the EE environment, it is convenient to describe its evolution as an initial *noisy phase* followed by a more *mature phase*. This division starkly highlights the two key specificities of the firms' environment in these transition economies: the extraordinarily high amount of uncertainty not controlled by the firms, and the nonstationarity in its level. Needless to say, the various types of uncertainty will not resolve simultaneously, and the division into two phases is only an abstraction facilitating the analysis.

The first years of the drive toward market economies involve considerable economic, legal and political uncertainty for firms:

• *Cost uncertainty.* The prices of inputs (labor, energy, raw materials, etc.) will be substantially modified. First, these prices are heavily distorted and will need to move toward yet unknown market prices. Second, the speed at which some of these inputs will be available is itself uncertain. For example, there are currently almost no accountants and lawyers trained to deal with modern corporations. Similarly it is hard to predict how fast entrepreneurial culture will pick up. Third, final market prices will depend on yet unknown governmental choices. For instance the cost of labor will be influenced by policies concerning wage subsidies, social security and unemployment insurance.

• *Demand uncertainty.* The demand for a firm's products will be unusually random in the years to come. It will depend on highly uncertain standards of living (themselves linked to, e.g., macroeconomic stabilization plans, lending by foreign countries, foreign exchange developments and housing policies) as well as on the extent of restructuring (layoffs, bankruptcies, speed of foreign trade liberalization . . .).

• *Financial uncertainty.* Capital markets must be created from scratch.[17] It is hard to know how long it will take to develop institutions and to train investment bankers, analysts and other financial experts. Another element of financial uncertainty is the treatment of inter-enterprise debts and arrears.[18]

• *Legal uncertainty.* It is widely recognized that legal changes related to property, contract, bankruptcy, antitrust and labor laws ought to be introduced as soon as possible. The desire to tailor the laws to the EE environment as well as the sheer burden of drafting the laws is likely to delay their introduction.

• *Political uncertainty.* For historical reasons, the ideology of future governments is more uncertain than in western countries. Consequently it is somewhat difficult to predict the tax structures and levels, the treatment of foreign assets and trade, the commitment to a hardening of soft budget constraints, the willingness to install a safety net, and so forth.

Another crucial feature of the EE environment is the need for a large scale-competition- and efficiency-oriented restructuring. Firms are highly integrated horizontally and vertically. As a rough approximation most industries are served by a national monopoly. And, previous input assurance concerns have led most firms to produce their own capital goods and other inputs, such as maintenance, repairs and transportation. Free markets therefore raise the two concerns of horizontal collusion and of vertical foreclosure of suppliers' and buyers' markets. Substantial restructuring will be needed to create market structures that resemble those of western economies (where anticompetitive concerns are serious, but pure monopolies are rare and firms are much less vertically integrated). This form of *competition-oriented restructuring* (to contrast it with *efficiency-oriented restructuring*, which is meant to improve firm management and discover synergies across units) will not be voluntarily undertaken by the private sector as it reduces profits. Many privatization proposals dismiss the issue by invoking, first, trade liberalization and the emergence of foreign competition and, second, antitrust legislation. While both policies will be useful ingredients of a competition policy, they by themselves are unlikely to be sufficient to create appropriate market structures for reasons discussed in Section 7. The creation of competitive markets is thus not an independent appendix to the privatization program.

Even ignoring competitive goals, massive breakups and reorganizations of the industries will still be needed for efficiency purposes, as the current structure of integration reflects historical and political considerations more than any economic rationale. Input management will undergo substantial changes. With labor hoarding estimated at above one-half of the work force and with the necessary adjustments in industrial structure, many employees will be laid off (which requires the quick establishment of a safety net and retraining programs)[19]. Large inventories of inputs will need to be eliminated.

6. The Eastern German Environment

Eastern Germany, like Eastern Europe countries, starts with poor capital, a lack of infrastructure, a polluted environment, and inefficient organizations. Its case is however quite different.

While the uncertainty in East Germany is substantial by western standards, it is smaller than that in Eastern Europe. For instance, the integration with West Germany offers somewhat better prospects for the import of "foreign" (understand here West German) expertise, and gets rid of legal uncertainty. Similarly, the tax treatment of foreign assets is constrained by West German laws.

On the competition side, goods available in West Germany are guaranteed access to East Germany. Thus, except for nontradables, anticompetitive concerns in East Germany are similar to those in most western economies.

The social impact of unemployment in East Germany, although substantial, is less severe than in Eastern Europe due to large transfers from West Germany. Furthermore, capital flows from West Germany cannot be hampered by the threat of taxation or expropriation. And despite some resentment toward the "Wessis", the psychological impact of ownership located outside the economic area seems limited. So, there does not seem to be any real obstacle to "foreign" ownership.

The benefits of integration for East Germany are accompanied with some constraints. Wages above the marginal productivity of labor[20] create problems of their own, in particular unemployment and difficulty to sell firms. And, whether a good or a bad thing, immediate unlimited entry of West German goods in East Germany has been unavoidable.

7. Implications for Eastern Europe

This section draws some implications of the brief discussion in Sections 3 and 4 for the EE environment reviewed in Section 5.

7.1. Implication A: Stock markets will work poorly in the noisy phase

We contend that the conditions that make the trading of stocks a somewhat successful institution in western economies will not be present in EE in the next few years. To see this, suppose that whatever policy is adopted leads to a somewhat liquid stock market and significant trading on this market.

Consider first the informational value of stocks for management control. There are several reasons why stock prices will very inaccurately measure managerial performance. On the one hand, price fluctuations will reflect the noise in the firm's environment more than the managers' value enhancement. The other side of the same coin is that stock market participants will focus on learning about government policy, and input, capital and labor market developments more than on monitoring managerial activity. [Surely, this type of learning reduces the uncertainty about the firm's exogenous environment and allows better control of managers, but, as argued in Section 3, the cost of this reduction in uncertainty is eventually borne by the firm's owners.]

On the other hand, market analysts in western economies rely on (besides industry studies) the firm's income statements to forecast their future earnings. Analysts must work through income statements' depreciation and amortization to assess the economic value of assets, and must estimate future tax liabilities from their (distinct) tax counterparts; in so doing they must adjust for firm specific definitions of variables. Thus market analysis requires accounting structures that are reliable, undistorted and relatively homogeneous across firms. It would be naive to expect these conditions to be met rapidly.

Still another reason to express doubts about a well functioning stock market is that it will take time to set up an efficient system of financial regulation. For instance it will be very difficult to fight insider trading without a modern system to keep track of transactions. Similarly, one would expect a fair amount of trading based on private information about forthcoming government reforms. It seems unlikely that a government that is engaging in so many reforms simultaneously will be able to introduce efficient financial regulation rapidly.

A final danger of active stock markets during the noisy phase is that garbled stock market prices may give the wrong signals for restructuring. For instance, the acquisition of one firm by another may be driven more by information that the former is undervalued than by the existence of synergies.

7.1.1. Corollary 1

The first corollary of Implication A is the need for a *stable ownership of firms during the noisy phase.* A stable core of owners is created, who hold on to their firms until the mature phase. We can consider several options in this respect.[21]

- *Public ownership* (Scenario 1 of the introduction). The State keeps control of the firms.
- *Entrepreneurship* (Scenario 3). The firms are allocated to a small number of individuals who run them as entrepreneurs.
- *Holding companies* (Scenario 5). This option creates an extra layer between firms and their final owners. A small number of holding companies own the firms, and they themselves are owned by all citizens. There are several variants on this: among them, mutual funds, privatization companies, investment banks and banks. The distinction refers to what the holding company is allowed to do during both the noisy phase and the mature phase. During the noisy phase, investment banks and banks are indistinguishable. They receive deposits and hold debt and equity positions in the firms. Mutual funds and privatization companies are also alike; they do not receive deposits and are pure equity holders. During the mature phase, banks divest themselves of their equity, but continue to receive deposits and to make loans (they are thus banks in the American sense); investment banks keep some equity in the firms and are thus engaged in the same activities as during the noisy phase (they are thus banks in the German or Japanese sense). Privatization companies[22] divest themselves of the firms during the noisy phase and disappear thereafter. In contrast, mutual funds remain equity holders after the opening of the stock market at the beginning of the mature phase. [Note that, by not divesting equity, mutual funds are to privatization companies what investment banks are to banks.] For concreteness, and unless we specify otherwise, we will think of holdings as being mutual funds, i.e., as being pure equity holders during both phases.[23] But we should keep in mind that there are some interesting variants on this.
- *Hands-on foreign ownership* (Scenario 6). The firms are purchased by a foreign enterprise or institution.

Each of these options can be accompanied by the distribution of non-tradable, minority stakes to workers and management. We discuss them sequentially.

- *Public ownership* with government officials on the board of directors raises the same incentive concerns as in western countries, where it is generally agreed that it should cover only a handful of industries. But public ownership raises more concerns in EE. The budget constraint is likely to be softer there; and as will be argued in Section 7.3, there is a higher danger of regulatory capture. However, such reservations should not obscure the fact that, if only because of the immensity of the privatization task, public ownership is and will be a pervasive phenomenon during the transition and that it is therefore important to design appropriate forms of regulation of public enterprises for the EE environment.

The incentives of the government officials to manage the firms efficiently during the transition period will need to be addressed. In particular, there is an important risk that the government be captured by the firms' employees. Labor hoarding is likely to remain, and wages to be way above market wages. An important difference with public enterprises of western economies is that, at least at the beginning of the noisy phase, there will be no obvious yardstick to compare the wages in the public sector to. Thus, government discretion concerning wages will be large and so will be the risk of capture.

• *The entrepreneurship scenario* (sometimes called "cowboy capitalism") has been recommended by some because it recreates the "robber barons" so prominent in the late nineteenth century expansion in the US. Its main appeal is that owners are directly involved in the firm's management, which alleviates agency problems. Despite this benefit, we find the option unappealing. Giving firms to entrepreneurs would be grossly unfair. And one can have doubts about whether the distribution of income could be corrected through adequate taxes. Moderate taxation would leave immense wealth to a handful of lucky entrepreneurs who inherit healthy firms or firms with market power. On the other hand, steep taxation has its own limits. It is likely to induce entrepreneurs to dissimulate their income by (wastefully) transforming it into perks. And, more fundamentally (even if income diversion can be prevented), there are two issues concerning the design of an optimal tax scheme: the tax scheme should be tailored to the firm's environment, which brings taxation closer to regulation; and in this very noisy environment it will be difficult to design appropriate schemes that both give appropriate incentives for efficiency and extract entrepreneurial rents. [This point, although phrased in terms of the government designing an incentive scheme for the entrepreneur, is quite general. The proposal of creating robber barons is often couched in terms of giving property rights to some highly leveraged entrepreneurs. The motivation for having the entrepreneurs borrow against future profits is, like for the taxation scheme, one of fairness. However, the very noisy environment will make leverage a dangerous policy. Firms will have a high probability of bankruptcy; furthermore, the usual moral hazard problems – decapitalization, choice of very risky projects – associated with situations in which the firm is likely to be, but is not yet insolvent are bound to surface.]

The last two objections we have to the entrepreneurial solution are linked with the choice of the entrepreneurs. Even more than in western economies, there is little information about who is likely to be a good entrepreneur. Choosing the wrong person may have disastrous consequences for a firm (this issue will also have to be addressed for managers of holding companies). The other issue is that the large potential rents associated with becoming one of the happy few will politicize the appointment problem (this is also true for the appointment of managers of holding companies, but the rents are smaller so that capture of the appointment process is a bit less likely). We do not have a good scheme to select entrepreneurs in a rigid, nondiscretionary way.[24]

• The creation of *holding companies* or their variants is meant to address the problems associated with entrepreneurs: in particular, the need to tailor incentive schemes to the firm's environment,[25] to increase the informational value of managerial performance, and to design a mechanism to remove bad managers. The holding company in charge of monitoring a firm will have some incentive to create an incentive scheme appropriate to the firm, and to remove bad managers. And, very crucially, it will be managing a portfolio of firms. Even though the aggregate portfolio will be quite risky, it will be less so than the ownership of a single firm: by the law of large numbers, firm-specific shocks are diversified away.[26] Also, the creation of roughly similar portfolios will enable incentive schemes to filter out some of the aggregate noise through relative performance evaluation among holding companies.

A serious concern with holding companies is that one creates an extra layer between the real owners of the firms (the citizens) and the firms. The problem of control of the managers of holding companies is a difficult, but important one and will be addressed later.

• A fourth governance structure guaranteeing a nondiffuse, stable ownership is *hands-on foreign ownership* (this is by and large the structure implemented by the Treuhandanstalt). There is not much to be added to the general discussion of incentives, as the governance structure is familiar from western economies.

Note that there is nothing new to the idea of creating a core of stable owners in a phase of uncertainty and restructuring. Stock markets have played a minor role in the early stage of the development of modern capitalism in the US. For instance, a few investment banks (such as the Morgan investment bank) played a substantial role before the 1933 Banking Act separating commercial and investment banks. Banker control over railroad trusts was commonplace.[27] Similarly, many of the utility systems were controlled by bank-related holding companies. Large "interest groups" such as DuPont, Mellon, and Rockefeller, dominated the corporate scene. The idea of holding companies or hands-on foreign ownership is to recreate similar conditions for restructuring without the distasteful implications for wealth distribution.

7.1.2. Comparison with Growth Companies

Comparing the governance structure within the holding company to known governance structures helps clarify its nature. Let us point at some analogies and differences with growth companies.

A firm controlled by a holding during the noisy phase and a growth company financed by venture capital both face very risky environments. They will not be traded on the stock market until a substantial fraction of the uncertainty about the technological and demand environment is resolved. In the meantime a major investor holds a substantial amount of equity in the firm: the holding in the first case, a venture capital partnership, a wealthy individual or an investment institution in the second case. This investor carefully monitors and exerts control over the firm.[28] The investor supplies substantial advice to inexperienced managers of the firm. He gives the money in several steps in order to be able to shut down the firm if necessary. Debt, which is very risky in this environment, plays a very minor role. In both cases, the rewards of the investor and the firm are delayed; and so is the public offering and the opening of the firm to new investors.[29]

Besides these many similarities, there is an essential difference between a subsidiary of a holding and a growth company: as we will later argue the incentives of the investor's and the firm's managers are likely to be low-powered in the case of a holding. The fact that the managers of the holding company face low-powered incentives (some stocks, but mainly relative performance evaluation, monitoring and career concerns) make the holding resemble the investment division of a financial institution more than venture capitalists or wealthy individuals. More importantly, the firm's managers face very low-powered incentives (mainly monitoring and career concerns) while the founders of a growth company face high-powered incentives (at the beginning of the relationship they may hold half of the stock of the company). The explanation for this discrepancy is not due to differences in the marginal productivity of effort; in both cases, managerial input is quite crucial to the growth of the firm. Two other factors seem to generate the discrepancy. First, the founders of a growth firm usually can finance a nonnegligible fraction of initial expenses through savings and personal bank loans. In contrast, the managers of big privatized EE firms cannot purchase a substantial fraction of their firm's capital; nor can they use leverage in this very risky environment. This means that they will own a much smaller fraction of their firm than their counterparts in the growth firm. Second, it is hard to make the firm's managers accountable for the value of its assets during the noisy phase in EE. Because of the current idiosyncratic structure of production, firms will need to be broken into pieces and reorganized. In the absence of meaningful transfer prices for assets, it is difficult to identify the managers' individual contributions. In contrast, managers of a growth company are in charge of a well-defined and stable property.

7.1.3. Corollary 2

The second corollary of Implication A is that *the firms' managers ought to be given low-powered incentive schemes.* On the one hand, profits will be very garbled measures of performance. On the other hand, in the (short-run) absence of a stock market, there is no measure of asset value and it is difficult to give managers explicit or implicit incentives to increase their firm's value.

[One of course can give incentives to managers based on the stock value after the stock market starts functioning, but the role of such incentives is quite limited by the delay in measuring asset value, and by the noise and the reorganization of assets occurring in between.] The difficulty in creating long-term incentives adds to the case that short-term incentives based on the firm's profit (bonuses) should be limited: managers who face primarily short-term incentives are prone to focus on current profits to the detriment of future profits (this effect comes on top of the reduction in the use of bonuses due to the high uncertainty about profits). So one is constrained to give low-powered managerial incentives across the board.

7.2. Implication B: Most competition-oriented restructuring ought to take place before privatization

As discussed in Sections 3 and 4, the private sector may undertake efficiency-oriented restructuring, but it will not promote competition because this would reduce profits. And, breaking up firms (horizontally and vertically) on the basis of antitrust laws has proved difficult in western economies and is likely to be a quagmire in countries without a tradition of antitrust enforcement. So it seems that competition-oriented restructuring ought to be undertaken before private ownership is introduced.

Competition-oriented restructuring of course need not affect all industries. Some will naturally attract a large number of firms and be fairly competitive on their own. Others can be made competitive by the opening of the country to foreign competition. We should not, however, view foreign competition as a panacea for monopoly power. First, it can only affect tradables. Second, the government may be captured by industries or else be pressured by trade deficits, and may impose tariffs or other forms of protection. Third, some (at least temporary) protection is likely to be justified in some industries; while not starting from scratch, many firms cannot compete on the international market at this stage and will need some protection to develop to a healthy level (this is the infant industry argument).

The corollary of Implication B is, as we have already noted, that *firms in industries that are potentially noncompetitive should be kept a while longer under public ownership before they are handed in to the stable private investors.*

Clearly there will be no time to fine-tune the breakup of firms. Only the most obvious and simpler divestitures ought to be implemented. Needless to say, mistakes in evaluating synergies between units or future market conditions will be committed in such a short time frame. For instance, it may be the case that the merger commission (to be created) will later allow the reunification of units previously broken up, because this is needed to face foreign competition. Yet we would expect some major competitive gains to be obtained by some simple breakups.

In our opinion, the main hurdle will be the government's commitment to carry out divestitures where these are needed. Pressures from firms' employees to keep the monopoly positions will be strong. The government may also be tempted to preserve the firms' monopoly power to make holding companies (or entrepreneurs, or future subsidiaries of foreign firms, depending on the case) more successful financially (this might be the EE equivalent of western experiences of not breaking up monopolies in order to derive more revenues from privatization).

One possibility to deal with this problem is to create a *divestiture commission* that would be composed of (a majority of) independent government representatives and (a minority of) representatives of foreign lenders and donors, who would be advised by domestic and foreign experts and industry delegates without voting power. Linking through moral suasion foreign aid[30] to a minimum effort to create competition might be an incentive for the government to undertake some competition-oriented restructuring. The government representatives could not be easily removed by their government (as is the case for instance of justices on the US Supreme Court[31]), and thus would be less subject to political pressure. The presence of representatives of foreign lenders on the commission might prevent some extreme decisions, and mainly would allow some monitoring of decision making.

7.3. Implication C: The threat of capture of government decision making by interest groups is, during the transition period, more serious in EE than in western economies

Since at least Montesquieu and the American Federalists, it has been well understood that strong safeguards must be put in place to prevent governments from serving the interests of specific groups. Many of these safeguards did not exist under the previous regimes and will take time to install: organization and rotation in the civil service, administrative procedures and regulatory hearings, independent administrative courts, checks and balances in government, development of a tradition of investigative reporting by the media, etc.... Furthermore, historical circumstances are likely to create a close relationship between regulator and regulated, similar to the one associated with the revolving door in western economies.

How will the threat of capture influence the transition process? We already mentioned the issue of the governments' commitment to domestic competition. The commitment to introducing foreign competition is also a serious issue. While the fragility of the industries seems to warrant some temporary protection, the process of trade liberalization may be captured and trade barriers never be removed. Protection, if any, should thus be accompanied with a clear, nondiscretionary timetable for liberalization.

Another implication of the idea is that it may be dangerous to give the government control over the holding companies (during the noisy phase). (These companies would be regular joint stock companies traded on the stock market, or else would disappear, in the mature phase.) The government could then force the holding companies to implement demagogic policies in the firms they control or to induce those firms to collude on the product market.

Yet another implication of the idea is that regulated firms ought to be subject to *low-powered* incentive schemes, which as we saw in Section 4 create little scope for discretion and thus capture.

Last, there should be a timetable for the privatization process to which the government would be committed. All its steps should be simple and clearly defined.[32] Overall, the corollary of Implication C is thus that *one should pay attention to the discretion left to regulators.*

7.4 Implication D: The main attraction of foreign aid for the transition process may not be expertise, but rather commitment and independence from interest groups

Governments and private sectors can use the aid of international donors and lenders to hire foreign expertise by themselves. The experts may be, but need not be supplied by the donors and lenders. A more specific attraction of foreign aid is that foreign institutions are likely to be freer than governments from capture by domestic interest groups, and it may well be that some amount of their involvement in the reform process would commit the countries to a right course of action.

Certainly, foreign involvement raises a familiar dilemma. The foreign donors and lenders are themselves not always free from pressure from the governments that finance them. Furthermore, they may push their internal agenda rather than the most appropriate policy for the country. There is thus a danger of relinquishing national sovereignty to foreigners. Some arrangement has to be found in each instance that preserves national sovereignty, and yet uses foreigners as partial safeguards against capture.

Let us mention two other cases in which foreign institutions might be used as a commitment device. First, they might be given voting rights (with possibly no claim to income) in *boards of directors of holding companies.* Other members of the board would be government representatives and delegates of shareholders (the citizens). Giving minority stakes to each of the three groups preserves national sovereignty; it also raises the possibility that the foreign institutions make the case for efficiency in board meetings and influence the possibly less experienced and informed delegates of shareholders.

Second, those international financial institutions that directly lend to the private sector (as will be the case for the European Bank for Reconstruction and Development, and is the case for the International Finance Corporation) may be used as a commitment to *harden the firms' soft budget constraint* during the noisy phase. Firms will need financing for new projects and maintenance. The financing by domestic banks, whether public or private, raises some problems, besides the fact that the banking system is not well developed and is in financial distress in some countries (including Poland). Public banks are likely to adhere to the long-standing tradition of the soft budget constraint. The government has an incentive to cede to managers and employees afraid of losing their jobs, and rescue insolvent banks and firms, leaving painful restructuring to future administrations.

The use of private domestic banks (without equity holding) raises the issue of their regulation. The large aggregate uncertainty makes insolvency of a substantial fraction of banks a real possibility. The threat of insolvency together with the prospect of being bailed out in case of trouble gives rise to moral hazard, with the banks continuing to lend to financially troubled firms in the hope things will get better in the future, and more generally engaging in risky projects. [The regulatory slippage in the US in the eighties illustrates how financial regulation can go awry even in a country with a long experience in the matter. The savings and loans were subjected to new and looser regulatory accounting principles and to lower capital requirements in order to allow insolvent institutions to continue. The hope was that they would recover and the motivation was to reduce immediate political costs.]

Financial regulation is no easy matter. To discourage excessively risky investments, one ought in theory to subject savings institutions to "risk-based capital requirements," with the requirements based on the estimated value of assets in different economic scenarios and being continuously adjusted. Even western economies are reluctant to adopt such flexible financial regulations because of the burden they impose on regulators, and because of the substantial discretion conferred upon them. It is quite difficult for regulators to estimate risks appropriately, and it is easy for them to misreport actual risks. One may have some doubts about the efficiency of banking systems in the near future for countries lacking a tradition of financial regulation.

The issue seems to be to find a way to give lenders an incentive to monitor firms and to stop financing them when they become insolvent. Such considerations should come to mind when defining a role for the EBRD. Will the EBRD have such an incentive? Should it play the role of a merchant bank, taking only minimal stakes itself and bringing in loans of private foreign investors? If it plays the role of a merchant bank, should it guarantee the private loans, and, if it does so, wouldn't the lack of incentives for private foreign debt holders to monitor firms justify centralizing loans and have the EBRD be the only lender? Or should the interests of private foreign debt holders be subordinated to the interests of the EBRD to give them an incentive to monitor? These are a few of the questions to be addressed here.

A conjecture is that the best use of foreign financing is debt rather than equity. Financing by domestic banks creates the two problems of commitment and regulation, which suggests some substitution by foreign loans. [A distinct motivation for foreigners lending rather than taking equity positions is that it would face a lower opprobrium in the EE countries.]

7.5. Implication E: The stock market must be appropriately introduced at the beginning of the mature phase

Even after the legal framework (ownership, contract, bankruptcy, antitrust laws, disclosure rules, etc.) is put in place, and professionals (auditors, analysts, managers, and so on) are trained, the stock market will not run smoothly overnight. We saw in Section 3 that the liquidity for the stocks is what creates an incentive for analysts to estimate the firms' values and to discover synergies. We would expect little liquidity in a stock market restricted to holding companies.[33] On the other hand, opening stock markets to individuals, to newly created firms and institutional investors, and possibly to foreigners is likely to create such a liquidity. While the final objective is to give wide access to stock markets, we must think about the consequences of immersing small investors directly into a market where stock prices have never been quoted. Big investors will be needed to invest in acquiring information about real market values. Sophisticated small investors, who will be unable to obtain detailed information, will be reluctant to trade with the informed big investors in the presence of such uncertainty about true values, as they are likely to lose their shirts. On the other hand, unsophisticated small investors (and there are likely to be many at the beginning given the lack of experience with stock markets) may not realize the risk they face. They would be the ones to create liquidity in the market. This goes against fairness and against the building of a popular trust and political support for the stock market institution. Furthermore, liquidity trading would create noise in the initial pricing of stocks (as it does in all stock markets).

Remark: An interesting parallel is that of a primary initial public offering by a company not yet quoted on the stock market.[34] A company that goes public in general selects an underwriter and both agree on an issue price. The registration statement submitted to the Securities and Exchange Commission (in the US) as well as presentations to institutional investors convey information to potential buyers. It is interesting to note that potential buyers are usually big, sophisticated buyers when the firm goes public and when therefore no previous price information can be reflected in the current price.

In contrast, initial public offerings associated with the privatizations in western economies (in the UK and in France, for example) have tried to reach small investors through substantial discounts (they also devised schemes to allow employees to buy shares in their firms on favorable terms – see Vickers-Yarrow [1990a] for a description of this in the case of the UK and Chile).

The problem of inception of the stock market in EE (under the corollary of Implication A that firms are controlled by a stable owner during the noisy phase) seems to be closer to that of US firms' going public than to that of UK state owned enterprises being privatized, and this for two reasons: first, the number of firms to be privatized is much larger than in the UK (the UK privatized only a dozen big firms in ten years); second, the design of the inception of the stock market must take into account the incentives of the firm's private owner before the stock market opens.[35]

There are several ways to introduce the stock market. For instance, in the hands-on domestic private ownership scenario, one can let the holding companies, and possibly foreigners, bid for firms at the beginning of the mature phase, with the proceeds of the auction going to the previous owners of the firms; the stock market would later be opened to the general public once prices have stabilized. To create some liquidity, one might for instance force the holding companies to divest some of their shares.

This brings us to a discussion of what goals the inception of the stock market in the mature phase must meet. Here are some desirable properties of associated auctions:

1. Generate information about firm value: the auction should yield a picture of asset value. This information is useful for assessing the relative performance of holding companies during the noisy phase as well as to set up appropriate incentive schemes for the firm's managers for the mature phase. As discussed above, little information will be generated by the illiquid market created by voluntary sales by the holding companies. A possibility is to set aside a fraction α of the shares of each firm of each holding to be sold at the inception stage, and on which the owning holding company is not allowed to bid.[36]
2. Create an appropriate structure of control with large, but not dominant shareholders.[37] One possibility for this is to set $\alpha > .5$, and prevent any bidder in the auction from acquiring a majority of shares.[38]
3. Give incentives for holdings to monitor and invest during the noisy phase: because the value of the firm's assets is partly reflected in the bids at the inception stage, giving the proceeds of the auction to the previous owner yields incentives to invest. However, it may be useful to let the holding keep a minority share in the firm ($\alpha < 1$) to give it further incentives to invest.[39]
4. Prevent cartelization: the selection of allowed bidders (other holdings, other domestic and foreign firms) should prevent the creation of interlocking directorates that would create horizontal collusion or vertical foreclosure in concentrated industries.

8. The Scenario of Hands-on Domestic Private Ownership Refined

The purpose of this section is to examine a scenario involving holdings.

8.1. The timing

We break each phase into "subphases" or "periods":

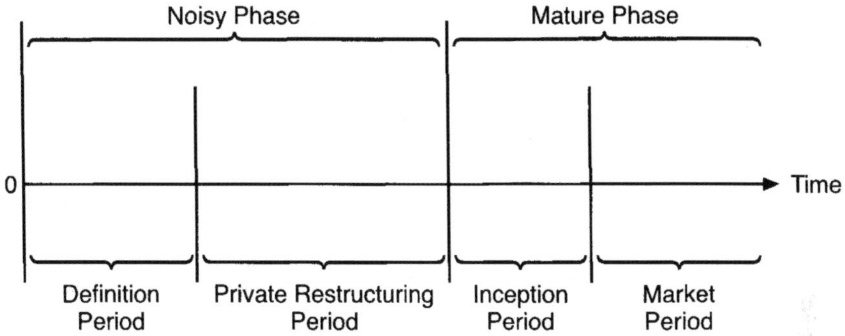

A. Definition Period. This period, among other things, reallocates capital.

1. A divestiture commission is created with independent representatives of government and representatives of international institutions on its board, assisted by domestic and foreign experts. The commission will perform the most obvious cases of competition-oriented restructuring.

2. Firms are divided into three groups by the divestiture commission. The first group consists of the firms in naturally competitive sectors or in sectors in which foreign competition will not substantially hinder the growth of firms. These firms will be allocated to holding companies as soon as possible. The second group consists of firms which will need to be broken up by the divestiture commission before being handed to the holding companies at the end of the definition period. The third group is composed of natural monopolies and will either remain under public ownership, or else be transferred to the holding companies and remain regulated in the long term.

3. A safety net is created to protect workers from the hardships created by the forthcoming private restructuring period.

4. The main elements of property, contract, bankruptcy and antitrust laws are enunciated and put into operation.

5. Holding companies are created and incorporated.

Their number depends on country size and available expertise. It must be large enough to obtain effective monitoring of the firms, to limit the holdings' political power, and to avoid interlocking directorates of firms in tightly oligopolistic industries (see below). But it must be small enough for the holdings to own similar and diversified portfolios.[40]

The shares of a holding company are distributed freely and equally to all citizens but will not be traded before the mature phase.[41] The holding company's board of directors includes representatives of the government, of international institutions, and of the shareholders (all with minority voting rights).[42] Directors have fiduciary duty and, like the holding company's managers (see below), are rewarded with stocks, with a strong element of relative performance evaluation.

The board of directors selects the holding companies' managers, and puts them on an incentive scheme. During the noisy phase, managers of the holding companies receive a salary. At the inception period, they are rewarded on the basis of the absolute performance of their holding company (through stock options) and, more importantly, through the performance of their holding company compared to the average performance of other holding companies. Low-powered incentive schemes, i.e., small stock options, seem appropriate. The main incentives for the holding companies' managers during the noisy phase, besides relative performance evaluation, are career concerns and monitoring by the directors. The managers can be fired by the board of directors, in which case they receive only a fraction of the final reward at the inception period equal to the length of their tenure in the holding company divided by the total length of the noisy phase.[43]

The holding companies are endowed with the shares of the firms to be privatized (in the middle of the definition period for the firms that do not need to be broken up, and at the end of the definition period for the others). There are two variants: (1) each firm is allocated to a single holding company, and (2) each firm is shared among several holding companies. We will consider the first variant for concreteness.[44] [As mentioned in the text, one can also consider a situation where holding companies are debt as well as well as equity holders. For simplicity, we develop the case of pure equity holding in more detail.]

Firms are allocated randomly to the holding companies to avoid capture as well as to roughly equalize the initial quality of portfolios among holding companies. In tightly oligopolistic industries with little prospect for intense foreign competition, firms are allocated to holding companies so as to prevent common ownership of product market competitors. Similarly, where there is a danger of foreclosure, common ownership of a vertical structure is avoided.

6. The managers of the firms are given employment contracts. Bonuses, stock options and relative performance evaluation are limited by the large aggregate and idiosyncratic uncertainty and by the fact that the firms may divest themselves of assets or receive assets from other firms of the same or another holding company. Where the reallocation of capital across firms proceeds quickly, the managers can be given some stock options and bonuses linked to the performance of their firm.[45] The main incentives for the firms' managers during the noisy phase are career concerns and, especially, monitoring by the holding companies.

7. Regulation of public enterprises and private regulated firms: as in the private restructuring period (see below).

8. A merger commission is created (possibly, the divestiture commission becomes the merger commission after having broken up firms).

B. Private Restructuring Period 1. Holding companies restructure firms; they make sure that labor hoarding is eliminated and that insolvent firms are shut down. They reallocate capital and eliminate inefficient vertical integration. They monitor the firms' managers in their attempt to organize production efficiently.

Holding companies may sell units or firms to one another subject to the approval of the merger commission when they have assets in the same industry. The sale of assets may be used by the holding companies to purchase other assets or may be invested in indexed bonds.[46]

2. The government completes the legal system.

3. The government sets up agencies to regulate the banking sector and the stock market. These agencies will later prevent insider trading, enforce disclosure and conflict-of-interest rules, monitor savings institutions, etc.

4. The government sets a timetable for trade liberalization and defines foreign exchange guarantees for the capital inflow.[47]

5. Firms put modern accounting structures in place.

6. Borrowing: the EE industries will need money for updating current technologies and for financing new investments. First, they may borrow western capital (from private lenders as well as from international institutions). As we noted earlier, the comparative advantage of foreign participation might be loans rather than equity holdings because of the commitment and regulation problems associated with financing by domestic banks. Furthermore, foreign equity financing is likely to be restricted on political grounds anyway. Because the EE economies will need substantial inflows of capital from western economies,[48] it seems natural that privatized firms look abroad for debt holders.

A second source of financing may come from private domestic savings (we we do not have much feel for how large these private savings will be during the noisy phase). An interesting issue is whether one should allow holding companies to receive deposits and channel them to firms, in which case the holding companies would be similar to the US investment banks of the early twentieth century.

Should the creditors (foreign and domestic) lend their money directly to the firms or indirectly through the holding companies? In the scenario considered here, with each firm controlled by a single holding, it would seem difficult to channel loans directly to the firms. A holding company would then have an incentive to strip some of its firms of their assets through low transfer prices for intermediate goods or physical assets charged to other firms of the holding company. To prevent this behavior, the holding company must be liable for its firms' debts, or, more realistically, the loans must be channelled to the firms through the holding company.[49] [Such stripping of the firms' assets is more difficult, although not impossible, if the firms are held by several holding companies with minority shares. In this case, direct lending to the firms becomes a possibility.]

7. Each holding company hires or trains domestic and foreign analysts, who start studying the potential of the firms (not only the holding company's) that the holding company will be allowed to bid on.

8. Regulated private firms (owned by holding companies) are subject to cost-of-service regulation. The standard for cost of service is variable cost plus a fair rate of return on the investment sunk since the beginning of the process. No attempt is made to assess the rate base (amount of capital) before the beginning of the process. Thus prices only reflect new investments. Price reviews are frequent (every six months, say) in order to adjust to a rapidly changing environment.[50]

Given that we have strong reservations about cost-of-service regulation in general, we will need to justify this regulatory recommendation in Section 8.2.

9. State-owned enterprises are also subject to some form of cost-of-service regulation. There are serious concerns about the management of these state-owned firms. For instance, the employees are likely to ask for high wages, which the government is likely to grant (this is a serious concern in private firms subject to cost-of-service regulation as well. But in those firms, the presence of private owners may alleviate this concern a bit). In a sense, this problem is the same as that facing state-owned enterprises in western economies, but some of the safeguards there, like the benchmark of market wages in the private sector and the control of ministries in charge by independent general accounting offices, are much weaker in the transition economies. Serious thought should be given to the creation of commitment mechanisms for disciplining state-owned enterprises.

C. Inception of the Stock Market. Holding companies, newly created firms and institutional investors, and possibly foreigners[51] bid on each firm. The proprietor of the firm receives the proceeds of the auction. Holding companies bid in units of currency. Those who have a negative balance after the auctions issue indexed bonds in the corresponding amount to the government. Those with a positive balance receive a corresponding amount in indexed bonds from the government. (Or else the holding companies balance their accounts among themselves.) Some constraints are put on the auctions:

First, a mechanism is set up to prevent interlocking directorates in tightly oligopolistic industries.[52] For instance, in an industry with two large firms, a simple-minded mechanism has half of the holding companies bid on one firm and the other half bid on the other firm.

Second, to induce trade among holding companies and therefore to create incentives to collect during the noisy phase information about the firm's value, a fraction of each firm can be earmarked for holding companies that did not own this firm before (the holding companies resemble "privatization companies" if this fraction is equal to 100 percent).[53]

A holding company's total asset value after the auctions is the value of its shares in the firms, plus the proceeds of the sales of shares of the firms they used to own, minus the cost of purchase of shares of firms that belonged to other holding companies. The auctions have thus created an initial value for both the firms and the holding companies, which will enable other economic agents to enter (or exit) the stock market in a less uncertain situation for stock prices.

D. Market Period

1. Immediately after the inception period the markets for the firms' and the holding companies' stocks are open to all: citizens (who can sell their shares of holding companies and buy shares of firms), foreigners (up to government restrictions), holding companies (up to laws on mergers and interlocking directorates enforced by the merger commission), and other participants. The holding companies' assets are thus now liquid.
2. The government and the (non-equity holding) foreigners lose their voting rights in the boards of directors of the holding companies.
3. Firms can issue equity and bonds and can borrow from (newly created) domestic banks.
4. The managers of firms and holding companies are presumably put on incentive schemes that are more powerful than those during the noisy phase.
5. Trade liberalization is completed according to the predetermined timetable.
6. Regulated firms are given more innovative and more powerful incentive schemes than cost-of-service regulation ("incentive regulation").

8.2 Discussion of the Incentives in the Scenario

A. Incentives of Firms. The prescription of very low-powered incentive schemes for managers of firms reflects the absence of a stock market as well as the large uncertainty about profits. Close monitoring by the holding companies is important at this stage. We would also expect managerial career concerns to play a role: during the noisy stage, there is much to be learned about managers both because managers lack experience running profit-oriented units and because previous education is often unrelated to (and therefore is a poor predictor of the ability in) the job. The labor market is thus likely to pay close attention to the managers' behavior, which gives managers incentives to try to fool the labor market by working hard. This career concern, however, will be operative only under two conditions: first, managers should be able to move easily to other jobs; second, the labor market must be able to tell apart the roles of exogenous shocks and of managerial contribution in determining managerial performance.

The prescription of giving more bonuses and stock options after the inception phase reflects the ideas that there is then less exogenous uncertainty and that the firm's stock market supplies a measure of the value of assets.

B. Incentives in Holding Companies. Managers of holding companies can be given stronger monetary incentives than their counterparts in the firms they control. First, portfolio diversification gets rid of some of the firm-specific noise. Second, the use of relative performance evaluation for holding companies eliminates some of the aggregate risk. Yet, the high level of noise in the environment limits the role of monetary incentives. Monitoring by, in particular, foreign institutions and (possibly independent) government representatives may therefore be quite important. Last, we would expect career concerns also to play some role in the noisy phase.

The reduction of noise in the mature phase allows even stronger monetary incentives and reduces the desirability of monitoring by the board of directors. It thus seems logical to phase out the former form of monitoring (attached to the absence of a market for shares of the holding companies). [Because the value of the holding companies can be continuously assessed by looking at the stock value of their shares in firms, monitoring by big shareholders or financial regulation seems less important than for firms or banks, respectively.]

C. Regulatory Incentive Schemes. Cost-of-service regulation has many unattractive features. Prominent among them is the firm's low incentive to reduce current cost or to introduce (nonmonetary) innovations. The firm benefits from the cost reduction for a short period until the next regulatory review, at which point the price is adjusted downward to reflect lower costs. Similarly the firm enjoys the benefits of an innovation only until the next regulatory review. This problem will be particularly serious in the EE environment: the many adjustments taking place in the economy (including input prices) require frequent price reviews for the regulated firm, which creates low incentives for cost reduction and innovation.

Cost-of-service regulation, the predominant mode of regulation in many countries until the eighties, has been rightly decried, and more powerful incentive schemes (profit sharing provisions, price caps) have been introduced in some industries, in particular in the US and the UK. Despite favoring incentive regulation in general, we would be reluctant to recommend its adoption during the noisy phase in EE. As discussed earlier, both the high level of uncertainty and the strong threat of regulatory capture call for low-powered incentive schemes such as cost-of-service regulation. Only when the uncertainty has been somewhat resolved and safeguards have been put in place to prevent capture can incentive regulation be introduced.

D. Incentives and Auctions. The design of the inception stage must reflect several goals as discussed in Section 7; in particular, it must give the firm's owner during the noisy phase an incentive to invest; it must also give holding companies an incentive to collect information about the firms they will bid on, so as to create a relatively accurate measure of asset values at the inception stage. The firm will have some incentive to invest if its owner (the holding company) receives the proceeds of its auction and carefully monitors the firm.

Managers of the firm will also be induced to invest by the nonstationarity of their incentive scheme: the low-powered incentives in the noisy phase reduce the cost of investment borne by managers, while the higher-powered incentives in the mature phase allow them to benefit from these investments.

Earmarking shares on which the firm's owner is not allowed to bid is one simple way of creating liquidity in the stock market. The motivation was developed in Section 7. Its main purpose is not to create liquidity per se, but to give investors incentives to acquire information about the value of firms.[54] Forcing a firm to divest some of its shares eliminates to some extent the lemons problem associated with the voluntary sale or issue of shares.[55]

9. The Hands-on Foreign Ownership Scenario

The scenario of sales to western firms or institutions is much simpler than the one previously described. Incentives in the privatized firms and their owners are basically those of a western-style M-form, say. The main debate is then about what type of auction to set up.

The simplest auctions take into account only the price dimension of bids; for instance the firm is sold to the highest bidder. In contrast, the auctions may reflect the fact that markets are distorted; like the Treuhandanstalt, the privatization agency may conduct multicriteria auctions, where the bidders' commitments to employment, investment or other variables play a role beside prices. Introducing nonprice dimensions in auctions is clearly superior when the privatization agency is well informed and benevolent. But, leaving aside the increased transaction costs, multicriteria auctions have some drawbacks.

First, in such auctions the privatization agency substitutes for other government agencies in its quest for macroeconomic adjustments. This requires for instance that it correctly estimates the shadow prices of unemployment and investment, and that it makes sure that its various managers and branches use consistent shadow prices.

Second, unlike first-price auctions, say, multicriteria auctions leave discretion to the managers of the privatization agency. Poor information, friendship with specific bidders or outright corruption may therefore have grave consequences for the efficiency of the auctions. This danger has long been recognized in the procurement arena in western economies. For instance, in the US, Department of Defense officials or managers of public utilities purchasing power from qualified cogenerators are constrained to clearly lay out the measurement methods for nonprice dimensions and the weights of the different criteria. While this still leaves them with substantial discretion, it is not clear how one could reduce this discretion without jeopardizing the efficient use of their soft information about nonprice dimensions.

In the case of sales of firms, variables like employment and investment in the firm are generally more objective ("harder information") than the quality variables (the contractor's reputation, quality, risk of bankruptcy, etc.) assessed in the western procurement examples just mentioned. It is possible to measure and to put weight on them. What is harder, however, is to write contracts that specify the levels of employment and investment *contingent* on the state of technology of the firm or the future levels of demand. Such contingent contracts with the privatization agency would be quite desirable in view of the large uncertainty facing the firms. Simply choosing firms on the basis of price and noncontingent price dimensions seems to constrain the firm's future decision making too much.

One may then ask why the privatization agency would not sell to the highest bidder and let other policies correct macroeconomic distortions. Such policies have the advantage of, first, ensuring consistency of corrections across firms, second, of reducing the discretion (and the load) of the privatization agency, and, third, of not constraining firms to a noncontingent path of actions. A possible justification for the use of multidimensional auctions is that the shadow prices of macroeconomic variables such as investment and employment may not be uniform. For instance, some workers, if dismissed, are less likely to find a job than others; similarly, some investments create jobs while some others substitute for labor. If the shadow prices established at the national level cannot be sufficiently specific to the type of investment or jobs, there may be a point in decentralizing their assessment for each particular firm to the branches of the privatization agency.

The choice between multicriteria auctions and first-price auctions combined with macroeconomic policies is illustrated by the case of Eastern Germany. While the Treuhandanstalt's policy is to conduct multidimensional auctions, large investment subsidies are distributed by the government.[56] Akerlof *et al.* (1991) argue for the use of first-price auctions combined with large labor subsidies[57] (75 percent of current wages, say) to offset the current labor market distortions. While some of its aspects can be debated[58] (for instance, whether subsidies should apply economy wide rather than to the firms derived from the combines, whether geographical arbitrage by firms will have a serious negative impact, or whether estimates of the cost of the program are accurate), the Akerlof *et al.* embodies the general point that more thought must be given in order to vindicate the cost in terms of lack of flexibility and consistency associated with multicriteria auctions.

10. Conclusion

We argued that two key specificities of the transition process are the unusually high level of uncertainty in the firms' environment and the nonstationarity in its level. From there followed our main points:

1. Stock markets cannot function well during the noisy phase. The large amount of noise as well as the absence of trained analysts and reliable accounting data will deprive stock prices from most of their information content. The environment seems to call for hands-on monitoring by a stable ownership.
2. Managers of firms and holdings must face low-powered incentive schemes during the noisy phase, which raises a concern about efficiency. Alternative incentive mechanisms must be devised: e.g., close monitoring of firms by holdings or foreign firms, and of holdings by independent directors; relative performance evaluation for holding managers and holding directors; career concerns for all.
3. Because of the asymmetry between preventing mergers and breaking up firms, market structure interventions to prevent horizontal collusion and vertical foreclosure are best performed before privatization. A divestiture commission ought to be given incentives (in particular be free from interest group pressure) to rapidly perform breakups in those industries where anticompetitive behavior is a concern.
4. Regulated firms should be given low-powered incentive schemes during the noisy phase to limit the level of rents as well as to respond to the high threat of regulatory capture. Incentives should be raised during the mature phase.
5. Because privatization ought to occur before the introduction of a stock market, specific plans must be made for the inception of the stock market, that reflect the considerations discussed in Section 7.5.

The purpose of this paper has not been to formulate precise policy recommendations. Besides the fact that our theoretical understanding is still limited, policy recommendations should be tailored to the industrial and political realities of each country. The issue is not only to quantify the various parameters of the theoretical analysis – e.g., the likely length of the noisy phase, the number of holdings, or the list of industries with potential market structure problems. It is also to adjust the theoretical framework to account for further fairness considerations, for the political economy of commitment[59] or from the difficulty in attracting foreign capital depending on the country's specificities.

Acknowledgements

This paper is part of a research program initiated by the Institute for Policy Reform. It builds on Tirole [1991]. The author is grateful to Philippe Aghion, Olivier Blanchard, Christopher Clague, Mathias Dewatripont, Stan Fisher, Alan Gelb, Paul Joskow, Mancur Olson and Rob Vishny for helpful comments.

Notes

1. As was approximately the case in many Eastern European countries before and at the start of the change in regime (see Hinds [1990]).
2. See, e.g., Fallenbuchl [1991] for an account of privatization plans in Poland.
3. See, e.g., the OECD survey on Hungary [1991] for more details.
4. See, e.g., Willig [1991]. Pittman [1991] contains an extensive comparison of the antimonopoly laws of these three countries and of the Russian republic.
5. As noted in Pittman [1991], the laws have some potential loopholes through clauses allowing agreements "necessary to conduct an economic activity ... and not inducing a substantial limitation of competition" (Polish law) or that "are intended to prevent the abuse of an economic superiority" (Hungarian law).
6. See, e.g., Akerlof *et al.* [1991] and *The Economist* of September 14, 1991 for recent accounts.
7. We include few theoretical references in this section and the next. See, for instance, Holmström and Tirole [1989] for some other references.
8. Gibbons–Murphy [1990] find evidence that implicit compensation of US chief executive officers (the revision in their pay and their probability of remaining in their position) is negatively and significantly related to industry performance.
9. See Mace [1971] for a negative assessment of the activity of boards of directors.
10. Hostile takeovers are almost unheard of in Japan. In the US, in 1986 (an all-time record) 40 out of the 3,300 takeover transactions were hostile tender offers. It is difficult to measure the indirect effect of takeovers on voluntary transactions (Jensen [1988]).
11. See Grossman–Hart [1980] and Shleifer–Vishny [1986] for discussions of how free riding can be partly avoided.
12. See Holmström [1982].
13. The following discussion and that of the next subsection borrow from Holmström–Tirole [1990].
14. See, e.g., Hart–Tirole [1990].
15. In the US the Hart–Scott–Rodino Act [1976] requires firms with assets or sales over $100 million to report all proposed acquisitions of assets valued over $15 million to the Department of Justice and the Federal Trade Commission. These agencies, who share the mergers evaluation, must react within some period of time (thirty days, plus the possibility of a second request for information) or let the merger be consummated (see, e.g., Posner–Easterbrook [1981, pp. 25–26] for details. This act reflects the philosophy of Section 7 of the 1914 Clayton Act according to which monopoly power must be thwarted in its incipiency. Similar rules exist in other countries. The European Court of Justice enforces articles 85 and 86 of the European Community competition law (concerning restrictive agreements and abuse of a dominant position) by making agreements that violate those articles (such as anticompetitive mergers) null and void. Firms must notify the European Commission to obtain an exemption.
16. This subsection is based on Laffont–Tirole [1986, 1989].
17. Existing banks are widely thought of as being unable to function in a market economy.
18. Interfirm credit is pervasive in EE. For instance, around 40 percent of the book value of the Polish companies to be privatized is in the form of outstanding liabilities from other enterprises (see Frydman–Rapaczynski [1990]).
19. See Aghion–Howitt [1991] for a theoretical analysis of the link between growth and unemployment.
20. The causes of the wage–productivity differential are discussed in Akerlof *et al.*

[1989]. The East German productivity is estimated at less than a half, and often at one third, of the West German one (see Siebert [1990]). The wage ratio between the two parts of Germany has risen from around one third at the wage conversion to one half and is on its way to one (agreements have been signed to achieve wage parity in three or four years in some industries).

21. We will not here consider scenario 2 of the introduction. Employee ownership has several drawbacks. It creates inequities between manufacturing and non-manufacturing sector employees, and across employees of the manufacturing sector (because of substantial differences in the productivity of capital). Furthermore, employee ownership creates the threat of low investment and decapitalization (on this, see Bradley–Gelb ([1982, 1985], Grosfeld [1990] and Lipton–Sachs [1990]).

22. See Blanchard *et al.* [1990], Saldanha–Milanovic [1990] and Siebert–Schmieding [1990].

23. "Mutual find" is a slight misnomer, because the term usually does not suggest a strong control over the firms, unlike what is envisioned here for the noisy phase.

24. Bidding for the right to become an entrepreneur would select former members of the nomenklatura (who own the wealth). On the other hand, competing on the basis of the amount of leverage one is willing to bear (instead of bidding an amount of money one is willing to pay up front to be an entrepreneur) will give rise to the agency problems analyzed in the literature on credit rationing.

25. Rausser and Simon [1991] argue that the firm's specificities should be reflected not only in the incentive schemes, but also in the very way it is privatized. They envision a hearing where the government would solicit information from intervenors in order to determine the method of privatization, the structure of access or control rights in the firm, etc. The holding-company method in contrast does not tailor the privatization process to the firm's specificities (beyond the fact that it falls in the large-industrial-firms category).

26. This argument is reminiscent of Diamond's [1984] description of the role of financial intermediaries.

27. For instance,

> very often the railroad reorganization led to the establishment of voting trusts, with very important powers given over to three trustees for some term of years (typically five), partly to assure the security holders that responsible management would be in charge *during the period of corporate revival.* Investment banker domination of these voting trusts was commonplace.
>
> (Herman [1981], p. 118, emphasis added)

28. According to Brealey–Myers [1988, p. 326], venture capital investors do not necessarily demand a majority on the board of directors. A common compromise gives an equal number of seats to the founders and to outside investors. Coutarelli [1977, pp. 18, 110] observes that the European venture capitalist does not seek a majority interest in the investee, but that they still exert substantial control (often, the venture capitalist becomes a majority shareholder by supplying further funds to the venture anyway).

29. Of course, some successful firms do not go public (examples include investment-banking firms such as Goldman, Sachs & Co., construction and engineering firms like Bechtel or stereo manufacturer Bose). These firms either are not capital intensive or else finance new investments through retained earnings and secured bank lines.

30. In this respect, the foreign representatives need not necessarily belong to institutions engaged in micro projects (European Bank for Reconstruction and

Development, International Finance Corporation) and could also belong to the World Bank, the IMF, USAID or lending countries. Some merger experts from the US Department of Justice or the European Commission might also be involved.

31. A distinction to be made is that independent civil servants in western economies often have a long tenure. Because the divestiture commission is meant to be ephemeral, there is a danger that, despite their independence, government representatives might be pressured by their governments through the threat of bleak future job prospects. A possibility is that the members of the divestiture commission be reallocated later to the merger commission.

32. By "simple," we mean "not informationally demanding." For instance, a regulatory rule of the type "charge marginal cost" looks simple, but is extremely complex to implement because it requires cost information that is hard to obtain. Informationally demanding rules give discretion to regulators and are prone to capture.

33. Once bilateral trades of assets to achieve synergies have taken place, it is not clear why holding companies should trade among themselves. The gain for one becomes a loss for the other, as discussed in Section 3.

34. See, e.g., Brealey-Myers [1988, pp. 329–332] for a description.

35. But there are also differences with initial public offerings of private companies. For instance, agency problems before the offering are less serious when only the entrepreneur and possibly a venture capitalist are involved than when the firm belongs to a holding. See Section 7.1.2.

36. There is a large literature on "common-value auctions" with information acquisition, that ought to guide the design of such auctions (e.g. Milgrom [1981], Lee [1982], Matthews [1984]). This literature has looked at simple auctions, in general the first-price auctions, and derived equilibria (Riley [1988] allows the winner's price to depend on the other bids and on the stock's future performance and might be particularly relevant here). A recurring theme of this literature is that bidders acquire too much information from a social viewpoint. This conclusion comes from the assumption that the information has no other role than redistributing income, which is the case if the value of the stock is exogenously given. Here, the information revealed by the auction has social value because it helps measure the previous owner's performance and initialize the managers' stock incentives. New theoretical work in this area linking ex post auctions with ex ante incentives would be most welcome.

37. The market may perform such an adjustment itself after the auction stage. The idea behind avoiding the formation of majority shareholders is to limit the need for costly controls to prevent minority squeeze outs following the auction.

38. Effective control may require less than 50 percent, depending on the distribution of shares.

39. Laffont and Tirole [1988], building on ideas in Williamson [1976], study the issue of investment in a repeated auction context, and show that to promote unobservable investments, the incumbent firm should be favored at the renewal state and that the power of his incentive scheme should grow over time. See also Stein's [1988, 1989] related work on managerial myopia. In the context of an auction with information acquisition, investments are partially, but not fully observed by the potential bidders.

40. A number of holdings implies a large number of firms per holding and, possibly, reduced monitoring of each firm. On the other hand, holdings should be given similar portfolios to be comparable; increasing the number of firms per holding improves comparability by reducing on average the ex post inequities in the distribution of firms to holdings. To accommodate these two goals, the holding companies might not be given firms in all industries but rather specialize in a subset

of industries. Their performance would then be compared with that of holdings with similar portfolios rather than with that of the average holding. Alternatively, one could have holdings own firms in overlapping subsets of industries, and design more complex relative performance to enlarge the comparison group. The concern about the holdings' political power relates to the existence of a few powerful groups with congruent interests. The congruence of interests is in part created by the desire to set up comparable portfolios.

Yet another consideration that may be relevant to the choice of number of holding companies is that there should be enough of them in order for incentive schemes based on relative performance evaluation not to lead to perverse incentives (with two holding companies, say, beating on the other holding company may become a goal in its own right, while with many holding companies, a holding company cannot affect the average performance of the others much).

41. The distribution of shares can await the mature phase as the plan is not to create an active stock market before then. It may still be the case that a secondary market opens during the noisy phase with the private sector exchanging options on the shares to be distributed. We would still expect trade to be substantially smaller in the noisy phase than if a regular market existed for the shares.

42. Because of the scarcity of trained private-sector businessmen, representatives of shareholders might be former members of the controlling ministries, professors, or the like.

43. This is to guarantee that firing managers does not per se increase shareholders' wealth. In western economies, managers often exercise their stock options when they quit or are dismissed. But they cannot do so in this scenario because the stock market is not yet active in the noisy phase.

44. Giving a firm to a single holding company prevents free riding in the monitoring of the firm. Giving it to several holding companies may increase the diversification of the portfolios of the holding companies; it also may offer a diversity of views and prevent disastrous reorganizations brought about by a single, incompetent team.

45. There is an argument for focusing on "external restructuring" first so as to create well-defined entities quickly. Managers will be somewhat reluctant to perform the "internal restructuring" (elimination of labor hoarding, reorganization of management and production processes, etc.); defining the boundaries of the firm early will make them more responsible and will allow small monetary incentives to complement monitoring.

46. Alternatively, they could distribute dividends to the shareholders. An accounting system would then have to be devised, that would keep track of dividends and compound them at the rate of interest so that the wealths of the holding companies can be compared at the inception period.

47. See Newbery [1990a,b] for a discussion of the sequencing of trade liberalization.

48. See, e.g., Frydman–Rapaczynski [1990].

49. US courts have long recognized that a corporation must have the authority to act in its own best interests to be identified as a separate corporation and be subject to limited liability in case of insolvency. For example, in a well-known case (Henderson *et al.* v. Rounds & Porter Lumber Co. 99F. Supp 376, US District Court, W.D. Arkansas 1951), a timber processor was forced to sell lumber at half the market price to a lumber company which owned half of its shares, and was led to insolvency. The judge ruled that the latter company was liable for the former's debts.

50. Not including historical capital into the rate base considerably simplifies the regulatory process. Yet cost-of-service regulation will not be a trivial exercise.

Multiproduct firms will need to allocate common costs to each output according to some arbitrary, fully-distributed cost accounting system. Other issues familiar from the regulation of US utilities will surface: the choice of the rate of depreciation for new investment, the determination of allowable costs and that of a fair rate of return.

51. There are arguments suggesting that foreign bidding will be limited, related to the deep-seated fears of a foreign takeover (Blanchard *et al.* [1990]), to the threat of expropriation of foreign capital, and to the problems caused by the appreciation of the local currency brought about by a large sudden inflow of capital (as was the case in Chile). But see also Section 2.

52. In the US, Section 8 of the Clayton Act [1914] prohibits interlocking directorates when these lessen competition substantially.

53. Setting aside a fraction for other holding companies is similar to a secondary public offering by a private company that looks to sell some of its existing shares. The remaining fraction gives rise to an auction in which the previous owner participates.

54. A concern is that the large number of auctions might induce the holding companies to rig bids. There are however some safeguards. First, the seller is not an outside seller such as the government, but one of the holding companies. Second, foreigners might be used as "potential entrants" to break the collusion.

55. See Akerlof [1970] for the general issue, and Myers–Majluf [1984] for the application to corporate financing. See also the discussion in Section 7.

56. There is a sempiternal debate about whether investment subsidies promote employment. They do if capital and labor are complementary. On the other hand, one can also envision scenarios in which firms invest in labor-saving technology.

57. They propose a "self-eliminating flexible employment bonus", that is phased out as EG wages grow.

58. See DIW [1991] for a critique of the proposal.

59. See Dewatripont–Roland [1990] for interesting considerations on the means to obtain political support for a reform and on some commitment aspects of reforms.

References

Aghion, P. and P. Howitt [1991] "Growth and Unemployment", Mimeo, DELTA, EBRD, and University of Western Ontario.

Akerlof, G. [1970] "The Market for Lemons: Quality and the Market Mechanism," *Quarterly Journal of Economics*, 84: 488–500.

Akerlof, G., Rose, A., Yellen, J. and H. Hessenius [1991] "East Germany in from the Cold: The Economic Aftermath of Currency Union", forthcoming *Brookings Papers on Economic Activity*.

Blanchard, O., Dornbusch, R., Krugman, P., Layard, R., and L. Summers [1990] "Reform in Eastern Europe and the Soviet Union," Mimeo, UNU-WIDER, Helsinki.

Borensztein, E. and M. Kumar [1990] "Proposals for Privatization in Eastern Europe", Mimeo, IMF.

Bradley, K. and A. Gelb [1982] "Motivation and Control in the Mondragon Experiment," *British Journal of Industrial Relations*, 19: 20–33.

Bradley, K. and A. Gelb [1985] "Employee Buyouts of Troubled Companies," *Harvard Business Review*, 121–130.

Brealey, R. and S. Myers [1988] *Principles of Corporate Finance*, Third edition, McGraw-Hill.

Courtarelli, S. [1977] *Venture Capital in Europe*, NY: Praeger Publishers.

Dewatripont, M. and G. Roland [1990] "Economic Reform and Dynamic Political Constraints," Mimeo, Université Libre de Bruxelles.

Diamond, D. [1984] "Financial Intermediation and Delegated Monitoring," *Review of Economic Studies*, 51: 393–414.

DIW (Deutsche Institut für Wirtschaftsforschung) [1991] "Lohnsubventionen – kein Ausweg aus der Beschäftigungskrise in Ostdeutschland" Wochenbericht 36/91 (prepared by H. Flassbeck, G.A. Horn and W. Schemeret).

Fallenbuchl, Z. [1991] "Polish Privatization Policy", *Comparative Economic Studies*, 33: 53–70.

Fischer, S. [1991] "Privatization in East European Transformation," Mimeo, MIT.

Frydman, R. and A. Rapaczynski [1990] "Markets and Institutions in Large-Scale Privatizations," WP no. 49, Center for Law and Economic Studies, Columbia University.

Gibbons, R. and K. Murphy [1990] "Relative Performance Evaluation for Chief Executive Officers," *Industrial and Labor Relations Review*, 43: 30S–51S.

Grosfeld, I. [1990] "Privatization of State Enterprises in Eastern Europe: The Search for a Market Environment," Document No. 90–17, DELTA, Paris.

Grossman, S. and O. Hart [1980] "Takeover Bids, the Free-Rider Problem and the Theory of the Corporation," *Bell Journal of Economics*, 11: 42–64.

Hart, O. and J. Tirole [1990] "Vertical Integration and Market Foreclosure," *Brookings Papers on Economic Activity*: *Microeconomics*, pp. 205–286.

Herman, E. [1981] *Corporate Control, Corporate Power*, Cambridge University Press.

Hinds, M. [1990] "Issues in the Introduction of Market Forces in Eastern European Socialist Economies," Mimeo, World Bank.

Holmström, B. [1982] "Managerial Incentives Problems: A Dynamic Perspective," in *Essays in Honor of Lars Wahlbeck*. Helsinki: Swedish School of Economics.

Holmström, B. and J. Tirole [1989] "The Theory of the Firm," Chapter 2 in R. Schmalensee and R. Willig (eds.), *Handbook of Industrial Organization*, Amsterdam: North–Holland.

Holmström, B. and J. Tirole [1990] "Corporate Control and the Monitoring Role of the Stock Market," Mimeo, Yale University and MIT.

Jensen, M. [1988] "Takeovers: Their Causes and Consequences," *Journal of Economic Perspectives*, 2: 21–48.

Laffont, J.-J. and J. Tirole [1986] "Using Cost Observation to Regulate Firms," *Journal of Political Economy*, 94: 614–641.

Laffont, J.-J. and J.Tirole [1988] "Repeated Auctions of Incentive Contracts, Investment and Bidding Parity, with an Application to Takeovers," *Rand Journal of Economics*, 19: 516–537.

Laffont, J.-J. and J. Tirole [1989] "The Politics of Government Decision Making: A Theory of Regulatory Capture," forthcoming, *Quarterly Journal of Economics*.

Lee, T. [1982] "Resource Information Policy and Federal Resource Leasing," *Bell Journal of Economics*, 13: 561–568.

Lipton, D. and J. Sachs [1990] "Privatization in Eastern Europe: The Case of Poland," Mimeo, Harvard University.

Lutz, M. [1991] "Eastern European Reforms and Transformations: Progressions and Progressiveness", paper presented at the 3rd International Conference on Socio-economics, Stockholm.

Mace M. [1971] *Directors: Myth and Reality*, Harvard Business School.

Matthews, S. [1984] "Information Acquisition in Discriminatory Auctions," in M. Boyer and R. Kihlstrom, eds., *Bayesian Models in Economic Theory*, Amsterdam: North–Holland, pp. 181–208.

Milgrom, P. [1981] "Rational Expectations, Information Acquisition, and Competitive Bidding," *Econometrica*, 49: 921–944.
Myers, S. and N. Majluf [1984] "Corporate Financing and Investment Decisions When Firms Have Information that Investors Do Not Have," *Journal of Financial Economics*, 13: 187–221.
Narayanan, K. [1991] "Bank Influence and Industrial Concentration: A Comparative Study of Post-War West Germany and Japan," Mimeo, MIT.
Newbery, D. [1990a] "Tax Reform, Trade Liberalization and Industrial Restructuring in Hungary," forthcoming in *European Policy*.
Newbery, D. [1990b] "Reform in Hungary: Sequencing and Privatization," forthcoming, *European Economic Review Papers and Proceedings*.
OECD [1991] *OECD Economy Survey on Hungary*, Paris
Pittman, R. [1991] "Some Critical Provisions in the Antimonopoly Laws of Central and Eastern Europe", US Department of Justice, D.P. EAG 91–10.
Posner, R. and F. Easterbrook [1981] *Antitrust*, Second edition, West Publishing Company.
Rausser, G. and L. Simon [1991] "The Political Economy of Transition in Eastern Europe: Packaging Enterprises for Privatization," Mimeo, UC Berkeley.
Riley, J. [1988] "Ex Post Information in Auctions," *Review of Economic Studies*, 55: 409–430.
Saldanha, F. and B. Milanovic [1990] "A Proposal for a Fast and Efficient Privatization of the State Sector," *The Privatization Review*, Fall, 20–30.
Shleifer, A. and R. Vishny [1986] "Large Shareholders and Corporate Control," *Journal of Political Economy*, 94: 461–488.
Siebert, H. [1990] "The Economic Integration of Germany: An Update", Kiel Discussion Paper 160a.
Siebert, H. and H. Schmieding [1990] "Restructuring Industry in the GDR," Mimeo, Kiel Institute of World Economics.
Stein, J. [1988] "Takeover Threats and Managerial Myopia," *Journal of Political Economy*, 96: 61–80.
Stein, J. [1989] "Efficient Capital Markets, Inefficient Firms: A Model of Myopic Corporate Behavior," *Quarterly Journal of Economics*, 104: 655–669.
Tirole, J. [1991] "Privatization in Eastern Europe: Incentives and the Economics of Transition", forthcoming, *National Bureau of Economic Research Macroeconomics Annuals*, MIT Press.
Treuhandanstalt [1991] "The Chance of the 90's: Investing in Eastern Germany", brochure.
Triska, D. [1991] "Why and How to Privatize in Post-Communist Countries (the case of Czechoslovakia)", Mimeo, Federal Ministry of Finance, Prague.
Vickers, J. and G. Yarrow [1988] *Privatization: An Economic Analysis*, Cambridge, MA: MIT Press.
Vickers, J. and G. Yarrow [1990a] "Economic Perspectives on Privatization," Mimeo, Oxford University.
Vickers, J. and G. Yarrow [1990b] "The British Electricity Experiment," Mimeo, Oxford University.
Williamson, O. [1976] "Franchise Bidding for Natural Monopolies – In General and with Respect to CATV," *Bell Journal of Economics*, 7: 73–104.
Williamson, O. [1991] "Institutional Aspects of Economic Reform: The Transaction Cost Economics Perspective", Mimeo, UC Berkeley.
World Bank [1988] *Techniques of Privatization of State-Owned Enterprises*. Volumes I, II, and III.

71

Privatization in Eastern Europe: The Case of Poland

David Lipton and Jeffrey Sachs

Source: *Brookings Papers on Economic Activity*, 2, 1990, pp. 293–341.

The transformation of the Eastern European economies into market economies requires comprehensive action on three fronts: macroeconomic stabilization, liberalization of economic activity, and privatization of state-owned enterprises.[1] Each of these is a monumental task. Nonetheless, privatization stands out as the most difficult and novel of the three, both conceptually and politically. There are enormous challenges in transferring state-owned property—which constitutes around 90 percent of industrial capital in Eastern Europe—to private hands in a manner that is rapid, equitable, and fiscally sound, and that accomplishes two fundamental goals: the efficient operation of the resulting private enterprises and the development of efficient capital markets.

The task of privatization in Eastern Europe is not widely understood in the West, partly because misleading analogies have been made to privatization in other parts of the world.[2] In a typical country that has recently "privatized" some state enterprises, only a handful of firms—perhaps up to a few dozen—have been sold by the government to the private sector. These sales may have made an important economic difference in some sectors, but they have not involved a fundamental transformation of the economy. The amount of capital transformed through privatization has generally been a small proportion of total business capital and national income, and the economies typically had large, private industrial and financial sectors before the privatizations.

In Eastern Europe, privatization is a very different task, involving nothing less than the complete redefinition of property rights for literally thousands of enterprises. Privatization means creating anew the basic institutions of a market financial system, including corporate governance of managers, equity ownership, stock exchanges, and a variety of financial intermediaries, such as pension funds, mutual funds, and investment trusts. The importance of such financial intermediaries can be gauged from the fact that institutional investors now hold more than half the value of shares in the United Kingdom,

Italy, and Japan, as well as more than half the value of the New York Stock Exchange.[3] The economic challenge, then, is to combine the redefinition of property rights with the creation of vital financial market institutions. The political challenge is also awesome: to design a mechanism for creating private property rights that can win broad, lasting social approval (and prevent special interests from paralyzing the process through a fight for the spoils).

Ironically, the rush of investment bankers and Western experts who have been proposing privatization strategies in Eastern Europe have not addressed the real needs of the privatization process. Not surprisingly, the bankers have focused almost exclusively on a *firm-by-firm* strategy not unlike the programs in which they have participated in other parts of the world. In Eastern Europe, however, this customized approach is likely to bog down for political, economic, and financial reasons well before a significant portion of state firms are actually privatized.

In this paper, we review the enormous scope of the privatization task, and suggest means for a rapid, efficient, and equitable transformation of state property into private property. Our focus will be Poland, where we serve as economic advisers. Some of the problems that we discuss are more urgent there than elsewhere. Particularly problematic for Poland is the fact that workers' councils are powerfully organized in many enterprises, and are fighting for worker self-management and against privatization. Nonetheless, most of the analysis of privatization in Poland applies throughout Eastern Europe.

We should offer one disclaimer at the outset. Even though we favor rapid privatization, we doubt that privatization will produce immediate, large increases in productivity or managerial efficiency. The real gains from private ownership will take years to manifest themselves—the length of time needed for managers to be upgraded, supervisory boards to gain experience, stock markets to improve the quality of valuation of enterprises, and real economic restructuring to take place. Nonetheless, we believe that in order to enjoy those enormous long-term gains, it is necessary to proceed rapidly and comprehensively on creating a privately owned, corporate-based economy in Eastern Europe.

Since privatization is such a vast topic, and cannot be treated comprehensively in a single paper, it is important to spell out what we will *not* discuss here. We do not discuss the problems of the "small-scale" privatization of retail shops and smaller industrial enterprises.[4] We will not touch on the socially complex question of *restitution* of property (or reprivatization as it is called in Eastern Europe) that was nationalized from the 1940s through the 1960s. We will not discuss the ground-up development of the private sector in Eastern Europe, which is at least as important, and in Janos Kornai's view, even more important, than the privatization of state enterprises.[5] Finally, we will say relatively little about the crucial question of managerial compensation, which can provide a vital link between the interests of managers and the interests of the owners of the enterprises.

The Debate over the Pace of Privatization

Perhaps the central debate about privatization in Eastern Europe concerns the feasible pace of an effective privatization strategy. Some authors believe that the potential efficiency gains from private ownership and private capital markets are so overwhelming that the process must be speeded up as much as possible. Advocates of rapid privatization are typically confident that even if quick privatization initially leads to an inappropriate distribution of ownership with, for example, too diffuse ownership, or firms in the wrong hands, then the capital markets will encourage a reshuffling of ownership through takeovers, mergers, and buyouts so that there is a proper matching of owners and firms. For these analysts, privatization should be undertaken as rapidly as possible, to reap the full benefits of private ownership.

Many authors who take this point of view have recently called for the free distribution of the enterprises into private hands as a way to speed privatization.[6] In Poland, the landmark study calling for a free distribution of shares in order to speed privatization is by Janusz Lewandowski and Jan Szomburg.[7] In Czechoslovakia, the minister of finance, Vaclav Klaus, and his deputy, Dusan Triska, have been outspoken advocates of rapid privatization through the sale of enterprise shares for vouchers. In Hungary, Tibor Liska has been an outspoken advocate of the free distribution of shares to the population. Other important and influential pieces are those by Manuel Hinds and Roman Frydman and Andrzej Rapaczynski.[8] Other researchers advocating rapid privatization through the free distribution of shares include Olivier Blanchard and Richard Layard, Fernando Saldanha and Branko Milanovic, and Anders Aslund. The president of the Hungarian-American Enterprise Fund, Alexander Tomlinson, has also proposed rapid privatization through the free distribution of shares.[9] *The Economist*, too, has advocated rapid privatization in this manner.[10]

For other analysts, privatization should take place at a more measured pace in order to ensure the development of effective enterprise ownership. In Kornai's view, the apparatus of the state

> is obliged to handle the wealth it was entrusted with carefully until a new owner appears who can guarantee a safer and more efficient guardianship. The point now is not to hand out the property, but rather to place it in the hands of a really better owner.[11]

Kornai believes that in order to bring about effective ownership, the enterprises should be sold carefully and mostly on a one-by-one basis, rather than freely distributed to the public.

We are sympathetic to the concerns that Kornai raises. As he stresses, the privatization strategy should focus on establishing effective ownership and corporate governance, rather than on simply transferring nominal ownership to the private sector. The secondary market for corporate control, which might operate, for example, through takeover bids on a stock market, will not be reliable enough to ensure efficient matches between enterprises and owners. Nonetheless, we believe that privatization can proceed faster than the one-by-one sale of enterprises would dictate. The process can be accelerated through the free distribution of shares in a manner consistent with the development of effective ownership.

One reason that we stress rapid privatization is that the current pattern of ownership in Eastern Europe is itself prone to massive inefficiencies. The potential costs of overly rapid privatization must be traded off with the high cost of maintaining the present system in which state-owned enterprises lack clear incentives (or actually have perverse incentives) in the face of the market forces now being introduced in Eastern Europe. But our reasons go beyond that, to the politics of privatization. In our opinion, the real risk in Eastern Europe is not that the privatization process will be less than optimal, but that it will be paralyzed entirely. We believe that unless hundreds of large firms in each country are brought quickly into the privatization process, the political battle over privatization will soon lead to stalemate in the entire process, with the devastating long-term result that little privatization takes place at all.

Consider the current political situation. While the state enterprises are presumably owned by the state, the various components of ownership—including the rights to use the property, to benefit from financial returns, and to dispose of the property—are in fact jointly held, in a shifting and imprecise way, among managers, workers, and the state. In this situation, workers and managers have incentives to wrest the income and assets of the firm away from the state, often in ways that are highly inefficient and politically explosive.

If property rights are not clearly defined in the near future, enormous energy will likely be wasted in a bruising fight over property rights. As in Argentina, for example, the nation's political and social energy will be spent defining the rules of the game, rather than operating efficiently within stable rules. Groups of workers and managers, both at the enterprise level and at the political level, will surely try to strengthen their claims (both legal and implicit) over the enterprises in ways that will further confuse the ownership structure. Their efforts may simply block the state's political and legal capacity to privatize the firms at a later date. Insiders such as influential bureaucrats and state managers might well use their positions to grab an inordinate share of the state property. Such actions could undermine the public consensus to proceed with privatization.

Workers' desires to block privatization may also increase rapidly in the near future if, as expected, unemployment rates rise sharply in Eastern Europe. Workers may assume, with some justification, that their job tenure will be undercut by the privatization of their firm. Even if workers in a particular enterprise do not actually block privatization, they may attempt to bargain with the government, demanding for example a cut in the enterprise's debts or various guarantees on employment levels, as their "price" for letting the privatization go forward. If the government becomes enmeshed in case-by-case bargaining, there will be no end in sight, given that hundreds of large enterprises must be privatized.

Our fears of paralysis are not hypothetical. In almost all countries where privatizations have been attempted, there have been major political obstacles to the case-by-case approach. These obstacles are likely to develop more rapidly in Eastern Europe given the thinness or, in some cases, the nonexistence of capital markets, the difficulties of valuation, the likelihood that privatizations will be followed by layoffs, and the sheer number of firms that must be privatized. Already, after just a handful of privatizations, Hungary has entered into a heated internal debate over political accusations that the privatization process is selling Hungarian assets too cheaply to the rest of the world. The first director of the Hungarian State Property Agency was fired in part because of the controversial flotation of shares of the tourist agency Ibusz on the Austrian stock exchange. In Poland, an increasingly powerful coalition of interests that favor worker management is already organizing itself against widespread privatization.

We propose a series of detailed steps to address the various pitfalls of privatization. At the outset, we recommend that hundreds of the largest enterprises be converted into Treasury-owned joint-stock companies. This step will ensure that the enterprise sector is indeed transformed into corporate form. Right from the start, some firms could be managed on a case-by-case basis (for instance, where a private bidder comes forward). Most firms, however, would follow a special track emphasizing the rapid distribution of shares. A portion of shares would be given at a low price or at no charge to workers, and another portion of shares would be transferred rapidly and free of charge to various financial intermediaries (such as mutual funds, pension funds, and commercial banks). Shares in these intermediaries will in turn be distributed or sold to households. Finally, the government would retain a portion of the shares of each enterprise and would gradually sell them off as a *block* to "core investors" who are to take a key role in management of the enterprise.[12] In this way, we hope to combine rapid privatization through free distribution with the advantages of case-by-case sales.

Current Ownership Patterns in Poland

The government of Poland aspires to an ownership structure like that of Western Europe. First, the bulk of the productive sector should be held in private hands. Second, the ownership of large enterprises should be predominantly in corporate form, with shares held by households, financial intermediaries, and other nonfinancial firms. And third, financial markets should be developed to facilitate the trading of shares.

As can be seen in table 1, the proportion of enterprise capital in state hands in Poland and the rest of Eastern Europe is vastly above the proportion in Western Europe.[13] Nowhere in Western Europe does the share of state ownership currently exceed 20 percent. Even the Social Democratic regimes in Scandinavia—which serve as role models for many politicians in Eastern Europe—have very little state capital, and almost none in the industrial sector.[14]

Table 1 Size of the state sector, measured by output and employment, selected countries (percent)

Country	*Output*	*Employment*
Command economies		
Czechoslovakia (1986)	97.0	...
East Germany (1982)	96.5	94.2
Soviet Union (1985)	96.0	...
Poland (1985)	81.7	71.5
China (1984)	73.6	...
Hungary (1984)	65.2	69.9
Market economies[a]		
France (1982)	16.5	14.6
Austria (1978–79)	14.5	13.0
Italy (1982)	14.0	15.0
Turkey (1985)	11.2	20.0
Sweden	...	10.6
Finland	...	10.0
United Kingdom (1978)	11.1	8.2
West Germany (1982)	10.7	7.8
Portugal (1976)	9.7	...
Denmark (1974)	6.3	5.0
Greece (1979)	6.1	...
Norway	...	6.0
Spain (1979)	4.1	...
Netherlands (1971–73)	3.6	8.0
United States (1983)	1.3	1.8

Source: Milanovic (1989), tables 1, 4 and 7.
a. Figures exclude government services, but include state-owned enterprises engaged in commercial activities.

State-owned Industrial Enterprises in Poland

Poland had 3,177 state enterprises in the industrial sector in 1988.[15] The country aims to privatize most or all of these firms, so that the ownership structure in industry will approach Western Europe's. As in Western Europe, privatization is likely to come first in industry and small-scale services, and then later and perhaps to a lesser extent, in utilities, communications, and railway transport. Privatization is typically more complicated in these latter cases, since the output markets in these sectors tend to be less competitive than in industry. Therefore, in these cases privatization must be accompanied by a regulatory apparatus for controlling the pricing and output decisions of the privatized firms.[16]

While some observers have worried that privatization in Eastern Europe should be delayed until after widespread demonopolization has occurred, we do not believe that monopoly power is an urgent problem in the industrial sector. Since most Polish industry is now subjected to strong international competition resulting from a policy of low tariffs and free trade, the problem of industrial monopoly is rather small even in sectors that are dominated by a few firms. Indeed, the Polish Ministry of Finance recently reviewed the competitive environment facing the 500 largest industrial enterprises and concluded that there are few cases, if any, where concerns over monopoly power should stand in the way of rapid privatization.

To some extent, the figure of 3,177 state-owned industrial enterprises exaggerates the task of privatization, since output and employment are concentrated in only the top few hundred firms. The size distribution of firms

Table 2 Poland: size distribution of state enterprises, 1990

	Sales[a]		*Net income*[a]		*Employment*[b]	
Number of enterprises	*Billions of US dollars*	*Percent of total*	*Billions of US dollars*	*Percent of total*	*Thousands of workers*	*Percent of total*
Top 100	18.1	39	2.9	43	711	18
Top 200	23.1	49	3.6	53	1,036	26
Top 300	26.5	57	4.0	59	1,261	31
Top 400	29.1	62	4.4	65	1,461	36
Top 500[c]	30.9	66	4.6	68	1,612	40
Total of socialized industrial sector	46.8	100	6.8	100	4,051	100

Source: Lista 500 and *Informacja Statystyczna*. Firms are ranked by sales.

a. Data are annualized from January–June 1990.

b. Employment refers to 1989 employment levels.

c. Sixteen firms have been dropped from the top 500 firms. We use the remaining 484 firms as a proxy.

by employment, output, and earnings is shown in table 2. Note that the top 500 firms, ranked by sales, account for 40 percent of employment, 66 percent of sales, and 68 percent of net income in the socialized industrial sector.[17] If most of the top 500 firms can be privatized, then an important part of the industrial sector, measured by employment, sales, and net income, will have been privatized.

It is useful to divide the task of privatization into three categories depending on the sizes of firms. *Large*-scale privatization refers to firms that are too large to be sold or distributed to a single Polish buyer. For these firms, privatization will require that ownership be vested in several groups of owners, or sold to a large foreign buyer. *Medium*-sized privatization refers to firms in which the majority stake can be sold to a single buyer, either through a management–worker buyout, or in a sale to an outside group. *Small*-scale privatization refers to very small firms, mainly in retail trade but also to some extent in the industrial sector. In these cases, privatization will be accomplished mainly by transferring ownership to the firms' workers, through a lease or an outright purchase.

As a working assumption, the Polish authorities are presently focusing on the 500 largest industrial firms as the universe for large-scale privatization, although the privatization program will simultaneously go forward for small-, medium-, and large-scale enterprises. Since large-scale privatization is the most difficult kind, and since such privatization will involve the bulk of the industrial sector, we limit our attention to these firms.

Legal and Political Aspects of Ownership

Many of the deepest problems of privatization arise from the ill-defined current ownership structure in Poland, and in the rest of Eastern Europe.[18] In Western thought, ownership entails several rights over a resource: the right to determine its use; the right to the earnings of the resource; and the right to dispose of the resource. In Eastern Europe, however, those rights are now rather vaguely distributed among the workers, managers, and state bureaucracies.

Under classical central planning, the state maintained all ownership rights. The enterprise had a "founding organ," usually a branch ministry, which maintained formal oversight of the enterprise. The enterprise's functions, of course, were largely determined by the central plan. It was during the process of reform communism (in Yugoslavia after 1948; Hungary after 1968; Poland after 1980; and the Soviet Union after 1985) that the situation became highly muddled.

Part of the process of reform communism in all these countries was the granting of increased operational and financial autonomy to the enterprise.[19] In Poland, these reforms were adopted in September 1981, with the Law on State Enterprises and the Law on Self-Management of the State Enterprises' Employees, just before the imposition of martial law. In theory, the enterprises were to become largely self-managing and self-financing, with less reliance on transfers from the state. Investment spending was to come increasingly from retained earnings, rather than from a state budgetary allocation. The enterprises were to develop more of their own work plans, with less top-down direction from the bureaucracy. In this way, enterprises were to become increasingly subject to market forces.

We know well that these decentralizing reforms in Poland, and elsewhere in Eastern Europe, were at best partial, and failed to create hard budget constraints for enterprises.[20] Under reform communism enterprises escaped from central planning into an endless series of negotiations with the bureaucracy over taxes, subsidies, prices, and output, rather than into a true market environment. Nonetheless, the devolution of power upon the enterprises did blur many of the ownership rights previously exercised by the central bureaucracy.

Workers' Councils

The reforms also raised the question of which group was to assume these ownership rights. In all countries, the formal answer was that *the workers of the enterprise* exercised responsibility for the enterprise, usually through a collective assembly of all the enterprise workers (like an annual shareholders' meeting), and through a representative workers' council, which was to govern the enterprise between meetings of the general assembly.

A workers' council in Poland is composed of fifteen workers who are elected by secret ballot for two-year terms. The councils are charged with "the formation of the enterprise's annual plans, investment decisions, changes in the scope of enterprise activities, acceptance and approval of the annual balance, and decisions on merger and enterprise dissolution."[21] In most enterprises, the workers' council has been given the power to appoint the manager. In enterprises of "primary importance," the workers' council has been given veto power over the choice made by the government.

Note that the development of workers' councils was not the only logical alternative for Eastern Europe, though it was universally taken to be the one most consistent with Marxist ideology. Another possibility, for example, could have been the classic state-owned enterprise in the British tradition, which is governed by an independent board of directors appointed by the government.[22] The board of directors possesses some operational independence from the government, and appoints the management, approves its plans, and monitors its performance.

Interestingly, privatization would now be much easier had enterprises taken the form of British state enterprises. In that case, the enterprise would already be in corporate form, and privatization would merely involve the transfer of control from the board of directors to new private owners. In the case of worker-managed firms, however, privatization requires a disenfranchisement of the workers' council at the same time that corporate governance is vested in a new board of directors.

In practice, the workers' council has played a lesser role, even under the communist system, than what had been set forth in the legislation. While workers' councils were set up in roughly 90 percent of Poland's state enterprises, it is commonly estimated that they have been fully effective in only about 15 percent of the enterprises, though these have typically been among the larger enterprises.[23] In many other firms, where workers' councils were not effectively organized, the state enterprise managers have acted with considerable independence, not only from the workers but from the state bureaucracy as well.

Consequences of Greater Autonomy for Enterprises

The Communist party, when it was in power, also played a key role in the management of the enterprises. Not only was the choice of managers heavily influenced by the "nomenklatura system," in which the party nominated politically acceptable directors, but also important decisions for the enterprise were referred to the "enterprise collective body," which was composed of the first secretary of the party, together with the managing director of the enterprise, the chairman of the trade union, and the chairman of the workers' council.[24]

After the collapse of Poland's communist regime, the independence of the enterprises increased enormously. The nomenklatura system collapsed, as did the direct intervention of the party in enterprise matters. In many enterprises, the workers' councils gained new strength, and ousted enterprise managers. In other cases where the workers' councils remained weak, the state managers inherited the powers previously held by the bureaucracy and the party. Although in March 1990 the rights of the workers' councils were reaffirmed, emphasizing that "the council must approve the decision by the enterprise to sell assets, to form or to enter into an existing trade company, to buy shares of stock in corporations, or to sell off shares in those corporations," there have been few legal changes in the power of the workers' councils.[25]

As the room for maneuver increased for the enterprises, the problems arising from the muddled ownership structure became acute. Workers and the managers gained control over the firm, but lacked the clear title to its assets; they therefore had the overwhelming incentive to appropriate the capital income of the firm and strip it of its assets. As Lewandowski and Szomburg put it, "There is still no one to lose anything from the decapitalization of state property."[26] For example, with increased freedom to set wages, workers' councils pressured managers to raise wages in order to absorb an increasing amount of the firms' cash flow. Liberalization in 1987–88, therefore, ushered in an enormous real wage explosion and a wage–price spiral.[27]

The possibilities for asset stripping became even more dramatic when various property laws were changed during 1988–89, the final period of communist rule. First, the private sector was liberalized, and state firms were allowed to do business with the private sector. Second, joint ventures with foreign partners were encouraged. As a result of the changes, managers quickly discovered ways to appropriate state property by making sweetheart deals with an outside partner in a process that quickly became known as "spontaneous privatization." Lewandowski and Szomburg call the process "legal parasitism."

Consider the case of joint ventures. The enterprises were given enormous freedom to enter into joint venture arrangements subject to little central control. Many state managers, particularly in firms without strong workers' councils, quickly realized that they could make deals with foreign partners. They would grant the foreign partner a highly favorable stake in the enterprise, and in return the foreign partner would grant the manager an attractive position in the new venture. The manager effectively traded the state property for personal gain.

Even more egregious cases ensued in which the state enterprises entered into contracts with newly established private firms in which the state manager had a personal stake. The manager might then lease to the private firm the plant and machinery of the state enterprise at highly favorable terms. The profits of the state enterprise would thereby be transferred to the private firm. These abuses became recognized by the general public in 1989, and led to an enormous storm of protest. The public realized that during the communist-managed transition to a market economy, the communist-appointed managers were appropriating the best property for themselves. The public's revulsion against spontaneous privatization was intense and surely helped to speed the demise of the old regime.

Since the start of 1990, Poland's industrial enterprises have had almost complete freedom with regard to pricing, production, and international trade decisions. Thus, the autonomy of the enterprises has been greatly enhanced. At the same time, though, administrative means have been introduced to cope, however imperfectly, with the anomalous ownership structure. Wage controls have been put in place to prevent enterprises from appropriating their own profits, and indeed the profitability of the industrial sector has increased markedly during 1990, despite a domestic recession.

While the government's oversight of joint ventures has been strengthened, there is anecdotal evidence to suggest that at least some joint venture arrangements still serve the self-interest of managers. Also, while new conflict-of-interest laws have been put in place to prohibit spontaneous privatizations through sweetheart deals, the effectiveness of these regulations is not yet clear. The government has also undertaken to review and reverse cases of conflict of interest that occurred in the past.

In some ways, however, recent reforms have made it harder, not easier, to define real claimants to the assets and residual income of a firm. On the one side, the government has drawn a sharper line between an enterprise's earnings and the state budget. Enterprises now receive fewer transfers from the state budget, and are allowed to retain more of their earnings after paying various corporate taxes. But they are not free to distribute those earnings through wage payments, without incurring substantial financial penalties under the excess wage tax law. And clearly because there are no private shareholders to whom the profits can be distributed, the residual income remains with the firm. There, the retained earnings can be used for only two purposes: to amass financial wealth or to make investment expenditures.

We can expect that unless the claimants of the residual income are quickly defined through the privatization process, management and workers will, through indirect means, find ways to enrich themselves. Some of the profits might be enjoyed through a reduced work effort, or through low-return investments, like new factory cafeterias, for example, that benefit the incumbents of the firm.

In yet a final facet of the ownership rights debate, most legal analysts in Poland believe that the state remains the holder of enterprise capital, but even this point has become muddled. The book value of the capital of the firm has been divided between the "founder's fund," which represents the initial capitalization of the firm, and the "enterprise fund," which reflects the book value of retained earnings. Some managers and workers' groups have asserted that the enterprise fund should be viewed as already belonging to the enterprise, while most legal scholars in Poland assert that the enterprise fund as well as the state fund belong to the state.

Privatization and Worker Management

The shift to a Western European ownership structure will require that enterprise governance be removed from the workers' councils and managers and be placed squarely with a supervisory board (or board of directors) controlled by the owners of the enterprise.[28] In essence, privatization requires first that certain ownership rights, now vested in the enterprises, and particularly in the workers' councils, be eliminated so that the property rights to an enterprise can be transferred to the real owners.

The transfer of power to private owners poses a significant political challenge to the governments of Eastern Europe, since support for worker control and worker ownership remains powerful in many enterprises and in some political circles. Not only was the worker management ideology validated in years of struggle against central planning, but it also enjoys well-organized support in enterprises that have active workers' councils. These councils now aim to strengthen their control and perhaps win outright ownership of the firms. In enterprises facing cutbacks in employment, many workers view their workers' councils as the best hope for avoiding layoffs and protecting workers' interests, if not the interests of the capital.

It is clear that for political reasons, and perhaps for ethical reasons as well, workers will have to be partially compensated for the transfer of control from workers' councils to private owners. After all, workers stand to lose some property rights because of privatization. The standard suggestion is that workers should be allowed to purchase a *limited proportion of shares* (20 percent according to the Polish Privatization Law) in their enterprise at a discounted price when the firm is privatized. The practical question is whether this concession will be politically palatable, at least enough so as to permit the privatization process to move forward smoothly. It is possible that even with the concession of favorable purchase terms for shares, some workers' groups will fight to slow the privatization process in order to assert their claims for complete worker control.

There are strong reasons, on grounds of equity as well as efficiency, for rejecting workers' demands to deliver greater firm ownership to them. To begin, workers were never really granted ownership of their enterprises in the communist reform process because that would have created vast and unjustifiable inequalities in income and wealth. Only 4 million of Poland's 18 million workers are actually employed in the state-owned industrial sector, so that less than one-fourth of the workers would have received any benefits from the full distribution of ownership to the industrial workers. Moreover, some workers are in highly profitable firms while others are in loss-making firms. To give the workers ownership of their respective firms would be highly capricious in its distributional consequences.

From an efficiency standpoint, it makes little sense for workers to own their own enterprises (or at least the capital in their enterprises), except in the case of small, labor-intensive operations. Worker ownership or labor–management tends to cut firms out of the capital markets. Outside investors often shun enterprises in which workers have a controlling interest, since the workers can act opportunistically to absorb all of the income of the firm in the form of wage compensation.[29] Moreover, it makes little sense for workers to hold most of their equity wealth in their own enterprise, since on diversification grounds they should hold their financial capital and human capital in separate investments.

Ironically, many supporters of U.S. employee stock-ownership plans (ESOPs) have traveled to Eastern Europe recently to organize support for worker ownership. In many ways, the effect has been pernicious. In the United States, the ESOP tends to promote a modest extent of worker ownership, almost always below the 20 percent threshold envisioned by the Polish authorities.[30] As shown in table 3, there are fewer than fifty industrial firms in the United States employing more than 1,500 workers in which employees own more than 25 percent of the shares. There are still fewer in which the workers own a majority stake in the enterprise. These firms account for a tiny proportion of the industrial labor force. Yet in Poland, the U.S. ESOPs have been used to support the political case for more complete worker management and ownership.

Table 3 United States: employee ownership of large industrial firms

Company	*Business*	*Persons employed*
	Ownership greater than 50 percent	
Science Applications	Research and development	10,000
Parsons Corporation	Engineering	10,000
Amsted Industries	Manufacturing	8,300
Weirton Steel	Steel manufacturing	8,100
Avondale Shipyards	Shipbuilding	7,500
W.L. Gore Associates	High-tech manufacturing	5,000
Simmons Company	Furniture manufacturing	4,900
Republic Engineered Steel	Steel manufacturing	4,900
Graybar Electric	Electrical equipment manufacturing	4,700
Treasure Chest Advertising	Printing	4,000
National Steel & Shipbuilding	Shipbuilding	4,000
Stebbins Engineering	Engineering	4,000
CH2M Hill	Engineering	2,300
Northwestern Steel and Wire Steel	Manufacturing	2,300
McLouth Steel	Steel manufacturing	2,000
Cranston Print Works	Textile printing	1,800
Okonite Company	Wire and cable manufacturing	1,700
North American Rayon	Rayon manufacturing	1,500
Total		87,000
Percent of total manufacturing employment[a]		0.4
	Ownership between 25 and 50 percent	
Phillips Petroleum	Petroleum	28,400
PMC Corporation	Industrial manufacturing	28,000
Tyson Foods	Chicken processing	25,000
Ashland Oil	Oil refining	22,800
USG	Construction material	22,000
Colt Industries	Industrial products	19,700
Olin Corp.	Chemicals/Defense	17,000
Hallmark Cards	Greeting cards	15,521
Lowe's Companies, Inc.	Lumber and hardware	14,700
CBI Industries	Energy and manufacturing	11,400
Stone and Webster	Engineering	10,000
Harcourt Brace Jovanovich	Publishing	8,000
Herman Miller Inc.	Furniture manufacturing	5,000
Dentsply International	Dental equipment	3,500
Applied Power, Inc.	Automotive equipment	3,400
Swank, Inc.	Leather goods	3,100
Anderson Corporation	Window manufacturing	2,800
Tyler Corp.	Cast iron pipes	2,700
H.K. Porter	Manufacturing	2,600
Nationwise Automotive	Auto supplies	2,200
U.S. Sugar	Sugar manufacturing	2,100
Granite Construction Co.	Highway and heavy construction	2,000

Table 3 Continued

Company	*Business*	*Persons employed*
Anthony Industries	Recreation products	2,000
CF&I Steel	Steel manufacturing	2,000
Quad/Graphics	Printing	2,000
Ormet Inc.	Aluminum manufacturing	1,700
E-systems	Electronics	1,500
Total		261,121
Percent of total manufacturing employment[a]		1.4

Source: "The Employee Ownership 100," National Center for Employee Ownership, May 1989, and U.S. Labor Department..

a. Total manufacturing employment in U.S. equals 19,167,000 employees.

The Polish Privatization Law

In June 1990, the Polish Parliament overwhelmingly passed the Act on the Privatization of State-Owned Enterprises, which is designed to be the guiding legislation for privatization. The act does not embrace a specific strategy for privatization, but rather sets a general framework that could accommodate a variety of strategies.

The history of the legislation is enlightening. In the fall of 1989, just after the Solidarity-led government ascended to power, it tried to introduce a Law on Transformation of State Enterprises, which would have converted state enterprises into joint-stock companies with the Treasury as the sole owner (this process is usually termed "corporatization," or sometimes, "commercialization"). This Transformation Law stalled in the Parliament and was ultimately withdrawn as a result of the objections of workers' groups, who rejected the state's claim to sole ownership of the enterprises.

The Mazowiecki government then went ahead with the Act on Privatization, which in many ways reflects the confused state of affairs. The new law allows for the transformation of state enterprises into Treasury-owned joint-stock companies, under the direction of a new Ministry of Ownership Transformation. The law also provides that the process should be approved by the state enterprise manager, the workers' council, and the founding organ. Thus, the enterprises are given a veto. The state, however, retains a trump card, since the Prime Minister, on the motion of the Minister of Ownership Transformation, can order the transformation of an enterprise. In the end, there remains the delicate balancing act between the interests of workers, managers, and the state.

The act has several other key provisos, but in general provides enough flexibility that the government has a wide range of options. Most of the legislation seems to envision a standard case-by-case privatization. Several articles in the act detail how shares are to be sold to the public, with the workers getting a half-price discount on up to 20 percent of the shares.[31] Once again, flexibility is built into the act by allowing the Council of Ministers (the executive body of the government) to permit State Treasury shares to be sold in a manner different from that specified in the act. The act also provides that shares might be distributed for vouchers, "scrip" issued by the government, but does not specify how that would be done. The deputy prime minister publicly stated during the debate on the law that the free distribution of shares, through one mechanism or another, would play some role in the privatization process.

During the period between corporatization of the firm and its sale, the enterprise is to be governed by a supervisory board of which two-thirds is appointed by the government, and one-third is elected by the workers. A maximum of two years can pass between the time of corporatization and privatization (defined as the point at which the state's holdings fall to less than half of the shares).

The law also restricts the role of foreign investors, who are allowed, in aggregate, to purchase up to 10 percent of the shares of an enterprise without restriction, but who must obtain government approval for ownership of more than that. The Mazowiecki government had stressed that it would be liberal in granting access to foreign investors, though it emphasized that the process must be controlled in order to prevent abuses and to monitor the extent of foreign participation in the economy. Since the law builds in so much flexibility, it is clear that politics, and policy choices, rather than the legal constraints of the new privatization act, will determine the pace and strategy of privatization.

In August and September of 1990, Deputy Prime Minister Balcerowicz publicly outlined the shape of the privatization program to be developed by the Mazowiecki government. The program would not be based on the case-by-case sale of medium- and large-scale enterprises through initial public offerings. Instead, the process of privatization would be accelerated by means of several techniques, including among other things the discount sales of shares to workers and a voucher system to place shares in the hands of the public.

Corporate Governance and Financial Intermediaries

A privatization program in Eastern Europe must do more than simply return enterprise ownership to private hands. The government should also strive to create an ownership structure that will effectively oversee the management of the newly privatized assets. That is, the government should foster an effective structure of corporate governance. Moreover, the government should encourage the development of financial intermediaries that will be important both for monitoring enterprises and for allowing the private sector to diversify the risks of property ownership.

We put enormous stress on creating adequate long-term oversight of management for two main reasons. First, there can be little confidence in the current managerial class in Eastern Europe. Many managers owe their positions to their Communist party allegiances rather than to their technical competence. Also, many competent managers won their positions because of their engineering expertise, which was crucial in a planned economy, rather than their ability to navigate the enterprise in the uncharted waters of an open market economy. Thus, an enormous effort will have to be made to evaluate current managers and to train and promote new ones.

Second, Eastern Europe lacks many of the individual and institutional actors that are normally involved in corporate governance in the West. Therefore, special care must be taken to assure that at least some institutions capable of effective corporate governance are created. In particular, unlike in normal market economies, Eastern European countries cannot rely on corporate oversight by any of the following: the original families and entrepreneurs that established an enterprise; outside directors who have a long involvement with an enterprise and understand its history and corporate culture; a vast financial press and investment analysis sector that investigates, reports, and evaluates management behaviour; or experienced regulatory institutions such as the Securities and Exchange Commission, which pursue investigations of malfeasance and which require various forms of disclosure that are widely analyzed by the investment community.

Our basic proposal, described in the next section, is that the ownership of most enterprises should be divided up in *tranches* among various groups and financial institutions that will each have an incentive to monitor the enterprise and promote sound management. In our proposal, a portion of shares is sold or given to workers; another part is transferred to pension funds and commercial banks; another part is transferred mainly to mutual funds that in turn will be owned by individual households; and another part is sold to a "core investor" group that commits both to hold a substantial proportion of the shares for several years and to manage the firm.

A Strategy for Achieving Effective Corporate Governance

There are two essential tasks in establishing effective governance of the productive capital now in state hands. The first, more urgent, task is to introduce a provisional system of corporate governance that can monitor a firm's management and prevent both managers and workers from squandering its capital income and capital assets before full privatization takes place. The second, longer-term task is to foster a structure of ownership in which the new private owners will be in a strong position to manage their newly acquired assets.

A vital, first step to privatization is the conversion of state enterprises into corporate form (their corporatization), in order to concentrate the property rights of the enterprise in a corporate board of directors appointed by the owners. Inevitably, given a realistic timetable for any privatization scheme, the initial boards of almost all enterprises will have to be appointed by the government, with the subsequent boards to be appointed by private owners as they emerge during the privatization process. To reduce the enormous administrative burden of creating a large number of corporate boards, the task should initially focus on the 500 largest firms.

The urgency of corporatization results from the complete inadequacy of the current structure of governance, in which the manager is completely unmonitored in most firms, or is monitored by workers' councils in others. We have stressed that the lack of effective governance has already produced enormous social, political, and economic problems that are likely to continue or worsen despite attempts at administrative controls.

The process of corporatization was one of the first steps in the recent German economic unification. The *Treuhandanstalt*, the state property trust, mandated the conversion of all 8,000 state enterprises into corporate form by administrative decree. So far, the Poles, Hungarians, and Yugoslavs have avoided this step for fear of running into political conflict with powerful workers' councils, known as "enterprise councils" in Hungary. These governments also fear being accused of politicizing the economy by attempting to reconcentrate control in the hands of the state.

In our view, the political risks of corporatization pale in comparison to the potential economic gains. If the principle is not accepted early in the privatization process, managers and workers' councils together with the state will likely end up bargaining over the terms for privatizing on a firm-by-firm basis, thus paralyzing the process. Moreover, without early corporatization there will be no effective way of replacing the most incompetent managers in those enterprises that have weak or nonexistent workers' councils. Since the boards of directors will monitor joint venture arrangements and other major corporate decisions, the ability to forestall "spontaneous privatization" will be greatly enhanced.

At the same time, the risk of politicizing the process through appointing boards of directors can be significantly reduced if first, the task is largely and visibly subcontracted to professional institutions, such as a consortia of Polish and international management advisory firms, and second, the initial board of directors is made provisional, until the enterprise is at least partially privatized (at which point, the new owners would assume some of the responsibility for forming the board of directors). In fact, Polish company law requires that the first board of directors be constituted for one year, while subsequent boards of directors be constituted for three-year tenures.

The long-term challenge of the privatization program is to create a structure of ownership in which the owners have effective control over the enterprises.

For example, if ownership of the enterprises is too widely dispersed, the individual owners will have little incentive to monitor management.[32] Moreover, it would be useful to match firms with appropriate owners in the privatization process itself, rather than relying on subsequent trading to establish the "right" owners for a firm. The market for corporate control through takeovers is highly flawed, with significant externalities and asymmetries of information. Therefore, the market cannot be relied upon to do a good job in matching potential owners and firms: many efficient takeovers may never be achieved, and many inefficient takeovers may be consummated.[33]

These concerns lead us to three principles for establishing effective long-term control over privatized firms. First, the privatization process should avoid creating an atomistic ownership structure for the large enterprises, in which hundreds of thousands or millions of owners each retain a small number of shares. Most ownership of the large enterprises should be held by intermediary agents such as pension funds, mutual funds, or commercial banks, or by large owners with concentrated stakes. This principle also conforms to the idea that small investors should hold diversified portfolios, through mutual funds perhaps, rather than shares in a single enterprise.

Second, the privatization process should be designed to foster at least one significant nonfinancial investor in each major industrial enterprise. This investor would hold around 20 percent of the shares, and would create a "stable core" of ownership of the firm, to use a concept developed in the French privatization process. In their privatizations of the 1980s, the French believed that their capital markets were too thin to rely primarily on public placements as the dominant method of privatization. They also lacked the investment banks that had guided public placements in the United Kingdom. Most importantly, there was concern that no single owner or ownership group would emerge with a significant stake in each enterprise.

Therefore, the French devised a scheme known as the "stable core." This involved soliciting a bid from a single investor, or group of investors working together, to buy 20 percent or more of an enterprise. This group committed a sum of money; prepared a management proposal; and submitted its financial bid. It also committed to hold its shares for at least five years. After reviewing the bids, the French government designated a winner to serve as the stable core. The winning bid was selected not only on the share price offered, but on the financial strength of the bidder, its reputation and experience, and the quality of its management plan.[34]

In Eastern European privatization plans, as in the French plan, governments would attempt to market a 20 percent block of shares in each enterprise to an investment group that could be domestic, foreign, or mixed. This group would be vested with significant representation on the corporate board in return for a requirement that the group hold the enterprise for a specified period of time, perhaps three to five years.

Third, the Eastern European countries should create a legal and institutional environment in which financial intermediaries play a more active oversight role than is typical in the United States and United Kingdom. The need for oversight by financial intermediaries results from the lack of other institutions or individuals in Eastern Europe that can be relied upon to help oversee an enterprise's corporate management. Thus, a great effort will be needed to economize on information that will be vital in corporate governance. Since banks, pension funds, and mutual funds will have such information, these institutions should also be assigned a major role in the governance process.

As a first step toward strengthening the hand of the financial intermediaries, the Eastern European economies should aim to develop universal banking, as in Germany and Japan,[35] where the commercial banks hold stakes in corporate assets and play active roles in the oversight of enterprises.[36] The new banks should place representatives on the corporate boards of directors, and strengthen their capacities to participate in the restructurings of troubled firms. Of course, qualified banks cannot be created at once, but it will be far easier to build up the operational capacity of a dozen large banks (perhaps through management contracts with foreign banks) than to rely on the decentralized oversight of thousands of individual enterprises.[37]

As a second step toward strengthening the oversight by financial intermediaries, newly created mutual funds and pension funds should be encouraged to appoint representatives to the boards of directors of enterprises in which they hold shares, and to create the institutional capacity to monitor closely a large number of firms. When the mutual funds and pension funds are initially licensed, for example, they could be required to present plans detailing how they will appoint directors to corporate boards and how they will develop the expertise needed to monitor these companies. One possibility is that they might subcontract the management oversight to an international management consulting firm.

The proposal that mutual funds and pension funds be so actively involved in corporate oversight may seem unusual, but it should be noted that several recent analysts have argued that the same change should apply in the United States.[38] One proposal in the U.S. context is for institutional investors to appoint a new class of professional, outside directors who would serve full time on a small number of boards of directors (perhaps six boards per person) for corporations held by the investors.[39] These new directors would constitute a "critical mass" on each board, but would serve together with traditional, outside directors (such as CEOs of other companies) and inside directors. The proposal for Poland is more natural in view of the fact that the newly developed financial intermediaries will have a much smaller task with regard to portfolio management than is usual in the United States. This is because the market for corporate shares will be considerably smaller and less liquid there than in the United States. Thus, they will have the time to focus somewhat more on corporate governance and rather less on portfolio management.

The Role of the Stock Market in Privatization

We doubt that the stock exchange can or should play a major role in the privatization process or more generally in the development of financial markets in Eastern Europe in the next few years. While each country will surely develop a stock exchange, the liquidity of the new exchanges will be low, and their capacity to raise corporate capital or serve as a market for corporate control will be highly circumscribed. Moreover, information concerning the fundamental valuation of firms will continue to be limited for many years, since firms will be operating for the first time in a market environment. Thus, we can expect that the markets will be subject to extreme volatility and will tend toward insider trading, not only because asymmetries of information will be pronounced, but also because the policing of the exchanges will be imperfect in the first few years. Nor are there likely to be many firms with a capital value that is large enough to support many institutional investors and small shareholders.

In general, the continental European economies rely much less heavily on stock markets than do the United Kingdom and the United States for raising and trading corporate wealth, and for gaining corporate control.[40] One sign of the smaller role of the stock market in Western Europe is the low number of listed companies in most European countries. Austria, for example, has only 81 listed Austrian firms; Finland, 78; Norway, 122; Sweden, 135; and Switzerland, 177.[41] In addition, hostile takeovers in these countries scarcely occur. There is little evidence to suggest, though, that this relative dearth of stock market activity has hindered effective corporate governance; many observers feel that the opposite is true: that active stock market trading encourages a short-term bias in managerial decisions. Given the difficulties of establishing an active stock exchange for a large number of firms, it seems safe to recommend that Eastern Europe follow the Western European lead, at least initially, and downplay the institutional role of the stock exchange.

A Strategy for Privatization

We now return to the basic question: how can a very large number of enterprises be privatized quickly while at the same time establishing an effective structure of corporate governance? We have argued that a large role must be played by new institutional investors, and a relatively small role by the stock market. We now describe a strategy for privatization that might be used for transferring ownership and control to private owners.

One key point in our strategy is that much of the privatization should be accomplished through the free distribution of shares to various groups, including workers, pension funds, and mutual funds, rather than through the sale of shares in an initial public offering (IPO), which was standard practice in the well-known British privatizations. In Eastern Europe, the free distribution of shares would help sidestep the difficult, costly, and time-consuming process of enterprise valuation, and recognize the scarcity of financial capital in private hands.

There is good reason to expect that the problem posed by asset valuation will be far more severe in Eastern Europe than it has been in the West. The economic environment is shifting in fundamental ways as the transformation into market economies proceeds. Not only is the domestic environment undergoing a profound change, but in several countries, international trade is being liberalized and currency convertibility has been introduced. The COMECON system governing trade and payments among the Eastern European countries will be revamped in January 1991. Furthermore, the legal and regulatory environment is changing. Indeed, the level of interest rates needed to discount future profits for the purpose of valuation could be greatly influenced by the strategy for privatization itself. As a result of all of these changes, many key relative prices have shifted and will continue to do so. Finally, in many enterprises there will be changes in the structure of management or in the management itself that will have profound effects on the value of the enterprise. These factors each pose fundamental conceptual problems for asset valuation and, taken together, cast grave doubt on the viability of privatization schemes that require careful valuation of assets as a prelude to the sale of most enterprises.[42]

Another key point in our strategy is that most enterprises should be privatized in a common manner, to avoid debates between the government and individual enterprises. To the extent that a common procedure is followed, it will be harder for individual enterprises to bargain for special advantages in the course of the privatization process. At the same time, however, it should be possible for an enterprise to proceed outside of the common procedure (for example, if it receives an attractive bid), and yet remain subject to various due process standards and government oversight.

Before detailing a method of privatization that uses the direct distribution of shares, let us consider the four fundamental limitations of IPOs in the Eastern European context. First, public offerings require a careful valuation of each firm, and a great deal of financial preparation. They tend to be time-consuming in normal circumstances, and would be far slower in Eastern Europe, where valuation of firms is nearly impossible and where the financial infrastructure for IPOs does not yet exist. Second, the financial capital currently in the hands of the public is a small fraction of the value of the enterprises to be privatized, assuming a reasonable market interest rate (and thus a reasonable price–earnings ratio for the firm). Thus, any attempt to sell a large proportion of the enterprises would create serious financial problems. Third, IPOs are typically used, as has been the case in Britain, to secure a widespread ownership of shares by small investors (in order to create "people's capitalism"). While this aim may be desirable, it does not generally produce an effective structure of corporate governance, and from a logistical

Table 4 Completed privatizations by method, various countries, 1980–87

Country	*Completed public offerings*	*Completed private sales*	*Completed worker/ management buyout*
Africa			
Equatorial Guinea	0	6	0
Gabon	0	1	0
Gambia	2	1	1
Ghana	0	1	0
Guinea	0	25	0
Ivory Coast	1	18	5
Mali	0	2	0
Mauritania	0	1	0
Niger	0	12	0
Senegal	0	4	0
Sierra Leone	1	1	0
Uganda	0	1	0
Zaire	0	0	0
Asia and the Pacific			
Bangladesh	4	1	0
Japan	3	2	0
Korea	2	5	0
Malaysia	2	5	0
Singapore	12	0	0
Sri Lanka	1	4	0
Taiwan	2	3	0
Thailand	1	1	0
Papua New Guinea	1	0	0
New Zealand	1	3	0
Europe			
Austria	2	0	0
Denmark	1	0	0
France	14	10	1
Germany	6	0	0
Italy	15	17	1
Netherlands	1	0	0
Spain	5	25	0
Sweden	1	1	0
Turkey	2	0	0
United Kingdom	13	18	12
North and South America			
United States	1	2	0
Brazil	6	46	0
Chile	12	24	1
Jamaica	2	22	3
Mexico	3	7	0

Source: World Bank, *Techniques of Privatization of State-Owned Enterprises*, vol. 1, *Methods and Implementation* (by Charles Vuylsteke), 1988, table 1, Annex E, pp. 169–72.

point of view is surely inappropriate for all but the largest enterprises. Fourth, reliance upon IPOs would lead to the privatization of only the most profitable enterprises, and leave the marginal or unhealthy enterprises—which are viewed as less marketable—in the hands of the government.

Let us consider each of these four points in more detail. Table 4 shows the total, worldwide number of privatizations through public offerings between 1980 and 1987, according to a World Bank study. The United Kingdom accomplished thirteen IPOs during this period, and the country with the largest number, Italy, accomplished fifteen. Many authors have discussed the laborious preparations involved in each IPO. Given that there is as yet no stock exchange in Poland, no Polish investment banks, and indeed no tradition of valuing enterprises for public sale, privatization through IPOs would likely be quite slow in Eastern European countries.

The normal problems of IPOs are greatly compounded by the shortage of public savings with which to purchase shares. Table 5 presents a rough illustration of the problem. We assume that the firms are valued as a multiple of annual earnings, with three alternatives considered: price–earnings ratios of 6, 8, or 10. In each case, the market value of the 500 largest enterprises is compared with the financial savings of private households, which consist of currency and bank deposits. Even for the lowest price–earnings ratio of 6, the value of the largest enterprises is roughly 2.5 times the current stock of savings.

Thus, the shares could not be sold quickly unless one of three things were to happen. First, the price–earnings ratio could fall sharply, leading to the sale of enterprises for close to nothing to those in the public who hold cash. Second, the government could lend money to the public for share purchases,

Table 5 Poland: capital value of the largest state enterprises, 1990 (billions of dollars)

Number of enterprises	*Net income*[a]	*Estimated capital value*			*Ratio to household financial savings*[b]		
		P/E = 6	*P/E = 8*	*P/E = 10*	*P/E = 6*	*P/E = 8*	*P/E = 10*
Top 100	2.9	17.6	23.5	29.4	1.6	2.1	2.7
Top 200	3.6	21.6	28.8	36.0	2.0	2.6	3.3
Top 300	4.0	23.7	31.6	39.5	2.2	2.9	3.6
Top 400	4.4	26.3	35.1	43.8	2.4	3.2	4.0
Top 484	4.6	27.5	36.7	45.9	2.5	3.3	4.2

Source: Authors' own calculations. Data were provided by the authorities and *Informacja Statystyczna*.

a. Data are annualized from January–June 1990.

b. Ratio includes household holdings of cash and domestic and foreign currency deposits in the banking system, which totaled $11 billion in mid-1990.

in the form of a grand leveraged buyout. Third, the enterprises could be sold mainly to foreigners. Of course, none of these alternatives would be remotely acceptable on a political or economic basis.

Interestingly, there is one case in which a country tried to sell a large number of enterprises very cheaply in the context of an enormous credit squeeze: Chile, during 1975–78, just after the coup that toppled Allende and brought Pinochet to power. There, 232 firms were rapidly sold to the public through leveraged buyouts. The outcome in Chile confirms the worst fears of such a process.[43]

Not only did the Chilean experiment produce weak firms and an undue concentration of wealth, but the government was (rightly) attacked for selling the firms at very low prices to the few financial groups that had some access to cash. According to Rolf Luders, a former Chilean finance minister (1979–81) and a strong advocate of privatization in general,

> The First Round [of privatizations] was carried-out in the midst of a deep structural transformation process, during which there was little interest on the part of foreigners to invest in the country, and which was accompanied by considerable political, social, and economic uncertainty. . . . These debt-led privatizations carried-out in an economically unstable environment, contributed to generate a considerable degree of *financial asset concentration, financial instability, and some important macro-economic problems*.[44] (Emphasis ours)

Ironically, because the newly privatized firms were undercapitalized and heavily indebted, many of them collapsed during the financial crisis of 1982–83, and had to be renationalized.

Our novel approach might rescue IPOs from the problem of limited purchasing power. The government might transfer purchasing power to the public in direct grants, rather than loans. This is the basic idea behind *voucher schemes*. The government issues purchasing power in a kind of voucher (scrip) that can be used solely to purchase shares. The initial distribution of vouchers can be made on an equal basis for the entire population, or according to other criteria. Care would have to be taken to ensure that vouchers do not become money substitutes, otherwise the issue of vouchers could lead to a sudden expansion of the money supply that is not synchronized with the sale of shares.[45] As we mention later, the voucher schemes are still likely to suffer from the other weaknesses of IPOs: their time-consuming nature and their inability to create an effective ownership structure.

In particular, the use of a voucher scheme in connection with IPOs may involve prohibitive administrative costs. If individuals swap vouchers for shares, the pattern of share ownership will involve a dispersion of holdings in small lots. A company worth $10 million—medium-sized by Polish standards—might be in the position of distributing only $300,000 in dividends per year (with a 15 percent rate of return and a 20 percent dividend payout ratio). If a voucher system involved the sale of 500 enterprises to 25 million adult Poles, it could well lead to 100,000 or more shareholders per enterprise. As a result, the administrative costs would leave few resources for profit distribution.

The discussion in Eastern Europe of privatization through IPOs has led to the notion that only profitable enterprises would be privatized. Accordingly, the marginal or unhealthy enterprises would be left to the government to restructure or liquidate. This proposition arises naturally from an approach to privatization based on the case-by-case sale of enterprises, because of the apparent difficulties of valuing and marketing enterprises that may not be sustainable. It would be preferable, in our view, for all enterprises regardless of their financial position to be corporatized and quickly put into private hands. There are several reasons not to leave the marginal and unhealthy enterprises in the hands of the state. First, these enterprises could remain in state hands for a long period as the government tries to determine whether restructuring or liquidation is appropriate. During this time, the enterprises would be targets for further asset stripping by an unrestrained management. Second, a corporate board of directors will be more competent and less subject to political pressures than the government in guiding the process of restructuring and, if necessary, liquidation.

An Illustrative Plan for Large-Scale Privatization in Poland

We now show how the considerations of the previous sections can be integrated into a single, workable plan. The goal would be to complete the privatization of the 500 largest state enterprises in Poland's industrial sector within a period of four years. While the privatization strategy of the Polish government is still evolving and is likely to change further after the presidential elections, we believe that it will share some—though certainly not all—of the features that we outline here. Indeed, we would like to stress once again that we have benefited from extensive discussions with Polish officials in crystallizing our own ideas.

To achieve a rapid privatization, a common track would be followed for most of the large enterprises. This has two advantages: the minimization of negotiation between the state and the individual enterprises; and the routinization of the process. Most firms would be privatized in tranches, with each "slice" of shares transferred or sold to a different kind of investor. A minority of firms would be sold outright in a standard kind of privatization (either a public offering or a private sale).

At the beginning of the process, each of the 500 largest enterprises would be corporatized—that is, converted into a joint-stock company with the shares initially issued to the state as 100 percent owner. An initial board of directors would be appointed according to the privatization law; two-thirds of the seats would be appointed by the government (most likely by a private investment group that would be hired to advise the government), and one-third of the seats would be elected by the workers. The initial board of directors would serve for one year.

A few enterprises would then proceed with a British-style privatization through IPOs, private sales, or auctions, though we do not discuss these enterprises in this paper. (The privatization law should leave room for individual firms to pursue these routes, especially when private bidders come forward.) The bulk of the enterprises would begin the privatization in tranches. The first tranche would be the transfer, or possibly sale, of shares to an enterprise's workers. The government could most simply mandate that the workers receive 10 percent of the enterprise shares for free (the law provides for the sale to workers of up to 20 percent of the enterprise for half price). The allocation of shares among the work force would be determined by the manager with the approval of the new corporate board. On this particular issue, it may be wise to require that the worker representatives on the board of directors also approve the share distribution plan among the workers.

In addition to the 10 percent distributed to the workers, around 5 percent of the shares would be reserved for compensation for the managers and the corporate board. Managers could receive stock options or outright share ownership as part of an incentive compensation package. We expect that the distribution of shares to managers, as part of their compensation package, could provide an important early spur to increased efficiency within the firm.[46]

The second tranche of shares, around 20 percent of the total, would be used to capitalize a new private pension system. The shares would be distributed to several new pension funds, which would in turn be distributed to enterprises and individuals in order to back retirement payments. Each pension fund would receive a portfolio of enterprises, and would be responsible for the active oversight of the corporations in its portfolio. It could also trade its shares.

During the following few years, enterprises would be "hooked up" with the new pension funds according to the size of the enterprise and the age and wage distributions of the employees. The basic idea would be for the state to scale back its own social security payments that are now made directly from the budget, and to increase the payments being made from the capitalized pension fund.[47] The actual transition from budgetary expenditures to payments by private pension funds could be phased in over a period of five to ten years. If the pension funds receive the income from 20 percent of the shares of the 500 largest enterprises, the annual earnings of the pension funds would equal about $900 million, or about 20 percent of the annual pension payments now being made from the central budget.

The use of share distribution to capitalize the pension system is not without complexity, and numerous logistical problems will have to be resolved in order to distribute claims in a fair way and reduce social security payments from the government in line with growing benefits from the private plans.

The third tranche would consist of 10 percent of the shares and would be used to capitalize the existing state-owned commercial banks and the insurance sector. Commercial banks would receive 6 percent of the shares (60 percent of this tranche) and would be expected to develop into active investors along German lines. At the same time, the commercial banks themselves would be converted into joint-stock companies and prepared for privatization.

The process of capitalization and commercialization of commercial banks would have two main benefits. First, as active investors, the commercial banks would begin to play an important role in scrutinizing the management of enterprises. Second, the capitalization would also help the banks to improve their weak balance sheets, which need recapitalization in any case. We estimate that with 6 percent of the shares in the 500 largest enterprises, commercial banks would receive a transfer equivalent to about 10 percent of commercial bank gross assets.

Privatization schemes that rely in large part on the free distribution of shares are sometimes said to be disadvantaged in that the government forgoes a large, potential revenue source. While this may be true when shares are distributed freely to workers or households, the revenue loss may not be incurred when public or quasi-public institutions are capitalized, as in the case of the pension funds and the commercial banks. The capitalization of the pension system will reduce the requirement for budgetary funding of the social security system by an equal magnitude. The capitalization of the commercial banks will likewise reduce a future claim on budgetary resources of the banks, by anticipating the need for a commercial bank recapitalization.

The fourth tranche will consist of 20 percent of the shares of the enterprises that will be distributed generally to the adult population of Poland (roughly 25 million). This part of the share distribution *will* cause a loss of wealth for the state sector, since the distribution to households will not be recouped by budgetary savings elsewhere. There are two prevailing models of how to distribute these shares. In one model, the shares of the enterprises would be distributed to several private investment trusts (which are closed-end mutual funds), whose shares in turn would be freely distributed to the adult citizens of Poland. After the initial distribution of the shares, the investment trusts would be free to actively manage their portfolios.

Each individual would receive one share in one of the investment trusts, so that if there were, say, ten trusts each would have around 2.5 million subscribers. The investment trusts would pass through dividends and other income to the shareholding public, after deducting the fund's expenses and fees. Each trust would be managed by a Polish entity, but would contract with a foreign advisory firm to assist in the establishment of the trust, in the active management of assets, and in the administration of dividend distribution.

An alternative model has suggested free distribution through vouchers. Individuals would receive vouchers with a fixed face value in the domestic currency. Shares would be tendered at a fixed price after a quick valuation. Households could either buy shares with their vouchers or buy claims on investment trust companies, which in turn would use the vouchers to purchase the tendered shares. The government could encourage the households to deposit their shares with the investment trusts as a sound method of diversification.

This second approach has won widespread support in Poland and is viewed as politically superior to the direct distribution of investment trust certificates, since it offers more choice to households. On the negative side, however, it is vastly more complicated, and could in fact greatly slow down the privatization process. With the voucher plan, unlike the plan to directly distribute investment trust shares, there must be a valuation of individual companies as well as a time-consuming public offering. In addition, the vouchers could be complex to issue and process.

The free distribution of investment trust shares could be completed within about one year, while the system relying on vouchers would probably take a couple of years more. In either case, after this phase is completed, the government will retain roughly 35 percent ownership in the partially privatized companies. A second board of directors would have to be formed upon the expiration of the one-year term for the initial board appointed by the government. The second board would be elected by the shareholders for a three-year period. The shareholder groups created by the pension funds, the banks, and the investment trusts would presumably dominate this board of directors and, thereby, firmly establish control over management. The board of directors could be elected by cumulative voting (essentially, proportional representation), to make sure that each of the major holders of shares places representatives on the supervisory board.

Following the free distribution of shares, any number of methods might be used to dispose of the remaining government holdings, including public offerings, private placements of shares, and further free distributions. Of course, if share sales are the predominant means of disposing of the last tranche, the government will have to undertake a careful valuation of each enterprise and prepare the sale. In addition, the government may wish to encourage enterprises and investor groups to come forward with privatization proposals in a decentralized manner, provided that each deal receives an adequate degree of scrutiny. In certain cases, the government may wish to retain a minority holding, and can look to Western European experience for an appropriate pattern of government equity positions in the corporate sector.

We consider the French concept of selling a block of shares to a stable core of investors to be an attractive technique for disposing of the last tranche. In the case of Poland, the government would entertain bids from domestic, foreign, or mixed investor groups. It should be possible to establish a stable core for most of the 500 largest enterprises and complete the privatization of these enterprises within a three-year period. The stable core would eventually become the primary investor group and, because it would be entrepreneurial in nature, would take a dominant role in supervising corporate management. In time, the supervisory role of pension funds, investment trusts, and commercial banks, although important, would no longer be the main force monitoring and controlling management behavior.

Central Features of the Illustrative Plan

We conclude this section by stressing what we regard to be the central features of the plan, and what we regard as illustrative but not fundamental. In our view, there are several key steps: corporatization that will establish the legal basis of the new economic system; a partial distribution of shares to workers and managers for political and incentive reasons; and the distribution of some shares to financial intermediaries such as banks and mutual funds, which will have some early responsibility for appointing corporate boards. Once this process goes forward for the bulk of the largest few hundred enterprises, it is not vital what fraction of shares the government holds; it could range from 30 percent to 50 percent of the enterprise. In the latter case, however, we would expect the government to be a silent partner in the day-to-day management of the enterprise.

We accept the proposition that long-term management of the enterprises will be enhanced if the government can sell a significant block of each enterprise to a core buyer. This will take time. The risks of waiting, however, will be significantly reduced if a large part of the enterprise is already in private hands, and if the preliminary struggle over the form of ownership, corporate versus worker management, for example, is decisively settled in favor of a corporate structure.

Conclusion

The most daunting challenge facing the countries of Eastern Europe today is the transfer of state property to private hands in a manner that is rapid, equitable, and fiscally sound. To achieve this in the Eastern European context is particularly difficult, because it requires the complete redefinition of property rights and wealthholding in the society, and the creation anew of the basic institutions of a market financial system. In this paper, we have reviewed the enormous scope of the privatization task, and suggested principles that should govern the process of privatization. We have used the case of Poland to illustrate the political, legal, and logistical problems that lie in the way of privatization. We have also suggested a concrete plan for privatization in Poland aimed at demonstrating how these constraints can be met and how the main economic objectives can be achieved.

Poland, and the other countries of Eastern Europe, must devise strategies for privatization that ensure that the transformation of ownership structure goes forward uninterrupted. The standard, case-by-case approach based on initial public offerings is prone to get bogged down for political, economic, and logistical reasons. An alternative approach is needed.

We are advocating the rapid conversion of state enterprises into corporate form and the distribution of tranches of shares to various groups in the population, including workers, commercial banks, pension funds, and mutual funds. This strategy differs substantially from the standard methods of privatization that have been used in the West: the sale of shares in an initial public offering and private placements to investor groups. The free distribution of shares helps to sidestep the difficult, costly, and time-consuming process of enterprise valuation, as well as the scarcity of financial capital in private hands in Eastern Europe. Morc importantly, corporatization combined with the free distribution of shares can occur quickly. Rapid privatization is needed to combat the inevitable social, political, and economic problems associated with the lack of corporate governance.

It is vital to establish effective governance quickly. The first, most urgent, task is to introduce a provisional system of corporate governance that can monitor the management and prevent the managers and workers from squandering the capital income and capital assets of the firms before full privatization takes place. The second, and long-term, task is to foster a structure of ownership in which the new private owners will be in a strong position to manage their newly acquired assets.

Comments and Discussion

Lawrence H. Summers: David Lipton and Jeffrey Sachs's excellent paper addresses what may be the most difficult aspect of economic transition in Eastern Europe—the privatization of large-scale enterprises. Lipton and Sachs make a powerful case for what might be called the rapid eclectic approach to privatization. They believe that the job must be done fast, and they believe that privatization can and should be used to help bring a whole set of new financial institutions into being. I label their approach eclectic because of the variety of branches of ownership—four or five—that they propose to create.

It has always struck me as odd that when Dan Rather provides only two economic statistics in a newscast, one of them is volume on the New York Stock Exchange. Lipton and Sachs are generally skeptical about the role of the stock market in developed economies. They condemn Western-style initial public offerings (IPOs) as an unfeasible and undesirable approach to massive privatization in Eastern Europe.

I think this skepticism about stock markets is warranted. Except in the

United States and the United Kingdom, the supply of publicly tradable equities is low relative to national income. In Germany, for example, the ratio is now about 20 percent and was less than 10 percent just a decade ago. In Italy, four companies comprise 60 percent of the total market value. And even Japan, after making adjustments for cross holdings, yields estimates of the "open" stock market of only about 60 percent of GNP before the market's rapid decline. The Eastern European situation is already unstable enough without adding stock market volatility. I have little doubt that the Lipton–Sachs rapid eclectic plan is better than the alternative: the world's most active IPO market.

My questions, and I do not claim to know the answers, are whether Lipton and Sachs propose to move too rapidly, and whether or not there are alternatives. More conservative reform strategies might reduce the risk of generating politically difficult regrets down the road. The case Lipton and Sachs make for rapid action turns heavily on the ambiguous ownership situation of current public enterprises and the resulting problems. They are particularly critical of spontaneous privatizations—essentially forms of self-dealing by managers—and of worker ownership, both of which lead to asset stripping. Their hope is that by establishing new and active owners these difficulties can be avoided. In my comments, I raise some questions about the blueprint Lipton and Sachs lay out. In assessing the risks of their strategy, it is important to remember that alternative strategies are risky as well. Slow, partial privatization could easily turn into no privatization. Policy judgments in this area depend as much on politics as on economics, and I have no basis for questioning those of Lipton and Sachs.

I think they put too little stress on the rule of law, and too much on what a board of directors, appropriately motivated, can accomplish. American corporations do much that is wrong, but they are rarely faulted for buying from companies privately owned by their managers or their relatives. The law, auditors, and some sort of cultural norm police corporate behavior, not monthly board of directors meetings. I would have thought that creating state corporations that are unambiguously owned by the state, and passing and enforcing tough conflict-of-interest laws, along with management compensation schemes that give managers a stake in profits, could alleviate the ambiguous ownership problem without the problems associated with rapid privatization. A nation whose legal infrastructure cannot stop blatant self-dealing by managers of huge enterprises seems unlikely to carry out any sort of corruption-free distribution of assets.

Lipton and Sachs hold out the hope that by distributing rather than selling assets, the difficulty of valuation can be sidestepped. I think this is a chimera. The banks, pension funds, and insurance companies, which would receive assets under the Lipton–Sachs plan, are or will be owned by people. If they get valuable assets, their ultimate owners will benefit; if not, their ultimate owners will not. Without a fair method of asset valuation, I do not see how they can be distributed equitably across different institutions. Excessively rapid distribution without accurate valuation will, I think, lead to blatant inequities down the road, between different banks and pension funds. If institutions are permitted to exchange blocks of shares, these effects will be accentuated.

Essentially the fairness aspect of the privatization dilemma boils down to the following. In the current climate of massive uncertainty assets have a low ex-ante value. If after everything, things work out well, there is a sense that those who received assets stole them, and there will be pressure for getting at the windfalls, pressure to undercut private property rights in the process. If after everything, things do not work out well, that is not a good outcome either. The only possible resolution is to delay selling or distributing assets until valuations become clearer. This is the practice of American companies when they spin off subsidiaries. They do not simply assume that the market will instantly give them a fair price.

What about the efficiency aspects? Here the Roman question *quis custodies custodiet*—who watches the watchers?—becomes central. One gets the sense reading their paper that they think that each of Gdansk's many Roger Smiths needs his own Ross Perot. The greenmail that Perot eventually received points up one difficulty with this image. The fact that he was a personal stakeholder, not a representative of a stakeholder, points up another problem. It is all very well to say that tough-minded owners are needed to make management do the right thing. The problem is that when owners are institutions, their representatives have agency problems of their own. Lipton and Sachs could do more to make it clear what the comparative advantage of bank and pension representatives will be in influencing management to do the right things, especially in the near term when banks and pensions are themselves state operated.

This "who watches the watchers" problem seems especially acute in the case of the "mutual funds plan" advocated by a number of observers of the Eastern European situation. Placement of all assets into ten pots rather than one and reliance on the law of large numbers to ensure fairness also raises the question of how enterprise managers will be watched. My guess is that mutual fund managers will find ways to self-deal too. They may sell assets to entities with which they have some involvement. They are also unlikely to vote themselves out of existence.

What then should be done? American venture capitalists recognize an important aspect of incentives. They are much more concerned with the fraction of an entrepreneur's net worth that he or she puts into a new venture, than with the total amount of money put in. It is the former not the latter that indexes the degree of commitment and is, therefore, relevant for mitigating moral hazard and adverse selection problems. This should be kept in mind when designing institutions in Eastern Europe.

Suppose that the Lipton–Sachs plan were modified to apply to only half of the shares in state enterprises, with the state passively retaining the remainder. The same creation of institutions could occur. Managers could still be compensated on the basis of performance. Board members could still represent institutions that would be large by the standards of owners in the capitalist world. Yet the risk of a wildly inequitable distribution would be reduced. Moreover, the state would maintain the ability to act if corruption set in.

More generally, the whole privatization area is fraught with uncertainty. At least from an economic standpoint, there is little to be gained and much that could be lost by the state giving up its ownership claims too quickly. In public finance courses, we often point out that if the corporate income tax really made the state a passive shareholder in enterprises, it would be wholly nondistortionary. Western corporate taxes are distortionary given depreciation schedules and the like. But it is natural to wonder when a new system is being crafted whether consideration should not be given to the state taking an equity stake as an alternative to levying a high rate of corporate tax.

An alternative device for hedging the state's bets is leasing assets or maintaining a debt interest in them. Both these schemes hedge against some form of disaster when they operate. They also reduce the risk of conferring windfalls unfairly. And they both offer the possibility of bringing in new profit-oriented management with a hard budget constraint. Relative to the state's maintaining an ownership share, these schemes have the disadvantage of creating inefficiency from conflicts of interest. For example, think of tenants' attitudes toward maintenance, or mortgage holders' attitudes towards risk taking. On the other hand, they have the virtue of increasing the sensitivity of private owners' rewards to their performance. The right approach will vary from case to case. But I would be very surprised if leasing and debt, which are barely touched on by Lipton and Sachs, do not have some role to play in an optimally designed privatization program.

Less than 100 percent privatization has the additional virtue of allowing time for aspects of industrial organization to be worked out. Lipton and Sachs are not worried about monopoly problems. Others are less sanguine. And there is the important issue of cross holdings. Automobile executives probably are in a better position to monitor tire company performance than anybody else. Should they be represented on the board? Would too much cross holding tend on the other hand to be anticompetitive? No one knows. Perhaps irrevocable commitments should be delayed until these issues and others like them can be more fully resolved.

The difficulty with allocating a larger role to the government is that slow privatization might simply serve as an excuse for maintaining the status quo. This would be disastrous. Yet, I do not see why the state's maintaining a substantial interest in the enterprises it sells off should benefit the managerial elite or current workers, if the state really keeps its interest passive and concentrates on policing corruption. This is, of course, an enormous if. A government that cannot reform itself cannot reform its economy. The worst thing that could happen in Eastern Europe is a U-turn on issues relating to private property.

General Discussion

Many panelists agreed that the crucial challenges for Eastern Europe's transformation were the privatization process and the creation of effective management structures for firms. However, some questioned certain parts of the authors' privatization strategy. Stanley Fischer doubted that the corporate boards of directors would have either the management expertise or the financial capital necessary to run companies without turning to foreigners. The lack of expertise would also limit the ability of banks and mutual funds to oversee corporations. Andrei Shleifer pointed out that in the United States mutual and pension funds do not participate in the governance of the firms in which they hold stakes. He also disagreed with Lawrence Summers's proposal that government should play an important oversight role at the beginning of the privatization process. He doubted that the government could be a "passive" owner and argued that it was sure to interfere in ways that would reduce the firms' efficiency. Jeffrey Sachs noted that Shleifer's doubts were widely shared in Poland.

Schleifer suggested that managers be given significant ownership stakes as a means of tying control and incentives. He also stressed the need for a stock market as an effective mechanism for sharpening these incentives and for sending signals to managers. Robert Barro reasoned that secondary markets for securities were particularly needed in Eastern Europe because such a large number of new shares would be distributed in a way not determined by markets. The form of the initial distribution would be less important if a functioning stock market existed that could reprice and redistribute securities after they were issued.

Benjamin Friedman reasoned that the debate over how to privatize wealth must explicitly consider the question of the distribution of ownership shares. He observed that the privatization process would have a strong impact on the way Poles felt about capitalism. In the Soviet Union, and presumably in Poland to a lesser extent, liquid assets are extremely unevenly distributed, and the people who have the most assets have often accumulated them by unsavory means. Without some constraints on the rapid redistribution of ownership, most stock would end up in the hands of these few, and the public's support for private ownership of property would be undermined.

Sachs responded that the Poles do envision an active role for the stock market—both in valuing claims and in providing incentives to management—but not necessarily a large role in the privatization process itself (that is, through public offering of shares). Although sympathetic to Friedman's view that trading should be restricted for a time, Sachs predicted that it would not be possible because of the strong desire of the Poles for the freest possible market economy.

Charles Schultze observed that many of the behavioral norms that are taken for granted in Western economies, particularly those informing relations between firms and workers, are conventions that have gradually built up because they were economically efficient. He cited both Robert Hall's finding that adult males exhibit very long job tenure for most jobs and Arthur Okun's models of the invisible handshake as evidence of the importance of such arrangements. Because newly liberated economies would have no such established conventions, the emerging new laws governing market relations may need to provide somewhat more social insurance and other protection than is now the case in Western economies.

Acknowledgements

This paper draws heavily upon the policy debate in Poland in recent months regarding strategies of privatization. As such, it has benefited enormously from extensive discussion with various officials and advisors of the Polish government, including Finance Minister Leszek Balcerowicz, former Minister of Ownership Transformation Waldemar Kuczynski, Stefan Kawalec, Jerzy Kozminski, Jacek Rostowski, Matthew Olex, Andrew Berg, Homi Kharas, and Joseph Bell. Of course, the views expressed here are strictly our own, and not those of the government of Poland. We also thank Janos Kornai and Lawrence Summers for very helpful discussions. Our work is supported by a project on economic reform in Eastern Europe at the World Institute for Development Economics Research (WIDER), of the United Nations University, Helsinki, Finland.

Notes

1. For a discussion of the authors' preferred strategy for making the transition to the market economy in Eastern Europe, see Lipton and Sachs (1990). For two other discussions of a comprehensive strategy for transition to the market economy in Eastern Europe, see Blue Ribbon Commission: Project Hungary (1990), and Kornai (1990).

2. There are, of course, exceptions. Trenchant recent analyses may be found in Kornai (1990) and Milanovic (1990). For an excellent overview of the privatization experience throughout the world, see World Bank (1988).

3. Cited in Milanovic (1990, p. 45). For evidence on the rise of institutional investors in the United Kingdom and Japan, see Cosh, Hughes, and Singh (1989). They report that in the United Kingdom, for example, financial institutions held 58.9 percent of the value of listed securities in 1985, up from 44.8 percent in 1976 (table 6, p. 16).

4. Small-scale privatization is moving forward in Poland. Approximately 17,000 retail outlets had been privatized through September 1990. It is still not clear, however, if the government will be able to achieve its target of privatizing roughly two-thirds of retail establishments during 1990.

5. The available evidence in Poland suggests a surge of private sector activity

during 1990, with high rates of return and the rapid establishment of new enterprises. According to the official data, approximately 360,000 new private enterprises had been established during January–November 1990. However, the data are subject to many biases. Many establishments are not registered in order to avoid taxes; other establishments are simply shell organizations created to reduce taxes for other related businesses.

6. Our own views have been influenced by several of the contributions mentioned in the text.

7. Lewandowski and Szomburg (1989).

8. Hinds (1990); Frydman and Rapaczynski (1990).

9. Tomlinson (1990).

10. *Economist*, July 21, 1990.

11. Kornai (1990, p. 82).

12. As we mention later, the idea of a "stable core" was central to the French privatization process in the mid-1980s. Notably, Kornai (1990, p. 91) has independently stressed the importance of such a stable core in his recent book.

13. These data are out of date and overstate the extent of state ownership in many cases, such as France and the United Kingdom, which have reduced the share in the 1980s.

14. In Poland, the social democratic faction within Solidarity argues for a more gradual, less free-market strategy of reform.

15. According to the official statistics, there were 231,000 private establishments in the industrial sector in 1988. These firms tend to be very small, with an average employment of 2 workers. Polish authorities estimate that the private industrial sector accounts for only about 5 percent of sectoral output, though this figure is almost surely understated by the high level of activity in the underground (and, therefore, underreported) economy.

16. For an extensive discussion of the difficulties and trade-offs involved in privatizing natural monopolies and other firms in noncompetitive environments, see Caves (1990) and Vickers and Yarrow (1988).

17. Sixteen firms have been dropped from the top 500 firms owing to a lack of adequate data on performance during the first half of 1990. We use the remaining 484 firms as a proxy for the top 500.

18. This section draws heavily upon the research of Gregory Moffatt (1990), of the Washington law firm of Hogan and Hartson. We thank Joseph Bell for sharing this research material with us.

19. While we focus on the phase of reform communism in Poland after 1980, in contrast to the period of strict central planning before that time, we should note that the extent of centralization and decentralization waxed and waned throughout the postwar period. In the early years after the war, workers' councils exercised some measure of management rights. These rights were largely lost with the Stalinist crackdown in the late 1940s, when the instruments of central planning were strengthened. There was a brief thaw in 1956 (at the time of Khrushchev's attack on Stalin at the 20th Party Congress), in which workers' councils were again invigorated. By 1958, however, they were once again demoted in real influence.

20. See the discussion on Kornai's concept of the soft budget constraint in Kornai (1990), as well as other references therein.

21. See Sajko (1987, p. 1372).

22. For an excellent discussion of the different forms of governance of state-owned enterprises, see Milanovic (1990).

23. See Rudolf (1988, p. 424).

24. Rudolf (1988, p. 426).

25. Reported by Moffatt (1990, p. 18), regarding the Amending Law on State Enterprises, March 9, 1990.

26. See Lewandowski and Szomburg (1989, p. 258).

27. The average real wage in industry increased by 15 and 12 percent in 1988 and 1989 respectively. See Lipton and Sachs (1990).

28. We do not rule out the possibility that workers might appoint a minority portion of the board as in the company law in many Western European economies. Poland's company law, which dates from the 1930s, does not have any such provision for worker representation.

29. For a sophisticated theoretical discussion of this point, see Dreze (1989). Dreze summarizes his findings as follows (p. 114):

> In economies operating with uncertainty and incomplete insurance markets, it is natural to find capital hiring labor [rather than labor hiring capital], because efficient labor contracts in capitalist firms are easier to draw and monitor than efficient equity contracts for labor-managed firms.

The point is that it is generally more efficient for capital owners to hire labor than for laborers to rent capital.

30. See Blasi (1988, table C-2, pp. 264–66), which reports the proportion of Fortune 500 companies owned by internal employee funds (ESOPs, retirement funds, savings funds, stock-purchase plans, and so on). There is no case in which an ESOP plan contains as much as 15 percent of the shares of a firm, and only 7 firms of the Fortune 500 have an internal stock fund of any kind that contains more than 20 percent of the shares.

31. The value of this discount is to be capped, however, at less than the value of one year's average compensation of the workers in the firm.

32. The seminal contribution linking dispersed ownership to ineffective corporate governance is Berle and Means (1932). An enormous debate has arisen concerning ways to solve the governance problem, and concerning the extent to which it is a problem. Some economists, such as Demsetz (1983), suggest that the problem is largely overcome in practice through a combination of managerial compensation based on stock prices and through an adequate size of share ownership by minority shareholders. Empirical evidence tending to support the Berle and Means hypothesis has recently been provided by Morck, Shleifer, and Vishny (1988). In particular, these authors show that an enterprise's market valuation (measured by Tobin's q) tends to be lower when management holds a very small share of the enterprise capital than when it holds a moderate amount of enterprise capital.

33. The main problem is that takeover bidders usually gain very little from a hostile takeover, and therefore often do not undertake the effort even when efficiency considerations would recommend it (see Grossman and Hart (1980)). On the other hand, some takeovers may go forward even when they are not justified by efficiency, if the takeover process results in a gain in wealth for the bidder not as a result of a rise in efficiency, but by a *transfer* of wealth from some stakeholders in the target firm. See Shleifer and Summers (1988).

Grossman and Hart showed that takeover bidders may be forced to raise the price of the takeover bid to a point that exhausts most or all of the potential financial benefits to them of the takeover. This is because the incumbent shareholders in the target firm have an incentive to free-ride on a takeover bid, by holding on to their shares if they believe that the enterprise will indeed become more valuable if the takeover bid is successful. Thus, in order for the takeover bidder actually to acquire a firm, the bidder must make an offer that is generous enough to tempt the incumbent shareholders to part with their shares. A recent empirical study of hostile takeovers tends to confirm that the bidder gains little in the takeover bid, while all of the gains are appropriated by the shareholders of the target firm. See Bhagat, Shleifer, and Vishny (1990).

34. For discussions of the French concept and development of the "stable core" (*noyau stable*), see Friedmann (1989a, 1989b).

35. In the recent debate about the short-sightedness of American and British firms, considerable admiration for the German and Japanese patterns of corporate governance has been expressed. The argument has been summarized as follows:

> Much recent criticism of the City of London by British industrialists is rooted in the belief that institutional investors are too willing to sell out to an opportunistic bidder without having due regard to the longer term strategy of incumbent management. Institutional fund managers, it is said, operate on a different time horizon from industrialists and are prone to behave as speculators rather than owners. Unlike the bankers who have played such an important role in corporate governance in West Germany and Japan, the insurance companies and pension funds which dominate the more equity-oriented markets of the English-speaking economies are remote from the boards of companies in which they invest. The resulting pressure on management for short term performance, it is argued, is inimical to capital investment and research and development.

(John Plender, "Malaise in need of long-term remedy," *Financial Times*, July 20, 1990)

The argument seems to have found a recent practical response as well. French commercial banks, for example, are now moving to emulate the German pattern of bank ownership of industrial capital (*Economist*, August 4, 1990).

36. Sheard (1989) contains an excellent discussion of the role of the commercial banks in corporate governance in Japan. Sheard explains how "the main bank provides an important substitute mechanism for what in effect is a 'missing' takeover market in Japan; or to put it somewhat differently, the main bank serves to internalize the market for corporate control" (p. 407). Sheard stresses that corporate governance by a main bank economizes on scarce information, a fact of enormous practical relevance in Eastern Europe today.

37. The large banks were created by the dissolution in 1989 of the state monobank. These banks are therefore still in the state sector, and have little actual experience in corporate oversight or loan analysis. But they will have to play a vital role in reconstruction in any event, and therefore will have to be built up in administrative capacity. The banks should receive shares of state enterprises, however, only when the banks themselves have a clear timetable for privatization and have a demonstrated program for enhancing their capacities to engage in corporate oversight. Initially, the shares could be transferred to each bank as a trustee of the government's shares, with the ownership actually shifting to the bank only upon privatization of the bank.

38. Some people have called for an even more active role for financial institutions by calling for the creation of holding companies that would immediately become majority owners of the state enterprises. Advocates of the holding company approach believe that it is crucial to create a dominant investor with a majority stake at once, and arrange later for the sale of shares that would transfer corporate control. In our view, it would be dangerous to entrust the ownership of a large number of state enterprises to a *single, untested financial institution*. Such an arrangement would, in all likelihood, exacerbate problems of market power and would impede restructuring and liquidation. Moreover, there would be no clear mechanism under which the

holding companies would ultimately divest themselves of the enterprises. As long as the holding company maintained its control, there would be a period of limbo during which time it would be difficult to create the financial institutions needed for a market economy.

39. See, for example, Geoffrey Owen, "Improving corporate governance: Independent directors with bite on the board," *Financial Times*, September 5, 1990, p. 21, reviewing the article by Ronald Gilson and Reinier Kraakman, "Reinventing the outside director: an agenda for institutional investors." Working Paper 66. Stanford, Cal.: Stanford Law School (August).

40. See Franks and Mayer (1990) for evidence that hostile takeovers in the stock market play a larger role in the United Kingdom than in Germany in correcting "managerial failure." In Germany, a change in management is not commonly associated with a change of ownership.

41. International Finance Corporation (1990).

42. If, on the other hand, valuation is done in a mechanical way, without close approximation to true economic value, privatization will inevitably generate large windfall gains and losses that can become focal points for political protest against the entire privatization process.

43. For three analyses of the debacle of Chilean privatization in the 1970s, see Luders (1990), Hansson (1990), and Yotopoulos (1989).

44. Luders (1990, p. 3).

45. It seems that the most effective way to ensure that the vouchers do not become near-monies is to limit their liquidity by issuing them in registered and nontradable form.

46. For a discussion of managerial compensation schemes and their effects on firm efficiency, see Murphy (1985).

47. In essence, the income for part of the retirement payments would come out of enterprise profits. These profits are now financing the accumulation of physical and monetary capital by the enterprises. It is likely that as the enterprises are pressed to pay out part of their earnings to the pension funds, the retained earnings of the enterprises would fall, with a consequent fall in domestic investment spending.

References

Berle, Adolf A., and Gardiner C. Means. 1932. *The Modern Corporation and Private Property*. New York: Macmillan.

Bhagat, Sanjai, Andrei Shleifer, and Robert Vishny. 1990. "The Aftermath of Hostile Takeovers." Discussion Paper 87. London: LSE Financial Markets Group (June).

Blasi, Joseph R. 1988. *Employee Ownership: Revolution or Ripoff?* Cambridge, Mass.: Ballinger Publishing Company.

Blue Ribbon Commission: Project Hungary. 1990. "Hungary: In Transformation to Freedom and Prosperity." Indianapolis: Hudson Institute (April).

Caves, Richard. 1990. "Lessons from Privatization in Britain: State Enterprise Behavior, Public Choice, and Corporate Governance." *Journal of Economic Behavior and Organization* 13: 145–69.

Cosh, A.D., A. Hughes, and A. Singh. 1989. "Openness, Innovation and Share Ownership: The Changing Structure of Financial Markets." Working Paper 74. Helsinki: World Institute for Development Economics Research (October).

Demsetz, Harold. 1983. "The Structure of Ownership and the Theory of the Firm." *Journal of Law and Economics* 26: 375–90.

Dreze, Jacques H. 1989. *Labour Management Contracts and Capital Markets: A*

General Equilibrium Approach. Oxford: Basil Blackwell.

Franks, Julian, and Colin Mayer. 1990. "Capital Markets and Corporate Control: A Study of France, Germany, and the UK." *Economic Policy* 10: 189–231.

Friedmann, Jacques. 1989a. "Sur l'experience de privatisation: et sur les noyaux stables." *Commentaire* 45: 11–18.

———. 1989b. "Lecture pronounced at the Israeli International Institute in Tel Aviv" (September 14).

Frydman, Roman, and Andrzej Rapaczynaski. 1990. "Markets and Institutions in Large Scale Privatizations: An Approach to Economic and Social Transformations in Eastern Europe." New York University.

Grossman, Sanford J., and Oliver D. Hart. 1980. "Takeover Bids, The Free-rider Problem, and the Theory of the Corporation." *Bell Journal of Economics* 11: 42–64.

Hansson, Ardo H. 1990. "Capital Market Development and Privatization." Helsinki: World Institute for Development Economics Research (July).

Hinds, Manuel. 1990. "Issues in the Introduction of Market Forces in Eastern European Socialist Economies." Washington: World Bank (March).

Informacja Statystyczna. 1989 and 1990, various issues. *Statistical Information Monthly*. Warsaw: Central Statistical Office.

International Finance Corporation. 1990. *Emerging Stock Market Fact Book*. Washington: International Finance Corporation.

Jensen, Michael C., and Kevin J. Murphy. 1990. "CEO Incentives—It's Not How Much You Pay, But How." *Harvard Business Review* 90: 138–53.

Kornai, Janos. 1990. *The Road to a Free Economy, Shifting from a Socialist System: The Example of Hungary*. New York: W.W. Norton and Company.

Lewandowski, Janusz, and Jan Szomburg. 1989. "Property Reform as a Basis for Social and Economic Reform." *Communist Economies* 3: 257–68.

Lipton, David, and Jeffrey Sachs. 1990. "Creating a Market Economy in Eastern Europe: The Case of Poland." *BPEA, 1: 1990*, 75–133.

Luders, Rolf J. 1990. "Chile's Massive State Owned Enterprise Divestiture Program, 1975–1990: Failures and Successes." World Bank Conference on Privatization and Ownership Changes in East and Central Europe (forthcoming).

Milanovic, Branko. 1989. *Liberalization and Entrepreneurship: Dynamics of Reform in Socialism and Capitalism*. Armonk, New York: M.E. Sharpe, Inc.

———. 1990. "Privatization in Post-Communist Societies." Washington: World Bank.

Moffatt, Gregory. 1990. "Memorandum: Employee Participation in State-controlled Enterprises in Poland, Hungary, Yugoslavia, Czechoslovakia and the Soviet Union." Washington: Hogan and Hartson.

Morck, Randall, Andrei Shleifer, and Robert W. Vishny. 1988. "Management Ownership and Market Valuation: An Empirical Analysis." *Journal of Financial Economics* 20: 293–315.

Murphy, Kevin J. 1985. "Corporate Performance and Managerial Remuneration: An Empirical Analysis. *Journal of Accounting and Economics* 7: 11–42.

Rudolf, Stanislaw. 1988. "The Objective Nature of the Democratization Process in the Workplace." *Comparative Labor Law Journal* 9: 399–431.

Sajko, Kresimir. 1987. "Enterprise Organization of East European Socialist Countries—A Creative Approach." *Tulane Law Review* 61: 1365–82.

Sheard, Paul. 1989. "The Main Bank System and Corporate Monitoring and Control in Japan." *Journal of Economic Behavior and Organization* 11: 399–422.

Shleifer, Andrei, and Lawrence Summers. 1988. "Breach of Trust in Hostile Takeovers." In *Corporate Takeover: Causes and Consequences*, edited by Alan J.

Auerbach. Chicago: University of Chicago Press.
Tomlinson, Alexander C. 1990, "Proposal for a Hungarian National Investment Trust." Washington.
Vickers, John, and Vincent Wright. 1989. *The Politics of Privatisation in Western Europe*, London: Cass.
Vickers, John, and George Yarrow. 1988. *Privatization: An Economic Analysis*. Cambridge, Mass.: MIT Press.
World Bank. 1988. *Techniques of Privatization of State-Owned Enterprises*. Volumes I, II, and III. Washington: World Bank.
Yotopoulos, Pan A. 1989. "The (Rip)Tide of Privatization: Lessons from Chile." *World Development* 17: 683–702.

72

Alternative Financial Approaches to Privatisation

Pawel H. Dembinski

Source: *Eco-Diagnostic Analyses and the University of Fribourg*, October 1990, pp. 1–19.

Issues

1. This paper aims to clarify the relationship between the financial system and privatisation in post-communist economies. More specifically, it considers the direction in which the financial system should evolve to facilitate the dismantling of the system left by 40 years of central planning and to ensure that the foundations of a market economy are laid judiciously.

It will not review the debate on privatisation in the various East European countries, since the literature on this subject is vast and in constant flux;[1] what it will do is to draw the financial implications of the various alternative approaches to privatisation. The method of privatisation adopted, and the structure and functioning of the financial system, obviously cannot be separated from one another. The post-communist economies in Eastern Europe are currently in the process of simultaneously remodelling fundamentally the financial system that they inherited from the centrally-planned economy, and preparing privatisation. However, in both the literature on the subject and in practice, the two issues tend to be treated in isolation from one another, and often by different institutions. In consequence, the debate on privatisation is often artificially reduced to ideological and/or highly technical matters. But the very fact that a smoothly-functioning financial system does not yet exist in these countries itself constitutes an opportunity to be grasped and offers the possibility of adopting solutions commensurate with the scale of the problems.

2. Nobody any longer contests the fact that the centrally-planned economy has ceased to function. Its brutal collapse was prompted by the sudden collapse of the logic that had underpinned it for decades.[2] However, although the logic has disappeared along with its ideological foundation, component elements of the system continue to survive in Eastern Europe. These may be divided into three distinct categories: structures, mechanisms and behaviour.

3. The replacement of one economic system by another predicates that, simultaneously with the introduction of a new logic – in this case that of the market economy – new structures, mechanisms and behaviour consistent with that logic must also be introduced. The transition to a market economy thus entails, in addition to the inevitable short-term disruption, the simultaneous introduction of new legal and institutional structures, the development of new mechanisms, and the promotion of new patterns of behaviour. If the transition is confined solely to structures, it is likely to remain a dead letter and, by the same token, the new logic will prove to be inoperative. If the transition does not embrace the entire system, it is likely to fail.

4. Mainstream economic thinking has to a large extent ignored these systemic problems for the simple reason that, at the level of abstraction at which it operates, it assumes that *homo economicus* is universal and that he acts in the same way in all circumstances. This is why the comparative study of economic systems, and "sovietology" in particular, have remained outside mainstream economics, which has tended to regard them as unscientific. The degree to which economic science was ignorant of these systemic problems was revealed when the world woke up, somewhat to its astonishment, to the fact that it was not enough to replace one set of economic principles by another for a market economy to start functioning spontaneously.

The transition to a market economy is a systemic problem, and should be approached as such. The task is to create, as quickly as possible, the embryo of a market system, i.e. to achieve, as quickly as possible, a minimum amount of consistency between structures, mechanisms and behaviour – some of which have been inherited from the past while others still have to be created from scratch – and market principles. As structures, mechanisms and behaviour gradually come into line with market principles, an economic system in the full sense of the word should start to emerge.

5. The main difference between the centrally-planned economy and the market economy is that the former recognises only one economic actor – the socialised sector; in contrast, a market economy requires a large number of independent actors. The basic meaning of the term "privatisation" is thus quite clear: it means stimulating and encouraging the emergence of private economic actors.

6. Although this basic feature of the centrally-planned economy – that it recognises only one economic actor – has tended to be overlooked in the discussions and the reforms implemented in the past two decades with a view to making enterprises more independent, it has left its imprint on all the elements that have been inherited from the centrally-planned system by the fledgling market economies in Eastern Europe. Although some of these elements do show similarities with the market economy, most often the

similarities are superficial. This is true of those elements that make up what is known as the "financial system".

7. In the post-communist context the relationship between the financial system and privatisation is difficult to ascertain because at this stage the concepts underlying them cannot be clearly defined. The following analysis seeks to clarify them and draw the implications for the financial system of two different privatisation scenarios: first, privatisation by divestiture i.e. the transfer of assets from the socialised sector to the private sector; second, privatisation by decapitalisation of the socialised sector and the simultaneous injection of capital into the private sector. Lastly, the practical, theoretical and political advantages and drawbacks of each scenario are compared.

8. The paper is divided into five parts. Part I summarises the basic features of a financial system in a centrally-planned economy. Part II examines some definitions of the term "privatisation". Parts III and IV outline the two alternative privatisation strategies: privatisation by divestiture and privatisation by decapitalisation. Lastly, Parts V and VI compare various features of the two methods.

I. The Financial System in Transition

9. According to a report by the World Bank, the basic functions of a financial system are to provide payment services, mobilise savings and allocate credit.[3] Households, businesses and governments use these services, which are provided by specialised institutions, particularly banks, brokers and insurance companies. But wide as this definition is, it is not valid for the financial system in a centrally-planned economy, which can be defined as follows: "Although a socialist financial system is segmented from the point of view of its economic functions and organisation, it nonetheless forms an organic whole. It constitutes an effective instrument for managing the socialist economy.

The components of this system are:

- the State budget;
- quasi-budgets, also called "specific funds";
- the finances of socialised enterprises;
- money-creating institutions (banks);
- insurance and other financial institutions.[4]

As this definition makes clear, all the institutions in a socialist economy, including enterprises, exist for the purposes of the final distribution of national income. In other words, the role of the financial system in a centrally-planned economy is much wider than in a market economy.

10. Households, and the rest of the world – which does not appear in the

diagram of the financial system in centrally-planned economies in the annex to this paper – are outside the socialist financial system as thus defined. Financial flows between households and the socialised sector are recorded under the "balance of households' expenditures and receipts". When the balance is negative this means that households' liabilities to the socialised sector have increased, while a positive balance indicates that the socialised sector's indebtedness to households has increased, either because lending by the sector is less than deposits or because households' money holdings have increased. It is important to note that under this system of accounting the private sector and households are regarded as being the same.

Financial flows between the rest of the world and the socialised sector are recorded in the balance of payments in national currency; however given that the currency is non-convertible, and given the pricing system in a centrally-planned economy, this balance bears no direct relation to a balance of payments in convertible currencies.

11. Although the socialist financial system no longer exists as such, it is worth recalling the principles that underpinned it so that it can be reorganised or dismantled all the more effectively. In centrally-planned economies, that part of the national product that was allocated neither to households' consumption nor to exports remained in the hands of the socialised sector, which utilised it primarily for investment. The role of the socialist financial system consisted in matching what could be called the "self-financing" of the socialised sector, and the physical counterpart of that financing, i.e. investment goods. The financial system enabled the planned economy to requisition the resources for what is known in Marxist terminology as the "process of large scale capital reproduction", i.e. the replacement and expansion of the productive capital stock that is the key to growth. An important feature of the planned economy, and one that is incompatible with a market economy, is that households have no control over the saving–investment process. In a planned economy the centre can decide the share of the national product that will be allocated to investment by fixing the share and value of national product earmarked for consumption. Thus, as long as the post-communist economies continue to exhibit this feature, they – and by the same token their financial system – will bear the imprint of a planned economy, and privatisation will remain a pious wish.

12. The socialist financial system has the following distinctive features:

12.1 It is a system of flows; it involves only current payments, since by definition transactions in assets are ruled out. In consequence, physical assets have no financial counterpart, either in the sense of securities or in the accounting sense. The acquisition value of productive capital appears in the accounts of socialist enterprises only for the purposes of calculating depreciation.

12.2. The debt relationships that are fundamental in a market economy, whereby one agent lends liquidity to another for a fixed term against security – usually an asset – and in return for a remuneration – cannot exist in the proper sense in the socialised sector. On the other hand, the system is such that agents in the socialised sector have an automatic borrowing facility; however, there is no way of recovering debts. In other words, in a planned economy debtors are at an advantage over creditors; by not settling a claim, an agent in the socialised sector not only creates a liability but also imposes it on other agents. Enterprises can thus lend between one another, bypassing the budget and the banks. Growing imbalances may lead the socialised sector to compel households to "lend" to it (see above), notably by monetising part of the total debt thereby created.

12.3. The financial system in the planned economy could function satisfactorily only as long as it could impose stringent discipline on payments between agents. In addition to the mechanism of control and regulation, two other instruments were used to reduce the risks of a surge in debt or inflation: the money supply was divided into several categories, and the liquidity of enterprises was tightly controlled.

The money supply was divided into three distinct categories: consumption, foreign trade and the socialised sector. Initially, each category was relatively independent of the other two;[5] this allowed each category to be balanced separately. But the reforms from the 1970s onwards increased the financial imbalances, and the interdependence between the categories of the money supply; the upshot was growing disorganisation of the financial system and the emergence of inflation.

12.4. From the purely institutional point of view, the financial system of the planned economies was underspecialised or not specialised at all. For example, it is impossible to identify the share of subsidies, loans, taxes and payments proper in the total flow of payments. The cause of the lack of specialisation, and hence transparency, of the financial flows in a planned economy, lies in the accounting framework within which enterprises operate and in the specific features of the price system.

13. The financial system inherited by the post-communist economies thus does not comprise a single element or institution that bears a resemblance to the financial system in a market economy. It is important to stress this, because the fact that the names are the same might suggest that we are talking about the same thing, when in fact they refer to very different things. To move to a market economy, it is therefore necessary to remodel fundamentally the financial system of the post-communist economies, and this irrespective of the method of privatisation that is adopted. Above all, it is necessary to:

13.1. Redesign the financial system so that it reflects the stocks as well as flows in the economy, which means setting in place the legal and institutional prerequisites for the creation of financial assets; essentially, this involves ensuring that physical assets are matched by financial counterparts.

13.2. Make enterprises autonomous accounting entities with respect to the financial system, which means not only creating an accounting system in which operating and asset accounts are quite separate, but also transforming enterprises from pseudo-economic actors into fully-fledged independent entities.

13.3. Lay down the broad lines of institutional specialisation; this involves classifying transactions by their function in the financial system, and then assigning them to institutions which should either be restructured in line with these functions, or set up from scratch. Leaving aside for the moment the question of the institutional charges required by privatisation and foreign debt management, four groups of specialised institutions should emerge from the current institutional confusion:

(a) private and public social security institutions: these would collect contributions, pay benefits and manage assets;
(b) budget institutions in the strict sense, comprising the central and local budget authorities with redistributive functions and responsibility for the provision of public goods;
(c) monetary authorities: these would be responsible for monetary policy and, to a certain extent, the supervision of banks and financial markets;
(d) financial intermediaries: their role would be to collect savings and to channel them into investment projects.

14. The financial system, being one of the instruments via which the transition to a market economy will be effected, should be restructured with an eye to the global aspects of the reform, and to the requirements of privatisation in particular. Political resolve at the highest level is thus absolutely essential in order to minimise the risk of bureaucratic trade-offs which, by watering down the transformation, could easily knock it off course. At this stage only the broad lines and fundamental principles of the new financial system should be laid down, matters of lesser importance being dealt with as they arise.

15. The transformation of the financial system is part and parcel of the overall remodelling of legal and institutional structures. It will provide the necessary framework for the establishment of economic relations consistent with the principles of a market economy, without actually creating the relations themselves. Both the mechanisms and, insofar as it is possible, the prevailing behaviour need to be modified simultaneously so that private actors can seize the opportunities opened up by the new structures. A new economic system will emerge only when the new structures, mechanisms and behaviour are broadly in line with one another.

16. This said, however, it should not be forgotten that, once the remnants of the planned economy have been dismantled, private actors will have to take over the process of transforming savings into investment that lies at the heart of any economy. Hence the need to underline once again the crucial importance of privatisation.

II. The Concept of Privatisation

17. The underlying ambiguities of the term "privatisation" become clear when it is applied to the post-communist economies.

Many recent studies of privatisation in the post-communist economies define it as the transfer of ownership of assets from the public sector to private economic actors, which ultimately means to households.[6] However, this is an implicitly static view of privatisation: the stock of productive capital is taken as given, and all that privatisation involves is a change, either total or partial, of ownership. The public sector "loses" assets, so to speak, to the private sector. Privatisation is thus perceived as being a zero-sum game.

Other studies, although admittedly not so many, focus on the dynamic aspect of the privatisation process. For example, Savas[7] says: "in the broadest and most philosophical definition, 'to privatise' means to rely more on the private institutions of society and less on the government to satisfy people's needs. Most narrowly, privatisation is the act of increasing the role of the private sector, or decreasing the role of government, in an activity or in the ownership of assets." The merit of this definition is that it puts the emphasis not on redistribution, i.e. the transfer of assets or activities from the public sector to the private sector, but on the increase in private activities. To privatise means to increase, by every means possible, the share of the private sector in the national product. The definition is thus broader than the previous, static one, according to which privatisation is a zero-sum game; it poses the problem of privatisation in the dynamic terms of a non-zero-sum game. It takes account of the increase in the capital stock resulting from privatisation, and makes it possible to envisage the expansion of private activity in low capital-intensive sectors.

18. The difference between the foregoing definitions of "privatisation" can be explained by the fact that the situations that gave rise to them were different: up to 1989 the question of privatisation arose solely in the context of Western economies or in some developing countries where it involved a transfer of State assets to the private sector. Until then the idea that privatisation could ever take place in Eastern Europe did not even cross the mind of sovietologists,[8] who were so busy monitoring the difficulties of the centrally-planned economic system that they did not see that it was in its terminal phase. The collapse of the East European communist regimes in 1989 created a new context in which the withdrawal of the State from the

economy – i.e. privatisation in the broad sense – became a top political priority, and an increased contribution by the private sector to the national product was seen as the prerequisite for a successful transition to a market system.

19. Under the pressure of events the meaning of "privatisation" thus became broader, and the transfer of assets from the public sector to the private sector became only one of the aspects or paths to privatisation. In the light of these developments Savas identified three strategies for privatising State enterprises, assets and activities: privatisation by divestiture (selling, giving away or liquidating State assets); privatisation by delegation (via contracting out, licences, subsidies, authorisation to perform activities previously conducted by the State, vouchers); privatisation by substitution (by default or withdrawal of the State, deregulation). According to this classification, transfer of State assets to the private sector is equivalent to a privatisation by divestiture, irrespective of the instruments used.

20. In the post-communist political context the principle of privatisation does not have to be justified as such. All the protagonists recognise that it is necessary rapidly to reduce the economic weight of what used to be called the socialised sector. There is thus agreement on the systemic objective. But there is far from unanimous agreement on the best way of achieving it.

Although in the long-term privatisation may make the economy more efficient from the standpoint of both allocation and production costs, analyses may differ as to the medium- and short-term effects. And when the institutional and financial feasibility of implementing privatisation is taken into account, opinions differ even further.

21. One of the main problems posed by privatisation, and one of the most difficult to resolve, is what to do with the assets currently held by the socialised sector. Two approaches are possible: privatisation by divestiture i.e. the State's assets and activities are transferred directly to the private sector, or privatisation by substitutions and delegation.

In the first scenario the assets themselves are transferred to the private sector, whereas in the second one a large proportion of the cash flow generated by the socialised sector is transferred to the private sector until the productive capital in the socialised sector has been completely depreciated. In the long run both scenarios have the same result: the State's assets are transferred to the private sector; but in the first scenario the transfer involves an injection of physical capital in the private sector, while in the second one it involves an injection of financial capital.

Hereafter the direct transfer of assets will be called "privatisation by divestiture", while the transfer of cash flow will be called "privatisation by decapitalisation", i.e. by capital dilution.

22. Turning to the technical aspects of privatisation, at the heart of the

debate on privatisation by divestiture lies the question of whether assets should be transferred directly or via the financial system; in contrast, privatisation by decapitalisation can be done only through the financial system. In both cases privatisation modifies the saving–investment process: in the case of privatisation by divestiture, the entire process is transferred to the private sector along with the assets themselves, while in privatisation by decapitalisation savings continue to be collected to a large extent within the socialised sector, and then transferred to the private sector, which thereafter takes over the investment process.

III. Privatisation by Divestiture

23. To transfer productive capital to the private sector, it is first necessary to:

(a) identify the object of the transfer;
(b) identify the parties to the transfer;
(c) create the appropriate financial instrument;
(d) determine the financial counterpart of the transfer.

23.1 In the centrally-planned economies, production and, to an even greater extent, productive capital, were in the hands of specialised economic agents which although they were called "enterprises" in fact bore only a superficial resemblance to the enterprises in a market economy. The question thus arises of what exactly should be transferred: enterprises in their existing state, enterprises that have been restructured or reorganised along market economy lines, or productive capital in the physical sense of the term. This difficulty is compounded by the particularly thorny problem of how capital should be valued in an environment in which prices and markets are fluctuating all the time, which has no capital market, and in which the role to be played by interest rates is still not quite clear.

23.2. The problem of identifying the parties to the transfer is that of determining from whom the assets should be transferred, and to whom. Numerous scenarios are possible, ranging from that in which the assets are transferred to holdings specially created for the purpose, to that in which individuals, particularly the employees of enterprises, receive the assets. But whatever the scenario, the legal framework of the enterprise – its form, structures, decision-making mechanisms, accounting system etc. – needs to be radically remodelled to allow the new owners to exercise effective management and control over their enterprises.

23.3. In the financial system of socialist economies, financial assets did not exist because titles of ownership as such did not exist. The return to a market economy, and particularly the transfer of physical assets from the socialised sector, predicates the reintroduction of titles of ownership. These titles can be either securities that represent a given share in the ownership of an enterprise, or securities with a nominal value – each enterprise's capital being equal to the sum of the nominal values of the securities issued. Titles of ownership would thus naturally take the form of shares, with voting rights allocated either proportionally or according to a special system. Decisions concerning the return on capital would be taken by shareholders' assemblies – i.e. they would be taken on a case-by-case basis by each enterprise. To avoid abuses, the law should protect small shareholders from systematic domination by large shareholders.

23.4. The financial counterpart of the transfer of assets also has to be worked out. There seem to be two possible solutions:

(a) Securities are offered for purchase at a price that is determined by supply and demand. It is for the State to decide the price and the terms of the subscription that are the best suited to the objectives sought. But given that the money holdings of households are limited, the higher the subscription price the slower the pace of privatisation will be.
(b) The government distributes or sells vouchers to the public. The Czechoslovak government favours this solution, and it is also being considered in Poland. This would mean that the shares of privatised enterprises would be denominated in coupons – or other units of account – and not in money. When an enterprise is sold, the government would withdraw some of the coupons from circulation. The advantage of using coupons for the initial placement of shares is that the initial placement would be technically separate from subsequent transactions in the private sector, which would be paid for in money.

24. Privatisation by divestiture also raises other questions:

(a) What would the proceeds from the sale of assets, or coupons, be used for?
(b) How would enterprises behave while awaiting privatisation?
(c) What are the chances of preventing excessive concentrations of shares in the hands of a few shareholders?
(d) What are the chances of the new shareholders exercising effective control over enterprises?

24.1. As regards the use to which the proceeds from privatisation would be put, there are several possibilities. They could be used for recapitalising banks; giving social security institutions the capital they need to start operating on a funded basis (like pension funds in market economies); enabling the government to pay off its debt to the central bank; reducing the foreign debt. Whatever the solution adopted, however, it would have a specific impact on the functioning of the domestic financial system.

24.2. Privatisation by divestiture will necessarily take a long time, and while it is taking place two types of enterprises – those that are already in the hands of the private sector and those that are still under State control – will exist alongside one another. Those in the hands of the private sector will be controlled by shareholders in accordance with the law; they will decide how the cash flow generated by the enterprise will be allocated – whether to replacement or expansion of capacity, reserves or dividends. In contrast, the cash flow of enterprises still under State control will be left in the hands of the present management, with probably less supervision by the government than at present. This could prompt the enterprises, however, to take ill-considered investment decisions,thereby squandering a significant proportion of their savings and saddling the economy with an unsuitable productive structure.

24.3. The debate on privatisation in general, and in East Europe in particular, attaches great importance to the distributive aspects of the process. All East European countries would like to move from a socialist economy to a Thatcherite-type property-owning democracy. This requires two things: (a) the initial distribution of assets would need to be as broad and equitable as possible; (b) shareholders would have to resist the temptation to sell their shares at the first opportunity.

An equitable distribution can be achieved by giving away the assets or by selling them on very favourable terms to certain categories of the population. However, this would deprive the State of a substantial amount of income and, even though it was intended to reduce social inequalities, it could generate more distortions than it did away with.

The initial distribution of assets could be preserved only by imposing very stringent constraints – by prohibiting shareholders from selling their shares, by placing limits on the transfers of shares, or by other legal restrictions. However, such measures would be imperfect and counter to the principles of economic freedom. An alternative method would be to increase the income of households sufficiently to ensure that that they would not be tempted to sell the assets that they had just purchased or received. Given that the most pressing concern of the populations of Eastern Europe is to increase their consumption, the danger is all the greater because the threat of inflation is ever-present.

24.4. But even if it proves possible to create a stable, widely-based class of shareholders, the question still arises of whether they could exercise effective control over the privatised enterprises. The lack of meaningful information about companies' accounts, the fact that it is extremely difficult to make forecasts about a company's subsequent development, the underdeveloped state of the media, and finally the total lack of business and financial sophistication among the population, would suggest that even if the legal framework existed, shareholders would be essentially passive. This would mean that in practice enterprises would be controlled either by large shareholders or by the proxies of small shareholders – probably banks, or even management funds of a new type.

To ensure that privatisation does not result in a situation where company managements are freed from any kind of control, proposals for concentrating shareholdings – in State holdings, pension funds, banks or other types of financial companies – have been put forward. But although these proposals may be technically feasible, they would result in an extreme concentration of economic power, and even of wealth. The upshot would be that, even though enterprises had been withdrawn from State control, they would still not have been privatised.

25. To sum up, privatisation by divestiture involves the transfer of existing enterprises to private shareholders, with shares issued against the existing assets. It follows logically that financial institutions and intermediaries capable of handling such transactions would be needed. The privatisation by divestiture scenario thus presupposes the creation of a market-oriented financial system with a banking sector consisting of universal banks.[9]

IV. Privatisation by Decapitalisation

26. In contrast with privatisation by divestiture, privatisation by decapitalisation of the socialised sector takes as its starting point the idea that it is not so much the existing assets of the socialised sector that should be transferred to the private sector as its capacity for creating new assets, i.e. its capacity for investment. Claiming that divestiture would merely put new wine into old bottles with all the possible adverse consequences, the advocates of privatisation by decapitalisation argue vigorously for the creation of new investment mechanisms. They thus put the emphasis not on the transfer of existing assets but on the creation of the prerequisites for the emergence of new economic actors.[10]

In the same way as the communist regimes exploited the agricultural sector and light industry to finance the growth of heavy industry, which in practice meant the dilution of their capital and the overcapitalisation of heavy industry, the privatisation by decapitalisation strategy would use the socialised sector to finance the development of the private sector. Just as the financial system of the centrally-planned economy was the instrument of State control over the economy, it is now necessary to build a transitional financial system that would promote the revival of the private sector while gradually reducing the weight of the socialised sector.

The problems to be solved with privatisation by decapitalisation are very different from those posed by privatisation by divestiture. They relate to:

(a) the framework within which the financial system would operate;

(b) the way in which cash flow would be siphoned off from the socialised sector;
(c) the use that would be made of this cash flow;
(d) the manner in which the private sector would exist alongside the socialised sector.

27. However, the prerequisite for privatisation by decapitalisation is a fundamental remodelling of the financial system that has been inherited from the planned economy. First of all, it would be necessary to set in place a legal framework setting out clearly the forms and internal organisation of the new enterprises, and the requirements in respect of initial capital provisions, management and supervision.

27.1. A proper accounting framework is an absolute priority. Asset and liability accounts would have to be separated from operating accounts, as is the practice in market economies. New firms would thus be able to offer security against loans. All new enterprises would be required to comply with the accounting framework, whereas enterprises in the socialised sector would be allowed to continue to apply the old accounting rules.

27.2. If new enterprises are to be set up in countries in which the private sector's financial resources are extremely limited, there will be a particularly large need for collateral to secure loans, notably insurance, especially life insurance, and mortgages: this will require major changes in property and rental law. Public or private investment banks should also be set up; their statutes should specify clearly their sphere of activity, i.e. the financing and the provision of advice to the new enterprises.

27.3. During the initial phase specialised investment banks would be the only sources of credit; they would thus play a key role in the new financial system. As financial markets gradually emerged, the specialised banks could become universal banks.

28. By its very principle, privatisation by decapitalisation is a financial process which consists of transferring resources from the socialised sector to the private sector. Profits and depreciation are siphoned off from socialised enterprises, slashing their capacity for investment. The choice of the mechanism for siphoning off their profits is thus of crucial importance: it can be done by taxation – using a scale based on the book value of the enterprise's physical assets – or by simply taking all or part of the profits and depreciation in accordance with a clearly-defined legal procedure.

If the taxation method was chosen, enterprises in the socialised sector would be divided into three categories: those which retained the capacity for investment even after being taxed; those which no longer had any; those which could not pay the tax. Although there would be difficulties in drawing up an appropriate scale, this method would have the virtue of being simple to implement.

Siphoning-off the cash flow would be technically more cumbersome since it would be necessary to deal with each enterprise on a case-by-case basis. Moreover, it would leave scope for negotiation and encourage enterprises to conceal part of their earnings. Its advantage would be that it would theoretically put all enterprises on the same footing.

In order to avoid too drastic a fall in State income, all enterprises, whether public or private, would have to pay the capital taxes currently in force. But only socialised enterprises would transfer their profits and depreciation funds to the institutions responsible for overseeing the privatisation of the economy.

Both techniques would in fact involve the use of methods perfected and used continually by the planned economy for directing investment flows to selected sectors. Notwithstanding the reservations that one may have about them, in view of the use that was made of them in the past, these techniques would be effective, simple to implement and would make the transition to a market economy much easier.

29. The cash flow siphoned off from the socialised sector should be channelled to ad hoc institutions or funds that would decide how they would be used. A new public institution would thus have to be created for collecting the payments from socialised enterprises and for allocating them. They could be used in several ways: they could be distributed to the public, used to constitute the capital of new investment banks or specialised institutions such as regional guarantee funds, mortgage banks, etc., or for financing low-interest loans or even direct subsidies to certain new enterprises.

The solution with the most to commend it in terms of theoretical purity would be to distribute the funds to the population. It would be possible to create "capital accounts" that households could not use for consumption purposes but only for setting up their own business or for buying a stake in new enterprises. Alternatively, the funds could be placed on bank savings accounts or used to buy government bonds. The drawbacks of such an arrangement are: the lack of a banking system capable of managing a large volume of capital accounts, the fact that it is not known whether households would want or have the ability to manage their assets actively, the danger that the economic power of existing banks would increase thanks to deposits which were no longer managed actively by the public.

It is essential to use the cash flow from the socialised sector to create investment banks, guarantee and mortgage banks that would allow new enterprises to get started and eventually to increase their borrowing capacity relative to that of other economic actors, particularly households. Initially, these credit institutions – which would be different from existing banks – would be in the public sector but would be run on a commercial basis as they are in many market-economy countries. It would be necessary to train the staff for them; this would be a big job, but could be done by international organisations with the support of Western professional associations; the French Banking Training Centre, for example, is already providing such training.

The cash flow generated by the socialised sector could also be used for financing low-interest loans or even subsidies to specific enterprises, sectors or regions. The drawback to this approach, however, is that it could dilute the real costs of privatisation, remove transparency from it, and create scope for favouritism, and thus prevent privatisation from being implemented properly.

30. Privatisation by decapitalisation would continue until the capital of socialised enterprises had been completely depreciated. This gives rise to two questions: (a) how would the socialised and private sectors exist alongside one another while privatisation was in progress; (b) what would happen to the socialised enterprises once their capital has been completely depreciated.

30.1. The corollary of privatisation by decapitalisation is that two distinct sectors would have to continue to exist during the transitional phase. The legal status of enterprises, their system of accounting, their latitude in respect of the use of profits, borrowing from banks and investment, would be different for each sector. The new legal framework would apply immediately and entirely to the private sector, whereas the socialised sector would continue to operate within the existing legal framework. Ultimately all economic activities would be transferred to the private sector and the rules applicable to the socialised sector would automatically cease to have effect. In short, the aim of privatisation by decapitalisation is to halt the development of the socialised sector and to promote that of the private sector.

Naturally, during the transitional period there would also be a dual financial system. Payments and short-term financing in the socialised sector would need to be concentrated among a few banks – such as those that already exist – whereas the financing of the private sector should be handled by new financial institutions operating on a commercial basis, although some of them could remain under State control. Households' savings should be collected and transferred solely to private sector institutions.

30.2. As privatisation by decapitalisation would be a gradual process, the question arises of what would happen to socialised enterprises once they had been completely decapitalised. In theory the community would have recovered its investment and the enterprise could be closed down, left in the hands of its employees, or sold off to outsiders.

In order not to squander the potential of certain socialised enterprises that are performing particularly well today, another alternative would be to allow them to continue to expand so as not to lose the footholds that they have acquired in markets, particularly in foreign ones. They should be leased to the private sector. Control of their management would be transferred immediately to the private sector in return for the payment of a monthly or annual charge calculated using a formula that would vary according to the length of the lease; the enterprise's assets would serve as security. When the lease expired, the private sector would automatically become owner of the enterprise. Investment by such enterprises should be financed solely by the private part of the financial system.

Convertible bonds could also be used by enterprises in the socialised sectors that wanted to continue to invest while at the same time paying the financial charges that privatisation by decapitalisation would impose on them. They could obtain the funds they needed for investment by issuing bonds, but solely in the private sector of the financial system; these bonds would be converted automatically into shares, at a date specified in advance, when cash flow ceased to be transferred to the private sector from the socialised sector.

An undoubted advantage of privatisation by decapitalisation over privatisation by divestiture is that it would allow bonds to be issued before shares were issued on a large scale. This advantage is a considerable one given the public's relative lack of financial sophistication.

V. Similarities and Differences between the Two Approaches to Privatisation

31. Although they have the same objectives, privatisation by divestiture and privatisation by decapitalisation differ in their approach. The main difference is that in one case the enterprises themselves are transferred to the private sector, while in the other it is their financial resources that are transferred. While the ownership of public enterprises could, at a stretch, be transferred outside the financial system, to transfer cash flow from the socialised sector to the private sector the financial system would have to be remodelled radically. The role that the financial system would play in one system is thus very different from that which it would play in the other.

The choice of the method of transferring assets from the socialised sector to the private sector, from among the numerous possible methods that are available will be determined by the objectives, which themselves will be influenced by considerations of distributional equity, the method chosen for valuating assets, and finally the end-use that is planned to make of the proceeds of the privatisation. Every privatisation scenario for Eastern Europe inevitably has to address these questions, although in the case of privatisation by decapitalisation only one of them really matters: that of the choice of institutional arrangements via which the cash flow generated by the socialised sector would be injected into the private sector. As regards considerations of distributional equity, these would be impossible to guarantee under privatisation by decapitalisation since the enterprises with the best prospects would need to be given priority in access to privatisation funds. Enterprising individuals who were able to set up an enterprise and to keep it going would automatically be in a privileged position. As for the valuation of assets, this question would not arise immediately under a privatisation by decapitalisation scenario, since it could be based on the book value of assets at a given date, linked to a reference index. At the same time, a capital market would develop in the private sector, allowing assets to be valued as in a market economy. In other words, the financial approach to privatisation – privatisation by decapitalisation – makes it possible to overcome two of the drawbacks to privatisation by outright transfer of assets from the socialised sector to the private sector.

The two approaches also differ in their vision of the national economy during the transitional period. Privatisation by divestiture would make it possible rapidly to unify the legal and accounting framework for socialised and private enterprises, whereas in the privatisation by decapitalisation scenario they would continue to be treated differently until the capital of socialised enterprises had been completely depreciated. The financial system would exhibit the same duality.

32. The shape of the financial system would be different under each of the scenarios. Privatisation by divestiture would require the creation of capital markets, the development of universal banks and possibly pension funds to manage vast share portfolios.

The emergence of a wide range of financial institutions – insurance companies, banks, regional funds and underwriting institutions that would operate in specialised markets reserved to professionals – would be essential to privatisation by decapitalisation. As private enterprises developed and gradually became stronger, in the medium term the first public share issues could be made, and companies that were performing particularly well could be listed on the stock exchange. Privatisation by divestiture thus requires a market-oriented financial system, whereas privatisation by decapitalisation requires rather a bank-oriented financial system which in time could evolve, as in most Western countries, into a market-oriented system.

Conclusion

33. This report shows that a successful transition to a market economy depends on the degree to which the privatisation scenario adopted, and the financial system set in place, complement one another. It aims to draw attention to the interrelationships that exist between the two, and to the margin of choice that still exists, since neither the method of privatisation nor the set up of the financial system have yet been decided. The situation both offers opportunities and presents risks: opportunities – since it is it possible to envisage comprehensive schemes commensurate with the challenges; risks – since there can be no guarantee today that the choice of method of

privatisation will be compatible with the choice of financial system in the post-communist economies.

The relationship between the financial system and privatisation was discussed with respect to two scenarios: privatisation by divestiture, i.e. the transfer of assets from the socialised sector to the private sector, and privatisation by decapitalisation of the socialised sector and the simultaneous injection of capital into the private sector. Under the first scenario a market-oriented financial system would be required, whereas a bank-oriented system would be more suitable under the second one.

The advantages and drawbacks of the two approaches were compared, and it was concluded that privatisation by decapitalisation offered the post-communist economies a better chance of developing private economic activities rapidly.

Notes and References

1. For a recent summary see Grosfeld, I., "Les perspectives de la privatisation en Pologne" and Hare, P.G., "Réforme de la réglementation régissant les entreprises en Hongrie", in *Economie Européenne*, No. 43, March 1990.
2. Dembinski, P.H., "*The Logic of the Planned Economy: The seeds of the collapse*", Oxford University Press, Clarendon Press, 1990.
3. World Bank, *World Development Report 1989: Financial Systems and Development*, Washington, 1989, p. 29.
4. Owsiak, S., *Bilans finansowy panstwa*, PWE, Warsaw, 1980, pp. 87–88.
5. Dembinski, P. "Quantity versus Allocation of Money: Monetary Problems of Centrally Planned Economies Reconsidered", *Kyklos*, Vol. 41, No. 2, 1988, pp. 281–300.
6. Grosfeld, I., "Privatisation of State Enterprises in Eastern Europe: the search for a market environment", mimeo, Delta, 1990, Paris; Hinds, M., "Issues in the Introduction of Market Forces in Eastern European Socialist Economies", World Bank Working Paper, 1990; Nuti, M., "Privatisation of socialist economies: general issues and the Polish case", mimeo, European University Institute, Florence, 1990.
7. Savas, E.S., "Taxonomy of Privatisation Strategies", to appear in *Policy Studies Journal*, 1990.
8. Some recent studies do not even mention the possibility: EEC/UN, *Economic Reforms in the European Centrally-Planned Economies*, New York, 1989; Economic Development Institute of the World Bank, *Financial Reforms in Socialist Economies*, Washington 1989; nor was it mentioned by more theoretical studies such as those by Brus, W., and Laski, S., *From Marx to Market: Socialism in search of an economic system*, Clarendon Press, Oxford, 1989.
9. Rybczynski, T., "Financial Systems and Industrial Restructuring" in *National Westminster Quarterly Review*, August 1988, and "Corporate Restructuring", ditto, August 1989.
10. Dembinski, P.H. "Reforming Post-Communist Economies", *The Banker*, August 1990. The studies by Ribnikar, I., also seem to reach similar conclusions: "Transition from Planned-Market to Market Economy", mimeo, 1990.

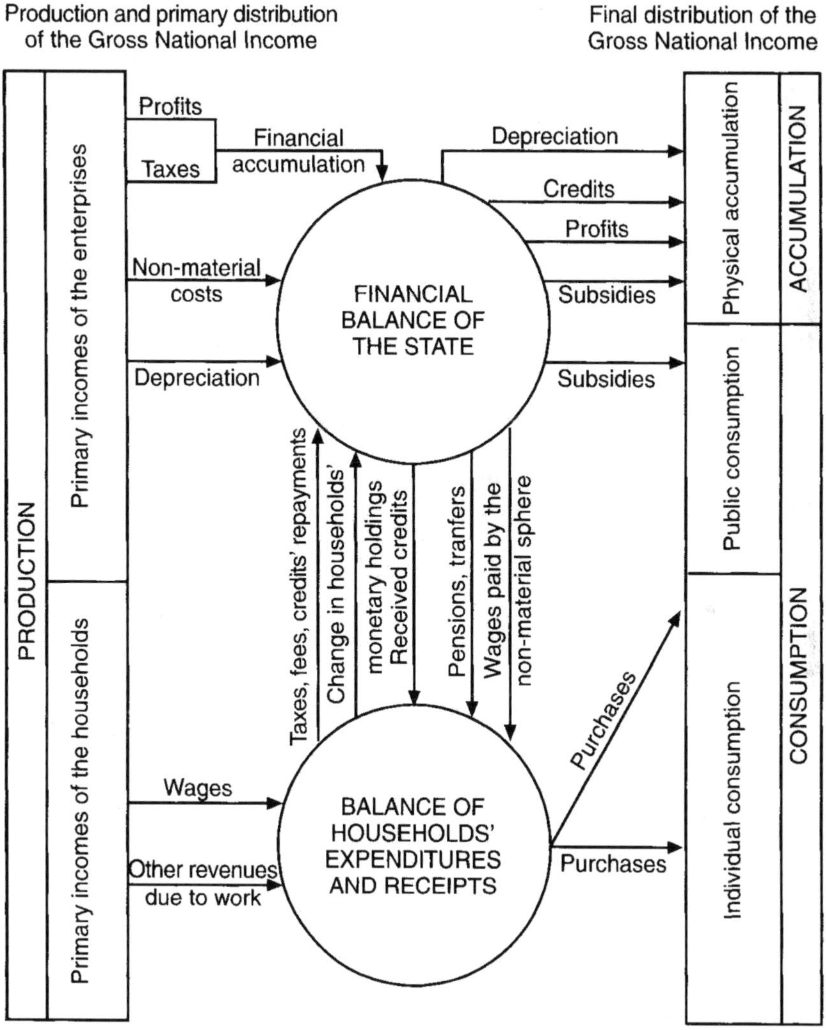
Production and primary distribution of the Gross National Income
Final distribution of the Gross National Income
PRODUCTION
Primary incomes of the enterprises
Primary incomes of the households
Profits
Taxes
Financial accumulation
Non-material costs
Depreciation
Wages
Other revenues due to work
FINANCIAL BALANCE OF THE STATE
BALANCE OF HOUSEHOLDS' EXPENDITURES AND RECEIPTS
Taxes, fees, credits' repayments
Change in households' monetary holdings
Received credits
Pensions, tranfers
Wages paid by the non-material sphere
Depreciation
Credits
Profits
Subsidies
Subsidies
Purchases
Purchases
Physical accumulation
Public consumption
Individual consumption
ACCUMULATION
CONSUMPTION

Figure 1

73

How Not to Privatize

Martin L. Weitzman

Source: *Rivista di Politica Economica*, December 1991, pp. 249–69.

The task of privatizing the formerly socialist economies of Eastern Europe (I include the Soviet Union, or the republics of the Soviet Union) is one of the most formidable problems ever encountered by economic policy makers. This monumental task stands at the center of the transformation process. All important aspects of economic theory and policy are involved, because the process of widespread privatization goes to the heart of what the capitalist system is all about.

As might be expected by the historical and intellectual dimension of the problem, various economists have begun to weigh in with various approaches, schemes, and proposals. It is important to recognize at the outset the enormous complexity of the privatization task that faces Eastern Europe. There is very little historical parallel that can be drawn upon for guidance. (Analogies with the limited privatization experience of capitalist economies are tricky and, as has been recognized by the more perceptive observors, downright misleading in many instances because the transformation of an entire system is under discussion in Eastern Europe. This is very different from the limited privatization experience within the fully developed market context of even a strongly privatizing Great Britain.) Economic theory is inadequate, silent, or ambiguous on many of the key issues. Political, social, and psychological elements are likely to be important relative to "pure" economic aspects. For all these reasons, and some others, it is difficult to lay out a clear strategy that commands agreement. There are few easy answers here and very little that is clearly "wrong" or "right". Every approach can be cogently criticized and most clever proposals can be countered by even cleverer counter-proposals.

All this notwithstanding, Western economists have arrived at a kind of a consensus of sorts on how to privatize in Eastern Europe. Stanley Fischer summarizes the standard advice as follows: "Small firms should be privatized by sale almost immediately, perhaps with some financing provided by the state. Larger industrial firms should be corporatized as soon as possible, moved out of the shelter of the ministries that now in principle control them, and put under the direction of corporate boards; shares should be distributed to some combination of current workers in the firms, current management, mutual funds, holding companies, banks, insurance companies, pension funds, citizens, and the government" (Fischer, 1991). I have no quarrel with the standard prescription for small firms. In practice, this part of the privatization process seems to be proceeding relatively well. Where I have some hesitation about the consensus view concerns the large firms. (This probably means something like the largest 500 enterprises in Poland and the largest 5000 in the Soviet Union.) And actually, privatization of large enterprises has been slow and erratic. So perhaps it is not premature to consider proposals along lines different from the standard holding company (or their equivalent) approach summarized above.

I think that it is worthwhile to stand back a bit from the fray of everyday proposals, arguments, and counterproposals in order to take a broader view. This "broader view" suggests to me that there is a certain misemphasis or misguidance in what has been put on the table so far. So my argument is not so much that wrong things have been proposed by wrong-headed individuals or governments, but more that the line of attack is somewhat off-center. This leads me to emphasize somewhat different aspects of the privatization problem and to put somewhat different weights on the appropriate solution concepts. Of course, what I have to say can also be legitimately criticized, and no doubt it will. At this drafting or framing stage of the argument I do not see great merit in going very deeply into specific institutional details of time and place, although, as I hope everyone recognizes, such details can in the end be at least as important to success or failure as the conceptual framework.

At the outset, I should clarify certain points. Despite the disclaimers, which I truly believe, about there being few demonstrably provable wrong or false positions about privatization policy, in the end, as a kind of short cut, I revert to somewhat stronger language and a more provocative tone in supporting my own position. My fundamental position is that privatization in Eastern Europe should be designed along simple, basic lines, avoiding the high-tech instruments of financial markets that are appropriate to advanced stages of capitalism. If you are learning to fly an aeroplane, your first lesson should be on a simple, basic, no-frills model, not a supersonic, state-of-the-art, extraordinarily sophisticated version, because there are too many things that can too easily go wrong with high technology in a low technology environment. In making this judgment I am somewhat influenced — perhaps overly influenced — by the Soviet experience. For different countries of Eastern Europe, at different stages of development and receptiveness, it may be appropriate to have different privatization strategies. Still, I think the overriding need for simplicity and directness in the initial private ownership structure of Eastern Europe has been insufficiently considered by economists and policy makers.

Anyone who reads the new privatization literature is bombarded by a welter of proposals centered around the mechanics of to-be-created mutual funds, holding companies, pension funds, financial intermediaries, and the like. While there is some debate about the details, the basic idea behind the mutual fund/holding companies idea is to create a politically palatable form of ownership that balances the efficiency requirements of correct incentives, informational needs, corporate structure, and so forth with the equitability requirement that the process of creating property rights should be viewed as basically "fair". This latter requirement is very important. Although there are others the essential argument for not creating property rights directly by handing the property over to the existing workers and managers and then letting things rip is that such a process, no matter how well designed or thought out, would be unfair. Various nomenklatura, mafia types, speculators, profiteers, and other undesirables, as well as workers who happened to be in the right place at the right time, will benefit from such a procedure, while the public at large will lose out. Indeed, there is apprehension that the assets of some enterprises may already be in the process of being stripped away illegally or unfairly. The circuitous route to creating property rights through artifically created entities, that look like mutual funds or holding companies in capitalist countries at advanced stages of development, is needed essentially in order to make the initial ownership distribution fair. The proper consideration of fairness has a crucial political dimension to it, but I think it is important to be clear that some extremely contradictory notions are involved here.

Capitalism is not a fair system and capitalists are not nice guys, at least not in their business dealings. Whether inadvertently or as part of a promotion strategy, this central fact has been massively camouflaged behind all the sanitized talk about transition to a "market system" with its justifiably well-publicized opportunities for initiative, entrepreneurship, and advancement. But perhaps this aspect has been overdone.

No matter how it is accomplished, there is no way that privatization is not going to end up with some unpleasant characters becoming relatively rich and some virtuous innocents losing out. This is what capitalism is all about. Under capitalism, society does not attempt to micromanage individual incomes, because to do that kills the goose that lays the golden eggs.

Under capitalism there is a lot of randomness, resulting in many undeserving winners and unjust losers. The winners in the new systems of Eastern Europe are likely to be correlated with the winners in the old systems of Eastern Europe, because there is a statistically significant, if not perfect, correlation between aggressive opportunists in both cases, and in the end there is not a whole lot that can be done about it.

The average East European is not getting this central message from the political leaders or visiting economists. The new system is not likely to end up looking pretty. Of course we will try, and our efforts will make some difference (should go the message), but no matter how well-intentioned or designed is the initial property distribution system, it is rapidly going to get out of control and yield unfair results. Of course there are good sides to capitalism, and that is why we are moving in this direction (should go the message), but there is also this inevitable bad side. As the system takes on a life of its own, as it succeeds, if it succeeds, we will not be able to maintain an impression of fairness no matter how well-engineered was our initial distribution of property. Within a relatively short time the losers are going to feel cheated in almost any case.

The historical experience of the actual development of real capitalism seems to have been forgotten in the rush to embrace the new hypothetical, sanitized "market system". In historical fact, so strong was the sense that capitalism, as it developed, was an unfair system, that this became the chief reason for the rise of socialism in the first place. Do I simplify? All right, I simplify. But the underlying, fundamental reason why over one third of the planet's population came to live under a Marxist–Communist centrally-planned economic system grew out of the perceived inequities of the capitalist system. It seems to me that not to attempt to meet this central issue head on is to be flirting with disaster. Maybe I am missing something, but I do not find much awareness or sensitivity to this set of issues in the new privatization literature.

What is being tried now in Eastern Europe is without precedent precisely because it is an attempt to create a just form of capitalism whole cloth, directly out of an existing previous system, skipping the intermediate stages. While there is a superficial plausibility about the enterprise, in the end it looks to me about as artificial in its way as market socialism was in its. In both cases there is the eerie similarity of a logically enticing possibility stalemated by the ahistoric nature of the endeavor, like a beautiful theory slain by an ugly fact.

Let me rush quickly to my main point, the better to back up and treat it in more detail. Even the best versions of the mutual-fund or holding-company type schemes are hopelessly complicated for a world without asset markets, valuations, profits, or even genuine accountants. The possibilities for manipulation, mismanagement, and neglect of the real in favor of the financial side of the economy are enormous. The new "owners" of the newly privatized enterprises would be far too diluted and distant to affect outcomes. The possibility of regulatory capture is too large. The intellectual and bureaucratic effort being put into fancy schemes for distributing property rights are out of all proportion to the effect they are likely to create.

What is needed is much closer to a fundamentalist approach. The initial property distributions should be as simple as possible, with hands-on owners as close to the enterprise as possible, not unlike the way capitalism actually developed. Any principle of distribution is going to be attacked as unfair, and squatter sovereignty seems to me as defensible a general position as can be taken. Let those who work the land and the machines own them, at least initially. There is plenty of historical precedent for this approach and it can command a great deal of political support, even if that support is not unanimous. The widespread in-group consensus of the new Western experts against worker ownership is typically knee-jerk reaction against a "third way" based on an inadequate understanding of the important role that worker ownership can and has provided for capitalism during times of transition and recession. Worker ownership is a powerful rallying cry that should be used — by centering it within a well-designed set of institutions and rules that allow for an orderly transition, through voluntary buying and selling, into other forms of ownership — rather than brushed off and disregarded.

The really important thing is not to squander scarce bureaucratic, managerial, and credibility resources on fine tuning a distribution process which in any event is rapidly going to get out of control and take on a life of its own. Instead, effort should be put into a well-designed system of ownership, defining exactly what title means, how people can buy, sell, and otherwise transfer property rights; and into a tight, well-managed progressive tax system. The emphasis should be on the classical approach of remedying inequalities through a well-designed and well-run progressive tax system, of which very little has been written or spoken, leaving the "capital markets" pretty much to develop on their own, with some limited guidance from the economic regulators on high. I repeat, the emphasis should be on an orderly framework allowing people to buy and sell property, and on a progressive income tax — not on mutual funds, holding companies, capital markets, and fine-tuned initial property distribution schemes.

1. Outline of a "Classical Approach" to Privatization

I want to go over in a more detailed outline, the main features of what I call a "classical approach" to privatization:

(1) capitalism is not a fair system and capitalists are not nice guys. East Europe should be buying into a "market system" not because of sanitized fantasies of a new utopia but because it is, or at least can be, better than the alternatives. It is extremely important for politicians, visiting economists, and prominent members of the population to speak loudly and clearly to this point. An inevitable by-product of the capitalist system is inequality, unfairness, and envy. A healthy variant of capitalism tries to minimize the inequality and unfairness, and develops an internal ethic that emphasizes keeping up with the Joneses rather than keeping down the Joneses, but there is no way of avoiding altogether the inevitable random elements that in the end make the system arbitrary and unfair. People need to deal openly and honestly with this subject, rather than keeping it hidden in the closet. Otherwise there is the very

dangerous possibility of massive disillusionment afterwards;

(2) no matter how well thought out are the initial distribution schemes, the private enterprise system will soon get out of control and wealth distribution will take on a life of its own;

(3) the initial distribution of property should be simple and quick. It should follow simple basic principles that are comprehensible to the most ordinary citizen. There is not much room here for fancy, complicated schemes based on misplaced analogies with advanced market economies that have well-developed capital markets, accounting systems, valuation procedures, and a long, continuous history of acquaintance with sophisticated market phenomena and high-tech financial instruments;

(4) in so far as possible, the privatization process should follow the historical analogy of how private property actually developed in the West. In almost all cases, direct, hands-on forms of ownership are to be preferred. The last market to worry about and pay attention to is the capital market. It is in no sense irrelevant, but merely less pressing than other issues;

(5) considerable intellectual and bureaucratic effort should be directed toward creating a viable legal and institutional framework that makes it easy for citizens to buy and sell property rights from each other, to consolidate properties, to dismember properties, and so forth. It is of the utmost importance that a well-defined framework be in place that facilitates the ability to transfer property so that the ultimate ownership pattern of a market capitalist economy can readily work itself out, since, I maintain, the government cannot engineer an ideal initial property distribution in the first place;

(6) probably the best single principle of initial property distribution is squatter sovereignty. Whoever occupies the apartment gets to own it. Whoever works at at a given workplace gets to own the means of production at that workplace. Collective farmers are given ownership of the land they work. There are an enormous number of problems, complications, ambiguities, injustices, and potential for going wrong with this approach to privatization; but the problems, complications, ambiguities, injustices, and potential for going wrong are significantly greater with other approaches, in my opinion, especially the ahistorical, artificial holding company/mutual fund type schemes. I will go over the relative advantages of my approach in more detail in the next section;

(7) the inevitable inequality that arises as true capitalist development proceeds should be dealt with by a well-designed and well-administrated progressive tax system. I believe it is difficult to overemphasize the importance of this issue, which has been largely overlooked or neglected in the standard economic discussions. On the one hand, the governments should be explaining loudly and clearly the inevitability of inequality, greed, and envy. On the other hand, the governments should also be explaining, loudly and clearly, that the principal approach to dealing with inequality is going to

be a broadly-based, well-designed, and well-administered progressive tax system, accompanied by a reasonable safety net program. Of course it can be said formally that the newly emerging market economies of Eastern Europe are currently developing, or at least discussing, new tax systems. They are going through the motions, but there is little inspiration. Relatively little intellectual or bureaucratic effort is going into the serious design or implementation of a progressive tax system. I am saying that this should be a central ingredient in the new economic order, the principle means of dealing with the inevitable income inequality that is going to arise. It is important to have in place an operational reporting system for all forms of income, a good data base, good auditing systems, competent and honest tax administrators, and so forth and so on. In my opinion this is where the scarce administrative talent belongs, not at designing and regulating the holding companies, mutual funds, stock markets, and other semi-fictional entities being bandied about;

(8) serious thought must be given to the subject of setting up a reasonable banking and credit system. But at this stage, given the scarce administrative and intellectual resources, I think that relatively little attention should be paid to stock markets, mutual funds, and all of that. As with the development of actual historical capitalism, if the process is generally successful then capital markets will emerge pretty much of their own accord. Of course they will need to be regulated in some fashion, but given the enormity of the immediate tasks that need to be faced in Eastern Europe, sophisticated capital markets are one of the last things to be worrying about. As I have been at pains to emphasize, I think the standard Western economist's approach has badly misplaced priorities on this aspect of the privatization process.

In the following section I want to discuss in more detail what I see as the important role of worker ownership and the advantages it has over the fancy, complicated mutual fund/holding company approach to distributing property.

2. Worker Ownership vs. Financial Intermediaries: Myth and Reality

In most cases the new Western experts on the transformation process in Eastern Europe are economists with little or no background in the field of comparative economic systems. In some instances that is no great disadvantage. It can even be an advantage because old, stereotyped ways of thinking are avoided. But sometimes, I believe, the lack of exposure to the theory and experience of comparative economic systems really hurts because there is only a superficial understanding of the role of certain economic institutions. Nowhere is this ignorance more problematical, I believe, than in misanalyzing the possible role of worker ownership in the privatization and transformation process. Worker ownership is dismissed in favor of far-fetched mutual-fund-like distribution schemes largely because of stereotyped, imperfect understanding of the role of worker ownership in a capitalist economy.

Although worker ownership and producer cooperatives are not exactly the same thing, for my initial purposes the two concepts can be lumped together; later, when it is more relevant, I will attempt to bring out the distinctions.

Worker ownership or producer cooperatives have a long history and carry a lot of ideological baggage that typically colors the views of analysts, both pro and con. Throughout history, sympathetic observors of producer cooperatives have seen in them the centerpiece of a system of democratic, decentralized, non-centrally-planned, "true" socialism. They have been viewed as the embodiment of decentralized equalitarianism, workplace democracy, cooperation, non-exploitation of labor, and other core values of the socialist vision. This romantic view of worker ownership can bring together strange bedfellows, since populist partisans of capitalism have simultaneously seen in worker ownership a "true" version of people's capitalism. Advocates of worker ownership claim to find in innumerable anecdotes and, sometimes, in formal studies, clear evidence of the superiority of this organizational form, e.g., in terms of productivity, appropriately measured.

The larger reality, of course, does not support this romantic vision. Throughout the history of capitalism, it is an overwhelming generalization that capital hires labor, not the other way around. Pockets of producer cooperatives exist everywhere, and occasionally they rise to a position of some prominence (more on this later), but it is a fair generalization to say that worker ownership has not served as a long-term driving force in any successful real economy. The country that has come closest to embodying the worker–management model, Yugoslavia, is widely held to be an economic failure. (To be fair, this judgment may be somewhat unearned because Yugoslavia has special problems, but the judgment is widely held nonetheless).

It is largely because of the perceived lack of survivability of worker-owned firms that they are shunned as a possible approach to large-scale privatization. There is also fear of the symbolism of what might be interpreted as an attempt at finding a "third way" after the "second way" proved to be so disastrous. It should be understood that the role I envision for worker ownership is not an attempt to find a "third way", but a practical means of getting to the "first way" faster and more reliably, I will argue, than the standard alternatives.

Why is there such an apparently limited real-world role for producer cooperatives in spite of a seemingly appealing, at least to some, ideology? This question was first posed in a serious way, and more or less answered, almost a century ago by the great Russian economist Tugan-Baranovsky in his comprehensive and influential book on cooperatives. Tugan was basically sympathetic to the cooperative movement, but felt it was important to address this question centrally and answer it honestly. The world has changed a great deal since that time, and we have many new experiences and a lot of new evidence, but I feel Tugan's approach has held up well.

There are a great many possible specific reasons for the seeming failure of producer cooperatives to become a dominant economic force. For example, it could be that capitalist society conspires against employee ownership, so that, e.g., it is more difficult for worker-owned firms to obtain capital from banks or to remain solvent. (The Israeli experience, where the Kibbutz form is actually favored and subsidized in innumerable ways, presents an immediate counter-example to the generality of this hypothesis; in spite of unquestionably preferential treatment, Kibbutz employment constitutes less than 3% of the labor force and has been steadily declining over time.) It could be that people actually do not like cooperative work life, or at least their children do not like it. Maybe risk aversion or portfolio balancing plays a role, although I personally doubt the empirical relevance of this hackneyed workhorse of economic theorists. A very likely specific candidate is that, for whatever reason, worker-owners do not work as hard as hired workers, or they do not react as quickly to market opportunities as more traditional capitalist organizational forms. Many other partial and specific possible answers exist.

Tugan-Baranovsky thought that although there could be some merit in the partial and particular arguments, such a broad-based phenomenon as the general instability of the producer cooperative form must be based on some general principle. If producer cooperatives failed so strikingly, always and everywhere, to become a dominant organizational form, that must be hinting at some deep-seated reason.

The reason Tugan uncovered has a strikingly modern resonance. Let me restate it in contemporary language.

Suppose there is some prevalent going wage at which ordinary capitalist firms are hiring. The concept of a "going wage" is not without its problems, but it clearly has meaning at some level of abstraction. The essential idea is that any worker can find employment at the going wage.

Consider next the situation of a typical producer cooperative. Suppose the producer cooperative is maximizing income per member. This means that the dividend or average income per member must equal the marginal income value of an additional extra member.

Generally speaking, there are two possibilities, either of which makes the producer cooperative an unstable form of ownership. Case one is that the dividend per worker is less than the going wage. Then there is an incentive for members to leave the cooperative and seek higher pay in the capitalist sector as hired workers. Even if cooperative members resist this temptation for ideological reasons, it is unlikely that their children will have the same commitment to resist the temptation of greater economic gain. When this occurs, the cooperative unravels.

The more interesting case, which requires a more subtle analysis, is the opposite situation. Suppose the cooperative is successful in the sense that the per capita dividend exceeds the going wage. Then there is a dilemma. Outside workers would like to join the cooperative as members because they can earn more money that way than as ordinary hired workers. But cooperative members will resist taking on new members because it will dilute their existing pay dividend (which equals the marginal value of an extra worker). If cooperative members could capitalize their good fortune and hire an extra outside worker at the going wage, they could divide among themselves the difference between the marginal value of labor and the going wage, and go on doing so until the marginal value of labor equals the wage. There is thus a temptation for a successful cooperative to capitalize itself and hire outside labor at the going wage. But in that case the organization ceases to be a worker-owned cooperative firm and has de facto transformed itself into a capitalist firm. Historically, there are a number of instances where exactly this has happened.

Thus, except in the rare case having probability measure zero that the cooperative dividend happens to equal exactly the going wage rate, forces are set in motion that dissolve the cooperative. The worker-owned cooperative is thus an unstable or transient organizational form.

The argument that Tugan-Baranovsky developed is a particular, and in my opinion convincing, application of Coase-like reasoning to a specific situation. The producer cooperative yields inefficient labor allocations which, by a reasonably simple reorganization, can be eliminated in favor of a Pareto improvement. Hence, this particular organizational form is unlikely to represent a stable solution.

The idea that worker-owned firms are fundamentally unstable does not, however, mean that they do not play a role in capitalist economic development. They do. There is ample empirical evidence that producer cooperatives live a counter-cyclical life cycle. During times of high unemployment, there are more worker-owned firms. During boom times there are fewer worker-owned firms. Worker-owned firms play a useful role in evening out the business cycle. They are unstable in a long-run steady state, but tend to grow and prosper in any disequilibrium situation where unemployed workers have few other job opportunities.

There are many actual instances of employee buyouts helping to save a community from devastating plant shutdowns. In a typical situation a company cannot maintain the operation of a particular plant or an enterprise because it is unprofitable. Workers are presented with the unpalatable option of either taking a pay cut or having the operation shut down, frequently with devastating results on the community. Whether from pride, inertia, the presence of a union, or human nature, workers typically find it very difficult to accept a wage decrease, even when it is economically justified. In such situations, the possibility of an employee buyout often plays a very important constructive role. When the employees buy out the company, the very first thing they must do, of course, is make themselves take a pay cut. If the former capitalist owners cannot make the enterprise profitable at the previous wage levels, the new worker-owners typically face exactly the same problem. However, for reasons that are not entirely explained by any known (to me) "rational" economic theory, when the workers are owners they are much more likely to be able to accept a "temporary" pay cut. Of course if the enterprise is doomed by long-term economic forces in the first place, the "temporary" pay cut becomes permanent and in the long run the labor force withers away toward better opportunities. But, and this is crucially important, in the short-run jobs have been preserved, a community has been saved, and output has been maintained. The employee buyout can play a very significant practical role in easing the transition from profitability to unprofitability, or, conversely, from unprofitability to profitability. This constructive countercyclical role is, I think, the main significance of employee ownership in a capitalist economy, and it is nothing to be sneered at.

Now when it comes to privatization in Eastern Europe, it is exactly this kind of transitional role that is needed everywhere throughout the economy, on a wide front. It is a natural, politically defensible, even popular gesture to give the enterprise to the workers. I am arguing that instead of trying to fight this natural inclination, the economic gurus should be going with the current. Let the workers have "their" factories. But there are to be absolutely no state bailouts or soft budget constraints. If the worker-owners can make profits, then more power to them. (Of course, they will have to pay higher taxes, according to the newly enacted and strictly enforced tax code.) If the worker-owners cannot make profits, then they will have to swallow the losses in the form of lower pay. In either case, a well-defined legal framework allows property to be sold or otherwise transferred by mutual consent between buyer and seller, and thereby facilitates transition to the ultimate ownership structure.

I believe the above squatter-sovereignty approach to be an intuitively plausible, readily understandable, commonsense approach to privatization that is far more likely to run smoothly and meet with acceptance than the alternatives. If one reads the recent Papal Encyclical *On Giving Capitalism a Human Face*, it should be apparent that giving to the workers the tools with which they work is likely to be a more acceptable approach to distributing government property for many Poles than the stock market simulation schemes dreamed up by Western economists. The mutual funds/holding companies approach strikes me as a particularly problematical scheme that is vulnerable to all manner of abuse.

First of all, it is hard for me to understand how this mutual funds/holding companies system can work at all. We are talking about economies where there are no competitive markets, no market values, no profits, no accounting tradition. Perhaps I exaggerate, but it is very hard for me to envision how widespread distributions of mutual funds that administer holding companies that administer other companies even makes sense as a concept in this environment, much less as genuine approach to property distribution having a realistic likelihood of succeeding.

I fear that with a lot of financial paper will come a lot of fraud. And with a lot of paper instead of direct hands-on ownership, in economies with underdeveloped capital markets will come a dilution or disincentive for real management. The paper pressures of ersatz ownership in economies with underdeveloped capital markets will, in the end, be too weak compared to the real pressure of genuine, direct ownership.

Then there is the not-so-slight matter of regulatory capture. Giving an enterprise to workers and then leaving them to fend on their own is at least a relatively clean-cut concept. Having amorphous, unproven, previously non-existent "holding companies" in charge of "regulating" an enterprise is about as murky an idea as can be imagined. The parent "holding company" is going to be under intense pressure from each of its infant enterprises to obtain special treatment, special funding, special status. The result, in my opinion, is likely to stalemate economic development into a horrible political battle of special interests. This whole approach seems to me to be asking for trouble because it has all the ingredients for a stagflationary impasse. It is really hard for me to imagine that serious economists have identified themselves with proposals to privatize Eastern Europe by creating ersatz mutual funds and holding companies to supervise formerly state-run enterprises. This entire approach is built upon a faulty ahistoric analogy with the most advanced forms of capitalism. Mutual funds, holding companies, stock markets, and the like were among the last institutions created by developing capitalism, and are predicated upon the firm existence of a host of more basic capitalistic institutions, conceptions, and traditions. It seems to me fundamentally implausible to launch a massive privatization campaign in formerly socialist countries based upon the most sophisticated instruments in the capitalist arsenal. What makes more sense to me is to base initial privatization upon the simplest possible ownership concepts, those that appeared earliest in history, are easiest to understand, and have firm political support among important groups of the population.

To summarize: the basic principle of initial property distribution should be simple and direct, and the distribution should be done quickly. A prime candidate for such a basic principle is squatter sovereignty. Initial owners of productive capital should be as close as possible to the actual operation of the enterprise. A lot of effort should go into creating reasonable, workable laws that permit the orderly sale or transfer of property rights. Then let the ultimate forms of property ownership evolve through natural selection processes of capitalist development. The very last set of issues to be worried about at an early stage concern the capital markets. Once truly private enterprises are created by giving the property to the workers, they should basically be left alone, and in no instances — without exception — bailed out by any governmental preferential treatment. All fairness issues are dealt with by a meaningful, well-designed, and well-administered progressive tax system coupled with specific supplemental safety net features for the aged and truly infirm.

I want to conclude this paper by contrasting the standard "consensus" mutual fund/holding company approach to privatizing large firms with my own "worker-ownership" approach.

3. The Mutual Funds/Holding Companies Approach to Privatization

The typical "consensus" approach to privatizing large firms in the formerly socialist countries of Eastern Europe presents approximately the following sequence of events:

(1) enterprises are corporatized. The enterprise is given a legal structure that resembles state owned enterprises in market economies. Accommodation of debts, typically by cancellation, is accomplished to enable firms to begin with a relatively clean balance sheet;

(2) the concept of "share ownership" of enterprises is given operational meaning. A legal and administrative framework is created that defines the rights and obligations of share ownership, and that determines how shares can be sold or otherwise transferred. Legitimate and illegitimate operations with shares are defined and enforcement mechanisms are specified and put into place;

(3) enterprise shares are issued and distributed. Various schemes differ in details concerning whether shares are given or sold, and to whom they are given or sold;

(4) holding companies are established to control the enterprises under their jurisdiction. Various schemes differ in emphasis and detail on the role of holding companies. In some versions the "holding companies" are just the enterprises themselves, so that in effect this stage is skipped;

(5) mutual funds of holding companies of enterprises, or mutual funds of enterprises, are established. Some proposals can become quite baroque at this point, so that it is sometimes unclear (at least to me) whether there are to be mutual funds of holding companies or mutual funds of enterprises, or some other combination;

(6) the mutual fund shares (which themselves consist of enterprise shares) are distributed by some mechanism to the population, with various segments of the population being favored under various particular schemes. Henceforth, decentralized market forces are supposed to shape events by playing themselves out, with some proposals advocating sunset laws that cause the holding companies to self-destruct over time;

(7) workers in the enterprises are essentially treated as hired labor and continue to be paid primarily in the form of wages. Enterprises are supposed to be subject to market forces directing output, prices, wages, bankruptcy, expansion, contraction, layoffs, hiring, etc.

The problems with this approach, as I see them, include the following:

(1) the owners are too far removed and too diluted to apply effective

pressure for profitability and to enforce hard budget constraints;

(2) there is a too-significant danger of regulatory capture by workers, regions, ethnic groups, etc.;

(3) the wage system will perpetuate a confrontational "us vs. them" mentality between workers and management/owners which could readily lead to an inability to control wages or effect plant shutdowns;

(4) in an environment where a great deal of restructuring is required, there is the too-real possibility of a stagflationary impasse;

(5) with a relatively complicated capital and ownership structure being imposed upon a relatively primitive capitalist economy without meaningful valuations, markets, notions of profits, or experienced accountancy, and with a lot of financial paper floating around, there is a too-large possibility of financial manipulation, fraud, volatility, and so forth. The outcome will not be seen as "fair" once the game begins;

(6) an enormous amount of scarce bureaucratic and administrative resources must be employed in establishing and administering the holding companies and mutual funds.

4. The Worker-Ownership Approach to Privatization

Steps (1) and (2) are basically the same as in the "consensus" approach, except that in (2) special attention is paid to the problems of beginning with worker-owned firms;

(3) shares are given to workers in the enterprise. Shareholders decide on governance structures, market strategies, work standards, whom to fire and hire, and so forth. Workers are legally entitled to sell shares or buy shares from outsiders or each other.

(4) wages per se are no longer paid by the government. Workers can pay themselves dividends, etc., as they see fit within the constraints of the budget;

(5) the enterprise is put on a hard budget constraint. No state subsidies are paid, or, at a minimum, state subsidies are phased out by a rigid time schedule.

The hope is that the worker-ownership approach makes for a better transition to a market economy by removing or blunting the criticisms of the last section. It is true that distribution by squatter sovereignty is "unfair", but on the other hand it can be viewed as a "natural" mechanism. (I have tried to argue that almost any initial distribution mechanism will likely come to be viewed as "unfair" and the more important thing is to be in a position to remedy the coming inequities by a meaningful progressive tax system). Under worker ownership, the workers themselves, or their agents, will have to control pay and negotiate plant shutdowns. The most acute "us vs. them" stalemates may be avoided. Ownership is more concentrated relatively close to management decisions and can put more immediate pressure on performance. Regulatory capture may be avoided. Hard budget constraints may be more acceptable. There is less opportunity for financial manipulation.

Gradually, over time, as shares of large enterprises are sold and bought, the ownership structure will change toward a steady state that will probably (hopefully) resemble that of a modern capitalist country.

There are many difficulties of worker ownership. But most of them spring from the soft budget constraint, not from worker ownership per se (Prasnikar Svejnar, 1991). Besides, what is being advocated here is not worker ownership as an end in itself, but worker ownership as a transition mechanism to full-fledged capitalism. As a transition mechanism, all I wish to claim is that worker ownership offers more promise than the alternative mutual fund/ holding company approach for privatizing large enterprises.

5. Concluding Comments

In preparing this paper I have tried to put forward something specific, the specific idea is that worker ownership has been dismissed too readily as part of a privatization strategy for large enterprises in formerly socialist countries. I have attempted to argue that, although there are no easy solutions here, the "consensus" strategy of marketizing through holding companies and mutual funds is fraught with danger. By comparison, worker ownership seems to me to be a less dangerous strategy, and therefore one that better deserves to be tried.

Bibliography

1. Blanchard O., Dornbush R., Krugman P., Layard R. and Summers L.: *Reform in Eastern Europe*, London, MIT Press, 1991.

2. Fischer S.: "Privatization in East European Transformation", MIT, *Working Paper*, n. 578, April 1991.

3. Kornai J.: *The Road to a Free Economy*, New York (NY), Norton, 1990.

4. Lipton D., Sachs J.: "Privatization in Eastern Europe: The Case of Poland", *Brookings Papers on Economic Activity*, n. 2, 1990, pp. 293–334.

5. Sachs J.: "Accelerating Privatization in Eastern Europe: The Case of Poland", Mimeo for *World Bank Conference*, April 1991.

6. Tirole J.: "Privatization in Eastern Europe: Incentives and the Economics of Transition", *NBER Macroeconomics Annual*, 1991.

7. Tugan-Baranovsky M.I.: *Sotsial'nyia Osnovy Kooperatsii* (The Social Foundation of Cooperation), Berlin, 1921.

9. Vickers J. and Yarrow G.: "Economic Perspectives on Privatization", *Journal of Economic Perspectives*, vol. 5, n. 2, Spring 1991, pp. 111–32.

PART XIV: Associated Issues

74

The State in Neoinstitutional Economics

Thráinn Eggertsson

Source: *Economic Behavior and Institutions* (New York: Cambridge University Press, 1990), Chap. 10, pp. 317–58. (Chapters, etc., cited within this chapter, refer to the original publication.)

1. Introduction

In Chapter 9, we examined the system of property rights in stateless societies, particularly how informal rules, values, and taboos constrain behavior and limit the waste associated with open access to resources. However, the embryonic institutional structure of prestate societies is not capable of supporting the complex exchange relationships among unrelated individuals that are associated with highly developed specialization in production and large markets, advanced technology, and time-intensive production patterns.[1]

Without the state, its institutions, and supportive framework of property rights, high transaction costs will paralyze complex production systems, and specific investments involving long-term exchange relationships will not be forthcoming. But the state is a two-edged sword: "The existence of a state is essential for economic growth; the state, however, is the source of man-made decline."[2]

Section 2 elaborates North's (1979) theory of the state, which was introduced in Chapter 3.[3] His approach is based on the modern theory of the firm (see Chapters 5 and 6) and emphasizes how transaction costs and agency problems affect political behavior and the structure of property rights. We present a formal version of a North-type model of the state (due to Findlay and Wilson), and consider various ramifications of the approach.

Section 3 is given to empirical applications of the theory. Our purpose is primarily to outline critical variables and suggest a research agenda rather than to settle debates in economic history and development. Following an introduction (Section 3.1), the link between political coalitions and property rights is examined in Section 3.2. The discussion is organized about Bates's study of markets and states in Tropical Africa. In Section 3.3, we consider the agency problems of the principals who control the state, illustrating, with studies by Winiecki, the issues of reforms and counterreforms in Soviet-type economies. Finally, Section 3.4 cites studies by several authors, and the case of early modern Europe, to discuss the links among methods of public finance, property rights, and economic outcomes. Predatory public finance, with its devastating long-term consequences, is seen as constrained optimization by rulers who have few choices.

The chapter's final section (4) looks at applications of Neoinstitutional Economics to the study of democratic institutions. Rather than surveying the emerging field of "neoinstitutionalism" within Public Choice and Political Science, the discussion is limited to two issues and two important studies that display the potential of the NIE approach in this area. First, we examine a formal model, by Denzau and Munger, of the importance of information costs for the behavior of legislators. Second, we consider a model by Weingast and Marshall that uses the new theory of economic organizations to explain the internal structure of the U.S. Congress.

2. Theory of the State: The Model

We turn now to a discussion of the state in the context of Neoinstitutional Economics. Our concern is with the interaction between the state and the system of property rights; the approach, which is due to North (1979, 1981), involves combining the economics of transaction costs and agency theory in a rational-choice analysis of political institutions and processes.

North's vision of the interrelationship between the state, property rights, and productivity can be described as follows. The stock of knowledge in society and the endowment of resources determine the technical upper limits for productivity and output, the economy's *technical production frontier*. However, for each structure of property rights there is a *structural production frontier*, which is reached by selecting, from the set of feasible organizations, those structures that minimize costs and maximize output. The set of feasible forms of economic organization is defined by the system of property rights (given the state of technology and other exogenous factors), and the system of property rights depends on the community's political structure. And, finally, some political systems create incentives that place the structural production frontier close to the technical production frontier; other political systems do not. Usually, a political change is required to move the structural production frontier closer to the technical frontier, and, therefore, a benefit–cost evaluation of economic reforms must include both the costs of political change and the costs of maintaining (enforcing) each system.[4]

Modern technology creates the potential for very high levels of productivity. These high levels of output cannot be reached without elaborate specialization in production and complex webs of exchange among unrelated individuals, extending across both time and space. In general, we can say that the more advanced the technology, the more complex the transactions, and the higher the transaction costs of utilizing the technology.[5] Appropriate structures of property rights are needed to reduce transaction costs of advanced technologies to manageable levels, and the state has a relative advantage in supplying the required structure: "The economies of scale associated with devising a system of law, justice, and defense are the basic underlying source of civilization."[6]

In sum, the willingness of individual owners to supply specific appropriable assets, essential for economic growth and full utilization of advanced technologies, depends directly on the social rules structure, including the availability of relatively consistent and impartial dispute processing by a third party, which in most cases can be supplied only by the state.

North (1981) argues that there is overwhelming historical evidence to support the proposition that states typically do not supply structures of property rights that are appropriate for placing the economy close to the technical production frontier. For example, he maintains that various historical cases of relative and absolute economic decline can be explained only as *failures of organization.* We now turn to North's theory of the state, which is intended to provide an explanation for such failures, and begin by examining the theory in terms of a formal model due to Findlay and Wilson (1984).[7]

Let us assume that an economy produces a composite commodity Y, which is supplied by private firms. The only inputs are labor services, L, and the services of a fixed capital stock, K. The input–output relationship is represented by a conventional production function, $f(L, K)$. However, the output of the economy can be enhanced by a third input, which we can call public order, P (the services rendered by the system of property rights). Public order can be supplied effectively only by the state, and government workers, G, are the sole input used. The production function for public order is $p(G)$, and the aggregate production function for a community where the state supplies public order can then be written as:[8]

$$Y = f(L, K)\,p(G) \tag{1}$$

Findlay and Wilson (1984) assume that the supply of homogeneous labor to the economy, H, is constant, and people work in either the public or the private sector. So we have:

$$H = L + G \tag{2}$$

Because the total supply of labor services is a constant, H, and $G = H - L$ we can write:

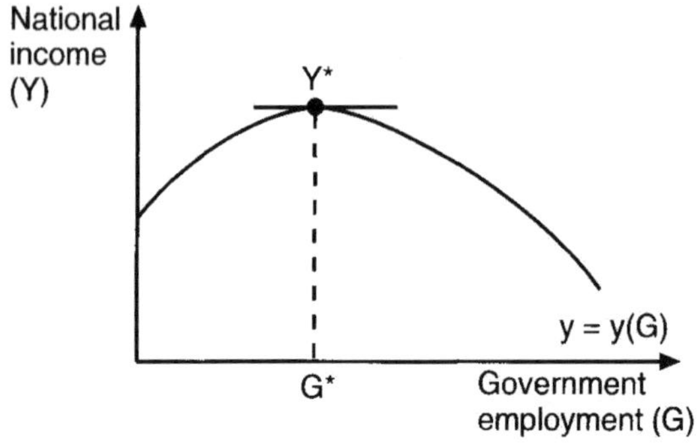

Figure 1 National income as a function of the level of public employment

$$Y = y(G) \tag{3}$$

In Figure 1, we graph the relationship between Y and G.[9] The graph shows how expansion of the public sector first increases the national output, Y, and then, after a point, reduces it. Maximum output, Y^*, is reached at a level of public employment, G^*, where the marginal products of workers in the public sector and in the private sector are equal.[10]

Contractual theories of the state, associated with Locke, Rousseau, and some of the traditional public finance literature (the Pigou–Meade tradition), view the state as a contractual arrangement among equals for providing productive public services. In terms of the Findlay–Wilson model, the level of G would then be decided in terms of a common goal. Let us assume that the goal is the one of maximizing the community's joint income, which calls for $G = G^*$. However, the state must tax in order to pay wages for G^* hours of work in the public sector (as the sector's output is a public good and cannot be marketed). Findlay and Wilson assume that the state levies a proportional tax, t, on all incomes. The government's tax revenue is equal to tY. Now the optimization problem involves finding both G^*, and the corresponding tax rate t^*, which exactly covers the government's wage bill (and balances the budget). It is assumed that the labor market is competitive, which constrains the wage to be the same in the public and private sectors: $W_G = W_L$. Figure 2 presents the revenue function and the expenditure function of a contractual state when $t = t^*$.[11]

North's model of the state is of another variety, a relation of Hobbes's predatory theory of the state, recognizing *both* the productive and the potentially predatory nature of government.[12] North defines the state as "an organization with comparative advantage in violence, extending over a geographic area whose boundaries are determined by its power to tax constituents."[13] The state is controlled by a ruler who monopolizes both

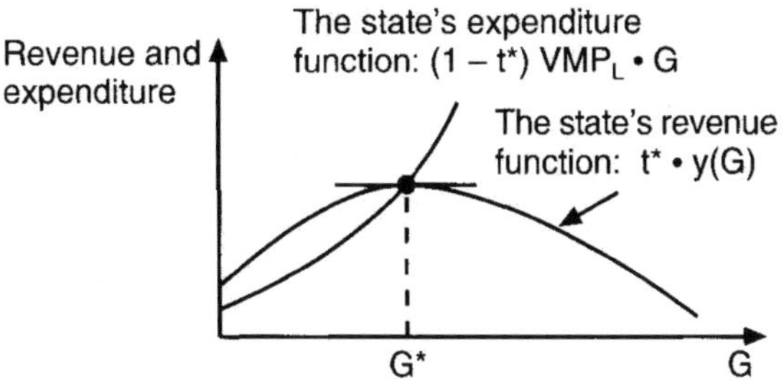

Figure 2 Equilibrium public employment in the contract state

the use of violence and the supply of public services and acts as a discriminating monopolist. The ruler has a long-term contractual relationship with his or her subjects, which stipulates the terms for the exchange of public services in return for taxes. The price that the ruler can set for such services is limited by the extent of his or her monopoly power. In particular, the ruler's ability to raise monopoly profits is constrained by three factors, the first being threats of entry from potential domestic and foreign rivals or, in other words, the availability to the subjects of substitutes for the ruler. As the availability of substitutes varies from one group to another, their ability to resist taxation also varies, and it is therefore rational for the ruler to follow a policy of price discrimination (e.g., exempt ranking members of the military from taxation and place heavy taxes on scattered, unorganized rural populations).

The second factor limiting the ability of the ruler to exploit his or her monopoly is rooted in the propensity for opportunistic behavior of the agents of the state who must be employed to provide public services and collect taxes.

The third constraining factor involves various measurement costs, particularly the cost of measuring the tax base.

The ruler maximizes his or her wealth, subject to the constraints listed above. Only after allowing for the requirements of survival does he or she take measures to increase the tax base. North's central point is that the ruler's maximization – constrained by survival consideration, agency problems, and measurement costs – easily can lead to methods of collecting taxes and systems of property rights that place the economy well inside its technical production frontier.[14] In extreme cases, the ruler's optimum strategy can give rise to structures of property rights that bring stagnation and economic collapse.

Now let us return to the Findlay-Wilson model. Their formal model does not capture the full flavor of North's theory, but some of the basic elements of that theory are represented in Figure 3. Let us assume that the ruler holds

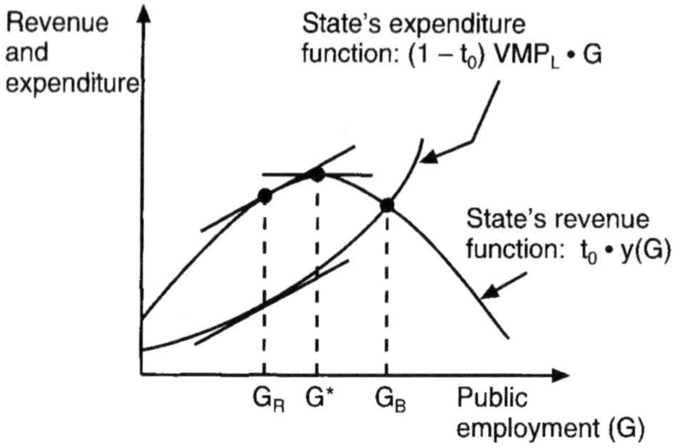

Figure 3 Failure to maximize national income when the tax rate is exogenous (t_0) or when bureaucrats are out of control

the power to tax but does not control the tax rate, *t*, which is exogenously set at t_0. We can imagine, for instance, that *t* is controlled by some representative body or is protected by custom stronger than the ruler. In terms of the formal model, the fixing of *t* at t_0 means that employment in the public sector is the ruler's only control variable. In Figure 3, the ruler seeks to maximize his or her wealth by selecting an employment level in the public sector, G_R, that maximizes the state's surplus of revenue over expenditure. By "expenditure," we refer to the net wage bill of the public sector. In the diagram, maximizing the surplus involves finding a level for *G* that corresponds to the greatest vertical distance between the tax revenue function and the expenditure function.

This elementary model gives us the following results:

1. G_R will always be to the left of G^*. As G^* corresponds to Y^*, the economy's maximum output, this implies that Y_R will always be smaller than Y*.
2. A higher value for t_0 raises the revenue function and lowers the expenditure function (by lowering the net income of government workers), and, similarly, a lower value for t_0 lowers the revenue function and raises the expenditure function. But the *ruler's* optimum size of the public sector, G_R, will never correspond to G^*, the level that maximizes the output of the economy; hence $Y_R < Y^*$.[15]
3. The ruler undersupplies public services to the economy. A move from G_R to G^* (and hence from Y_R to Y^*) appears to be Pareto efficient. The output of the economy could be maximized by changing the rules of taxation. For example, rather than being provided with residual tax revenue, the ruler could be given the revenues either from a lump-sum tax

or from a separate proportional tax on incomes. The change could provide simultaneously a greater net tax revenue for the ruler and a higher after-tax income for the subjects. North argues that such adjustments are often blocked by measurement costs, the costs of contracting, and power politics.

4. Finally, let us assume that the ruler is not fully in control of his or her agents, the public-sector workers. For instance, the chiefs of bureaus in the state bureaucracy may seek to enhance their power and prestige by increasing their staff. One scenario might involve public-sector employment expanding out of control until government wages have eaten up all tax revenues. In Figure 3, this point is reached at G_B. The state now oversupplies the economy with public services, and again we have $Y < Y^*$.

3. Theory of the State: Applications

3.1. Introduction

If an economy is to operate close to its technical production frontier, economic agents must be given the appropriate incentives. Incentives depend on the structure of property rights, and the state has a central role in determining the structure of property rights. The actual incentives and structures, which are required to place an economy close to its technical production frontier, will depend on the available technology and other circumstances, but certain generalizations can be made. The structural frontier of an economy will depend on the following factors:

1. The degree to which decision makers bear the full social costs and benefits of their actions. In general, productivity is enhanced when the system of property rights encourages decision makers to internalize the full costs and benefits of their actions.[16]
2. The degree to which present and future ownership rights are clearly defined and secure and the extent to which disputes over ownership and contractual performance can be settled in an orderly manner and at a low cost. Secure property rights encourage investors to increase the economy's stocks of productive capital.
3. The degree to which the structure of property rights contributes to the lowering of both the cost of measuring valuable margins of assets and commodities and the cost of transferring from one owner to another the ownership rights over resources. Structures that lower the costs of transacting can move the economy closer to its technical production frontier.
4. The degree to which the state directly assigns ownership rights to assets to the uses of highest value in situations where high transaction costs prevent voluntary exchange. A state that uses a neoclassical criterion of

wealth maximization in settling disputes over conflicting uses of resources can contribute to higher productivity.

The theory of the state presented above gives various reasons for the propensity of states to create property rights that are inconsistent with economic prosperity, but all the explanations are derived from the joint effects of information and transaction costs, on the one hand, and struggles over the distribution of wealth, on the other. As North (1981) notes, "Under the condition of zero transaction costs, the ruler could always devise first an efficient set of rules and then bargain for his rents, but this postulate from welfare economics simply ignores positive transaction costs, which is what the game is all about."[17]

Below we apply the theory of the state to examine how *political coalitions*, the state's internal *agency problems*, and systems of *public finance* affect the structural production frontiers of economies. Although empirical studies are used to illustrate these issues, our purpose is not to settle debates in economic history but rather to highlight critical linkages among political systems, property rights, and economic performance, and outline an important research agenda for Neoinstitutional Economics.

3.2. Political Coalitions and Property Rights in Tropical Africa

All rulers depend on the support of influential social groups to maintain their power. We do not attempt here to present a comprehensive theory of political coalitions, but the discussion elsewhere in the book suggests the following points: other things being equal, the political weight of social groups is directly related to the strength of their economic base. Second, the costs of collective action tend to be relatively high for large groups, especially when the members are scattered over large geographical areas, and high costs of collective action reduce the political influence of a group. Third, rulers will often divide and rule by strategically supplying goods and property rights to select individuals and groups.[18] Fourth, as North has emphasized, a common ideological fervor, for instance, arising from a pervasive sense of unjust treatment, lowers the cost of collective action and increases the political weight of groups.

Our interest in political coalitions derives from the link between the structure of coalitions and the property rights systems that result. Usually, the ruler (or the ruling group) of a state must deal with individuals and factions that possess substantial bargaining power. An increase in the bargaining power of a group often leads to demands for renegotiating the group's contract with the ruler, and changes in the structure of the social contract can affect economic performance.

Throughout history, changes in population and military technology have been a driving force behind shifts in the bargaining power of social groups. In his *Structure and Change in Economic History*, North (1981) uses historical examples going back to the city states of Mesopotamia and the kingdoms of ancient Egypt to illustrate a chain of causation, which begins with changes in population and military technology and ends with new economic organizations and outcomes.

For example, North argues that in the past, shifts in bargaining power caused by changes in military technology were a major (but not the only) causal factor in the rise of pluralistic government:

> The transformation of the Greek city-state from monarchy to oligarchy to democracy (in the case of Athens) occurred as a consequence of a change in military technology (the development of the phalanx) which could only be accomplished with a citizen army; the price the ruler paid was a dilution of his rule-making powers. Similarly in early modern Europe, alterations in military technology (the pike, the longbow, and gunpowder) led in some instances to the delegation of rule-making powers to parliament or Estates General in return for the increased revenue needed for survival.[19]

In turn, pluralism has various implications for property rights, which are explored by North (1981). In the modern era, North sees pluralism and changes in the control of the state rise primarily from the "Second Economic Revolution," namely the systematic development of science and its application to technology in the nineteenth century. However, he makes clear that no simple one-way line of causation dominates. In fact, economic growth (or lack of it) often has feedback effects on relative prices and the bargaining power of social groups, and no simple model explains the complex interactions involved in political and economic change.[20]

In the remainder of this subsection, we turn to an examination of the static (rather than dynamic) relationship between political coalitions and economic variables, using as an illustration Bates's (1981) study of *Markets and States in Tropical Africa*, which addresses the political origin of economic stagnation and decline in various African states.[21]

Economic structures and economic outcomes in Tropical Africa are far from being uniform, but certain generalizations can be made. The industrial structure of these countries is characterized by dependence on the production and export of cash crops, yielding products such as cocoa, coffee, palm oil, sisal, and cotton. Recently these vital industries have entered a path of stagnation, and Bates reports "that during the 1970s the volume of agricultural exports from all of Africa has declined."[22] Furthermore, the states of Tropical Africa, just like so many states in the Third World, have embarked upon a course of industrialization that has given rise to a small, state-sponsored manufacturing sector, which is sheltered from foreign competition and often from domestic competition as well. The production methods tend to be excessively capital intensive as a result of various government subsidies for capital inputs, and high costs and low quality make the products uncompetitive on world markets.

Bates's (1981) study of political structures in Tropical Africa reveals that three groups form the ruling coalition: individuals associated with the state bureaucracy (including members of the armed forces), firms of the state-sponsored capitalist sector, and local industries (firms that process agricultural products). Furthermore, and this is of crucial importance, all these groups seek privileged access to the resources of farmers. In fact, the position of urban workers (a small minority) is stronger than the position of farmers (the majority of voters) because of the state's concern with urban riots.

Bates (1981) also reports on the structure of property rights generated by political alliances in Tropical Africa, particularly the structures found in the markets for agricultural outputs, agricultural inputs, and domestic manufacturing products. He cites a variety of evidence suggesting that:

1. In these countries the system of property rights is very unfavorable for farmers.
2. The system tends to favor urban dwellers, bureaucrats, owners of manufacturing firms, and local industries.
3. The state has strong preferences for direct controls rather than measures that affect incentives indirectly through changes in relative prices; the state also has strong interest in mammoth projects, apparently for reasons of prestige.
4. The state uses *selective incentives* for evoking support for the government in the countryside – for example, through strategic allocation of agricultural inputs, such as fertilizers, and rural services (schools, hospitals, etc.).
5. The state is ready to use violence against political entrepreneurs who try to capitalize on rural discontent.

Let us consider more closely the status of farmers who produce the vital cash crops and the disincentives that they face. In the output market, the producers of cash crops are usually required to deal exclusively with state-sponsored *monopsonies* (state marketing boards or agencies), which offer low prices for the products. The marketing boards, which were established during the colonial period and initially were used to stabilize prices, are now major instruments of taxation. At present, the farmers receive only a fraction of world-market prices for their products, and the bulk of the marketing boards' net incomes is transferred to the ruling coalitions rather than plowed back into the rural sector.

Although rural dwellers form a majority of the voting population, they have relatively little political influence, for example, compared with individuals belonging to the small manufacturing sector. There are several explanations for this. In the rural sector, the cost of collective action is high, selective incentives (political rationing of inputs and social services) weaken the resolve of potential leaders to take action against the governing coalition, and the state uses force to quell political entrepreneurs who seek to make political capital out of rural discontent. However, even though the farmers do not organize in opposition to the ruling coalition, they can minimize the losses of an adverse system of property rights by economic adjustments.

In Chapter 4, we discussed how owners of resources respond to restrictions on their property rights (e.g., to rent control) by minimizing, subject to the relevant constraints, the potential dissipation of nonexclusive income. Similarly, African producers of cash crops, when faced with severe restrictions on the right to income from their assets, adjust the use of these assets so as to maximize their value under the new constraints. Bates finds that the adjustments include withdrawal of inputs from the production of cash crops, the substitution of unregulated food crops for regulated products, the allocation of labor time to work outside agriculture including migration to urban areas.[23] The adjustment has been massive and the economic costs have been large: even though the farmers have sought to maximize the private value of their assets by shifting them into new uses, according to the criterion of social productivity these are inferior uses. In Tropical Africa, the system of property rights works against the region's vital industries, and, in many cases, the economic impact has been devastating.

3.3. Agency Problems and Soviet-type Economies

If a state is to prosper and stay close to the economy's technical production frontier, it must have the political strength to adjust the structure of property rights to changes in the economic environment. However, adjustments are often blocked by *agents of the state* who believe that reforms threaten their self-interest. When structural changes are expected to raise society's aggregate wealth, both ruler and subjects may find it in their self-interest to offer state agents compensation for expected losses and to attempt to buy their compliance. Yet high transaction costs are likely to prevent such side payments. For the proponents of structural change, the transaction costs in question include not only the costs of collective action, such as the problem of free riding, but also the cost of making credible commitments to the agents. For their part, the agents fear that yielding privileges and strategic positions, even in return for reasonable compensation, will weaken their bargaining position and eventually lead to an uncompensated loss of all privileges through political action.[24]

Below we use the history of economic reforms in Soviet-type economies to illustrate how agents serving the state's ruling group can obstruct structural change. The discussion draws on a series of articles by Winiecki (1986a, 1986b, 1986c) dealing with the Soviet Union and the other Soviet-type economies (STEs) of Eastern Europe.[25]

In our times, centrally managed STEs are of great significance in terms of the world economy, and the study of STEs is a field to which Neoinstitutional

Economics could make important contributions. In the STEs, the principals ruling the state attempt to manage the industrial sector and, partly, the agricultural sector of their economies as a single gigantic firm.[26] The evolution of the centrally managed economy can be compared to the evolution of the corporation in the Western economies; each form of organization has shaped the economic history of the twentieth century. In the West, the introduction of marketable shares and complex capital markets lowered the potential for debilitating agency costs in the corporation, which has flourished as an organizational form despite the separation of ownership and control.[27] In STEs, the institution of the Communist Party, one of the most significant institutional developments of this century, made it possible to manage complex economies from the center.[28]

The structure of the STE has a unique feature: branching from the center of the Soviet state are two organizational trees, populated by party apparatchiks and agents of the multilevel management bureaucracy.[29] The parallel hierarchies are designed to lower the transaction costs of managing an industrial economy as one administrative unit, and the double structure remains the singular characteristic of the STEs. In this scheme, party agents monitor agents on the management bureaucracy and report back to the center. The party apparatchiks also have the important role of selecting managers at all levels, using loyalty to the principals and the Party as the overriding criterion for selection. In addition to these two sets of agents, the rulers of the STEs rely on the agents of the police and the military – in all, four agency networks.

This organizational form, chosen in the late 1920s and early 1930s by the leaders of the Soviet Union, was well suited for rapid mobilization of resources, forced industrialization, and for taking advantage of economies of scale in various basic industries. In spite of high agency costs, the system was suited for extensive growth, and it served the leaders well: There are few who question the military and economic might of the Soviet Union. However, Winiecki (1986a) and other observers argue that for some time the basic organizational structure of the STEs has been dysfunctional from the viewpoint of the ruling groups of the STEs for two reasons: the cumulative effects of the system's *agency problems* and *increases in transaction costs* caused by changes in the technological environment.

First, there is the *cumulative* effect of an incentive structure that does not encourage cost minimization in the production sector but emphasizes meeting (volume or value) output quotas.[30] The long-run effects of these incentives on the economic structures of the STEs stand out, for example, when we examine their resource intensity per unit of output. Winiecki (1986a) compares energy intensity and steel intensity per U.S. dollar of GDP in East European STEs and West European market economies, and finds that the resource intensity is 2–2.5 times higher in the STEs. Furthermore, time series studies show that the resource intensity of market economies *decreases* as they mature whereas the

STEs do not display a comparable trend.[31] In addition to rising resource intensity, Winiecki (1986a) analyzes various other malfunctions that are endogenous to the central management system and over time cause mounting difficulties. For example, the STEs display high and increasing transport intensity in freight ton-kilometers per unit of GNP compared with market economies, even after allowance is made for differences in income per capita, and the STEs' ability to compete in international markets for industrial products seems to have fallen over time, whereas the evolving industrial structure of these countries has created increasing demand for imports of industrial inputs.[32]

Second, changes in the technological environment have raised transaction costs and rendered the organizational structure of the STEs dysfunctional. The hierarchical central management structure of the STE works best when (1) final outputs have relatively few quality dimensions; (2) when the vertical phases of processing a commodity are few; (3) when there are substantial economies of scale at the enterprise level; and (4) when the technology does not require horizontal linkages between enterprises with each unit acting as both supplier and purchaser of inputs.[33] However, recent technological developments have worked against the central management structure:

> The trend in the world economy during the 1970s and the 1980s has been for industries in which vertical relations predominate (steel, cement, bulk chemicals) to be replaced as an engine of growth by industries in which enterprises are typically linked horizontally and act as both suppliers of inputs and purchasers of outputs from each other. These less material-using, more value-adding industries (electrical and non-electrical engineering, instrument making, fine chemicals) where complex, non-linear intra- and inter-industry linkages predominate depend much more for their performance upon features that are the antithesis of central planning.[34]

In sum, the long-run effect of central management appears to be economic stagnation.[35]

For some time, the leadership of the STEs has been aware that their economies may be on a path of long-term decline and there is no turning around unless the command-rationing system is replaced with decentralized management in the state sector and/or an expanded private sector. In order to restore their economies, the leaders have introduced a series of reforms but with little or no success. Winiecki (1986c) advances the thesis that the reforms have been sabotaged primarily by middle-level agents of the party and the management bureaucracy. The reason is simple: the common theme of the proposed reforms is the replacement of commands with autonomous parameters, such as prices. Bureaucrats, who are asked to implement reforms where parametric adjustments replace command-rationing by agents of the state are, in fact, asked to show inventiveness in making themselves obsolete and forego the *rents* which their current property rights give rise to.

There are two reasons why middle-level agents of the Party and the management bureaucracy have a strong interest in keeping the basic institutional structure of the STE intact. First, the Communist Party apparatus holds property rights over managerial positions in all administrative and enterprise units through the *nomenklatura* system. A competitive market for managers would represent a huge transfer of wealth away from Party functionaries.[36] Second, the agents benefit from an elaborate system of kickbacks involving managers primarily of industrial enterprises. The STEs have been characterized as *shortage economies*, and the kickbacks tend to be goods and services in short supply provided at list prices or at even lower prices, bypassing the rationing-by-waiting system. A detailed description of the system of privileges enjoyed by the agents of the two networks is found in any text on the Soviet system, but the basic point is that these privileges are *system-specific to the STEs*: the management agents and their monitors, the Party apparatchiks, are substitutes for the decentralized systems of parametric adjustments, and the rewards they enjoy arise from their monopoly over top positions and opportunistic behavior which the center is unable to control.[37]

However, as Winiecki (1986c) emphasizes, the privileges accruing to members of the other two networks of agents, the military and the police, are system-specific not to central management but rather to *autocratic* forms of government. As the STEs enter a path of long-term decline, the call for a fundamental change in the structure of property rights comes from both the rulers and the public, whereas the military and the police either are largely neutral or support change, and opposition comes primarily from two segments of the ruling stratum: party apparatchiks and management bureaucrats.[38]

The first signs of slowdown in Eastern Europe were seen early in the 1960s, but the traditional sources of extensive economic growth were still available and partial economic reforms still worked. Difficulties in the 1970s were met with Western technology and credit, but by the 1980s the choice seemed to involve radical political change or economic decline: by themselves, investment expansion, technological change, changes in industrial composition, and more international trade could not revive the failing European STEs.[39] If political reforms are to create conditions for sustained growth they must involve a system "of checks and balances constraining the freedom of party apparatchiks to interfere in and sponge the economy. . . ."[40]

A survey of attempts at reforms in European STEs reveals the following:[41] first, attempts to decentralize these systems, beginning shortly after the death of Stalin in 1953 and accelerating in recent years, have not removed control by party apparatchiks over economic enterprises, particularly control over appointments to managerial positions.

Second, the strategy employed by agents of the state who seek to preserve the nomenklatura and the kickback system varies, depending on political constraints such as the extent of public discontent. At times, the agents have been able to ensure from the start that the reforms are no more than pseudo-reorganization. For example, a program of reforms may involve shedding a few middle-level organizations but adding other comparable institutions or limiting the number of obligatory plan indicators for enterprises but adding new classes of "orienting" and "auxiliary" indicators.

Third, in other instances, reforms have raised the cost to the agents of controlling enterprises, rather than eliminating their control. For example, although direct commands have been eliminated, the agents' right to ration inputs has been retained; alternatively, commands and rationing have been abolished but not the right to appoint and dismiss managers of enterprises. In many cases, the agents have managed partly to reverse this process, thus confounding the situation by creating uncertainty about the effective structure of property rights.

Finally, only in Hungary have both formal commands and rationing been abolished, but still the party apparatchiks remain in control:

> Thus, since the market did not substitute for central planning, the void was filled by "suggested" auxiliary or orienting indicators covering the whole range of enterprise activities, and bargaining between managers and economic bureaucracy for change in the value of these indicators, by informal rationing and bargaining for inputs, by participation of economic bureaucracy and party apparatchiks in the preparation of enterprises' "autonomous" plans, as well as by an amalgam of disguised or undisguised, formal or informal, persistent or ad hoc interference in enterprise activity.[42]

The analysis above suggests that a necessary condition for increasing the dynamic efficiency of the STEs is to destroy, in its present form, the now dysfunctional monitoring agency, the Communist Party, which previously was the key to the system's success. One suggested scenario has the Party somehow fade into the background; another scenario has the ruling strata form a coalition with the military and the police against the Party, turning the systems into market-oriented dictatorships.[43]

3.4. Public Finance and Property Rights: The Case of Early Modern Europe

Long-term investments tend to be vulnerable to appropriation and forthcoming only when potential investors see present and expected future ownership rights as reasonably secure. The question of stable exclusive private ownership rights is not an issue in the STEs, where the state, through its agents, directly controls major physical investments.[44] However, in countries where ownership of the means of production is decentralized, the stability of private ownership rights is of critical importance for the performance of the economy.

The way in which the state conducts its finances affects the definition and stability of exclusive rights. Predatory public finance creates de facto incomplete exclusive rights, and wealth-maximizing individuals respond to uncertain property rights by making various adjustments to minimize the risk of appropriation. These adjustments tend to lower the level of investment activity and change its nature.[45] In other words, predatory public finance can move the economy's structural production frontier away from its technical production frontier.

In Europe, during a period of 200 years ending in the mid-seventeenth century, the nation-state rose from the ruins of the former feudal/manorial structures. The gradual emergence of the nation-state was in response to various forces, including military technology, which had increased the optimal size of the political unit and multiplied the state's military and bureaucratic expenditures.[46] However, as the crown was typically constrained by an archaic revenue system, and as the costs of measuring the tax base were high, the early nation-state suffered chronic financial deficits and relied heavily on credit.

To repeat, in addition to political constraints, measurement and other transaction costs limited taxation. Land was taxed, but high transaction costs restricted taxes on the growing wealth of the merchant class except when large volumes of trade passed through a few specified points, such as ports in the case of English foreign trade. As for income taxes, the concept of annual income was still poorly defined and the costs of measuring incomes were high. Later developments of organizational forms in business and associated commercial law required the definition and measurement of annual incomes and reduced the costs of effective income taxation. Similarly, general property taxes were impeded by the high cost of maintaining measures of current property values: the measurement cost fell later when property, to a considerable extent, came to be in the form of transferable securities. And, finally, an unsophisticated monetary and banking system, along with economic and political considerations, limited inflationary financing through manipulation of the money supply.[47]

In order to survive, the typical ruler resorted to predatory public finance, which created uncertainty about property rights, reduced the tax base and lowered the crown's credit ratings, and further weakened the state's ability to finance its activities. For instance, in early seventeenth-century England under the Stuarts prior to the Civil War, public finance involved the sale of crown lands to raise revenue, the sale of monopoly rights to industries, the sale of peerage and knighthood, the seizure of goods for public purposes without paying the owners the full market value of the goods, the sale to specific individuals of the right to dispense with certain public rules, and outright confiscation of private property. The Stuarts also secured loans under force of threat and, later, unilaterally rewrote loan contracts to make the terms more favorable for the state.[48]

There is ample historical evidence to show that predatory public finance has often shrunk the state's tax base, reduced its credit and tax revenues, and contributed to economic decline.[49] Therefore, let us recall why a rational ruler might ever resort to such self-defeating measures. First note that, according to the theoretical model of the state presented in the second subsection of this chapter, a ruler who is not constrained by competition, agency problems, and measurement costs will seek to maximize the state's tax base.[50] However, in the real world, rulers do face the constraints just listed: their control (ownership) of the potential tax base is incomplete and uncertain, and, under certain circumstances, dissipation becomes rational behavior for a wealth-maximizing ruler.

Although the constraints of competition and transaction costs often create incentives for rulers to dissipate the state's potential wealth, the addition of *further constraints* can both create stable property rights and increase public and private revenues. A ruler who appropriates the quasi-rents from investments, initially made by private investors who believed that ownership rights were secure, can be compared to an opportunistic party to a private long-term contract. In our discussion of the nature of the firm (Chapter 5), it was pointed out that reneging on contracts, holding up investors, and confiscating their quasi-rents not only curtails vulnerable investments and reduces wealth, but also makes it worthwhile to make arrangements that prevent appropriation.[51]

There are two fundamental ways of protecting quasi-rents. One is vertical integration, which, in the political arena, is the road of Soviet-type states and many developing countries: the state acquires the vulnerable assets. The other approach is to constrain potential appropriators. Potential appropriators can either make credible commitments and bond themselves by means such as long-term contracts and collaterals ("hostages"), or they can be deprived of power and have constraints forced on them. The early history of the nation-state provides examples of both kinds of constraints.

The case has been made that relative economic success or failure of the countries of Europe in the past 200 or so years is related to the resolution of the financial crisis in the early nation-states.[52] In some instances, the crisis was resolved through the emergence of representative government, the distribution of powers, an independent judiciary, and other institutions supportive of secure property rights. In other cases a centralist bureaucratic tradition evolved, and dissipating property rights structures became institutionalized. Furthermore, during the colonial era, the European powers exported their alternative systems which thus came to affect world development.[53]

Finally, let us briefly consider the different responses of England and France to the financial crisis of the early nation-state.

> A king could rely on loans to tide the government through a war; but facing the awesome task of repayment, he required fiscal revenues. The necessity to establish a regular source of revenue to repay war loans influenced and then determined the relationship between the state and the private sector.... In most cases the crown was initially forced to grant to 'representative" bodies (Parliament, Estates General) control over tax rates in return for the revenue they voted. In some instances these representative bodies retained this privilege; in others, they lost it. This last point requires special emphasis and further elaboration since it is the key to future differential patterns of development which we observe within Europe.[54]

North and Weingast (1987) examine how constraints were forced on the English crown during the seventeenth century, leading to the separation of powers and an independent judiciary. Toward the end of the century, various changes were made in the way in which the government sought credit, and the new institutions, including the Bank of England, ushered in modern capital markets. The new political institutions and the fiscal revolution made credible the government's commitment to honor its credit contracts, and the new structures demonstrated how: "Rules that can readily be revised by the sovereign differ significantly in their implications for performance from exactly the same rules when not subject to revision."[55]

The new limits on the crown's ability to control property rights, and the balance of powers, increased enormously the government's capacity to borrow at very low rates of interest. Furthermore, the new institutions not only took away the crown's incentives to renege on its contracts, but also lowered the cost to private individuals of making credible commitments to long-term contracts among themselves. Looking beyond the seventeenth century, "It is clear that these institutional changes underpinned the drive towards British hegemony and dominance of the world. England could not have beaten France without its financial revolution. These changes also provided the institutional underpinnings of the industrial revolution."[56]

In fifteenth-century France, Charles VII unified France after the devastations of the Hundred Years' War. To finance the pacification of the country and the recovering of more than half his claimed kingdom, the representative body, the Estates General, granted Charles VII special power to tax. However, the sovereign's control over public finance outlived the emergency, and the crown retained rights to grant and alter property rights until the Revolution.[57]

For lenders an unsecured loan to sovereign, who is above the law and cannot be sued, is a risky venture. Hicks (1969) shows how European sovereigns sought to make credible commitment to repayment by pawning physical assets such as crown jewels and royal estates and, more importantly, by pawning less tangible assets such as the right to collect certain taxes, the right of appointment to high offices, the right to monopolize trade, and the right to claim tax exemptions.[58]

Root and Ingberman (1987) discuss how the crown, during the Old Regime in France, sought to make credible commitments to lenders. The commitment technology evolved from using a few financial families as intermediaries, to relying on bureaucratic corporations. The financiers, who made a network among themselves through intermarriage, were not above the law, and could be held responsible if the king failed to honor his debts. However, the crown's abuses of the financiers created incentives for their organizing themselves into corporations in order to increase the cost to the crown of repudiating its debts and to constrain kingly discretion. "Among the intermediaries the king called upon were the traditional corps: the village communities, the guilds and the provincial estates. In return for official recognition and privileges, these corporate groups acted as bankers for the sovereign."[59] Typically, the privileges involved the assignment of monopoly rights protected by the state and the right to tax the movement of goods at the local level.

However, the king's claim to absolute power undermined the government's fiscal credibility. In the eighteenth century, France could not make credible commitments to a national bank (an experiment that failed), the old practice of selling tax exemptions had come to a dead end, and the country could not satisfactorily finance its wars. The French were aware that institutional change in England, including the separation of powers, and a fiscal revolution, had put English finances on a sound footing, and major social and political reforms were needed in France to raise tax revenues and improve the government's credit standing:[60] "Informed members of the public insisted on the need to subject economic policy to public discussion and to design institutions that would limit the crown's discretion over finance. The discussion of how to design such institutions led to the Revolution [of 1789]."[61]

We conclude with a few generalizations. First, society's stock of institutional capital changes through obsolescence and new investments, but changes tend to be marginal. Existing institutions shape the course of future institutional developments. Second, credible commitment by the state to stable property rights both promotes private investments and lowers the transaction costs to the state of raising revenue. In modern nation-states, such commitments seem to require an effective separation of powers. Finally, generalizations about the separation of powers are hard to make. In history, the separation of powers has depended partly on factors, such as the existence (or nonexistence) of a standing army controlled by the crown, structural features of the economy that affect the transaction costs of regular taxation, and various domestic and foreign political factors, which affect the bargaining strength of social groups.

4. The Institutions of Representative Government and Transaction Costs

4.1. Introduction

In the industrial democracies of our times, public rules prescribing exchange in factor and output markets have multiplied in the past 100 years. In general, there is vast involvement by the state in economic life, spanning both the definition and the enforcement of property rights and direct allocation of resources. Ultimately, a behavioral theory of representative government and its institutions is needed to explain the allocation of resources in modern industrial states.

The positive study of representative government has been the domain of two related disciplines, Political Science and Public Choice. The Public Choice school extends the rational-choice model to the study of politics, and since the 1960s the economic approach is increasingly used by political scientists in general.[62] The early work applying the rational-choice model to politics tended to mirror neoclassical economics in that transaction costs were assumed to be zero and the role of institutions was neglected. Furthermore, the scholars of the 1960s and 1970s rediscovered, and became preoccupied with, the classical voting paradox.[63] According to the voting paradox, outcomes are unstable under majority rule because a new majority preferring some other alternative can always be found.[64] In fact, Schwartz (1987) surveys this literature and concludes that almost all collective choice environments are unstable.

As we discussed in Chapter 3, when this topic was introduced, actual political outcomes are not as unstable as the early rational-choice models suggest. Recently, political theorists have reintroduced institutions into their models and, using the tools of Neoinstitutionalism, sought to explain how rules constrain legislators and induce stability:

> The importance of procedural rules became more obvious in all sorts of rational-choice models of politics. Students of Congress argued that creating subject-area committees in Congress, with a seniority rule for determining committee chairmanship, resulted in quite different outcomes than an alternative set of internal procedural rules based on, for instance, party discipline. ... Rational-choice theorists became fascinated with examples which demonstrated the coercive nature of such institutional rules on group choice.... [W]ith the renewed interest in institutions came a renewed interest in history, since institutions (as opposed to individual attitudes and behavior) seemed grounded in history.[65]

The next logical step for political theorists was to apply the tools of Neoinstitutionalism to the question of how the institutions themselves were chosen. This work has just begun.

It is beyond this book to give a comprehensive view of attempts to use the tools of NIE to endogenize the political outcomes and institutions of representative government.[66] Our task in this section is to suggest the potential of our approach to political theory through the example of two studies. The first study attempts to model formally the role of transaction costs in explaining how the influence of interest groups and the behavior of legislators depend on the nature of the assumptions about the cost of information. The second study uses NIE and the new theory of business organization to explain the internal structure of the U.S. Congress.

4.2. Information Costs and Interest Groups

The interest-group theory of legislation was introduced in Chapter 3. The puzzle of an excessive influence over legislators by a relatively small special-interest group was explained informally in terms of an asymmetrical distribution of information and by the majority group's high costs of collective action relative to expected benefits. Denzau and Munger (1986) have formalized these issues in a model that shows how policies chosen by legislators, and the influence of organized interest groups, depend on the assumptions that are made about the availability of information to voters.[67]

In the Denzau–Munger model, legislators maximize votes (V). The legislators' activities are constrained by a scarce resource, effort (E), an exogenous variable. Each legislator allocates her $\bar{E}$ to various activities so as to maximize the chances of reelection. A legislator can affect the votes of her geographical constituency in three ways: (1) by policies and actions directed explicitly to benefit the district's unorganized constituency; (2) by promoting policies of interest groups that don't vote – policies that may be liked or disliked by the voters; and (3) by advertising and otherwise controlling the flow of information to voters.

In order to control the flow of information to her voters (through advertising and other forms of campaigning), the legislator requires resources R. R is available only from nonvoting interest groups in return for support in promoting their policies, P. A legislator produces policy results by allocating some effort E_i to policy P_i. The legislator's effectiveness in getting results is represented by a production function, $P_i(E_i)$. The productivity of legislators varies both from one person to another and, for an individual, across policies. For example, the productivity of a legislator is relatively high for policy P_i, if she is a member of a legislative committee with jurisdiction over P_i.

Any policy, P_i, can increase or decrease the welfare of the legislator's geographical constituency. The legislator will support a policy that affects potential voters negatively, only if by doing so she can raise advertising revenue, R, from organized groups. Therefore, the model also contains both a revenue function, $R_i(P_i)$, representing the prices paid by organized groups for services rendered; and a production function, relating votes to advertising expenditure, $V(R)$.

The legislator's optimization problem involves allocating effort, $\bar{E}$, to policies and services for the geographical constituency, P_u, and to policies, P_i, favored by organized groups in order to raise advertising revenue, R. We assume that there are only two organized interest groups, each promoting a single policy program. Then a legislator maximizes the following equation:[68]

$$V = V[P_u(E_u), P_1(E_1), P_2(E_2), R] + \lambda(\bar{E} - E_u - E_1 - E_2) \qquad (4)$$

Now consider two extreme assumptions about information available to voters: (1) *rational ignorance*, and (2) *full information*. The concept of rational ignorance implies that voters find it costly themselves to collect information about the activities of their representative and depend for information on her advertising. In the limit, when all information comes from the legislator (a case of pure rational ignorance), the response function for voters is $V(R)$, and Eq. 4 becomes:

$$V = V\{R_1[P_1(\bar{E}_1)], R_2[P_2(E_2)]\} + \lambda(\bar{E} - E_1 - E_2) \qquad (5)$$

In situations depicted by Eq. 5, interest groups control the legislator's activities, and her production function for producing alternative policies, $P_i(E_i)$, becomes the central issue. Pressure groups will seek out legislators with high productivity in their policy area (committee chairpersons, individuals with expert knowledge in the field, etc.) in an attempt to minimize the resource cost of obtaining and preserving favorable laws and regulations.[69] Note, however, that the model exaggerates the power of interest groups over legislators in a world of complete rational ignorance. A legislator does not have a monopoly over the flow of information to the geographical constituency. If she can advertise, so can her political competitors, and the news media also polices the actions of incumbents.[70]

Next consider the implications of introducing a world of full information where, at no cost to themselves, all the members of a constituency have full knowledge of the activities of their representative. As there is no room for manipulating information, political advertising by the legislator is pointless. Therefore the vote productivity of advertising resources, R, falls to zero, and interest groups have nothing to offer the legislator.[71] R drops out of the voters' reaction function, which becomes:

$$V = V(P_u, P_1, P_2) \qquad (6)$$

Furthermore, a legislator will not allocate effort to policies P_1 and P_2 unless they directly promote the welfare of her constituency, which means that a legislator will represent only the interests of her voters.

In real life, the situation lies somewhere between the assumptions of rational ignorance and full information. Denzau and Munger (1986) point out that various phenomena, ranging from political advertising, preferences by members of the U.S. Congress for positions on committees, and the behavior of organized interest groups, are inconsistent with both extreme assumptions. Well-funded interest groups are, indeed, influential, as a result of positive transaction costs, but their influence is constrained by the geographical constituency because some information does filter through to the voters, and voters do react.

4.3. Transaction Costs and the Structure of Democratic Institutions

In Chapters 6 and 7, the tools of Neoinstitutional Economics were used to explain the structure of firms and contracts in various markets in terms of cost minimization. We emphasized how measurement and enforcement problems may prevent owners of valuable resources from realizing potential gains from trade, and also how trade can be thwarted by the difficulty of foreseeing future environments and writing contingent contracts when exchange has a substantial time dimension. Incomplete contracts give rise to opportunistic behavior. When the gains from exchange cannot be realized because of high transaction costs, traders have an incentive to lower these costs by introducing new institutions, which constrain and prescribe individual action. These new institutions include, for example, vertical integration, franchising, or the traditional entrepreneurial firm.

It is reasonable to believe that the NIE approach may be useful also in modeling the structure of political institutions under representative government, but work in this area has just begun. As we just said, the introduction of the rational-choice model into political science in the 1960s was, in part, a reaction to the old institutionalism. The early work tended to emphasize exchange across implicit or explicit markets, ignored transaction costs, and did not focus on the structure of institutions or their constraining influence. Recently, this has changed, and scholars using the label Neoinstitutionalism have begun to apply the tools of NIE to the study of government. For example, the twenty papers by various authors in *Congress: Structure and Policy* (1987) provide a good summary of the current understanding of the institutional structure of the U.S. Congress.[72] The authors represent different schools of thought, but, in one way or another, the papers are concerned with the effect of institutions on individual behavior, particularly institutional innovations in Congress that organize the business of legislating, the effects of institutions on policy choices, and how the U.S. Congress designs institutions to control the execution of delegated authority.

A model of the organization of the U.S. Congress by Weingast and Marshall (1988) illustrates the potential of the NIE approach to democratic institutions.[73] A great variety of interests are represented in a legislature, but few have the automatic support of a majority of the members. If we assume that reelection is the primary goal of legislators, and that the promotion of appropriate policies enhances their reelection, then legislators can gain by trading votes: a legislator seeks votes for bills that make the largest positive impact on her reelection in return for giving her vote to bills with minimal negative impact on her election fortunes.

The pioneering studies of vote trading (logrolling) all assume implicit or explicit markets in votes.[74] Although these studies have provided valuable insights, Weingast and Marshall (1988) argue that they fail to account for the high transaction costs of exchanging votes. In fact, the organizational structure of legislative bodies can (at least in part) be explained in terms of designs for lowering the transaction costs of exchanging votes and building coalitions. Let us pause and consider why transaction costs of trading votes should be high.[75]

First, legislators, unlike traders in markets for goods and services, cannot rely on third-party enforcement of their agreements. Legislator A who reneges on her promise to vote for the bill of legislator B (in return for some favor) cannot be taken to court for breach of contract.

Second, legislators A and B may agree to support each other's policies, but the voting on their bills need not take place simultaneously. Legislator A may vote for B's bill, but B may refuse to return the favor weeks or months later, when A's bill comes up for voting.

Third, many things can happen before A's bill comes up for voting, such as changes in the preferences of voters who benefit by the bill or other political circumstances. Legislator A may need to amend her bill to protect her reelection chances, or the new circumstances may create incentives for B to ask for changes in the bill. In either case, asymmetrical information makes it hard for each legislator to judge whether the other's behavior is opportunistic or a genuine response to changing circumstances.[76] High transaction costs preclude the writing of complete contracts that cover all contingencies, and the role of repeat play and reputation in facilitating enforcement is undermined.

Fourth, the flow of electoral benefits from their programs to legislators A and B need not coincide in time. A's program may involve dams and bridges, and B's program may constitute a new regulatory agency. Once the dams and bridges are built, A can join a new coalition and vote for a bill abolishing B's regulatory agency and deprive him of future benefits.

These factors can impose high costs on exchange and limit trade, but Weingast and Marshall (1988) use the new theory of the firm to analyze how institutional structures within the U.S. Congress help make agreements between members enforceable and facilitate the forming of durable coalitions. The committee system is the centerpiece of their model, and the basic features of the analysis are summarized below.[77]

In Congress, the political agenda is divided into clearly defined jurisdictions. Committees are assigned property rights over jurisdictions, and they control what alternatives, if any, to the status quo, come up for vote by the whole assembly. The system also involves rules for proper amendments.

Legislators compete for positions on committees that best suit their reelection chances. The competitive process reveals the legislators' preferences, and the assignment of committee positions reflects these preferences. Seats on committees cannot be traded, and members keep their positions as long as they wish, subject to their reelection.

A committee is an agent of the whole legislature, and various rules are designed to constrain the power of committees in order to limit agency problems. The most important of these constraints is the requirement that committee proposals must command a majority of votes in the legislature to become public policy.

Now reconsider the previous example of an exchange of votes for dams and roads in return for votes in support of a new regulatory agency, and the possibility that legislators may renege and abolish the agency once their dams and roads have been built. With the committee system in place, the original coalition that supported the regulatory agency had to include a majority of members on the committee with jurisdiction over the relevant regulations. Even when a new majority emerges in Congress for revoking the regulations, the committee can use its veto power over changes in the status quo and refuse to bring bills to the floor for vote. A new majority on the *committee* is required to bring about a change in this area.

Furthermore, the committee system limits opportunistic behavior in vote trading, when voting is not simultaneous and some legislators have an incentive to renege by rewriting the original bill. The committee, which has jurisdiction in the area, can control which of several alternatives, supported against the status quo by a majority, comes up for voting. The committee system does not solve all problems, and agreements across committees are still costly (and this should affect the structure of jurisdictions), but the assignment of property rights over jurisdictions, through a process of competition and self-selection, lowers the cost of forming coalitions and enforcing agreements.[78] The institutionalization of the system gives permanence to policies.[79]

Finally, Weingast and Marshall (1988) suggest that the transaction costs of trading in legislative IOUs can also be reduced with the help of a party system in the legislature. In fact, a strong committee system may be a substitute for strong political parties and party discipline. Enforcement through reputation and repeated dealings is more effective in the case of political parties than individual legislators, provided the parties control the access of their members to political resources.

Notes

1. This point has been made by North, for example: North, Douglass C. (1987). "Institutions, Transaction Costs and Economic Growth." *Economic Inquiry 25* (No. 3): 419–428.

2. P. 20 in North, Douglass C. (1981). *Structure and Change in Economic History*. New York: W. W. Norton. To a large extent this chapter is based on North's theories of the relationships among the productive forces of an economy, the structure of property rights, and the political system.

3. North, Douglass C. (1979). "A Framework for Analyzing the State in Economic History." *Explorations in Economic History* (July): 249–259.

4. The argument could also be stated in terms of growth rates – that is, how fast the production frontier moves out under alternative systems of property rights. Note that we treat technology and population as exogenous variables in this chapter, although these factors are fundamental sources of economic and political change. The NIE approach suggests that the rate of investment in technological change is inversely related to the investors' cost of capturing the potential returns on their investments. However, except for general statements, economists working in the NIE tradition have not contributed important new theories of population and technological change.

5. But note that technical change also works to lower transaction costs – for example, by advancing the technologies of measurement and communications.

6. North (1981) [op. cit., note 2], p. 27.

7. Findlay, Ronald, and Wilson, John D. (1984). "The Political Economy of the Leviathan." Seminar Paper No. 285. Stockholm: Institute for International Economic Studies. Their model can be used to discuss alternative positive theories of the state in terms familiar to economists.

8. It is assumed that $p(0) = 1$. Therefore, in a stateless society the community's production function would be $Y = f(L, K)$.

9. It is assumed that $p_g > 0$, $p_{gg} < 0$, and that $f(L, K)$ is homogeneous of the first degree in L and K.

10. The optimization problem is comparable to that of a firm that operates two plants and must divide its fixed labor force between the two plants so as to maximize output.

11. The government's expenditure function reflects the equality of wages in the two sectors, $W_G = W_L$, and also the assumption that wages in the private sector are equal to the value of the marginal product of private sector workers, $W_G = W_L = VMP_L$. Note that the public sector workers are also taxed. The expenditure function is then $(1 - t^*)VMP_L G$. The revenue function can be written as $t^*Y(G)$.

12. North (1981) [op. cit., note 2] concedes that the contract theory can serve as an explanation of the origin and the productive function of the state. However, the nature of the social contract is likely to change over time as events influence the potential power of the contractors. A look at the state in history does not suggest that "contracts among equals" is an appropriate characterization of the relationships involved. Also note that the introduction of transaction costs and agency problems (for instance, bureaucrats out of control) can alter the outcome of the contract model and make it less ideal than suggested by Figure 2. In fact, transaction costs blur the distinction between the contractual and predatory models.

13. Ibid., p. 21.

14. North provides a recent statement of his theory in North, Douglass C. (1984). "Government and the Cost of Exchange in History." *Journal of Economic History 44* (No. 2, June): 255–264.

15. An optimizing ruler will increase G while marginal revenue (incremental tax revenue) is greater than marginal cost (the addition to the wage bill). The ruler will never take the economy to the point where Y peaks (to Y^*), because at that point marginal revenue ($t \times$ the change in income) is zero, but the marginal wage cost of expanding the public sector will always be positive, given Findlay and Wilson's assumptions.

16. This statement may not be true if our definition of output is the same as found in standard national income accounts that fail to account fully for various spillovers such as pollution. "Economic organization that induces economic growth may very well do so by internalizing the benefits and externalizing the costs and hence raising the private rate of return to 'productive' economic activity at the expense of costs lumped on other groups in society." North (1981) [op. cit., note 2], p. 62.

17. Ibid., p. 28.

18. Of course, no one can be excluded in the case of pure public goods, but many goods supplied by the state are not public goods.

19. North (1981) [op. cit., note 2], p. 30.

20. Furthermore, in explaining collective action, North (1981) puts a major emphasis on changes in ideology – that is, people's stylized view of the world, particularly their conception of fairness. When political changes are brought about by voluntary actions of large groups, North argues that strong ideological beliefs are instrumental in overcoming the free-riding problem. He has criticized Marx for both neglecting the free-riding problem in his analysis of group (class) action, and for overplaying the role of production technology in political change prior to industrial revolution. See North, Douglass C. (1986). "Is It Worth Making Sense of Marx?" *Inquiry 29* (No. 1): 57–63.

21. Bates (1981) emphasizes that, in addition to domestic political causes, there are other complementary explanations of agricultural shortfalls in Africa. (p. 2) Most of the data used in his study are drawn from the English-speaking territories of West Africa. Bates, Robert H. (1981). *Markets and States in Tropical Africa.* Berkeley: University of California Press.

22. Ibid., p. 2.

23. Bates reports that African states have strong interest in low food prices for their urban populations. However, attempts to push food prices below equilibrium market prices have met with little success. Plans to channel food crops through monopsonistic marketing boards have not been successful because of high enforcement costs. (In the case of cash crops for export, enforcement is usually manageable, as the transaction costs of controlling exports are usually relatively low.) Furthermore, most of these countries lack foreign monies to purchase food on international markets.

24. The same reasoning also applies to the behavior of members of political coalitions who obstruct changes in property rights, even when they are expected to increase the community's total wealth.

25. Winiecki, Jan (1986a). "Are Soviet-Type Economies Entering an Era of Long-Term Decline?" *Soviet Studies 38* (No. 3, July): 325–348; idem (1986b). "Soviet-Type Economies: Considerations for the Future." *Soviet Studies 38* (No. 4, October): 543–561; idem (1986c). "Why Economic Reforms Fail in the Soviet System: A Property Rights-Based Approach." Seminar Paper No. 374. Stockholm: The Institute for International Economic Studies.

26. See our discussion, in Chapter 2, of the Soviet economy as a single firm.

27. These issues are discussed in Chapters 5 and 6.

28. See p. 240 in Lindblom, C. E. (1977). *Politics and Markets: The World's Political Economic System.* New York: Basic Books.

29. For details of the organization of the Soviet system, see for example, Nove, Alec (1986). *The Soviet Economic System*, 3rd ed. London: Allen & Unwin.

30. The emphasis on output quotas at the expense of cost minimization represents a constrained choice by the leadership of an STE for whom it is too costly to measure all margins. The resulting problems are good examples of what we referred to as *moral hazard*, in Chapter 2 when the theory of agency was introduced. The lack of regard for costs by enterprises in STEs has given rise to the term, *soft budget*

constraints. See Kornai, Janos (1979). "Resource-Constrained Versus Demand-Constrained Systems." *Economica 47* (No. 4) 801–819. Furthermore, the incentive structure of STEs does not encourage innovation, which becomes increasingly troublesome as these economies catch up with advanced industrial economies and economic growth depends increasingly on complex technological industries.

31. The high resource intensity of the STEs is partly related to their lack of specialization. All the small STEs of Eastern Europe have followed Stalin's model of national self-sufficiency and each built a self-contained industrial base without regard for economies of scale and comparative advantage. Also, high transaction costs make it attractive for each enterprise to be self-sufficient rather than rely on the central-management mechanism for inputs. Therefore, Winiecki refers to the *twofold lack of specialization* in STEs. Winiecki (1986a) [op. cit., note 25], p. 337.

32. Ibid., pp. 337–340. Also note that "by the late 1970s the source of labor provided by the shift of agriculture into industry had largely dried up. On the other hand, intra-industry movement of labor from slow- to fast-growing branches in a basically autarkic economy is almost non-existent" (p. 329).

33. Ibid., pp. 326–327.

34. Ibid., p. 328.

35. "The predictable outcome has been stagnation of real – as distinct from officially reported – economic growth, higher inflation – open, hidden, and repressed – and falling living standards, with the latter affected more strongly than overall growth by decision makers' preferences, the working of the central planning mechanism, and the necessity to pay foreign debt." Winiecki (1986c) [op. cit., note 25], p. 543.

36. By a "competitive market for management" we imply a system in which selection is based on managerial skills rather than loyalty to the Party. Winiecki (1986c) argues that in the STEs the pool of talent included in *nomenklatura* is below average competence relative to the pool of talent that non-STEs can draw on to fill positions of management. He maintains that entry into nomenklatura is characterized by adverse selection. Ibid., p. 7.

37. Reforms face the strongest opposition in industry, as the most lucrative management positions are found there. The STEs have been relatively more successful in reforming agriculture. Ibid., p. 12.

38. Extensive economic reforms in the STEs would require the introduction of equilibrium prices. It is not clear how the general public would react, at least in the short run, if a large increase in prices replaced rationing by waiting. Opponents of reforms have also warned that they will increase inequality. Winiecki reports that in Poland the price of a car on the free market is 110-130 percent higher than list prices. Winiecki (1986b) [op. cit., note 25], p. 11.

39. Winiecki (1986b) gives the details of this argument.

40. Ibid., p. 558.

41. See Winiecki (1986c), op. cit., note 25.

42. Ibid., p. 24. Winiecki (1986b) argues that the high living standards of Hungary, relative to the other STEs, are explained by a decision by the top leadership, responding to the massive uprising in 1956, to give higher priority to consumer goods. The emphasis on consumer goods predates the first Hungarian reforms. Hungary shows the same structural weaknesses as the other STEs, according to Winiecki.

43. In this context, Winiecki (1986c) speculates whether the Chinese Cultural Revolution managed to weaken the power of the middle-level Party apparatus and lay the groundwork for the successful replacement of commands with parameters, and elimination of the Party's control over management positions in enterprises, or whether counterreformation is unavoidable.

44. However, the delegation of investment decisions by the state raises a host of agency problems, as we touched upon in the previous subsection.

45. See our discussion, in Chapter 4, of common and incomplete property rights. The adjustments to reduce the risk of appropriation are likely to involve several margins, such as type of technology employed, time profiles of investments, type of inputs used, and nature of commodities produced. One possible reaction is to avoid long-term investments altogether.

46. "Whether the development of an exchange economy was a sufficient condition for expanding the optimum scale of warfare or [whether] technological innovations augmented the scale may still be argued. What cannot be argued is that it expanded. As a consequence, the conditions for political survival were drastically altered. Survival now required not only a large army, but a trained disciplined fighting force supported by costly equipment in the form of cannons and muskets. The age of the armored knight with lance passed; the age of chivalry was ended. Warfare on land and at sea (where the size and armaments of naval ships increased dramatically) had dramatically altered the size of the financial resources necessary for survival." North (1981) [op. cit., note 2], p. 138. See also Tilly, Charles, ed. (1975). *The Formation of National States in Western Europe*. Princeton: Princeton University Press.

47. See "The Finances of the Sovereign," Chapter 6 in Hicks, John (1969). *A Theory of Economic History*. Oxford: Oxford University Press.

48. See pp. 5–9, and 21–22 in North, Douglass C., and Weingast, Barry R. (1987). "Constitutions and Commitment: The Evolution of Institutions Governing Public Choice in 17th Century England." Working paper. St. Louis: Washington University. The European sovereigns, as a rule, were not creditworthy. They frequently repudiated their promises, creditors (particularly minorities) were persecuted and expelled from their country, and outright bankruptcies were not unusual. "The Spanish declared bankruptcy in 1575, 1596, 1607, 1627, and 1647." See p. 1 in Root, Hilton L., and Ingberman, Daniel E. (1987). "Tying the King's Hands: Credible Commitments and Royal Fiscal Policy During the Old Regime." Working paper. Philadelphia: University of Pennsylvania.

49. For example, the selling of monopoly rights over major industries will bring stagnation in the long run, and extensive selling of tax-free status will limit future tax revenues. "Parting with State property, and parting with taxing power, obviously weaken government." Hicks (1969) [op. cit., note 47], p. 87.

50. The wealth of his or her subjects is the potential tax base of a ruler. The dissipating ruler can be compared to fishermen in an open-access fishery or landlords subject to rent controls. See our discussion in Chapter 4.

51. For an authoritative discussion of these issues see Williamson, Oliver (1985). *The Economic Institutions of Capitalism*. New York: Free Press.

52. See North, Douglass C., and Thomas, Robert (1973). *The Rise of the Western World: A New Economic History*. Cambridge: Cambridge University Press; North, Douglass C. (1981), op. cit., note 2; idem (1986a). "Institutions, Economic Growth and Freedom: An Historical Introduction." Political Economy working paper. St. Louis: Washington University.

53. North examines divergent institutional change in England and Spain in early modern Europe and discusses how these structures influenced property rights in British North America and Spanish imperial policies in the Indies and Latin American colonial development. North (1986a), op. cit., note 52.

54. North (1981) [op. cit., note 2], pp. 140–141.

55. North and Weingast (1987) [op. cit., note 48], p. 1.

56. Ibid., p. 28.

57. North (1981) [op. cit., note 2], pp. 148–150.

58. "There is indeed not much difference between pawning an asset, with little prospect of redemption, and outright sale. Thus borrowing against a tax-farm slides into selling tax-farms; and that slides into selling exemptions from future taxation." Hicks (1969) [op. cit., note 47], p. 87.

59. Root and Ingberman (1987), p. 14.

60. For a discussion of why a parliament has less incentive than a king to default on government loans, see Root and Ingberman (1987) [op. cit., note 48], pp. 19–20.

61. Ibid., p. 26.

62. For an early classic in the Public Choice field, see Buchanan, James, and Tullock, Gordon (1962). *The Calculus of Consent*. Ann Arbor: University of Michigan Press. A pioneering application of the rational-choice model to government is found in Downs, Anthony (1957). *An Economic Theory of Democracy*. New York: Harper and Row. The early public choice literature is surveyed by Mueller, Dennis C. (1979). *Public Choice*. Cambridge: Cambridge University Press.

63. The Marquis De Condorect discovered in the eighteenth century the paradox associated with majority-rule decisions.

64. The theoretical literature dealing with the instability of outcomes in voting is reviewed by Schwartz, Thomas (1987). "Votes, Strategies, and Institutions: An Introduction to the Theory of Collective Choice." In McCubbins, Mathew D., and Sullivan, Terry, eds. (1987). *Congress: Structure and Policy*. Cambridge: Cambridge University Press.

65. See p. 8 in Knott, Jack H., and Miller, Gary J. (1987). *Reforming Bureaucracy: The Politics of Institutional Choice*. Englewood Cliffs, N.J.: Prentice Hall.

66. We refer the reader to leading journals, such as *Public Choice, American Journal of Political Science*, and *American Political Science Review*. Also, some twenty papers representative of the neoinstitutional approach are found in McCubbins and Sullivan (1987), op. cit., note 64.

67. Denzau, Arthur T., and Munger, Michael (1986). "Legislators and Interest Groups: How Unorganized Interests Get Represented.' *American Political Science Review 80* (No. 1, March): 89–106.

68. Note that in the following equation $R = R_1(P_1) + R_2(P_2)$. Also note that E_u represents the effort that the legislator allocates to the promotion of policies and services for her geographical constituency, P_u.

69. Denzau and Munger derive from their model that "the more adept the legislator is at producing policy services for a group, the lower the minimum price he will require for doing so." Denzau and Munger (1986) [op. cit., note 67], p. 97.

70. Ibid., p. 100.

71. It is assumed that the legislator cannot use R for personal consumption.

72. McCubbins and Sullivan (1987), op. cit., note 64.

73. The remainder of this section is based on their study. See Weingast, Barry R., and Marshall, William J. (1988). "The Industrial Organization of Congress; or, Why Legislatures, like Firms, Are Not Organized as Markets." *Journal of Political Economy 96* (No. 1): 132–163.

74. For example, see Tullock, Gordon (1967). *Towards a Mathematics of Politics*. Ann Arbor: University of Michigan Press; Wilson, Robert (1967). "An Axiomatic Model of Logrolling." *American Economic Review 59* (June): 331–341; and Koford, Kenneth J. (1982). "Centralized Vote-trading." *Public Choice 39* (No. 2): 245–268.

75. Weingast and Marshall (1988) [op. cit., note 73], pp. 137–142.

76. The resulting problems of measurement reduce the effectiveness of investment in reputation as an instrument of lowering the transaction cost of trading in legislative IOUs. Weingast and Marshall (1988) emphasize, however, that reputation comple-

ments formal legislative institutions rather than substitutes for them. Ibid., pp. 141–142.

77. See ibid., pp. 143–148.

78. Note that the membership of a committee does not change except after elections to Congress. The decision to move between committees is comparable to an investment, and is taken only in response to substantial changes in the legislator's environment. Weingast and Marshall (1988) report empirical evidence which "supports four implications that follow from our model of legislative institutions but do not follow from a simple market exchange mechanism. First, committees are composed of 'high demanders,' that is, individuals with greater than average interest in the committee's policy jurisdiction. Second, the committee assignment mechanism operates as a bidding mechanism that assigns individuals to those committees that they value most highly. Third, committee members gain a disproportionate share of the benefits from their policy area. This appears to hold across widely differing policy jurisdictions. Fourth, there exists important evidence supporting a comparative statistics prediction of the model, namely, that as the interests represented on the committee change, so too will policy, with the interest of the non-committee members held constant."

79. One question remains. Why do the legislative institutions themselves survive? If outcomes depend on institutions, why don't majorities first vote to change the institutions and then vote for the policies they favor? The reader is referred to Chapter 3, where these issues were introduced. Note that political institutions can be seen as a set of complementary capital goods, some involving time-consuming investments in understanding the nature of outcomes generated by the institutional complex. An institutional change at one margin can destroy capital values at other margins. Institutions do change, but usually in response to fundamental changes in the environment.

References

Bates, Robert H. (1981). *Markets and States in Tropical Africa*. Berkeley: University of California Press.

Buchanan, James, and Tullock, Gordon (1962). *The Calculus of Consent*. Ann Arbor: University of Michigan Press.

Denzau, Arthur T., and Munger, Michael (1986). "Legislators and Interest Groups: How Unorganized Interests Get Represented." *American Political Science Review 80* (No. 1, March): 89–106.

Downs, Anthony (1957). *An Economic Theory of Democracy*. New York: Harper and Row.

Findlay, Ronald, and Wilson, John D. (1984). "The Political Economy of the Leviathan." Seminar Paper No. 285. Stockholm: Institute for International Studies.

Hicks, John (1969). *A Theory of Economic History*. Oxford: Oxford University Press.

Knott, Jack H., and Miller, Gary J. (1987). *Reforming Bureaucracy: The Politics of Institutional Choice*. Englewood Cliffs, N.J.: Prentice-Hall.

Koford, Kenneth J. (1982). "Centralized Vote-trading." *Public Choice 39* (No. 2): 245–268.

Kornai, Janos (1979). "Resource-Constrained Versus Demand-Constrained Systems." *Economica 47* (No. 4): 801–819.

Lindblom, C. E. (1977). *Politics and Markets: The World's Political Economic Systems*. New York: Basic Books.

McCubbins, Mathew D., and Sullivan, Terry, eds. (1987). *Congress: Structure and Policy*. Cambridge: Cambridge University Press.
Mueller, Dennis C. (1979). *Public Choice*. Cambridge: Cambridge University Press.
North, Douglass C. (1979). "A Framework for Analyzing the State in Economic History." *Explorations in Economic History* (July): 249–259.
——— (1981). *Structure and Change in Economic History*. New York: W. W. Norton.
——— (1984). "Government and the Cost of Exchange in History." *Journal of Economic History 44* (No. 2, June): 255–264.
——— (1986a). "Institutions, Economic Growth and Freedom: An Historical Introduction." Political Economy working paper. St. Louis: Washington University.
——— (1986b). "Is It Worth Making Sense of Marx?" *Inquiry 29* (No. 1): 57–63.
——— (1987). "Institutions, Transaction Costs and Economic Growth." *Economic Inquiry 25* (No. 3): 419–428.
North, Douglass C., and Thomas, Robert (1973). *The Rise of the Western World: A New Economic History*. Cambridge: Cambridge University Press.
North, Douglass C., and Weingast, Barry R. (1987). "Constitutions and Commitment: The Evolution of Institutions Governing Public Choice in 17th Century England." Working paper. St. Louis: Washington University.
Nove, Alec (1986). *The Soviet Economic System*, 3rd ed. London: Allen & Unwin.
Root, Hilton L., and Ingberman, Daniel E. (1987). "Tying the King's Hands: Credible Commitments and Royal Fiscal Policy During the Old Regime." Working paper. Philadelphia: University of Pennsylvania.
Schwartz, Thomas (1987). "Votes, Strategies, and Institutions: An Introduction to the Theory of Collective Choice." In McCubbins, Mathew D., and Sullivan, Terry, eds. (1987). *Congress: Structure and Policy*. Cambridge: Cambridge University Press.
Tilly, Charles, ed. (1975). *The Formation of National States in Western Europe*. Princeton: Princeton University Press.
Tullock, Gordon (1967). *Towards a Mathematics of Politics*. Ann Arbor: University of Michigan Press.
Weingast, Barry R., and Marshall, William J. (1988). "The Industrial Organization of Congress; or, Why Legislatures, like Firms, Are Not Organized as Markets." *Journal of Political Economy 96* (No. 1): 132–163.
Williamson, Oliver (1985). *The Economic Institutions of Capitalism*. New York: Free Press.
Wilson, Robert (1967). "An Axiomatic Model of Logrolling." *American Economic Review 59* (June): 331–341.
Winiecki, Jan (1986a). "Are Soviet-Type Economies Entering an Era of Long-Term Decline?" *Soviet Studies 38* (No. 3, July): 325–348.
——— (1986b). "Soviet-Type Economies: Considerations for the Future." *Soviet Studies 38* (No. 4, October): 543–561.
——— (1986c). "Why Economic Reforms Fail in the Soviet System: A Property Rights-Based Approach." Seminar Paper No. 374. Stockholm: The Institute for International Economic Studies.

75

The Wider Share Ownership Programme

Paul Grout

Source: *Fiscal Studies*, 8(3), 1987, pp. 59–74.

I. Introduction

The Conservative Government has committed itself to a policy of wider share ownership aimed at reversing the decline in direct share ownership by individuals that continued throughout the 1960s and 1970s. It is now possible to identify a series of complementary measures that, *ex post*, can justifiably be referred to as a programme. These consist of incentives for employee share ownership, incentives for all employee option ownership, incentives for discretionary employee and management share options, and Personal Equity Plans. It can be argued that there are also indirect incentives for individuals in terms of the pricing of the privatised companies and we shall consider this issue in this context.

Our purpose here is to discuss this specific UK programme, although it is clearly impossible to discuss it independently of privatisation. We shall not discuss the general theoretical issues of the role of wider share ownership in economic performance; this is analysed in Grout (1987b). The paper will begin with a discussion of the recent experience and some brief comments on international comparisons. We then discuss in turn the various aspects of the programme before turning our attention to diversification and transactions costs.

II. Recent Experience

The Conservative Government inherited a position in 1979 where the number of adults directly owning shares had fallen from a little over 7 per cent in 1958 to 4.5 per cent. It was against this background that the wider share ownership programme was introduced. By 1983 the proportion of adults owning shares had only risen to 5 per cent. Today almost one in five adults directly own shares in their company. The last four years have differed dramatically from the previous four years because of the large-scale privatisations in the latter period (British Telecom alone attracted 2,051,373 individual shareholders (excluding employee shareholders)). The British Telecom flotation not only presents a change in the fortune of the wider share ownership programme, but also represents a major change in the policy itself. The programme is, with hindsight, a well-integrated package aimed at different groups, e.g. shares for the man on the street via privatisations, shares for employees encouraged by various schemes, options for higher management, and attempts to deepen the share base with Personal Equity Plans. In practice, however, the programme developed less clearly. Until the flotation of British Telecom, the emphasis had concentrated almost exclusively on provision of shares and options for employees (there was nothing even specifically available for top employees). With the arrival of British Telecom, the government was faced with the problem of bringing to the stock market the largest ever flotation. To reduce the probability of failure, efforts were made to attract small investors who had previously not purchased shares. This policy was a great success. The flotation went smoothly with investors receiving a significant premium. As a result, the idea of promoting 'popular capitalism' was born. The government shifted its emphasis towards promoting wider share ownership in this general form, and from this point on it is reasonable to describe the policy as a well-defined programme.

Between 1963 and 1981 the proportion of the stock market directly owned by individuals fell from 54 per cent to 28 per cent. This decline was almost entirely accounted for by the growth in large institutional shareholders; that is, insurance companies, pension funds, and investment and unit trusts. Furthermore, the proportion of wealth held in shares had declined consistently throughout the 1970s. As we have indicated, the position has changed since then. A survey conducted in January and February this year estimated that, surprisingly, 19½ per cent of all adults in the UK were shareholders. Furthermore, the proportion of personal wealth held directly in shares has been rising slowly since 1982. This has been a dramatic change. Although measures to promote employee share ownership helped reduce the decline in share ownership, it is the privatisation programme that has almost single-handedly turned the tide. For example, it is estimated that the flotation of British Telecom alone attracted one million shareholders to the market who had never owned shares before.

It is not widely recognised, however, that this move towards wider share ownership is of a very specific form. Although the value of shares owned directly by individuals is rising rapidly, it is not rising as rapidly as the value of shares owned by the institutions. Consequently, the proportion of the stock market directly owned by individuals continues to fall. The reason this is happening is that, although many more people now own shares than before, they own a very small number. Table 1 shows the results of a recent survey

Table 1 Number of companies in which shares are held

Number of companies in which shares are held	*Percentage of shareholders*[a]
1	59%
2	15%
3	5%
4+	18%

[a]Percentages do not sum to 100 because of 'don't know's.

Table 2 Value of shareholdings (for positive respondents)

Value of shareholdings	*Percentage of shareholders*
Less than £500	34%
£500–£1000	19.4%
£1001–£3000	18%
£3001+	30%

indicating number of types of shares owned (Dewe Rogerson (1986)). More than half those sampled held shares in only one company; less than a fifth held shares in four or more companies. Table 2 shows the value of shareholdings, using calculations based on the Stock Exchange (1986) survey.[1] Again the figures confirm the low number of shares owned. The interesting feature of the recent growth in share ownership is that although it involves a surprisingly large number of people, it is almost as thin as it possibly could be. This is important because as a result of this pattern of ownership, whether or not we believe that we have increased share ownership depends on the definition used. If we mean by an increase in width of share ownership that the total share ownership is less concentrated, then it is unclear whether this is being achieved. The large institutions are taking a large proportion, implying more concentration, but the declining remainder is being spread out more equally. This is a classic problem in inequality measurement to which there is no hard and fast answer. On the other hand, if we measure an increase in share ownership by the growth in the number of people owning shares, then it is undoubtedly the case that the policy has been successful in achieving wider share ownership.

It is helpful to put these figures in an international context. The country that has recently seen the fastest rise in direct and indirect share ownership outside the UK is France. This is because of the Loi Monory scheme. This allowed a family to deduct (for tax purposes) up to FF5000 a year (plus FF500 per child) to be invested on the stock market for at least five years.[2] The proportion of households investing in listed securities rose from 7 per cent in 1977 to 17 per cent in 1982. The interesting feature of the Loi Monory experience was that the bulk of the money was invested in mutual funds (i.e. unit trusts) whereas the emphasis in the UK wider share ownership programme has been to increase direct ownership (with a limited exception in Personal Equity Plans). In the UK there are 3.8 million unit trust holders compared with 8.5 million direct shareholders.

In the US 20.1 per cent of the US adult population own shares directly or indirectly through mutual funds, a figure that is rising slowly. In Canada 18 per cent of the adult population own shares or mutual funds. In Japan approximately 6 per cent of the adult population own shares while in Australia it is 9.2 per cent, and in Holland 9.2 per cent of all households own shares. Compared with these figures, the UK has a large spread of share ownership, particularly bearing in mind that the US and Canadian figures include mutual funds. This may suggest that further additions will become harder and harder to achieve.

1. Employee Share Ownership

The main fiscal incentives to create wider employee share ownership are the profit-sharing schemes introduced in the Finance Act 1978 (and frequently amended). If a company introduces a scheme, it is allowed to set shares aside (in trust) for employees where the value per employee must not exceed £1250 or 10 per cent of earnings (subject to a ceiling of £5000) per year. All full-time employees must be eligible to enter the scheme and a fraction of profit is usually set aside to purchase shares (limited to a maximum of 5 per cent before tax by the Investment Protection Committees). The fiscal advantage of receiving remuneration through this arrangement is that if the shares are held in trust for five years then the employee pays no tax. If he sells them after four years then he pays income tax on 75 per cent of the value of the shares. If he sells before this date then the full 100 per cent of their value is treated as income, although it should be pointed out that the employee is barred from selling the shares for the first two years. There are now 645 of these schemes in the UK and the number is barely growing (approximately 6 per month). Employee share ownership has also been a major feature of privatisations: Table 3 shows the proportions of employees taking up and/or buying shares in the privatisation programme.

The benefits of employee share ownership can either be of the type that improve efficiency with given inputs or alter the bargaining strengths of the parties in imperfect labour markets (see Grout (1987a); Estrin, Grout and Wadhwani (1987) and references therein). Also employee share ownership offers a way of treating existing employees (or 'insiders') in a different way from potential employees (or 'outsiders'). The argument is that insiders have some monopoly power, because it is expensive to replace them with workers

Table 3 Percentage of employees taking up and/or buying shares in company

Company	*Percentage of employees*
British Aerospace	74%
Cable and Wireless	99%
Amersham International	99%
National Freight	36%
British Telecom	96%
British Gas	99%
British Airways	94%
Rolls-Royce	96%

outside the firm, and they cannot convert this into higher wages. If others could be employed at lower wages then it would be profitable to do so. One method of doing this is to pay inside workers a wage plus a share arrangement but exclude the newly recruited worker from the share arrangement. The means to treat insiders and outsiders differently is already available in the existing UK legislation on employee share ownership. For example, a wedge between insider and outsider payments arises whenever new employees are not eligible for shares under the 1978 scheme until they have been employed for some time. If employees' pay consists of a base wage plus some fixed value of shares then the discounted cost of an additional worker under this scheme will be less than the pay of an existing worker. The existing workers will not lose by the employment of new workers either in the short or in the long run. The difference between the cost of the new worker and the cost of an existing employee increases, the larger is the share of wages paid in shares, the larger the period before a new worker is eligible for shares and the higher the turnover of employees. For example, if the average duration of employment is ten years, an employee is eligible for shares after three years and 10 per cent of the wage is paid in shares, then (discounting at 5 per cent) the cost of a new employee is 95.4 per cent of that of an existing employee. The main advantage is that existing employees do not lose from expanded employment and are less likely to resist such schemes. The existing UK legislation allows a company to delay provision of shares to new employees for up to five years. The time periods used vary: Surgical and Extel are two companies that require the full five years whereas Barclays Bank only require one year. In the UK about 40 per cent of all companies require three years or more service (Wider Share Ownership Council (1986)) and this represents a significant asymmetry of treatment between insiders and outsiders. Although this is unlikely to have a major impact on employment given existing levels of employee share ownership, it is an employment-enhancing process that is more significant the greater the extent of employee share ownership.

A problem of wider employee share ownership is that it may create diversification problems. The problem is twofold. First, by placing a significant proportion of wealth in one company, one is bundling instead of diversifying risks. Second, one is investing in an asset that is positively correlated with one's income and obviously a sensible investment policy is to invest in assets that are negatively correlated with income. This problem will be even worse if profit-sharing rules are introduced, because then the correlation of income and wealth will be very large. This suggests companies may have to choose between employee share ownership or introducing profit sharing. Attempts to do both may meet with considerable resistance from the work-force.

2. Employee and Managerial Share Options

The incentives to encourage option ownership are twofold – the all employee Save-As-You-Earn (SAYE) Share Option Schemes (1980 Finance Act) and the so-called Executive Share Option Schemes (1984 Finance Act). Options are distinct instruments from shares but it is conventional to consider these schemes as part of the so-called 'popular capitalism' programme. A (call) option is a right to purchase a share at a pre-specified price (the exercise price) on a specified date. The holder of the option can decide whether or not to purchase the share on the specified date. This creates an asymmetry and it is this asymmetry that makes options such useful instruments. The holder of an option will not purchase the shares if the market price on the specified day is below the exercise price. Therefore, in this case the value of the option is zero no matter how much the difference between the exercise price and the share price. If the market price is above the exercise price then the option holder will make a profit of the difference between the two prices. Therefore, if one is given an option on a share, one cannot make a loss from falling prices but can make a profit from rising prices. In contrast, if one directly owns the share then one faces losses if the price has fallen and will gain no more than the option holder if the price has risen. For this reason options are valuable instruments, the value of which can be calculated from the underlying share value (although this clearly requires other information, notably the volatility of the share).

The Savings-Related Share Option Scheme when introduced by a company allows an employee to take out a five-year SAYE contract of between £10 and £100 per month.[3] At the same time as the employee takes out the contract, the company is required to grant options to the employee with total exercise price equal to the total amount that will be saved over the five years (including interest). The exercise price per share must be at least 90 per cent of the share price on the date the options are granted. If such a scheme is adopted by a company then it must be available to all full-time employees. The fiscal advantage for the employee is that the gains are taxed as capital gains and not income. There are 635 of these schemes in the UK (again there is relatively slow growth, of about 12 new schemes per month).

The option scheme introduced in the 1984 Act does not have to be made available to all employees. If a company introduces such a scheme it is free to choose which of its full-time employees are granted options. Typically companies have reserved these options for top management and they are often referred to as 'Executive Share Options'. The company is allowed to grant options to an employee with a total exercise price up to £100,000 or four times salary, whichever is the greater. The advantage of these schemes for the employee is that, provided the options are exercised after three but before ten years, then the only liability for the employee is to capital gains tax. If the options are exercised outside this limit then full income tax applies to all gains. The exercise price for these options must be set at least as high as the share price on the day that they are granted. The legislation allows for a new set of options to be granted as soon as a set of options is exercised, but the Investment Protection Committees insist that only one set of options per employee is granted every ten years. There are 2318 of these Revenue-approved schemes operating in the UK and their number is growing at a rate of about 60 per month.

Although there are far more of the 1984 schemes than the 1980 schemes operating in the UK, there are very few people involved. In the majority of cases, fewer than 50 employees will have these share options. It is not surprising to see why they are popular. Figure 1 plots the value of an option with share price equal to exercise price (i.e. at the money) against time to expiry date. If we consider an employee earning say £100,000 per year, he will receive options with a typical value of £240,000 under the scheme (assuming 4 per cent dividends). Since these are taxed as capital gains instead

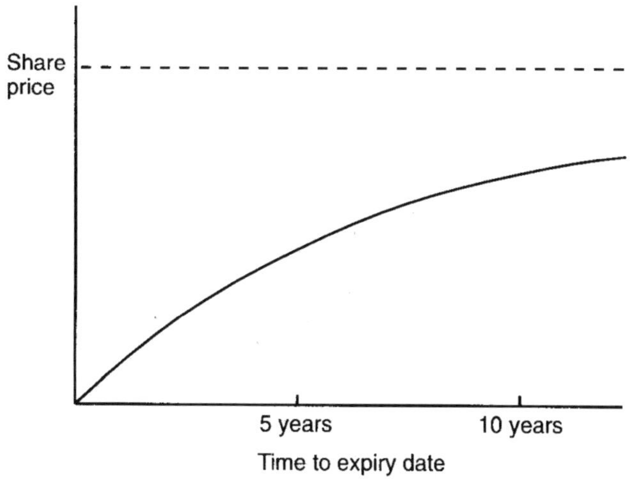

Figure 1 Value of at the money option as a function of time to expiry date (zero dividends)

of income, this is equivalent to an income payment of £420,000. The SAYE options are also valuable. An employee taking out a five-year contract of £100 per month will receive options with a typical value of £3,300. Surprisingly, the average take-up rate of these schemes is only 14 per cent (Wider Share Ownership Council (1986)), although this figure is considerably higher for most recent privatisations. This is a most attractive financial package offered to employees and it is disappointing to have such a low response.

The main argument for options, particularly managerial options, is that they increase effort. This is particularly important if there is a widening of share ownership, because such a widening may increase the managerial discretion in firms. In this respect the 1984 Executive Share Option Scheme is an integral part of the package. A major disadvantage of payment by options, however, is that the manager has an incentive to pick very volatile investments because of the asymmetry in returns that we have mentioned above. This type of problem is likely to be greatest when the exercise price is set very high at the start of the period.

3. Personal Equity Plans

A Personal Equity Plan (PEP) allows one to put up to £2400 per year aside for the purchase of equities, and provided capital gains and dividends are left in the fund they will not be taxed. Not all the money has to be put directly into equities: up to £600 per year can be placed in unit trusts; however, investment trusts are allowable in this limit. PEPs offer a chance to build up a large amount of wealth over a long period. The major fiscal advantage is for investors who pay or are likely to pay capital gains tax and who have a high marginal rate of tax. The scheme has only been operating for a few months but one would expect that these schemes are unlikely to attract large numbers of new investors to the stock market. Their role is probably best viewed as an attempt to deepen the share base amongst existing holders. The schemes do offer a permanent fiscal advantage to holding shares. It is unfortunate that similar permanent benefits are not available to employee shareholders who, because of diversification problems, have a strong argument for long-term fiscal benefits.

4. Privatisations

The role of the privatisations is somewhat different from the policies outlined above. On the one hand, privatisations have been the major force behind the achievement of wider share ownership, and yet there are few specific explicit advantages to encourage ownership. There have been general and specific benefits for employees in the companies and there have also been additional share bonuses (for example, 1 for 10) for individuals who have bought at the time of privatisation and held on to shares for a specified period (or general discounts on future purchases from the privatised industry). Apart from these features, however, there has been nothing to attract people to purchase shares in privatised companies. Despite this fact, they have been exceedingly popular. It is often argued that one of the reasons is that the government is buying wider share ownership by deliberately floating the shares at below their market value. If this is true then the cost of this can be viewed as a direct financial inducement which is equivalent to the advantages associated with the schemes that we have already considered. To discuss this issue, it is helpful to set the pricing of these assets into context. In the most simple economic framework without uncertainty, the general financial implications of privatisation are no different from government borrowing. To see this, consider a simple example where an economy raises £100 billion per year from a nationalised industry, which is used to pay for various services. Suppose now that the government wishes to invest in a project that it will pay for by borrowing money with repayments of, for convenience, exactly £100 billion a year. This project has created a commitment to raise taxes or future borrowing of exactly £100 billion per year. Now suppose that instead of borrowing money, the government decides to sell off the nationalised industry. In a perfect capital market the price of the industry will be exactly equal to the cost of the investment project. The project is, therefore, fully paid for by the sale of assets but now, of course, the government loses its right to the flow of profit from the nationalised industry and must make this up with further taxation and borrowing. The sale has created for the government a commitment to raise future taxes or borrowing of £100 billion a year, a figure exactly equal to their commitment if they had borrowed money instead of selling the industry. In this simple example, borrowing or selling assets are interchangeable activities. If a future government prefers the borrowing solution then it can simply borrow money to pay for the repurchase of the industry on the stock market.

We must look at the deviations from this simple textbook story to find the benefits and costs of the privatisation and wider share ownership programme. First, the price the government may receive from the industry may be greater than the present value of the future profit flows from the industry to the government. One reason is that the privatised company may follow a different pricing policy from that which the government would have pursued, and the company is more valuable for that reason. Assuming the government operates for society's well-being, then the increase in share price will not compensate for the loss in future welfare. Another reason for a higher share price is that the privatised companies may be far more efficient than their nationalised counterparts. The additional revenue raised for this reason is clearly beneficial. This particular supply-side aspect is one of the main arguments that the present government has emphasised for privatisation. There are reasons, however, why the price may be lower than the discounted flow of potential profits. One can be seen by returning to our simple example. One way for the government to raise its money once it has sold the asset is to tax away the profit of the company or simply repurchase the assets at below market price. A government cannot precommit itself not to do this and this must affect the pricing policy. The possibility of this reduces the price that can be obtained for the company. Notice that in this case the price that can be obtained for the company will be higher, the harder it is for the government to tax away the profits in the future or to repurchase the assets at below their market value. Essentially, any policy that is available now to precommit future governments will increase the present value. Wider share ownership may play a role here. Because the assets of privatised companies are sold to the general public in large quantities, one can argue that it may be politically damaging for a future government to purchase the assets back at below the full market price. Therefore, wider share ownership may reduce the probability of this occurring which will, consequently, increase the price that can be obtained for the company. If this argument holds good then it may be possible that the increase in the price achievable in the market may be greater than the cost of achieving wider share ownership and the present value of the possible lost revenue in the future.

The feature about the price differences mentioned so far is that, in an efficient market, there is no reason for the offer price to differ from the opening market price. However, one final reason why the government may not receive the discounted value of future profits is the desire of the government to widen the share base. The argument that is often made is that the government is deliberately setting the offer price below the predicted market price to attract the small investor. It is possible to exaggerate these discounts in relation to the equivalent figures for private flotations. The price has to be set about two weeks before the shares come to the market and therefore some leeway has to be built in to allow for the risk of changes. The larger the flotation the greater the risks, and therefore independent of any wider share ownership aspects we would expect a larger leeway to be associated with privatisations because of their size. It is less clear, though, whether there needs to be a larger leeway if one measures the difference between the best estimate of the price on the first trading day and the offer price as a percentage of the offer price. Also it is unusual for private flotations to have partly paid shares and, consequently, the ratio of the end-of-first-trading-day price to share price is quoted as a percentage of the full share price. In contrast, privatisations have typically been paid in instalments and the profit as a percentage of the initial instalment is quoted. To compare with the private flotation equivalent, the fully paid-up price is a better measure. This reduces the gain percentage terms by at least a half. Finally, the privatisations face the problem that the companies are household names and, for reasons that are rather unclear, this traditionally creates an additional uncertainty about the correct price to pitch. This problem occurs in the private sector too. For example, at the time of writing, the most recent flotation has been the Sock Shop Company. This is a well-known small retail company. The shares rose to 290p on the first day compared with an offer price of 125p.

Table 4 Profit per share at end of first trading day

	As percentage of full price	*As percentage of partly paid price*
British Telecom	33%	86%
British Gas	9%	25%
British Airways	35%	68%
Rolls-Royce	36%	73%

The difficulty is to gauge the valuation of the small purchaser who seems to have highly elastic demands in certain ranges. Finally, one should mention that all the privatisations have occurred against a backdrop of a bull market and, applying the assumption that markets are efficient, then flotation during a bull market should have higher stagging profits than normal. It is only the discount over and above normal that should be attributable to purchasing wider share ownership. Table 4 shows the first day profit following the four most recent privatisations, expressed both as a percentage of the part-paid and as a percentage of the fully-paid offer prices. These should be compared with figures of 5.3 per cent (offers for sale) and 7.3 per cent (tenders) for private flotations (listed issues) as a whole. These figures put the discounts associated with privatisations into context. It is also interesting to note that the other major sale by the government during this period was a large part of Cable and Wireless. In this case there already existed a share price on the market. Were the government aiming to purchase wider share ownership then this would have been an ideal opportunity to come to some arrangement that generated a significant discount for applicants.[4] However, on this occasion the share price at the end of first day trading stood at 303p compared with an offer price of 300p, and the offer was not heavily over-subscribed. Therefore, we can conclude that the stagging profits available on privatisation issues, although significantly larger than average, are not, when placed in context, quite as spectacular as is frequently thought. Of course, there are also additional costs that have to be taken into account: for example, the heavy advertising campaigns that are aimed at potential individual shareholders. These reduce the information-type costs involved with learning how to buy and sell shares, and could be interpreted as a transfer from the government to individuals.

III. Diversification and Transaction Costs

One of the main arguments given against direct ownership of shares is that most individuals cannot diversify significantly if they choose to own shares directly because of transaction costs and information costs. In contrast, if they invest in a mutual fund (i.e. a fund that buys and sells shares) then the transaction costs are much smaller because the fund can take advantage of economies of scale in dealing. Also, because information is a public good, mutual funds are able to spend less money per head researching into companies and yet produce 'more' information per head than can individuals acting independently. It is clear that in an efficient capital market without transaction costs, more diversification is better than less. Figure 2 plots a typical expected portfolio variance against the number of securities, if they are purchased randomly (i.e. naive diversification); see Elton and Gruber (1977). The variance drops dramatically and by the time the portfolio has ten securities the variance is less than 25 per cent of the variance of a one share portfolio. Thus the variance argument can be overemphasised. (Notice, however, that the variance is still over 50 per cent more than that which can be obtained with total diversification, i.e. owning all shares.) Furthermore, if shares are held for long periods without revision then the diversification arguments are of less significance. Also the presence of transaction costs reduces the number of assets it is optimal to own. Consequently, except for individuals with a very small quantity of wealth, the inability to achieve widespread diversification of shares is unlikely to be a major problem.

Indeed, individuals seem to diversify less than is optimal even when transaction costs are taken into account. We have already highlighted how few companies are present in a typical share portfolio. In a study of wealthy investors (mean wealth $¼ million in 1978) King and Leape (1984) found far less diversification than expected and far less than could be explained by transaction costs.

There is, however, a difficulty with diversification but this is not centred on shares but on other assets. Typically, individuals do not diversify their jobs but

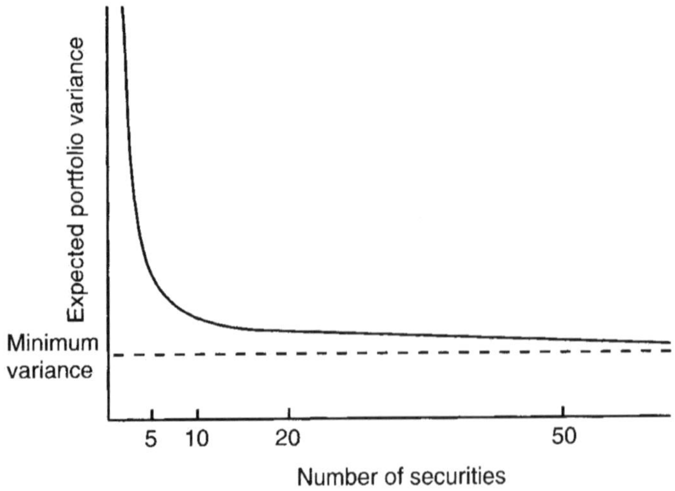

Figure 2 Naive diversification

are tied to one company. For someone earning his exact opportunity cost there is no problem. However, for any worker who has firm-specific skills that are reflected in his wage or who has some monopoly position (perhaps because inside employees cannot be easily replaced), there will be a firm-specific element to future earnings that will not be diversified. This will leave a large proportion of the workers' wealth (his discounted future firm specific earnings) dependent on the success of one company. Individuals also are not diversified on their housing asset. The transaction costs are very large, which prevents rapid movement in to and out of the asset, and, of course, the problems with the rental market make diversification (so that one's wealth depends to only a small extent on the housing market) almost impossible.

A final form of lumpy wealth that should be discussed concerns pensions. Typically, pension funds invest heavily on the stock exchange; therefore it may appear that individuals are already heavily exposed to the stock market. While this is true for some pensions, it is not generally true for most company pensions. The reason is that most occupational pension funds, although invested on the stock market, do not relate their returns to the market. In the 1970s when the market dropped heavily, companies entered to top up these funds and in recent years, with the market rising rapidly, companies have taken contribution holidays which, of course, increase their profits. Consequently it is the employee's company that bears the risk of the stock market rather than the holder of the pension. For this reason it is really housing and firm-specific income that are relevant.

Therefore, we can conclude that although individuals will be able to protect themselves against a great deal of firm-specific risk on the stock market, their overall portfolio is likely to be highly concentrated in some assets. In general, this makes the mutual fund versus direct ownership argument difficult to answer. The usual risk-spreading arguments, economies of scale in transactions and the public good element of information all indicate that mutual funds would dominate direct ownership. On the other hand, the individual is far from diversified elsewhere in his portfolio; therefore, he may gain from choosing specific shares and sectors because their performance may be negatively correlated with the undiversified elements of his portfolio. In this case each shareholder would need an individual specific portfolio and direct ownership may be the only way to achieve this.

Is direct ownership of shares likely to be a growing form of personal wealth? On the one hand it is certainly the case that many small shareholders are still holding their shares in the privatised companies. For example, as we have seen, at the time of flotation there were 2,051,373 individuals holding shares in BT and on 31 May 1986 there were still 1,566,790 individual holders (excluding employee holdings in trust). Of course, it is possible that most of these may not be the original holders; however, it is clear from Table 5 that there are still a staggering number of small holders, three-quarters of all holders having less than 800 shares. One presumes most of these must be the

Table 5 British Telecom shareholders (May 1986)

Number of shares	*Number of holdings*	*Percentage of total number of holdings*
1–399	457,144	29%
400–799	760,582	48%
800–1599	337,733	21%
1600+	26,342	2%

original holders at the time of flotation. It is not, however, universally true that many individual shareholders stay with the company after privatisation. The most spectacular case where this has not happened is Amersham International. In this case 263,000 applications for shares were received, there were 63,760 successful applications but by last year there were only 6572 shareholders, barely more than 10 per cent of successful applicants (all figures excluding employee shareholders). We have argued, however, that Telecom and post-Telecom privatisations have been part of a general programme to achieve wider share ownership and that this could not be said of earlier privatisations. Consequently, one would not expect the holding rates for Telecom (and later privatisations) to be the same as for the pre-Telecom cases, and it would be misleading to try to read too much into the pre-Telecom experience. Does this imply that the new shareholders are likely to become holders of more shares in the future, particularly of non-privatised companies? There is little evidence of this although it is clearly very early days, particularly given that privatisations are occurring at regular intervals and individuals wishing to buy more shares can choose to wait for another privatisation and avoid transaction costs.

There is, however, an alternative interpretation of the evidence. It is possible that many of the holders may simply see themselves as being in the position of traders with no information and with high transactions costs. The transactions costs are very high for small traders. For example, on £600-worth of shares a provincial stockbroker will probably charge something of the order of £23.50 in and £23 out (assuming these are not in the same account), i.e. almost 8 per cent to enter and leave the market. In an efficient market the price of shares reflects all available information and should prove on average to rise in line with other assets over time. With large exit transactions costs small traders may simply choose to hold the particular share as a passive investor. If this is the case then the widening of the share base may stop as abruptly as it started, once there are no more major assets to be privatised. At present it is difficult to assess where the long run trend is going.

Acknowedgement

The author is grateful to the Stock Exchange for supplying information.

Notes

1. Table 2 relates to data collected in late 1985. Since then there have been several privatisations. It is unclear how the figures will have changed because, on the one hand the minimum offer in British Gas was set very low, but on the other hand the value of privatised companies has risen very rapidly.
2. These figures relate to 1978 when the scheme was introduced.
3. The SAYE contract can be extended to seven years in certain cases.
4. Cable and Wireless was involved in this offer for sale so there would have had to be two separate offers rather than a joint one.

References

Dewe Rogerson (1986), survey conducted for Trustee Savings Bank.

Elton, E.J. and Gruber, M.J. (1977), 'Risk reduction and portfolio size', *Journal of Business*.

Estrin, S., Grout, P.A. and Wadhwani, S. (1987), 'Profit sharing and employee share ownership', *Economic Policy*, 4.

Grout, P.A. (1987a), 'Employee share ownership and privatization: some theoretical issues', paper presented to the AUTE Conference, 1987.

——— (1987b), 'Wider share ownership and economic performance', *Oxford Review of Economic Policy*, forthcoming.

King, M.A. and Leape, J.I. (1984), 'Wealth and portfolio composition: theory and evidence', no. 68, Taxation, Incentives and the Distribution of Income ESRC Programme, London School of Economics.

Stock Exchange (1986), 'The changing face of share ownership', London: Stock Exchange.

Wider Share Ownership Council (1986), report by Copeman Patterson prepared for the Wider Share Ownership Council annual forum.

76

The Regulation of Privatized Monopolies in the United Kingdom

M.E. Beesley and S.C. Littlechild[1]

Source: *RAND Journal of Economics*, 20(3), 1989, pp. 454–72.

Summary

This article examines the experience in the United Kingdom with the regulation of privatized monopolies. Its conclusions are (1) that there are significant differences between RPI – *X* (or price-cap) and US rate-of-return regulation, which provides greater scope for bargaining in the former system; (2) that UK regulators have taken seriously their duty to promote competition, but that the existing economic literature is of limited help in this task; (3) that price regulation is likely to be more effective where technology is changing slowly and/or where there are many firms in an industry, whereas the promotion of competition is indicated where technology is changing rapidly; and (4) that the case for RPI – *X* price-cap, rather than rate-of-return regulation, is strongest in telecommunications, gas supply and electricity supply and least strong in gas and electricity transmission grids.

Introduction

Since 1979, the Conservative government has transferred over two dozen public enterprises into private ownership. Most of them previously operated in more or less competitive industries, but three of the largest – namely, British Telecom (BT), British Airports Authority (BAA) and British Gas (BG) – had market shares approaching 100 per cent for their core activities. These three companies now operate under licences containing many obligations and constraints. Independent regulatory authorities, each headed by a director-general, monitor and enforce compliance with licence conditions. The impending privatization of the water and electricity industries will follow a similar pattern, although in these two industries there will be a number of successor companies rather than a single major one. Thus, in the UK there is now a set of five major privatized industries which (in the US context) would normally be thought of as regulated utilities.

The statutory duties of the regulators include protecting the interests of producers (licensees), of consumers of various kinds, and of employees and third parties (e.g. environmental concerns). The wording varies but, for present purposes, three main objectives may be identified in the respective privatization Acts: (1) to ensure that all reasonable demands are met, and that licensees are able to finance the provision of these services; (2) to protect the interests of consumers with respect to prices and quality of service; and (3) to enable or promote competition in the industry. Strictly speaking, the duties of the regulator are not a direct obligation to achieve the stated objectives, but rather require the regulator to carry out his or her statutory functions in the manner which he or she believes is best calculated to achieve these objectives.

Economists may find it helpful to analyse privatization as the instrument of change in a cost-benefit appraisal. The privatization Acts, and in particular the duties of the regulators, may be interpreted as consistent with a formal aim of maximizing the present value of expected net benefits to consumers plus producers, subject to a minimum profit condition and to various constraints on the distribution of benefits to ensure Pareto efficiency (i.e no major interest group is to be made worse off). The problem then faced by each regulator is to interpret this general criterion and make it operational. In particular, the regulator has to balance the interests of present and future consumers, both against each other and against the interests of present and future producers.

This chapter examines the experience of the United Kingdom with regulation of privatized monopolies. In particular, we consider: (1) whether the form of price control adopted is significantly different from US rate-of-return regulation and how far this constitutes an advantage; (2) how regulators have tackled their duty to promote competition and what mode of economic analysis is most appropriate for this; and (3) under what circumstances each of the two main regulatory duties is likely to be performed most effectively and what this implies for government policy.

Price Control

Rate-of-return regulation is well established in the USA. There have been numerous variants across jurisdictions, across industries, and over time, but for present purposes the key features of 'traditional' rate-of-return regulation may be characterized as follows (see Phillips 1969).

The regulated company files a tariff when it wishes to revise its prices. For an agreed test period ('frequently the latest 12-month period for which complete data are available' (Phillips 1969)), the company calculates operating costs, capital employed and cost of capital. The regulator audits these calculations and determines a fair rate of return on capital employed. These data plus assumptions about demand are used to calculate the total revenue requirement. This determines the *level* of the tariff. The *structure* of the tariff has to avoid unfairness and unjust or unreasonable discrimination. The tariff therefore has to be approved on a line-by-line or service-by-service basis, which typically requires the allocation of common costs on the basis of, for example, output, direct costs, revenues, etc. An approved tariff generally stands until the company files to change it, usually on the grounds that the achieved rate of return has become inadequate.

When making its plans for privatizing British Telecom (BT), the Department of Industry's original intention was to adopt a modified rate-of-return regulation. After further discussion and investigation, however (Littlechild 1983), a control on prices, or price-cap, was finally adopted and variants of it have been used for the other privatized utilities.

The key features of this price control are that, for a pre-specified period of four to five years, the company can make any changes it wishes to prices, provided that the average price of a specified basket of its goods and services does not increase faster than RPI – *X*, where RPI is the retail price index (i.e. the rate of inflation) and *X* is a number specified by the government. At the end of the specified period, the level of *X* is reset by the regulator, and the process is repeated.

Rate of Return versus RPI – X

The pros and cons of rate-of-return regulation versus RPI – *X* and other schemes have been frequently discussed (e.g. Littlechild 1983, Vickers and Yarrow 1988, Johnson 1989). Briefly, the main arguments for RPI – *X*, as originally spelled out in the context of privatizing BT and subsequently repeated in other cases, are threefold. First, RPI – *X* is less vulnerable to 'cost-plus' inefficiency and overcapitalization (the 'Averch–Johnson effect'). Because the company has the right to keep whatever profits it can earn during the specified period (and must also absorb any losses), this preserves the incentive to productive efficiency associated with unconstrained profit maximization. Part of this expected increased efficiency can be passed on to customers, via the level of *X*. Prices are therefore lower than they would be under rate-of-return control, without producers being worse off. Second, RPI – *X* allows the company greater flexibility to adjust the structure of prices within the basket, and in principle there is no constraint on prices outside the basket. This is of particular importance where, as with British Telecom, initial prices were thought to be considerably out of line with relative costs, yet 'optimal' prices could not be immediately determined and achieved because of inadequate knowledge of costs and demands, as well as political constraints on speed of adjustment. Third, RPI – *X* is simpler to operate by the regulator and the company. It is more transparent and better focused on the parameter(s) of greatest concern to customers, hence providing them with greater reassurance.

The main counterargument against the incentive and efficiency claim may be summarized as follows. The level of *X* must in practice be set, and repeatedly adjusted to secure a reasonable rate of return. If not, allocative inefficiencies will arise (from prices being out of line with costs), and there will be political pressures from company or consumers. If the criteria for revising *X* are left unclear, this will increase the cost of capital and/or discourage investment. Clear guidelines must therefore be laid down, or must emerge from precedent, for resetting *X*. These guidelines will have to embody an explicit feedback from cost reduction to (eventual) price reduction. This will negate the superior incentive effects claimed for RPI – *X*. Specifically, companies may believe that the short-term advantages of increased efficiency and lower costs will be more than offset by a tougher *X* and therefore lower prices in the next period, and may even induce an adverse change of *X* within the current period. In this view, RPI – *X* is merely a special form of rate-of-return control, embodying no significant net advantage over the US approach on grounds of economic efficiency.

It is also questioned whether RPI – *X* involves as much price flexibility and transparency as claimed. It is further suggested that greater price flexibility may be a disadvantage rather than an advantage, since it allows cross-subsidization which is allocatively inefficient and may be used anti-competitively.[2]

The key questions to pose in this section are thus whether in practice RPI – *X* makes any difference to regulation and, if so, whether the differences are beneficial. Our aim is to assess how RPI – *X* has actually operated in the United Kingdom. We make no attempt to assess its potential effectiveness in or appropriateness for the USA.

Setting and Resetting X

In assessing these arguments, it is necessary to understand the procedures for setting and resetting *X*, and to appreciate the similarities and differences between them.

The RPI – *X* constraint is one of many conditions in the regulated company's licence, all of which are initially set by the government. Unlike the other conditions, it has a limited duration, typically five years, and there is no formal constraint on the magnitude of *X* in any subsequent period. The regulator may modify any licence condition at any time by agreement with the licensee. If the licensee does not agree, the regulator may refer the matter to the Monopolies and Mergers Commission (MMC) and has the authority to modify the licence if and only if the MMC finds the licensees to be acting against the public interest. (With certain exceptions, the licensee has no power to refer possible licence modifications to the MMC.) Renewal of the RPI – *X* constraint, whatever the level of *X*, is equivalent to a licence modification.

The initial level of X is set by the government at the time of privatization, *as part of the privatization process*, whereas X is reset by the regulator *as part of the continuing regulatory process*. This has three important implications.

First, the initial level of X is set as part of a whole package of measures, whose parameters affect the costs, revenues and risks of the regulated company. Some of these parameters pertain to the design of the price control itself, including the duration of the price constraint, its scope in terms of goods and services included, what costs (if any) are allowed to be 'passed through' into prices, and whether constraint is calculated on the basis of historical or expected performance. All these parameters are embodied in licence conditions. Other parameters pertain to the wider regulatory framework, including what other non-commercial obligations or constraints are put on the company, what steps are taken to encourage or restrict competition, what policies are adopted towards suppliers, and so on. Both sets of parameters are fixed by the government more or less simultaneously in full acknowledgement of the interactions and trade-offs between them. They are gradually firmed up and made more precise in the run-up to privatization, culminating in the determination of certain key parameters, including X, prior to publication of the prospectus, a few weeks before flotation. (The striking price of the shares is determined later in this last period and will be heavily influenced by the anticipated changes in the stock-market level to the flotation date.)

In contrast, the resetting of X takes place in a context where these parameters have already been determined. Admittedly they could be changed, and in practice some have been, but to make substantial and unexpected changes would have potentially adverse effects on the company's cost of capital and hence on prices to customers. Moreover, in so far as any proposed changes pertain to the company's licence, if the company does not agree to the changes, the regulator may not wish to run the risk of an unsuccessful appeal to the MMC. There are thus fewer degrees of freedom in resetting X.

Second, the initial level of X is set by the government as owner of the company, whereas X is reset by a regulator who does not own the shares. The government as owner can choose, if it wishes, to take lower proceeds in return for, say, lower prices to customers. The regulator does not have that extra degree of freedom: any shift in favour of one interest group (such as customers) will be at the expense of another group (such as shareholders). The regulator is constrained by the expectations of shareholders and customers, which were established at privatization, and his or her discretion is limited to whatever range is deemed acceptable (or can be so presented).

The third difference between setting and resetting X, which reinforces the previous two, relates to the effect on the company's share price. In both cases the level of X will influence the share price via its effects on expected net revenue streams, so the stock market in fact decides the yield to shareholders. At the time that X is initially set, however, this effect has to be conjectured.

It is not known with any certainty how potential investors will evaluate the company put before them. Nor is there any market valuation of the previous or alternative arrangements with which to compare it. After privatization, however, the views of investors are clearly reflected in the company's traded share price, with its accompanying dividend yield, price earnings ratio, relative risk factor β, etc. A *change* in the stock market's evaluation of the company, following any action by the regulator, in particular the revision of *X*, can be immediately observed in the change in share price. If the market regards the regulator's decision as favourable to the company (i.e. more favourable than expected), its share price is marked up and its cost of capital falls; the opposite happens if the decision is regarded unfavourably. The regulator cannot ignore this consideration in his or her decisions, and it reinforces the greater constraints on resetting *X* than on setting it initially.

To summarize, when setting *X* initially there are many degrees of freedom. *X* is just one of numerous parameters chosen simultaneously in the light of the political and economic trade-offs involved. There is nothing unique, optimal or mechanical about the initial choice of *X*. When *X* is reset, there are significantly fewer degrees of freedom. Nevertheless, there invariably *are* degrees of freedom open to the regulator.

The following two examples will illustrate the above procedures and provide further insights into the characteristics of the RPI – *X* approach.

Setting *X* for Manchester Airport

The Airports Act of 1986 provides for economic regulation of 'designated' airports. At privatization, the Secretary of State designated BAA's three London airports and specified RPI – *X* regulation with *X* = 1 per cent. He also designated Manchester Airport, but delegated to the Civil Aviation Authority (CAA), as regulator, the task of designing Manchester's regulatory constraint. The Airports Act required the CAA, in turn, to seek the advice of the MMC.

Since Manchester Airport was not to be privatized, but was to remain in the ownership of The Manchester City Council, in important respects the considerations involved were different from those where *X* is set or reset for a privatized company. None the less, there are useful insights to be obtained from the MMC report because it sets out in some detail its reasoning on RPI – *X*. (Note that the MMC in this context is an 'advisor' to the regulator, not the regulator itself, and by convention the MMC's report is its only means of conveying that advice.)

The MMC recommended that RPI – *X* be adopted rather than rate-of-return control, for the kinds of reasons given earlier. The Airports Act set the review period as five years, and the MMC was advised that the scope of price control had to comprise landing, parking and passenger charges, but not baggage handling charges. The MMC exercised judgement on four main parameters apart from the level of *X*. It recommended:

1 that there be a single basket for all three charges rather than (say) three separate baskets or additional subconstraints on prices;
2 that the formula be based on a 'tariff basket' (as used for British Telecom), with weights reflecting revenues in the previous year rather than on a 'revenue yield' (as used for BAA) involving predicted revenue per unit and a subsequent correction factor;
3 that no special allowance be made for passing-through costs associated with changes in (non-economic) government regulation, except for three-quarters of any additional airport security costs; and
4 that the present levels of airport charges (which some users claimed were too high) were the appropriate starting point for the formula.

In proposing a level for *X*, the MMC's procedure was first to examine four important issues: future traffic growth, the timing and financing of capital expenditure (particularly the construction of a second terminal), the development of (unregulated) commercial income, and the scope for cost reduction and productivity increases. After exploring a range of alternative assumptions, it adopted those used by the company itself (except on 100 per cent self-financing policy), albeit commenting that some of these assumptions were rather cautious. On the basis of the adopted assumptions, it used the company's financial model to make predictions, for each year over a five-year horizon, of four financial magnitudes (operating profit before and after interest and tax, net current assets, and shareholders' funds) and five financial ratios (gearing or debt–equity ratio, self-financing ratio, interest cover, dividend cover, and return on capital employed). The MMC then 'looked for a value of *X* which would give the necessary degree of protection to users of the airport while leaving the company in a financially sound position and able to carry through its capital expenditure plans' (see MMC 1987). It recommended that $X = 1$ per cent.

Note that the MMC approach was explicitly based on *future predictions*, and a central problem for the MMC was to decide what those predictions should be. It felt that Manchester's assumptions were often cautious, but had no firm basis for making alternative assumptions. (Over time, a regulator would aim to secure an independent source of information on these matters, and the CAA has begun to do so, as have the other regulators in their own areas. We discuss this point further on pp. 219–22.)

This forward-looking approach also applied to the financial calculations. The rate of return on (historic) book capital was only one of nine financial projections and ratios that the MMC looked at. It was projected to decline steadily from the present 18.8 per cent to 9.0 per cent at the end of five years. The MMC merely commented that these rates of return were considered 'consistent with our assessment of the company's financial soundness, which is also reflected in the other projections' (see MMC 1987). Thus, in order to assess the future yield to shareholders, the MMC found it necessary to go beyond a single historic cost ratio.

The CAA proposed to accept the MMC's recommendations. Manchester Airport then appealed to the CAA, arguing for $X = 2$ per cent (i.e. RPI–2) and a revenue yield approach. Other interested parties also made representations. The CAA upheld $X = 1$ per cent but granted Manchester Airport's request for revenue yield. The CAA report hints at the bargaining situation in which it found itself but, in giving its verdict, does not quantify (for example) the differential effect on future cash flows of revenue yield versus a tariff basket approach (see Civil Aviation Authority 1988).

Setting and Resetting *X* for British Telecom

At a late stage in the privatization of British Telecom in 1984, three parameters remained to be determined: the contents of the 'basket' (i.e. the coverage of the price-cap), whether to allow unrestricted resale of BT's leased lines, and the level of *X*. The third parameter had clear implications for prices and proceeds, but so did the other two. Unrestricted resale would allow competitors to use low-priced BT circuits to undercut high-priced BT phone calls: this would mean lower prices, revenues and proceeds. Restricting the basket to local calls and connection charges, for which the monopoly was thought to be strongest, would leave little scope for price reductions. Indeed, British Telecom argued that local calls and connections were already underpriced. On the other hand, incorporating inland trunk calls – where competition was pending, prices were already considerably in excess of costs, and technological prospects were for yet lower costs – would give scope for greater average price reductions across the basket as a whole. (International calls, though known to be highly profitable, were not a serious candidate for inclusion at that time, perhaps reflecting the government's unwillingness to provoke issues of international liberalization at a time when only the USA was clearly pursuing similar policies.)

There was considerable negotiation, involving a wide range of *X*s. (This has been repeated in subsequent privatizations.) The eventual outcome was a package comprising no resale, inland trunk calls in the basket, and $X = 3$ per cent. The detailed calculations on which this figure was based have not been published. (Nor, for that matter, have any of the calculations of other *X*s by government departments.) The offer price for BT's shares was set to ensure that there would be demand from a large number of small shareholders and employees. After flotation, the share price was duly bid up by institutional shareholders, who had excess demand at the offer price.

As BT's profits increased, the question was raised whether they were excessive, even though its prices were within the RPI – *X* constraint. The regulator published an assessment of the appropriate rate of return for BT to earn, concluding that the then observed level of 18 per cent on book value was about right (Director-General of Telecommunications 1986). (For a debate on the adequacy of this assessment, see Beesley *et al.* (1987) and Carsberg

(1987).) BT, in fact, held its prices below the permitted maximum for two years. The regulator also commented on BT's changing price structure, suggesting that rebalancing between inland trunk and local call prices had gone far enough. The regulator's staff published an analysis of price structure based on Ramsey pricing (Culham 1987), although this was viewed with caution by the regulator himself.

The resetting of *X* in 1989 was preceded by a consultative document (Director-General of Telecommunications 1988a) in which the regulator invited comments and suggestions for modification to the whole framework of BT's price control, such as substituting rate of return for RPI – *X*, using revenue yield instead of tariff basket, changing the coverage and duration of RPI – *X*, and so on. Each of these would have required a change in the licence, and therefore allowed the possibility of a challenge by BT and reference to the MMC. An agreement was reached. The regulator reduced the duration of the subsequent review period from five to four years (to reflect the uncertainties involved and BT's own investment planning horizon), slightly extended the coverage of the price-cap (to include directory services), and increased *X* from 3 per cent to 4.5 per cent. He rejected the options of including international calls in the basket, but indicated that he would keep this area under review. He gave no detailed explanation for his choice of *X*, beyond indicating that rate of return was the most important criterion, but not the only one. The other factor mentioned was the financing of investment. He stated that in determining *X*, he had considered the effect on growth in earnings and borrowing, as well as on rate of return (Director-General of Telecommunications 1988b).

The regulator noted that he had taken some account of current cost accounting results. Perhaps a decision based entirely on such a valuation would have indicated higher prices and therefore a lower *X*, which would have been favourable to BT. In explaining his position, however, the regulator stated that current cost accounting should not be used as the sole basis of regulation unless it was also used as the main basis of reporting to shareholders. BT was evidently unwilling to do this. Nor did BT think it advantageous to challenge the decision on *X*, which would have meant submitting to an MMC investigation. As it happens, BT's share price did not move significantly after the announcement, suggesting that changing *X* to 4.5 per cent did not alter the stock market's expectations of BT's future profit stream.

One may surmise that the regulator focused the issue of the future level of *X* on BT's prospective or possible gains in productivity. By making effective use of the degrees of freedom open to him in redefining the formula and of BT's unwillingness to challenge his decision, the regulator was able to get agreement to a higher *X* than would otherwise have been possible. He thus set a target for efficiency, which BT was constrained to follow; he did not base his judgement primarily on evidence of what had *previously* happened in the industry.

Incentives and Efficiency

In light of these two examples, but also taking into account the experiences of the other industries, we may now address the argument on incentives and efficiency.

RPI – *X* and rate-of-return regulation have certain common features. Both accept the need to secure an adequate return for the company's shareholders in order to induce them to continue to finance the business, without conceding unnecessarily high prices at the expense of customers. Nevertheless, there *are* significant differences between the two systems, which give RPI – *X* a potential advantage with respect to incentives and efficiency.

First, RPI – *X* embodies an exogenously determined risk period between appraisals of prices, whereas rate-of-return regulation makes the duration of this period endogenous. Admittedly, US regulatory commissions have tended not to intervene when profits are increasing, provided that prices are not increased (Joskow 1974), but the company can file for a new tariff whenever its performance diminishes, which may be quite frequently. This last is not possible in the UK. The regulator can propose a modification of *X* within the risk period. BT's regulator considered doing this, but he decided not to. Apart from the disincentive effects, there would have been a risk of not getting MMC support for a contested licence modification. BT's regulator also reinforced the concept of an exogenous risk period by reducing its duration from five to four years to limit the extent of uncertainty during the period and stressed that any mid-term review should be limited to major unexpected events outside the company's control (Director-General of Telecommunications 1988b).

Second, RPI – *X* is more forward looking than rate-of-return regulation. The latter tends to be based on historic costs and demands, with adjustments for the future limited (at most) to an adjustment for inflation or the extrapolation of historic trends.[3] In contrast, RPI – *X* embodies forecasts of what productivity improvements can be achieved and what future demands will be and is set on the basis of predicted future cash flows.

Third, there are more degrees of freedom in setting *X* than are involved in rate-of-return regulation. The latter system does allow flexibility (e.g. on the basis of asset valuation, the definition of the rate base, treatment of work in progress, etc.) but it would seem difficult to change these decisions repeatedly. *X* is initially set in the context of negotiations about the whole regulatory framework, including the coverage, duration and form of the price constraints, the extent of non-commercial obligations, the restrictions on competition, and the permissible rate of adjustment from inherited pricing policies. In resetting *X*, the regulator has fewer degrees of freedom, but none the less can modify (at least at the margins) any aspect of this framework and in practice has done so.

Fourth, in setting *X* the UK regulator has more discretion and less need to reveal the basis for decisions than does his or her US counterpart. The US tradition is to place all evidence and reasoning in the public record. In the UK, there is less pressure for due process. The UK regulator is deemed to be a person to whom public policy may be safely delegated, subject only to judicial review on the question of whether his actions are legitimate in terms of the Act. In the UK, neither governments nor regulators have given detailed reasons for their decisions on *X*. This reduces the basis for challenge (by company, competitors or customers).

The consequence of these four differences – exogenous risk period, forward-looking approach, degrees of freedom, and less requirement to explain – is that there is greater scope for *bargaining* in RPI – *X* than in rate-of-return regulation. The level of *X* can reflect negotiations with the company, not only about the scope for future productivity agreements, but also about other matters affecting the company's future, including the details of the price constraint formula, the rate at which competition is allowed to develop, the provision of information, and so on. In short, *X* may be thought of as one of several variables in a political and commercial bargaining process.

It is not suggested that UK regulation is conducted, or even perceived, primarily in terms of bargaining. Nor, on the other hand, is it claimed that there is *no* scope for bargaining in US rate-of-return regulation. Spulber (1989), for example, explicitly characterized US rate hearings as a bargaining process between consumers and the regulated firm. The hearings economize on the transaction costs of forming consumer coalitions and bargaining directly with the firms. The regulatory commission establishes rules for negotiation and mechanisms for the resolution of conflict, selects the issues that are open to debate, acts as arbiter and 'may select an outcome especially if bargaining does not yield a unique solution' (p. 270). Spulber also notes that 'rates are often set *indirectly* through decisions on methods of estimating costs, demand, and rates of return' (p. 272). These insights are not inconsistent with our own assessment. Our claim here is simply that the UK approach offers greater and more direct scope for bargaining, with a correspondingly more active role for the regulator.

There is an important implication for incentives and efficiency. The exogenous risk period and the forward-looking approach mean that the company is not deterred from making efficiency improvements either by fear of confiscation *within* the period or by the belief that allowed *future* prices will simply be an extrapolation of past costs. The regulator can take an independent view of the scope for productivity improvements and can use the discretion and degrees of freedom open to him or her including the absence of a requirement to justify decisions in detail, to negotiate a better deal than would otherwise be possible.

Whether the difference between RPI – *X* and rate-of-return regulation is significant depends on whether the regulator is able to use the additional bargaining power effectively. This depends upon the underlying scope for efficiency improvements and upon the extent and quality of the information available (see Vickers and Yarrow 1988). These factors will differ from one industry to another. We take up this issue in the final section of this chapter.

Price Flexibility

Traditional US rate-of-return regulation requires each price to be individually approved. Changing a price requires filing a new tariff. In principle, RPI – *X* allows any price to be changed at any time, subject only to the price-cap on the average price within the basket. The coverage of the price-cap is approximately 37 per cent of BAA's total revenue, 57 per cent of BT's, 63 per cent of BG's, and probably 95 per cent or more of the water and electricity companies. Again, in principle, there is no constraint on prices outside the basket.

In practice, the regulated companies are typically more constrained than this. BAA has subconstraints on its two major airports; the public electricity suppliers will have separate constraints on their distribution and supply activities; and BT gave a written undertaking (outside the licence) to limit the rate of increase of residential line rentals to RPI + 2. The regulator has since added an additional constraint for BT's private circuits and brought directory services into BT's basket; non-discrimination provisions have also been added for gas. There are also informal constraints: BT's regulator indicated that the rebalancing of trunk and local call prices had, in his view, gone far enough, with the threat of explicit control via modification of the licence. There is always an incentive for a regulator to increase control by refining and extending the basket.

On the other hand, the rebalancing problem was in part attributable to the definition of BT's basket (which included competitive as well as monopoly services) rather than to the RPI – *X* concept itself. As Johnson (1989) has suggested, a key task during each formal review is to redesign the basket(s) to reflect (changing) market conditions.[4] BT's regulator did not in fact press his concerns on relative prices and, in particular, did not adopt the Ramsey pricing philosophy examined by his staff. Any new contested constraint would, in any case, need MMC approval. In effect, the burden of proof is on the regulator to show cause why the rebalancing of prices should not occur. The opposite applies in US rate-of-return regulation, where the burden is on the company to justify the price changes it proposes. There seems no doubt that RPI – *X* allows greater pricing flexibility for the regulated company.

Whether this flexibility constitutes an advantage or a disadvantage depends upon how much need there is for price flexibility (e.g. to reflect changing conditions), how much information is available to the regulator for determining prices in detail, and what other instruments are available for dealing with anti-competitive pricing (e.g. non-discrimination provisions). Again, we return to these issues in the final section of the chapter.

Transparency: Cost Pass-through and the X *Formula*

As privatization has been extended from BT to other utilities, questions have arisen as to whether the simple RPI – *X* constraint is appropriate for industries with different cost and demand structures. For example, should certain costs be passed through into prices, and should the price-cap be based on historic or predicted parameters? Decisions on these questions have implications for profits and proceeds, consumer prices and economic efficiency, as well as having an effect on transparency.

Cost Pass-through

An essential feature of any price-control scheme is the provision to be made for costs which are considered outside the control of the regulated company's management. Several options are available. A simple RPI – *X* constraint, based on expected costs, would expose the company to greater risk, thereby increasing the cost of capital and reducing proceeds. Setting a lower (less stringent) value of *X* would provide a greater margin against risk, but would imply higher prices for customers. Shortening the review period would reduce risk, but also would reduce the scope and incentive for cost savings; the cost of review would also be incurred more frequently.

The fourth possibility is to allow increases in specified costs to be passed through to customers as they occur. This does not eliminate the risk, but simply transfers it from company to customer. It therefore reduces the incentive of the company to seek lower cost or less uncertain sources of supply – for example, by signing fixed-price contracts with suppliers – and increases that incentive for customers. To the extent that prices vary more directly with costs, there may be an increase in allocative efficiency at the expense of productive efficiency. There is a reduction in transparency because of the added complexity in the regulatory formula and the reduced predictability of prices.

UK practice has varied. Both BT and BAA have zero pass-through (except for three-quarters of the unforeseen additional cost of airport security). The price controls in the other three industries make significant provision for pass-through: for BG the costs of buying gas; for the water authorities, the costs of meeting any unforeseen government commitment such as new EC directives (subject to a minimum threshold set at 10 per cent of turnover); and for public electricity suppliers, the costs of purchasing electricity from the generating companies. In the latter case, a yardstick provision (relating a proportion of pass-through to the costs of the industry as a whole) is also envisaged.

Tariff Basket versus Revenue Yield

Another feature of price control is the precise rule for determining allowed price changes. BT's rule is based on the concept of a 'tariff basket', whereby price changes must be such that the average price of the services in the basket, as weighted by *observed* usage in the *previous* year, does not increase by more than RPI – *X*. The water industry has a similar rule. In contrast, price regulation for BAA and BG (and prospectively for the privatized electricity companies) is based on a 'revenue yield' approach, whereby price changes must be such that the *forecasted* average revenue per unit of output (e.g. per passenger or per therm) in the *next* year does not increase by more than RPI – *X*. The necessary forecasts of output are made by the regulated company itself, and the formula involves an additional correction factor to repay or recoup any deviation between prediction and outcome.

The relative incentive effects of each type of formula have been debated and are not unambiguous, although it has been suggested that the revenue yield approach is more open to strategic behaviour by the regulated firm (see Cheong 1989). Revenue yield may be expected to reduce the risk to the regulated company in two ways: it smooths, over time, the average revenue per unit and gives the company (via determination of the forecasts) greater control over the total level of revenue. As with cost pass-through, however, this simply transfers the risks to customers and may reduce the company's incentive to seek a less variable pattern of income. There is also less transparency as the regulatory formula becomes more complex and future price changes less predictable.

In sum, the record on transparency is somewhat mixed. BT's simple RPI – *X* constraint is still in place, but three of the other utilities make heavy use of cost pass-through, and three have revenue yield constraints based on expectations declared by the regulated companies themselves. Such features reduce transparency and efficiency, though they may protect profits and proceeds or may allow a tougher *X* on prices. In the absence of transparency, protection for customers has to depend upon faith in the regulatory process rather than upon an explicitly guaranteed outcome. In this respect, cost pass-through and revenue yield are similar to rate-of-return regulation.

The Promotion of Competition

The promotion of competition is not traditionally associated with the regulation of utilities in the USA. The regulatory commissions have a long record of resisting entry, and it has been persuasively argued that the real purpose of regulation was to protect incumbents from competition (Stigler 1971, Jarrell 1978). Admittedly, competition issues have loomed increasingly large in telecommunications, especially since the 'above 890'[5] decision in 1969. The FCC has been concerned lately with protecting entrants from various forms of anti-competitive pricing. None the less (and in contrast to anti-trust policy) there is nothing in US utility regulation approaching a statutory duty to promote competition.[6]

The UK regulator's duty to promote competition reflects in part the fact that it is not possible to move from a nationalized monopoly to a competitive industry in a single step. The regulator needs the authority and duty to complete the process of transition (as does the Secretary of State), otherwise obstacles to competition might remain in place.

The emphasis placed on this duty differs greatly between industries, depending upon the scope for entry afforded by the underlying technical and market conditions. At one extreme, potential competition is very limited in water supply, sewage disposal and airports.[7] The promotion of competition has a correspondingly small place in the Airports Act of 1986 and the Water Act of 1989. At the other extreme, the 1984 Telecommunications Act and the associated licences are, to an important extent, addressed to the pace at which competition in telecoms is permitted to develop. The regulator has a potential role in the licensing of entrants, specifying the terms on which rivals have access to BT's network and other facilities, and constraining BT's pricing policy (which might encourage or deter entry). Analogous provisions are embodied in the Electricity Act of 1989 and licences. To a lesser extent, this is true of the Gas Act of 1986 and licence, where the role of the regulator in promoting competition in gas supply has subsequently been strengthened as a result of the MMC report on that industry.

The duty to promote competition cannot be taken in isolation. The regulator needs to take into account a variety of other economic, social and political considerations. Specifically, he or she has duties to secure the financing of licensed activities and protect the interests of consumers. In most situations, different policies will be indicated, depending upon the weight given to each duty. We now give two examples of how regulators have in practice resolved this issue. We then consider the appropriate mode of economic analysis and suggest a direction for future research in order to improve the effectiveness of regulation to promote competition.

An Illustration from Telecommunications

When Mercury wished to interconnect with BT, it was unable to agree on terms, and the regulator, in accordance with BT's licence, was called upon to adjudicate.

One option, stemming primarily from the duty to protect the interests of customers and using traditional welfare economic concepts, was to attempt to calculate levels of interconnect charges which maximized allocative efficiency. This would have required a detailed calculation (for each possible level of interconnect charges) of Mercury's likely outputs in relevant markets, BT's consequent costs and losses in revenue, and the effect of these revenue losses on BT's prices and outputs. Mercury's market share would fall out as a residual from this exercise. However, the approach would beg the question of how to determine Mercury's output reaction function, and Mercury's implied strategy of entry and growth would not necessarily be consistent with promoting competition.

An alternative option was to begin with the duty to promote competition and therefore to examine the impact of the interconnect decision on Mercury's strategy. This would have meant looking at the situation from Mercury's perspective. The margins it could secure were central to its prospects for building up its voice (and other) telephony business. Favourable access to BT's local distribution system meant that Mercury's customers could get not only the benefits of lower prices for calls made over Mercury's long-distance system, but also discounts on virtually all calls delivered by BT. Furthermore, the prospects for future entrants could be expected to depend on the terms achieved for Mercury. Of course, the interconnect charges to be paid by Mercury and others were only part of the story about predicting entry. The effects on BT's costs, revenues, prices and outputs also needed to be taken into account. Nevertheless, the thrust of this approach is quite different from the allocative efficiency approach, and it would be surprising if its policy implications were the same.

Oftel's *Annual Report for 1985* simply noted that the Director-General 'established the prices, based on BT's costs, which should be paid by MCL (Mercury) to BT for use of its network'. No explanation of this cost basis was given, perhaps to avoid any statement that might evoke a test of the decision by the courts. It is widely felt that the phrase 'based on BT's costs' has to be taken with a pinch of salt. There was almost certainly no attempt to run a model of allocative efficiency. The essence of the matter was that the regulator either had to provide sufficient inducement for Mercury to enter the market, or his decision would put at risk a central point of the government's strategy – that Mercury should become a serious competitor. The regulator's decision does seem to have established a key condition for future effective competition. When it came to the crunch, therefore, the regulator did not let considerations of allocative efficiency stand in the way of a judgement about the promotion of competition, although the precise basis for this judgement was not given.

An Illustration from Gas

The second example is found in the MMC's 1988 report on gas. There had been numerous complaints against BG's policy of discriminating in price, according to whether its customers had access to an alternative fuel (typically oil). These customers, industrial consumers of substantial quantities of gas, lay outside the RPI – X price-control basket, but were nevertheless within the regulator's general duty to enable competition. The privatization acts empower a regulator to refer any practice to the MMC. The regulated companies are also subject to general competition law, and it was in fact the Director-General of Fair Trading who referred BG to the MMC.

It is well known that, from an allocative point of view, price discrimination may have certain desirable properties. It can lead to greater output and aggregate value of output than a uniform monopoly price.

Perfect discrimination yields an output and aggregate value of output precisely equal to that of perfect competition. Nevertheless, the MMC opposed BG's policy of price discrimination, primarily because it would deter new entry.[8] The MMC acknowledged that the prohibition of price discrimination was likely to make some customers worse off, and would limit BG's ability to compete against the oil companies. However, it believed that these disadvantages would be outweighed by the improved prospects for new entry which would be necessary to create 'gas-on-gas' competition, to which the MMC attached great importance.

This conclusion was consistent with the regulator's own view as given in evidence to the Commission. The MMC found BG's policy to be against the public interest and accepted the regulator's suggestion that BG should be required not to discriminate in price. It recommended specific provisions against discrimination to be incorporated in BG's licence. The regulator subsequently negotiated a licence modification of this kind. (Similar non-discrimination provisions have been incorporated into the draft licences of the electricity companies.)

Economic Analysis of New Entry

The two examples presented above indicate that regulators have taken seriously their duty to promote competition, and that in so doing they have implicitly gone beyond traditional welfare economics. We now consider what the problem of promoting competition involves, and what kinds of economic analysis might be most helpful in that task.

Promoting competition involves facilitating the entry of new competitors, including the entry of existing competitors into new parts of the market. To do this effectively involves three main steps. The first is to assess the likely pattern of entry over the foreseeable future. This will require a prediction of likely changes in technological and market conditions, since these will often provide the necessary opportunities for entry. The second step is to identify decisions that the regulators themselves can make in order to change the regulatory framework, and to assess the likely impact of these changes on the future pattern of entry. Examples of these regulatory decisions (in the British system) are the licensing of new entrants, identification and prohibition of anti-competitive practices, determination of interconnect or common carrier (use of system) charges, collection and publication of relevant information, and so on. The third step is to choose which regulatory changes to make. Other things being equal, the preferred changes are those likely to have the greatest positive impact on entry. This is not always an obvious calculation, however, particularly since the whole time path of entry must be considered. The telecommunications duopoly policy, for example, reflects in part the view that where an entrant has to make a large cost commitment it is more likely to enter, the less swiftly is a subsequent entrant able to attack the same market (Carsberg 1987).

In order to promote competition, the regulators' essential task is to assess the relation between their actions (which will include regulatory changes as well as determining disputes and constraining prices) and the probability that entry will actually occur. They will need to consider the scale and time path of entry and its impact on all the parties involved as well as on other potential entrants. It will prove impracticable to analyse all the possible avenues and problems of entry simultaneously, however, if only because the regulators' time and resources are necessarily limited. The regulators therefore have to be selective, that is to take a view about where entry might be most likely, if encouraged, and hence most effective in producing net benefits to consumers and producers, as they will be refined by the impact of entry.

What kind of economic model is most helpful in doing this? It is natural to begin with the same comparative static welfare economic approach that is conventionally used to analyse the problem of price control. This model takes as given (1) the relevant cost and demand functions, and (2) the extent of competition in the market, which essentially depends on the conditions of entry. These assumptions are used to trace the implications for (equilibrium) prices, outputs, profits, number and size of firms, and so on. It is then asked: what kinds of constraints on the regulated firm will maximize aggregate net surplus subject to securing adequate protection for various classes of consumers? Rate-of-return regulation is set firmly in this world. There is an extensive literature aimed at determining optimal pricing and investment rules that maximize allocative efficiency, taking costs and demands as given.

RPI – *X* requires the relaxation of the first assumption. It does *not* assume costs and demands are given or known: indeed, the problem is to provide adequate incentives for the company to discover them. The aim is to stimulate alertness to lower cost techniques and hitherto unmet demands. The emphasis is on productive rather than allocative efficiency (and even the RPI – *X* price-cap reflects distributional rather than allocative considerations). This is an Austrian world rather than a neo-classical one. (Austrian is here defined broadly to include both Leibenstein's familiar *X*-efficiency on the cost side and the corresponding *Y*-efficiency on the demand side proposed by Beesley (1973).)

The problem of promoting competition requires the relaxation of the second assumption. Here, the extent of competition and the conditions of entry are not given: the essential regulatory task is to ascertain what they are and how they might be changed. The object is to choose the regulatory policy which will maximize new entry, subject to adequate protection of the interests of producers and present consumers. Nor are costs and demands assumed given or known. Indeed, one of the means of promoting competition is precisely to *shift* potential entrants' assumptions about the costs and possibilities of serving new markets, and one of the expected benefits of entry is a shift in the incumbents' own assumptions about these parameters.

Substantial recent literature on potential competition and contestable markets analyse the relationship between conditions for entry and price. At least one textbook on regulation (Spulber 1989) is more concerned with entry and competition than with static welfare analysis of pricing for a protected monopoly. There have also been important developments in the economic analysis of strategic behaviour (Dixit 1982).

In practice, however, these models are of limited use for the task of promoting competition. Although they analyse the effects of any given entry conditions, they do not help to identify what the entry conditions *actually are* in any particular situation, nor what the entry conditions *would be* as a result of any particular regulatory change. Thus, they are of limited assistance to the regulators in assessing how much entry will take place, and where, when, and by whom, as a result of different regulatory policies.

Briefly, an alternative approach would run as follows. In order to identify the entry conditions obtaining at any time, and to predict the consequences of a change in policy, the regulators need to start from the question: where and when will entry be *profitable*? This in turn requires looking at the situation from the point of view of the potential entrant. Given its assets, knowledge, resources, its ability to buy at current input prices, and the pricing and product policy of the incumbent(s), what parts of the existing market can it profitably develop? What (if any) better contracts with respect to cost, including superior productivity, can it establish? Where have incumbents missed possibilities for adding value or been unable for various reasons to supply? How will incumbents react to its entry? Can it survive their response? In short, what advantages does it have over the incumbents, and how long will these advantages last? The answers to these kinds of questions determine the central calculation for an entrant: the equity that the entrant needs to ante-up in order to be a player in the game (i.e. its risk capital reflecting its potential sunk cost if unsuccessful), and its potential net revenue stream if successful (the reward for taking the risk).

Admittedly, the models referred to earlier assume profit maximization, but they do not ask where the profit is coming from. They deal with profit in a purely formal way which does not highlight the need for information about entry and gives little help to the regulators in identifying the relevant factors in practice. Future research might usefully reflect the Austrian insistence on profit as the engine of capitalism and, in particular, on the exploitation of hitherto unforeseen profit opportunities as central to the continuing market process (Schumpeter 1950; Kirzner 1973, 1985). Examination of actual rather than hypothetical situations is also necessary, as Coase (1988) has long argued. Applications of the proposed approach (e.g. Beesley (1986) on airlines and Beesley and Laidlaw (1989) on telecommunications) suggest that there is more scope for promoting competition than has hitherto been recognized.

Regulatory Effectiveness

We argued in the second section that the RPI – *X* system offers more scope for bargaining, especially on productivity, than rate-of-return regulation. The importance of this depends upon the potential for productivity improvements and on the information available to the regulator to exploit this situation effectively. We also argued that RPI – *X* offers the company more flexibility in pricing. Whether this is an advantage or disadvantage depends on the need for price changes, on the information available to the regulator, and on the existence of alternative instruments of policy. In the third section we noted the UK regulator's explicit duty to promote competition, which in practice has been taken very seriously. Regulatory effectiveness depends upon the scope for new entry and, again, on the information available to the regulator.

In order to carry out the twin tasks of controlling prices and promoting competition, the regulator thus needs to acquire adequate information concerning the scope for cost reductions and the extent and effects of new entry. The regulator will also need to transmit information to incumbents and potential entrants, in order to improve both efficiency and the prospects for entry. The generation and dissemination of information are therefore at the heart of regulatory effectiveness.[9]

Various devices intended to give companies the incentive to provide the regulator with relevant information have been suggested in the recent economic literature.[10] Typically these devices are set within the context of a given technology and product line: innovation and entry are not encompassed. Once the latter phenomena are admitted, it becomes apparent that the information which the regulator acquired is ephemeral: over time, it gradually becomes obsolete and needs to be replenished. Thus, if the regulator is to succeed in either of the two tasks – controlling prices or promoting competition – he or she needs to acquire information at a rate faster than that at which it decays. The feasibility of doing this depends on two main parameters.

First, there is the rate at which the underlying technological and market conditions change. The slower the change, the more likely the regulator will gradually come to acquire more relevant information and will be in a position to set realistic productivity targets (and, for that matter, performance standards) and determine allocatively efficient price structures for the regulated utility. The regulator will also be able to assess the effects of new entry more accurately. Where the underlying rate of change is slow, new entry is less attractive. In these circumstances, there is likely to be greater payoff to controlling prices than to promoting competition. Conversely, the faster the underlying rate of change in the industry, the more likely it is that the regulator's knowledge will decay faster than he or she can replenish it, and hence the less likely it is that he or she will be able to control prices efficiently.[11] However, rapid change provides the very circumstances in which new entry is feasible. Hence, in these circumstances, the regulator's priority should be to promote competition rather than control price. In the longer term, as the industry becomes more competitive, this will tend to reduce the need for price regulation.

The second main possibility of the regulator acquiring information faster than it decays is where there are multiple sources of information. Where there are many companies in an industry, even though they necessarily differ one from another, they may be sufficiently similar that the regulator can use the performance of one as an indication of what another could achieve. This yields a basis for setting efficiency targets in an RPI – *X* price-control scheme. In these circumstances, the regulator's priority is to ensure that the laggards improve to match the (observed) performance of the leaders, while providing sufficient incentive for the leaders to stay ahead and blaze the way for the next round of target setting. The threat of takeover (if either the leaders or the laggards lapse into managerial slack) is an important aid in this endeavour. Conversely, where there is only one company in an industry, the regulator is more dependent upon that company for information, and his or her effectiveness in bargaining for productivity improvements is thereby reduced.

The prospects for generating information for regulatory purposes should therefore be an important argument in a government's decisions about the structure of the industry and the nature of the regulatory regime. Where the underlying rate of change is slow, there will be information advantages in creating and maintaining many similar firms for purposes of comparison.[12] Of course, it is economically efficient to do this only where the benefits of greater information are expected to outweigh any economies of scale or scope. This is more likely to be the case where a regulated industry is mainly an aggregate of several local monopolies (as with airports and local distribution networks for gas and electricity) than where the natural monopoly element is itself on a national scale (as with bulk transmission grids for gas and electricity).

An Illustration from the United Kingdom

These ideas may be represented in a 2 × 2 matrix. In Tables 1 and 2, the columns represent the underlying rate of change in technology (and market conditions), classified as 'Low' or 'High', while the rows represent the number of regulated companies in the industry, classified as 'One' or 'Many'. Each regulated industry, or part thereof, can be located in one of the resulting four cells.

Table 1 shows the matrix as it appears today for the five regulated utilities in the UK. The foregoing analysis indicates a policy of promoting competition in telecoms, gas supply, and electricity generation and supply. Water and electricity distribution provide the most promising conditions for price control. The difficulty of the single regulated utility presents itself in airports, electricity transmission, and gas transmission and distribution.

Table 1 Present position

	Rate of change of technology	
	Low	*High*
Number of regulated firms:		
Many	Water Electricity distribution	
One	Electricity transmission Gas transmission and distribution Airports	Telecoms Electricity generation Electricity supply Gas supply

Table 2 Potential position

	Rate of change of technology	
	Low	*High*
Number of regulated firms:		
Many	Water Electricity distribution Gas distribution Airports	Telecoms Electricity generation Electricity supply Gas supply
One	Electricity transmission Gas transmission	

The structure of those industries characterized by a low rate of technological change could only be altered by government legislation (and clearly many other factors would need to be considered). Where there is a high underlying rate of change, however, the promotion of competition – at its simplest, by licensing new entry – would shift those industries in the one-firm cell into the many-firm cell. With the development of competition, specific industry regulation would become less necessary; whatever needed to be done to help keep competition active might well be performed by the anti-monopoly legislation common to all industries. In other words, deregulation might be indicated.

Table 2 shows the situation that could result in the United Kingdom if the policies discussed were put into effect. In telecoms, gas supply, and electricity generation and supply, the regulator's role of promoting competition would be paramount, perhaps via general competition policy rather than by specific regulation. In water, airports, and gas and electricity distribution, an emphasis on price control would be indicated, with prospects of success. The problematic areas would be national transmission grids for gas and electricity. Paradoxically, because transmission is so crucial to supply, regulatory attention in these natural monopolies would need to focus also on the promotion of competition in upstream and downstream markets via the terms to be set for the use of transmission facilities. So for electricity and gas transmission (and distribution too) the dual role of the regulator might be expected to continue in the foreseeable future.

RPI – X versus Rate of Return Revisited

Future research might usefully assess US and UK regulatory systems in terms of the ideas suggested in this section, comparing their abilities to generate and use relevant information, depending upon rate of technological change and number of regulated firms. We may illustrate this by re-examining the initial question of the relative merits of RPI – *X* and rate-of-return regulation with respect to incentives and efficiency. We argued that RPI – *X* is indeed different because (*inter alia*) it incorporates a fixed risk period within which gains above the productivity bargain can be kept by the regulated firm(s). These productivity gains are potentially larger at the time of privatization than subsequently. They are also potentially larger the more rapidly technological conditions are changing, and where there are many different firms, with leaders blazing the way for laggards to follow.

Relating these considerations to the five regulated utilities, it follows that the case for RPI – *X* price control rather than rate-of-return regulation is strongest in telecoms, gas supply and electricity supply, where technology is indeed changing. If the aim is to 'hold the fort' until competition arrives, as Beesley and Littlechild (1986) put it, RPI – *X* will do this with greater potential productivity gains. At the other extreme, where there is less prospect of a shift in technology and only one firm in the industry, as with the electricity and gas transmission grids, there is less scope for bargaining about the potential for improvements in efficiency and no built-in mechanism to give the regulator scope for bargaining via directly relevant comparisons. Here, the grounds for preferring RPI – *X* are least strong.

In the remaining industries, notably water, gas, and electricity distribution, there is a strong reason for preferring RPI – *X* initially, given the potential productivity gains on privatization and the regulator's potential for generating superior information to that available to the companies taken separately. Admittedly, if there is indeed a low underlying rate of change in technology, both the scope for improvement and the discrepancies between companies may be expected to reduce over time, and in practice an RPI – *X* regime may gradually become indistinguishable from that of rate-of-return regulation. However, a permanently low underlying rate of change cannot be taken for granted. For the present, RPI – *X* seems to offer advantages.

Notes

1. We gratefully acknowledge helpful comments by Stanley Besen, Jan Acton, and a referee. It was written before the authors were associated with the Office of Electricity Regulation and does not necessarily represent the views of that office.

2. Other issues lie beyond the scope of this chapter. For example, is has been suggested that RPI – *X* may offer less incentive to maintain service quality (Vickers and Yarrow 1988; Besen 1989). The framework of regulation needs to be designed accordingly and the acts and licences do in fact reflect this consideration.

3. 'Commissions base costs upon a test year due to the need for certainty – the need to avoid unresolvable factual disputes that threaten lengthy proceedings, arbitrary decisions, and court reversals. Although last year's prices will differ from likely future prices, at least they are known. One thereby avoids what would be an endless and unresolvable argument about what future costs will probably be' (Breyer 1982). 'The Commissions have been hesitant to make future forecasts of consumer demand, often preferring instead to assume that the test period demand conditions will hold in the immediate future' (Phillips 1969). Joskow (1974) noted that 'a few commissions have begun to cautiously use "projected" test year results, allowing companies to predict cost and demand conditions one or two years ahead', but this does not appear to have become standard practice. Automatic adjustment mechanisms are widely used, however (Joskow 1974; Spulber 1989).

4. The possibility of a company cross-subsidizing competitive uncapped services out of monopoly-capped services is frequently mentioned in the literature (e.g. Johnson 1989; Besen 1989; Spulber 1989) but to date this has not been a major issue in UK regulatory experience.

5. In 'Allocation of frequencies in the bands above 890 Mcs', 27 FCC 359 (1959), the Federal Communications Commission authorized the licensing of private communications systems to give large users an alternative to obtaining service from AT & T. Although this decision had little immediate effect, it set the stage for the introduction of Specialized Common Carriers, such as MCI, which eventually led to the competitive supply of ordinary long-distance telephone services.

6. The text by Phillips (1969) devotes just two and a half of its 774 pages to the then novel concept of strengthening the forces of market competition.

7. Competition *for* the market, via franchising, has been much discussed (see Vickers and Yarrow 1988; Spulber 1989), but is beyond the scope of this chapter.

8. 'By relating prices to those of the alternatives available to each customer, it places BG in a position to selectively undercut potential competing gas suppliers; this may be expected to act as a deterrent to new entrants and to inhibit the development of competition in this market' (MMC 1988, paragraph 8.38(b)).

9. Like the market participants, the regulator needs to be alert to hitherto undiscovered opportunities for profit, deriving from both the cost and demand sides. Kirzner (1985) has argued that 'nothing within the regulatory process seems able to simulate, even remotely well, the discovery process that is so integral to the unregulated market'. Our argument is not that the regulatory process is more effective than the competitive market process. (As indicated, the regulator has some advantages and some disadvantages compared to market participants.) Rather, our argument is that an effective regulator needs to be alert in order to promote greater alertness in markets that are not (yet) competitive.

10. See, for example, the surveys and references in Vickers and Yarrow (1988) and Spulber (1989).

11. Beesley and Glaister (1983) argued that this is the case in the taxicab industry.

Wiseman (1957) has long argued that the very notion of an optimal price is untenable once uncertainty and change are admitted.

12. When dealing with mergers, the Water Act of 1989 embodies instructions to the MMC to this effect.

References

Beesley, M.E. (1973) 'Mergers and economic welfare', in Arthur Selden (ed.) *Mergers, Takeovers and the Structure of Industry*, IEA Readings, no. 10, pp. 73–80.

—— (1986) 'Commitment, sunk costs and entry to the airline industry: reflections on experience', *Journal of Transport Economics and Policy* XX (2), May, 173–90.

—— and Glaister, S. (1983) 'Information for regulating: the case of taxis', *Economic Journal* 93: 594–615.

—— and Laidlaw, B. (1989) *The Future of Telecommunications: An Assessment of the Role of Competition in UK Policy*, Research Monograph no. 42, London Institute of Economic Affairs.

—— Gist, P. and Laidlaw, B.H. (1987) 'Prices and competition on voice telephony in the UK', *Telecommunications Policy* 11, 230–6.

—— and Littlechild, S. (1986) 'Privatization: principles, problems and priorities', in *Lloyds Bank Review*, July 1983.

Besen, S.M. (1989) *Statement Submitted by the National Cable Television Association*, in Federal Communications Commission CC Docket no. 87–313, 3 August.

Breyer, S. (1982) *Regulation and Its Reform*, Cambridge, Mass.: Harvard University Press.

Carsberg, B. (1987) 'Regulation of British Telecom', *Telecommunications Policy* 11, 237–42.

Cheong, K. (1989) 'The British experience with price cap (RPI – *X*) regulation', *Nera Topics*, London: NERA.

Civil Aviation Authority (1988) *Conditions as to Airport Charges in Relation to Manchester Airport under Section 40 (3) of the Act*, CAA Report, London, 25 February.

Coase, R.H. (1988) *The Firm, The Market and The Law*, Chicago: University of Chicago Press.

Culham, P.G. (1987) 'A method for determining the optimal balance of prices for telephone services', Oftel Working Paper, no. 1, March.

Director-General of Telecommunications (1986) *Review of British Telecom's Tariff Changes, November 1986*, London: Oftel.

—— (1988a) *The Regulation of British Telecom's Prices*, A Consultative Document, London: Oftel, January.

—— (1988b) *The Control of British Telecom's Prices*, London: Oftel, July.

Dixit, A.K. (1982) 'Recent developments in oligopoly theory', *American Economic Review* 72, 12–17.

Jarrell, G.A. (1978) 'The demand for state regulation of the electric utility industry', *Journal of Law and Economics* 21, 269–95.

Johnson, L.L. (1989) 'Price caps in telecommunications regulatory reforms', *RAND Note* N-2894-MF/RC, January.

Joskow, P.L. (1974) 'Inflation and environmental concern: structural change in the process of public utility price regulation', *Journal of Law and Economics* XVII (2), 291–328.

Kirzner, I.M. (1973) *Competition and Entrepreneurship*, Chicago: University of Chicago Press.

——— (1985) 'The perils of regulation – a market process approach', in I.M. Kirzner (ed.) *Discovery and the Capitalist Process*, Chicago: University of Chicago Press.

Littlechild, S.C. (1983) *Regulation of British Telecommunications' Profitability*, London: Department of Industry.

Monopolies and Mergers Commission (1988) *Gas*, Cm 500, London: HMSO.

——— (1987) *Manchester Airport p.l.c.: A Report on the Economic Regulation of the Airport*, Report MMC 1, Civil Aviation Authority, London, December.

Oftel (1986) *Report of the Director-General of Telecommunications (Annual Report 1985)*, London: HMSO, June.

Phillips, C.F. Jr (1969) *The Economics of Regulation*, Holmwood, Ill.: Irwin.

Schumpeter, J.A. (1950) *Capitalism, Socialism and Democracy*, 3rd edn, New York: Harper & Row.

Spulber, D.F. (1989) *Regulation and Markets*, Cambridge, Mass.: MIT Press.

Stigler, G.J. (1971) 'The theory of economic regulation', *The Bell Journal of Economics* 2, 3–21.

Vickers, J. and Yarrow, G. (1988) *Privatization: An Economic Analysis*, Cambridge, Mass.: MIT Press.

Wiseman, J. (1957) 'The theory of public utility price – an empty box', *Oxford Economic Papers* 9, 56–74.

77

Privatization in the United States

Ronald D. Utt

Source: *Privatization and Economic Efficiency: A Comparative Analysis of Developed and Developing Countries*, eds A. F. Ott and K. Hartley (Aldershot: Edward Elgar, 1991), Chap. 5, pp. 73–86.

1. Introduction

For much of the world, privatization is synonymous with divestiture – the process whereby a well-defined government-owned and operated commercial enterprise such as a shipyard, telecommunications company or agricultural estate is transferred to private sector owners and operators. The privatization programme in Great Britain under Prime Minister Thatcher is perhaps the best known and most successful privatization programme where major divestitures of large, well-defined commercial enterprises with extensive holdings of physical assets have occurred over an extended period of time. Similarly successful programmes in France, Bangladesh, Jamaica, Honduras and Costa Rica have also followed this pattern, and the ambitious intentions in Mexico, Argentina and the newly-freed East European countries will also rely largely on the process of divestiture.

For the most part, the emphasis on divestiture rather than contracting-out and vouchers is appropriate for these countries because their governments had come to acquire an extensive array of commercial enterprises during the middle decades of this century. In the postwar era, successive socialist governments in Europe nationalized scores of industries as part of a scheme to guide the economy more directly, or for the simple expedient of preserving employment in otherwise bankrupt and obsolete industries. In the developing world, the poor, newly-independent countries of Africa and Asia saw state ownership of commercial enterprises as a key ingredient of a strategy of economic growth. Many adopted a policy of nationalizing the few foreign-held firms leftover from the colonial era and created many new ones as part of an overall development strategy to concentrate resources in the industrial sector. For the most part, these state-directed development schemes were failures and many of these countries now see privatization as a way of enhancing their development prospects by shifting toward greater reliance on free enterprise and competitive markets. Thus, for such countries a privatization process that relies chiefly on divestitures is the foundation of any transition from state control to market direction.

For a variety of reasons, the United States seldom succumbed to the temptation to nationalize its commercial enterprises, relying instead on the process of regulation and changes in the tax laws to encourage the attainment of an ever-changing series of national economic and social goals. With the exception of inconsequential fringe political parties, mainstream political and economic thought among both liberals and conservatives, Democrats and Republicans had as its foundation a strong commitment to the capitalist model and the concept of private property. As a consequence, the US government has generally avoided the ownership and operation of commercial enterprises, leaving it with very few state-owned entities suitable for the more traditional forms of divestiture as has occurred in Great Britain and elsewhere.

2. Divestiture Opportunities in the US

There are, of course, several major commercial-like enterprises owned and operated by the government and these have frequently been suggested as ideal targets for privatization through divestiture. These include AMTRAK, the government-run rail passenger service that the government acquired and re-established in 1972 when the privately-owned rail companies abandoned their passenger service because of persistent financial losses and the belief that such a service could never be made profitable. AMTRAK requires subsidies of around $600 million per year and former President Reagan proposed its privatization in several of his budgets. The Tennessee Valley Authority (TVA), a major producer of hydro-electric power for the middle south of the United States, is also a potential candidate for privatization. TVA was created during the Great Depression of the 1930s to provide electricity, investment and jobs to one of the most economically depressed regions of the nation. It has always been owned by the government, and although not well managed (it lost more than $10 billion in a failed attempt to establish an ambitious nuclear programme), there are no official intentions to privatize it nor any such studies underway. The chief reason for this stems from the likely political opposition that would greet such a proposal. TVA's customers have access to low cost, subsidized electricity and fear that privatization would eliminate this.

Another major commercial enterprise owned by the government is the uranium enrichment facilities in Oak Ridge, Tennessee and Portsmouth, Ohio. Created during World War II to provide the plutonium for the first atom bombs, these facilities went on to provide much of the enriched uranium used in nuclear power generation facilities throughout the free world. At one time these two facilities were the sole supplier of enriched uranium but they now must compete with newer enterprises in Europe, and will soon have to compete with the Japanese. Although the Reagan Administration actively explored options to privatize these facilities, political opposition from a variety of sources continues to prevent any meaningful divestiture of this programme. At present, these facilities operate under contract by a major American corporation.

Another divestiture that has been actively pursued, but without much success, is that of the Naval Petroleum Reserves, comprising oil fields in Wyoming and California, that were acquired by the government early in this century to assure a reliable supply of oil to the fleet at a time when it shifted from coal to oil and when the availability of commercially-provided oil supplies was still somewhat uncertain. The advent of a thriving private oil supply market quickly rendered this concept both uneconomic and obsolete, yet the government held on to the assets and now sells all of the oil produced on the commercial market. Although efforts to privatize these fields have had important support from the President and many in Congress, political obstacles have prevented it from occurring and the reserves are likely to remain in government hands for the foreseeable future.

Perhaps the greatest divestiture opportunity confronting the government is of the United States Postal Service, the government corporation holding a legal monopoly on the delivery of first and third class mail. Although no serious effort beyond US Office of Management and Budget proposals has been considered, the Postal Service is really nothing more than just another commercial information system, albeit a costly and inefficient one. In the provision of those mail services where the private sector is allowed to compete – bulk packages and overnight mail – the private sector offers better service at lower costs, and has captured more than 90 per cent of both markets. Employing over 900000 workers and with revenues approaching $50 billion per year, the US Postal Service offers the best target of opportunity for a divestiture that could markedly improve the mail service available to the American people. But again, as in the cases described above, major political obstacles confront any effort to alter the current institutional arrangement. Chief among them are the 900000 postal employees and managers whose high wages and low productivity would be materially altered if the postal service were to be privatized and subjected to competition along all product lines. In his last budget proposal, former President Reagan suggested a phased-in, four-part postal privatization plan, but it was largely ignored and the Administration of President Bush has chosen not to pursue the privatization of this unwieldy enterprise.

The final major divestiture opportunity is the extensive holdings of land, mostly in the western United States and Alaska, by a variety of government departments, including the Departments of Agriculture, Interior and Defense. Altogether the government owns and manages 770 million acres, a portion of which is leased for mining, timber, and oil and gas drilling. Although government land sales were a common occurrence in the 19th century, environmental and conservation concerns prevent such sales today, and each year Congress provides funds to purchase even more land to prevent economic development on privately-owned tracts that possess some environmental interest. Proposals to conduct selected sales of some Federal land holding were made in the early 1980s but the public outcry was so fierce that the proposal was withdrawn and is not likely to resurface in the foreseeable future.

Although the above listed divestiture opportunities focused on those entities that the government has failed to privatize, there have been a few notable successes. In 1986, the Reagan Administration successfully privatized Conrail through a major share offering to the public. Conrail was a government corporation created in 1979 to take over the rail freight service of the bankrupt Penn Central. Providing the only freight service for the economically vital northeast section of the country, it was feared that the bankruptcy of this system would lead to a severe disruption of business and increased unemployment, and for this reason the government took over the rail line, created a government corporation to run it and invested substantial amounts of money to improve service. Unlike the other government corporations, the law that was enacted by Congress to create Conrail included the commitment to return it to the private sector once profitability was restored. This occurred in the mid 1980s, and in 1986 Conrail was sold to private investors for $1.6 billion, far less than what the government had invested in it to make the system viable and ultimately self-sufficient. Beyond this, the only other divestiture was the sale of the National Consumer Cooperative Bank in 1982. The bank was an ill-conceived lending institution established under the Carter Administration, whose purpose it was to foster the growth of cooperatives among urban and suburban consumers.

3. Beyond Divestitures

Other than those few commercial-like enterprises still controlled by the government, divestiture opportunities at the Federal level are quite limited and will never form the major component of a comprehensive privatization programme in the US. There remain, however, numerous other opportunities for privatization that, collectively, could entail a major transfer of activities from the Federal government to private sector providers. At the same time, there are also many other opportunities, including extensive divestitures, that could be accomplished at the state and local government levels. This section will focus on the remaining privatization opportunities at the Federal level that could be accomplished through either contracting-out or vouchers.

Although the Federal government is involved in the production of very few obviously commercial products or services, it is extensively involved in the reallocation of income through a variety of transfer schemes, and it does provide tens of billions of dollars' worth of basic public services to the public at large. Both of these activities are amenable to privatization through either contracting-out or through vouchers.

3.1. Vouchers

Vouchers represent the earmarked equivalent of a cash payment from the government to some qualified beneficiary for the acquisition of some specified product or service from private sector providers. How vouchers work can best be illustrated by the Food Stamp programme which is the government's chief means of ensuring adequate diets for those with low incomes. Individuals and families are eligible for food stamps if their incomes fall below a certain level deemed necessary to ensure some measure of an adequate diet. Once eligible, recipients receive each month from the government a packet of food stamps that are sufficient to provide food for the month. The stamps look like cash, are denominated in dollars, and can be exchanged at par at virtually all privately-owned food stores for food products. The food store, in turn, deposits them in a bank where they are credited in dollars to the store's account, at par, and the bank then returns them to the government for cash. Using vouchers, the government's only direct involvement is the verification of eligibility and the monthly distribution of stamps. The private sector does the rest, freeing the government from having either to distribute bulk food to the poor, as it did until the early 1960s, or operate subsidized food stores for those in need. Through such a system, administrative costs are kept low, inefficiencies minimized and most of the money spent on the programme goes directly to those in need.

For the most part, voucher programmes are the chief means by which the Federal government provides basic social services to the poor or to other groups deemed worthy of assistance. Health care for the elderly is operated through a quasi-voucher system called Medicare. Eligible beneficiaries are free to go to the doctor and hospital of their choice at their discretion and arrange for whatever care and procedures are required. The doctors and hospitals then bill Medicare for costs incurred. To maintain some control over programme expenses, Medicare establishes price caps for many common procedures and also requires cost sharing with the patient. Many private insurance companies offer supplementary coverage for those costs and fees not covered by Medicare. A similar programme, called Medicaid, provides health care coverage for the non-elderly poor. All other Americans are responsible for their own health care and/or insurance, although most are protected by insurance schemes provided by their employers. By utilizing private sector providers, the government is free of the administrative burdens associated with owning and managing tens of thousands of hospitals, and employing hundreds of thousands of doctors, nurses and support personnel. Again, by taking advantage of the efficiencies of the competitive market, most government health expenditures go directly to the targeted beneficiaries.

Federal financial support for higher education (beyond Grade 12) is offered through vouchers and loan programmes that provide eligible students with the financial means to select and attend the educational institution of their choice. The origins of this approach go back to 1948 when the government created the GI bill to assist the veterans of the Second World War in obtaining a higher education as a reward for their service to the nation. In the early 1970s the concept was extended to virtually all eligible students through vouchers or loans, and such support now accounts for nearly half of all tuition received by all universities and colleges. As in the cases discussed above, the student is free to choose from among thousands of private and public accredited institutions of higher education. And as in these other voucher programmes, the government is free of the management and ownership responsibilities associated with running a vast education system and establishing a variety of curricula. More importantly, competition is encouraged among the providers of higher education, and educational and curriculum diversity flourish. Unfortunately, the application of privatization principles does not extend down to the elementary or secondary education levels, and the difference in quality between America's higher education system and the other levels is striking. This will be discussed further in the next section on state and local government privatization opportunities.

Another important voucher programme that has been only partly implemented is the use of vouchers to provide housing for lower income households. Traditionally, the US has provided shelter for those in need by constructing and operating – through local housing authorities – public housing projects comprised of several multi-family buildings concentrated in urban neighbourhoods. The public housing programme has long been recognized as a failure. It is a very expensive programme that reaches only a portion of those eligible and provides those that do manage to get in such projects with substandard housing subject to abuse and rapid deterioration. The programme also encourages racial segregation and frequently concentrates the poor in areas of the city infected with high rates of crime. In the 1970s the Department of Housing and Urban Development began experimenting with housing vouchers as an alternative to government managed housing.

Under the voucher system, which now serves thousands of households, an eligible household receives a housing voucher that entitles them to rent the privately-provided apartment of their choice up to a certain dollar amount. The dollar amount varies from city to city and is calculated by surveying the local market to determine the minimum monthly rent required to obtain an apartment on the private market that meets certain minimum standards. Once the government certifies the household's choice, the eligible household receives a monthly voucher that they then turn over to their landlord, who then turns it in to the government for cash. The advantage of the programme is that it allows the beneficiaries to select the neighbourhood of their choice, promotes integration and diminishes the concentration of the poor in densely populated public housing projects. The added advantage is that the costs are between a third and one-half of the cost of public housing, and it removes government from the real estate management business for which it is poorly equipped. Although President Reagan attempted to shift the bulk of government housing assistance to vouchers, political obstacles prevented this, and the Administration of President Bush appears to be gradually retreating from the commitment to use vouchers as the chief form of housing assistance to the poor.

For the vast majority of Federal income support and transfer programmes, vouchers have become the chief means by which the government delivers assistance to the poor or to other eligible groups. The advantage of vouchers is that they allow for a division of responsibilities among the institutions involved in a way that can promote the highest efficiency and lowest cost per dollar of benefits actually provided. With vouchers, the government determines eligibility and provides the money, while the efficient private sector operating in competitive markets provides that product or service. With the exception of veterans' health care and most federal housing assistance, vouchers are now the main vehicles for providing basic welfare services to those in need.

3.2. Contracting-Out

Contracting-out is the process whereby government hires, under contract, a private firm to perform, over a defined period of time, some specific service that might otherwise be provided by public employees using government equipment and facilities. Contracting-out is most appropriate for those governmental functions whose value can only be defined in terms of a franchise to perform a certain function such as accounting, rubbish removal, building security, vehicle maintenance, and so on. Typically, government will decide that some particular service might be better provided by the private sector. It then defines the task and the services to be provided and allows private sector companies to submit bids to perform the service according to government specifications. If the private firms' bids are below what the service is costing the government to provide, then government costs can be reduced by contracting with the private sector to perform the service under government oversight.

In principle, the government's formal commitment to utilize the services of the private sector whenever contracting can save money without a diminution in service is required by way of a series of Executive Orders that go back as far as 1955. These Executive Orders, revised and reissued as recently as late 1987, require government agencies to establish ongoing review and contracting procedures for all of the services they perform that are also available from the private sector. In practice, however, most agencies resist the requirement and only a small fraction of such government services are ever even reviewed for possible contracting opportunities.

The Reagan Administration attempted to expand the use of this programme by issuing a new Executive Order that established quantitative goals for each agency and created a new Office of Privatization in the Office of Management and Budget to oversee the programme and monitor agency performance. At the same time, to give agencies an added inducement to engage in contracting, the Office of Management and Budget reduced each agency's budget allocation by the amount estimated to be saved through the required contracting. Thus, agencies would either have to contract-out or reduce the services they provided. As a result of these changes in the programme, agencies scheduled substantially more programme reviews under the procedures laid down in an Executive Office document entitled 'Circular A-76'. Circular A-76 details the procedures that agencies must follow in making cost comparisons and competing the government workforce against bids from private contractors. The circular also provides for a variety of protection for the existing government workforce.

In the year prior to these changes (FY 1987), 12900 positions were competed under the procedures of Circular A-76, but this rose to 14900 positions for FY 1988. Undoubtedly, the new programme was a considerable success and several agencies that had not engaged in any cost comparisons and contracting in over a decade were induced to implement ambitious programmes. Unfortunately, officials in the Bush Administration have been less aggressive than their predecessors in managing the programme and agency commitments to contracting have diminished significantly in response, with an estimated 4000 positions scheduled for 1991.

The diminished commitment to contracting-out through the A-76 process is unfortunate because the numerous government studies of the programme that have been conducted over the past decade consistently demonstrate significant cost savings at no measurable diminution in the quantity or the quality of the service provided. On average these studies demonstrate that government services contracted-out to private firms under conditions of competitive bidding yield savings of 30 per cent over what the service had cost previously when provided by government employees. At the same time, when the government department manages to retain the contract under the same competitive process, the savings average around 20 per cent over what the service had cost previously. Thus, regardless of whether the service is actually privatized, the force of competition generally leads to significant cost savings. In a 1987 study, the US Congressional Budget Office estimated that the work being performed by 1.4 million federal workers could be contracted-out to the private sector. Based upon actual average cost savings from contracting, this could lead to budgetary savings in excess of $11 billion per year if all commercial positions were put out to competitive tender through the A-76 process.

To date, much of the A-76 competitions have been limited to routine services such as janitorial work, grounds-keeping, vehicle maintenance and data processing. However, some government agencies have applied the process to more sophisticated tasks and the results have been just as rewarding. The Department of Housing and Urban Development and the US Environmental Protection Agency have both contracted-out their departmental libraries to private firms. The Department of Defense has been the most innovative in pursuing contracting opportunities, relying on contractors to provide such sophisticated services as aircraft maintenance, management of supply depots, operation of the Defense Early Warning System (DEW Line) and many other sensitive tasks.

As in the case of so many other privatization opportunities in the US, political obstacles are the main limit on extending the contracting-out programme to its full potential. Confronted with the prospect of losing their jobs or having to work under more productive conditions, government workers often respond to the prospect of a scheduled A-76 review by attempting to have their elected representative in Congress thwart the effort through enactment of explicit legislative prohibitions on contracting. To date, Congress has enacted well over 50 such prohibitions including most recently a sweeping series of limitations on the extent to which the Department of Defense can contract-out civilian tasks. In what only can be described as some of the most bizarre prohibitions to exist in a free country, several laws actually prohibit government employees to discuss the privatization of certain Federal enterprises during working hours. Other legislative proposals that would broaden such limits are now under consideration in Congress and the Bush Administration is on record opposing them. Nonetheless, the process of contracting-out will remain controversial and political obstacles will continue to thwart efforts to expand the programme to take advantage of the many cost-saving opportunities that exist. With opposition intensifying and with the elimination of the Privatization Office in the Office of Management and Budget, it is likely that the volume of contracting-out conducted at the Federal level will continue to decline.

4. Privatization at the State and Local Level

State and local governments in the United States play a very active role in the provision of many basic services to the citizen. Local governments are largely responsible for primary and secondary education, and the construction and operation of public works such as waste water treatment, water supply, road construction and repair, mass transit and airports. State governments are also involved in these activities as well as others such as prisons, higher education and highways. Because these governments are more closely involved in the provision of basic services and because their tax revenue sources are more limited than those at the Federal level, opportunities to provide services efficiently and save money are often pursued more seriously than they are at the Federal level. As a result, privatization has made greater inroads at these levels of government.

In addition to the more aggressive pursuit of contracting opportunities, State and local governments are experimenting with a number of innovative privatizations that could lead to dramatic changes in how traditional government services are provided. For example, a dozen states have enacted legislation to permit the existence of privately-owned and managed prisons that operate under contract to the states' correctional department. At least one privately managed facility exists in each of these states and about a dozen other states are actively considering legislation that would allow them to utilize private prison facilities. With the exception of several short-term facilities to hold illegal aliens prior to deportation, private prisons are explicitly forbidden at the Federal level as a result of recently enacted legislation. Indeed, that same legislation also forbade the Department of Justice to conduct a small number of pilot projects to test the feasibility of the concept. Nonetheless, the Department of Justice is actively studying the privatization alternative and it is likely that the rapid growth in the US prison population and the limited Federal funds available to construct new prisons will ultimately force the Congress to give this alternative more serious consideration.

Elsewhere, several states are actively planning to permit the existence of private toll roads as a way of alleviating growing vehicular congestion in major metropolitan areas. A new private business called the Virginia Toll Road Company will soon begin construction of a private toll road in the Virginia suburbs of Washington DC. The government of California has agreed to go forward with several private toll roads and the governments of both Illinois and Colorado are giving serious consideration to permitting private toll roads in their states. Although such roads are relatively common on the European continent, the existence of an active Federal highway construction programme since the 1950s has discouraged the emergence of private competitors. However, as Federal funding has diminished while transportation needs continue to grow, more and more states are looking to the private sector to provide the resources and expertise needed to expand and improve their highway systems.

Airports represent another area of opportunity for state and local governments. Although all major airports in the United States are owned and operated by regional public authorities that are created and managed by the local governments served by the airport, these airports receive significant amounts of Federal funds for construction and improvement. They also receive significant amounts of local funds as well as private funds from the participating airlines and other private entities. For the most part, major US airports are operated on a commercial basis with significant participation from the private sector, although there is growing interest throughout the country and within the US Department of Transportation to increase this level of private participation.

The chief problem confronting the air transportation system is the rapid growth in air traffic since the system was deregulated in the late 1970s and the inadequate facilities to accommodate this rise in traffic. The last major airport to be completed in the US was the Dallas/Fort Worth airport in 1974. Although numerous improvements and expansions have been conducted at the existing airports, the nation is quickly approaching the point where completely new facilities will have to be constructed. Given the limits on government funds in an era of large budget deficits, local airport authorities are beginning to look to the private sector to take on greater responsibilities. The city of Chicago, for example, is now giving serious consideration to using the private sector to finance and own the third major airport that will soon be constructed in the region. Similarly, the city of Denver gave serious consideration to a private airport, as did Minneapolis. At the same time, several municipalities are conducting feasibility studies on the advantages of selling their existing airports to private investors. Atlanta is reported to have received an offer to purchase its airport, and officials in Los Angeles are reviewing options to privatize their international airport, LAX. Recently, an effort was made by the city of Albany, New York to sell their airport to a private management firm, Lockheed Air Terminal, but the US Department of Transportation prohibited the transfer. However, a modified version of the proposal may receive approval in the future.

Waste water treatment facilities represent another area where privatization may soon come to dominate. Although there are perhaps three dozen private or semi-private facilities in communities throughout the United States, the vast majority are municipally-owned and operated and are constructed with financial support from the Federal government. In recent years, however, persistent Federal budget deficits have forced major reductions in the programme and government grants are now being replaced by government loans. Still, the amount of financial resources that will be made available is woefully short of the funds needed to construct new facilities and rehabilitate older ones in order to meet the water quality standards of the Federal mandates under the Clean Water Act. The US Environmental Protection Agency has recently reported that an investment of $83.5 billion will have to be made in deficient existing facilities to bring them up to Federal standards. Because this greatly exceeds the amount of financial resources that all levels of government could commit to the task, more and more cities and communities will be forced to join in partnership with private financiers and developers to construct the needed waste water facilities.

In addition to the creative use of privatization techniques to construct and operate a variety of public works, state and local governments have also been in the forefront of innovative uses of contracting-out to provide basic services.

The city of Phoenix and the county of Los Angeles have operated very aggressive contracting programmes that force the existing government departments to compete with private sector providers. Phoenix, for example, regularly competes its municipal trash collection with for-profit businesses. The county of Los Angeles has contracted-out many services to the private sector and is now in the process of completing an employee buy-out of the dental clinic it operates to serve the poor. Interestingly, the plans to sell the dental clinic to the dentists employed there have led to numerous enquiries from employees in other departments seeking to become the owners and operators of their facility. One of the more innovative local privatizations occurred many years ago in the Phoenix suburb of Scottsdale where the city's fire department was contracted-out to a private firm at considerable savings. Other typical local contracting-out opportunities include date processing, road repair and maintenance, hospital management, particularly in the emergency rooms, ambulance service, grounds-keeping and building maintenance and cleaning.

In contrast to the pursuit of innovative privatization opportunities for public works and infrastructure, State and local governments remain reluctant to extend this process to another area where they have a major responsibility – the provision of primary and secondary education (Grades 1–12). For the most part, the provision of education services is a key responsibility of local government, with oversight, curriculum and some funding provided by the state governments. Although private schools and schools with religious affiliation also provide primary and secondary education, most students attend locally financed and managed public schools.

Over the last decade there has arisen a deep concern about the quality of the education that is being provided by the public schools. By most measures of educational attainment, there is every reason to believe that there has been a marked deterioration in the quality of the students that graduate from the public school system, particularly in the large, urban systems with concentrations of minority students. Efforts to reverse this trend have not been successful, notwithstanding the vast amounts of time and money devoted to the task, and student test scores continue to tumble. Recognizing the problem may lie in the basic institutional arrangements that characterize the public school system, many education experts have come to believe that the current system of local educational monopolies with captive clients needs a strong dose of competition and better accountability for the services, or lack thereof, that they are expected to provide.

The failure to achieve any measurable progress from the reforms attempted over the past decade have led a number of education experts to contend that it is the basic institutional structure of the system, particularly the absence of any meaningful competition, that has created the problems, and that a fundamental and comprehensive overhaul of the system is needed if improvement is to be achieved. More and more, these experts are recommending various forms of competition as the kind of fundamental reform needed. One set of reform proposals being discussed involves the provision of education vouchers to all eligible students to be used at the school of their choice, including private schools and those with religious affiliations. Although this approach has been widely rejected by the educational establishment, led by the many teachers' unions and professional associations, the idea is slowly beginning to make inroads and several states and communities are giving the idea a serious review. Recently, the legislature in the state of Wisconsin enacted a law that would create a demonstration programme that would provide vouchers to 1000 low income students to attend the private school of their choice. To date, objections by Wisconsin's Superintendent of Public Instruction have prevented the programme from being implemented.

While vouchers represent the most dramatic form of competitive reform, other school districts are experimenting with other mechanisms that provide greater choice within the public schools system. Although resistance to such experiments remains fierce, such reform proposals are gaining ground and will likely be more common in the future.

78

Privatisation: A Policy in Search of a Rationale

J. A. Kay and D. J. Thompson

Source: *Economic Journal*, 96(1), 1986, pp. 18–32.

Privatisation is a term which is used to cover several distinct, and possibly alternative, means of changing the relationships between the government and the private sector. Among the most important of these are denationalisation (the sale of publicly owned assets), deregulation (the introduction of competition into statutory monopolies) and contracting out (the franchising to private firms of the production of state financed goods and services). This paper principally examines the sale of government industrial assets – which has now become both the most striking and the most controversial element of the programme. However, its analysis has implications for other means of privatisation – and indeed its conclusion is that these should have greater priority.

The paradox of privatisation is that the view that it contributes to economic efficiency is derived from the belief that private sector managers are subject to incentives and disciplines different from, and more demanding than, those which apply to their public sector counterparts. If this were so, then it would be expected that the prospect of privatisation would be distinctly unwelcome to the management concerned. But without the consent, or acquiescence, of these same managers privatisation of any sort is a difficult and protracted business. As a result, measures of liberalisation, or deconcentration, associated with privatisation – those which offer most in terms of potential gains in efficiency – are also those on which major concessions have been made to win management support for the political process of privatisation. In section VI we describe how this has happened in industry after industry.

I. Privatisation in the UK

The volume of asset sales by central government has increased progressively from £370 million in 1979/80 to £1,142 million in 1983/4; the sale of British

Telecom (£3,900 million, with payment staged over three fiscal years), and also Jaguar and Sealink, has substantially boosted receipts in the last year. Up to 1983/4 only a few public enterprises had been transferred to the private sector; a substantial part of the receipts from asset sales arose from other sources, such as the sale of tranches of shares in British Petroleum and of leases of motorway service areas. Many of the enterprises which were transferred to the private sector operated in markets where private sector firms were dominant (e.g. National Freight Corporation).

The increase in the sale of disposals has also seen a change in their pattern. The largest, the sale of British Telecom, involved a public sector monopoly – a dominant enterprise which enjoys substantial, although reduced, protection from competition by statutory restrictions on market entry. This is also true of other industries for which the government is now developing proposals for privatisation – British Airways, British Airports Authority, British Gas and regional water authorities.

It is clear that the government sees the denationalisation of public industry serving a multiplicity of objectives (Moore, 1983). One purpose is to improve the economic performance of the industries concerned. Another is to resolve the persistent problems of management and control which have made the relations between government and nationalised industries one of the unhappier elements of British public administration. Privatisation is a radical remedy for these problems, although perhaps less radical than it appears at first sight if it involves the retention of a network of regulatory relationships between government and industry. The Treasury is greatly interested in the revenue which can be obtained from privatisation. Although the objective is rarely articulated, privatisation may also be seen by the government as a means of disciplining the power of public sector trades unions. A final objective is the promotion of a kind of popular capitalism through wider share ownership.

At different times each one of these objectives has been sacrificed for others. However the fact that a policy has a variety of objectives, and that these may at times conflict, is not in itself a criticism of that policy. But the reality behind the apparent multiplicity of objectives is not that the policy has a rather sophisticated rationale, but rather that it is lacking any clear analysis of purpose or effects; and hence any objective which seems achievable is seized as justification. The outcome is that no objectives are effectively attained, and in particular that economic efficiency – which is at once the most important of these and the most difficult to attain – has systematically been subordinated to other goals.

In section II, we consider how the emphasis in the economic analysis of public enterprise has shifted from the normative welfare economics of the 1940s and 1950s to the positive property rights approach of the 1970s and 1980s, and what these theories suggest for the relative performance of public and private firms and competitive and monopolistic market structures. Section

III reviews empirical evidence on these issues. This analysis stresses the importance of competition, and in section IV we consider how this might be promoted in the public sector. Sections V and VI examine the principal obstacles – concern for revenue and the interests of management.

II. Ownership, Competition and Performance

Why should we expect differences in the performance of private and public industry? When an industry is privatised, the managers of the new private firm are, literally, the same people as those who managed the old public firm the day before (although in telecommunications and airways management changes have been introduced with a view to privatisation). Thus any change lies not in the character or abilities of the management but in the constraints and opportunities with which that management is faced.

A statutory framework for British nationalised industries was established in the legislation which brought many of today's state enterprises into public ownership immediately after the second world war. This prescribed objectives only in the most general of terms, and saw the role of nationalised industry managers as that of trustees of the public interest. For twenty years thereafter, most of the economic literature on nationalised industries followed the tradition established by Hotelling (1938) and prescribed the pricing and investment criteria which such trustees would wish to follow. It is now apparent that at no time did this literature have any important influence on what nationalised industries actually did.

An early and perceptive critic of the Hotelling analysis was Little (1952), who was concerned by its neglect of appropriate incentives to productive efficiency. He anticipated the burgeoning literature on business management, which would stress increasingly that efficient organisation required that managers be given specific objectives and their performance monitored in relation to them – see Drucker (1974) for an influential popularisation. Little recognised the dangers of an environment in which objectives were ill-defined, and in which it was very difficult to determine ex post whether or not they had in fact been achieved. These arguments were to be developed as part of the economic theory of property rights, which was to elaborate a positive rather than a normative view of managerial behaviour (see Furubotn and Pejovich, 1972, for a survey). Public sector managers could be expected to respond to the particular personal incentives with which they were faced. Such incentives might lead to a desire to maximise the scale of operations of the business, subject to any external financial constraint, or to seek a quiet life untroubled by changes in working practices or difficulties in labour relations, rather than to pursue a nebulous public good.

Dissatisfaction with the performance of nationalised industries led to repeated attempts to prescribe more specific objectives. These came in White

Papers in 1961, 1967 and 1978, and a common theme to all was greater emphasis on commercial rather than public interest considerations and the introduction of more extensive financial controls. Despite the intentions of the authors of these papers, detailed scrutiny by government of day to day activities of nationalised industries has tended to increase rather than diminish, and their autonomy in investment and planning decisions, and in industrial relations, has been steadily eroded.

But if neither exhortation to pursue the public interest nor increasing central control has provided an appropriate control structure for nationalised industries, is there reason to believe that privatisation will do better? We are concerned with incentives to both productive and allocative efficiency. Productive efficiency requires that whatever is done should be achieved at minimum cost; allocative efficiency implies that what is done meets consumer needs at prices which reflect the costs of provision. Encouragements to achieve efficiency may come from the product market, or the capital market, or both. The product market may be one in which consumers can transfer their custom to other firms; the capital market can impose the threat of bankruptcy or of takeover.

A firm in a competitive product market has incentives to allocative efficiency, if the market price reflects the value of its output – which implies that external effects and distributional consequences are unimportant. If it can go bankrupt, it must also achieve productive efficiency. But if the firm does not face direct competition for the goods and services it sells, it is likely to set higher prices and to relate these prices to the intensity of competition in its different markets as well as to the relative costs of production. Thus it is unlikely to achieve allocative efficiency and the pressure on it to be productively efficient is also reduced.

It is important to recognise that it is the belief that private ownership would not achieve allocative efficiency which provided, in many cases, the rationale for nationalisation. Either the industry was inevitably characterised by monopoly or else there were non-commercial objectives, such as external benefits, which implied that some outputs should be produced even if they failed to cover their costs. It is possible, however, that the opportunity to remedy these allocative weaknesses may be outweighed by losses in productive efficiency, and clear that the first candidates for privatisation – telecommunications, gas, airways – are industries where these non-commercial objectives are comparatively unimportant. But they are all industries in which competition is severely limited, either by the nature of the product or by a history of statutory restriction. Do private firms which do not face competitive product markets have greater incentives to productive efficiency than their public counterparts? The property rights approach, which leads to scepticism about the effect of injunctions to promote the public good on public managers, also recognises that the managers of large private firms have little direct interest in the profitability of the organisation for which they

Table 1 Ownership, competition and efficiency incentives

Can the firm go bankrupt?	No	No	Yes	Yes	Yes
Can it be taken over?	No	No	No	Yes	Either
Is the product market competitive?	No	Yes	No	No	Yes
Incentives to – allocative efficiency?	No	Yes	No	No	Yes
productive efficiency?	No	No	No	Yes	Yes
Kind of firm	Publicly owned monopoly	Publicly owned competitor	Large private monopoly	Smaller private monopoly	Competitive private firm
Example of firm	British Airports Authority	Electricity showrooms	British Telecom	British Aerospace	Many

work. Their natural concerns are with their own salaries, with the survival and growth of the firm, with its size and with the public esteem and reputation which it enjoys. All these things will be influenced by profitability, but they are distinct from profitability. A firm which has market power will have freedom to pursue alternative goals, and its managers too may seek to increase the scale of their operations or to minimise the degree of change to their customary working practices. Such freedom is limited if the firm is at risk from takeover, which is the principal means by which the capital market puts pressure on a private firm to maximise profit.

These propositions yield the classification of Table 1 (based on Forsyth, 1984). It is competitive, privately owned firms which have incentives to achieve both productive and allocative efficiency. Privatisation tends to promote productive efficiency, competition allocative efficiency. The incentive to productive efficiency comes from the requirement on private firms to achieve profits – to stay in business in competitive product markets, to avert the threat of takeover from the 'market for corporate control' (Manne, 1965). If, however, there is little competition in the product market if the risk of bankruptcy is slight, and if the risk of takeover is also minimal, the pressures of the market affect a private sector manager no more than his public sector counterpart.

III. Public and Private Performance: Evidence

Evidence on the comparative performance of public and private enterprise is somewhat piecemeal, and drawn from a variety of different sources (see Borcherding *et al.*, 1982 and Millward, 1982 for surveys). There are several, interrelated, problems in making meaningful comparisons. One lies in finding a suitable test-bed; particularly in the United Kingdom many of the activities carried out in the public sector are simply not undertaken by the private sector. Moreover, public corporations may have some non-commercial objectives and these may bias comparisons of efficiency. Where outputs are not sold in a competitive market (typically the case for public corporations) appropriate measures of output may need to be devised. Public corporations may sometimes face different input prices as a consequence of being in the public sector; they may have access to cheap capital as a result of explicit or implied government guarantees, but may be requested to purchase more expensive domestically produced inputs.

The most comprehensive comparison of public and private performance in the United Kingdom is that carried out by Pryke (1982); he was able to compare three activities where services were provided by both the public and private sector – airlines, ferries and hovercraft, and the sale of electricity and gas appliances. In each of these activities Pryke's analysis showed a picture of a more profitable private enterprise increasing its market share at the expense of the public sector. In cases where comparisons of cost levels and efficiency were feasible, Pryke's analysis generally shows the private enterprises in a favourable light. Pryke concludes that the public enterprises he has studied have been badly managed and that the main explanation for this poor performance is a weakening of incentives resulting from public ownership.

It is not difficult to be persuaded that the public enterprises which Pryke has studied have been run inefficiently. In the particular case of airlines a variety of studies have confirmed that British Airways is not an efficient airline either by the standards of other United Kingdom based operators or relative to other national flag carriers (see Ashworth and Forsyth, 1984, for a summary). But it does not necessarily follow that public ownership is the cause of BA's poor performance. The detailed comparisons reported by Ashworth and Forsyth showed the (public) Air Canada to be the most efficient airline in their sample. However Air Canada operates in the competitive North American airline market, and is the only publicly owned firm to do so. In contrast many of British Airways' routes are closely regulated by agreements on numbers of operators, fares and capacity. Low efficiency may therefore be the result of the environment within which the firm operates rather than the structure of ownership.

The necessity – and difficulty – of distinguishing the effects on performance of ownership and competitive market conditions is reinforced by Pryke's other examples. Privately owned European Ferries are more efficient than the (then) publicly owned Sealink. However, a number of other private firms have unsuccessfully entered this market. The most recent is P & O Ferries who, after several years of losses, sold their operations to European Ferries as part of a restructuring of operations consequent on threatened takeover of the parent company. The implication is that private firms are not necessarily intrinsically more efficient, but that market pressures are more effective at weeding out poorly performing firms in the private sector than in the public.

Similar, observations apply in gas and electrical appliance retailing. Pryke's comparisons are with successful private firms with increasing market share. It might be argued (as the utilities concerned did) that showrooms serve not just to market appliances but also to collect bill payments and provide a centre for advice which has the effect of promoting greater safety. Although these arguments are not wholly convincing they underline the difficulties in making fair comparisons between the public and private sector where external costs or benefits arise. It is, however, clear that a private firm which did not have the opportunity of cross-subsidising its retailing activities from its supply monopoly would not continue to operate showrooms at the cost levels of these nationalised industries; either costs would be reduced or the activities abandoned. The attitude of a privatised, but still monopolistic, British Gas to its showrooms can therefore be seen as a litmus test of the impact, if any, of privatisation on the industry.

Local authority refuse services have recently been opened to competitive tender in some areas of the United Kingdom. There are cases where substantial reductions in costs appear to have been achieved although there are also cases where the contracted standards of service have not been maintained or where contractors have been unable to fulfil their contract. The most detailed study of the costs of refuse services in the United Kingdom (Audit Commission 1984) emphasises the *diversity* in the efficiency performance of public suppliers in different locations. It is clear from the Commission's analysis that an efficient supplier (public or private) should be able to undercut substantially the costs incurred by the least efficient local authorities. But the Commission also concluded that the most effective local authorities (the top 25%) achieved cost levels as low as those of the private contractors they investigated.

Thus it does not seem that there is anything intrinsically superior about performance under private ownership. There are efficient and inefficient public enterprises, and efficient and inefficient private enterprises. But if product markets are competitive, lower efficiency is penalised by falling market share and low profits. If capital markets are effective, this in turn leads to withdrawal from the industry by unsuccessful private firms. Thus market disciplines do more to improve the performance of the private sector than the public. It is not ownership as such, but the interaction of ownership and competition that promotes efficiency. The few direct tests of the introduction of competition between public and private firms support this. An analysis of electricity supply in the United States (where public and private firms operate together) has shown that where individual utilities are in competition costs are generally lower (Primeaux, 1977). Another American study of the costs of refuse collection (Savas, 1977) demonstrated that where competition was introduced between public and private suppliers the difference in costs between the two sectors was largely eliminated in a short time period.

Thus evidence of superior private sector performance comes largely from competitive markets. What happens when these market disciplines are blunted? Public ownership is common when competition is unlikely – as with the 'natural monopolies' of gas, water and electricity distribution – or where it is restricted by regulation as happens for airlines and many other means of transport. The credit rating of companies in these industries reflects the scale of their operations and their monopoly of product markets rather than their efficiency, and the threat of takeover is made insignificant by the size of the company or by regulatory restriction. Two very different cases in which public firms appear to perform markedly better than private firms – American electric utilities (Pescatrice and Trapani, 1980) and German insurance companies (Finsinger and Pauly, 1985) – share two important common features. Both are subject to detailed price and profit regulation, and in both the private sector is dominant and the share of the public sector relatively small. The higher costs of private firms are partly explained by the over-capitalisation and excessive marketing expenditures induced by the regulatory regime.

A variety of other studies yield a mixed pattern of findings. In a regulated market, privately owned British Caledonian is more efficient than publicly owned British Airways, but also smaller. A comparative study of water utilities in the United States (Crain and Zardkodhi, 1978) showed substantially higher costs in the public sector. The authors' analysis suggested that the methods used to regulate private water utilities had resulted in inefficient over-capitalisation (the Averch–Johnson effect); however, they concluded that any loss of efficiency resulting in this way was substantially outweighed by over-manning in the public sector.

Canada has two competing railroad networks – the privately owned Canadian Pacific and the publicly owned Canadian National. Australian internal flights are dominated by the public Trans-Australia Airlines and the private Ansett Airlines of Australia. In both cases, government policy has imposed a regulatory regime which has sought to maintain a balance between private and public sector operators and in both cases (Caves and Christensen, 1978, Forsyth and Hocking, 1980: see also Davies, 1971) investigation has shown very little difference between their performance.

It will be apparent – as was suggested by the structural analysis of section III – that no simple generalisation about superiority of private sector performance can be sustained. But there is support for the review that the efficiency of all firms – public or private – is improved by a competitive environment. The regulation of private firms which do not face competition sometimes distorts incentives in ways which lead to higher costs levels than those of directly controlled public enterprises. The consequence is that under competition private firms are likely to do better, but if there is little competition regulated private firms do not perform better than public firms and may do worse. It follows that privatisation into an uncompetitive environment is likely to be positively harmful, in particular if the resulting firm is small enough to be at serious risk from takeover. Privatisation will tend to improve performance in a company only if supported by liberalisation; and if the two conflict, liberalisation is decidedly to be preferred.

IV. Promoting Competition

There are several obstacles to the promotion of competition in the nationalised, or formerly nationalised industries which would exist even if such competition was the primary objective. Many were nationalised precisely because some element of market failure was characteristic of the industry's performance. Several are 'natural monopolies'. Some are statutory monopolies – entry has long been the subject of legal restrictions. Others have objectives which are not commercial, or are intrinsically unprofitable. Most industries have elements of all three.

Natural monopoly is most obvious in those industries which involve distribution networks – local telephone services, gas, electricity distribution (but not generation), water supply. In each of these the costs of providing two competing networks would not be a great deal less than twice the cost of provision through a single system. This is less true of telecommunications where technology is rapidly widening supply possibilities, but the others are certainly natural monopolies for the indefinite future. These are not only natural monopolies, but sustainable monopolies (see Sharkey, 1982 for an exposition of the recent theory of natural monopoly). This means that it is both inefficient for competition to emerge, and improbable that it will in fact emerge.

The new theory of contestability (Baumol *et al.* 1982) draws further attention to an old solution to these problems. If it is not possible to have competition for the product, why not have competition for the monopoly through franchising? (Chadwick, 1859, Demsetz, 1968). One variant would simply auction rights to the monopoly. This gives incentives to productive efficiency – the winner of the auction is the producer who maximises the gap between revenue and costs – and it solves the income distribution problems posed by the existence of private monopolies, but it does not deal with the allocative consequences of the high prices of monopoly. The Chadwick–Demsetz auction awards the franchise to the bidder who quotes the lowest price, and it is easily shown that this can give appropriate incentives to allocative as well as productive efficiency.

The issue is more complex where there are more dimensions to the product than price but, in fact, the products of distribution monopolies are not at all complicated ones. Franchising is the solution which has been pursued in most newly established monopolies – television wavebands, North Sea oil exploration licences, and most recently (and most closely analogously) in cable (Hunt, 1982). In principle, it has also been applied in telecommunications, where the 1983 Act provides for the licensing of telecommunications suppliers, but it is fanciful to imagine that British Telecom's 25 year licence is likely to be in serious danger of non-renewal. Franchising does, however, raise problems of its own (see Schmalensee, 1979 for a sceptical review). Two of the most serious of these are how to organise an efficient franchise bidding system and how to ensure a transfer of assets on termination consistent with appropriate incentives to invest, but not to over invest, in fixed assets (Domberger, 1985).

Other nationalised industries, in no sense natural monopolies, have been protected by the establishment of statutory monopoly. Airlines and buses are obvious examples; and the utilities have often achieved statutory protection for parts of their business that are not natural monopolies, such as the provision of subscribers' apparatus in telecommunications. The obvious response of a government concerned to promote competition is to repeal the restrictive statutes, and some such liberalisation has occurred in telecommunications, coaching and electricity.

But, as these examples show, deregulation is not enough. An incumbent firm which has achieved dominance in a period of statutory protection enjoys considerable advantages – technical, financial and political. The case of express coaches (Davis, 1984) is a telling illustration. Deregulation of coaching services in 1980 resulted in some price reductions (substantial in some cases) and innovations in the provision of new types of service. The liberalised market however remained dominated by a single operator, National Express, a subsidiary of the publicly owned National Bus Company. Prior to deregulation, National held monopoly rights to the majority of routes. It is possible that National's continued pre-eminent position in the market reflects favourably on its efficiency in meeting competition. It seems likely, however, that it has been able to build upon advantages arising from its position as a dominant incumbent to reduce the threat of competitive market entry. As owner of city centre coaching terminals it has been able to refuse access to competitors, and to exploit its financial strength to outlast comparatively small rivals in periods of intense price competition.

These financial and technical advantages are reinforced by the political skills and influence which incumbents have normally acquired. The most striking examples come from aviation. After British Airways' success in persuading the government to reject the Civil Aviation Authority's proposals for restructuring the industry (CAA, 1984), it would clearly be unwise for competitors to assume that the CAA can provide effective protection against predatory activity by BA. The point is reinforced by reference to the specific allegations of predation made against BA in the case of Laker Airways. The case was brought in the US Courts. It was strenuously opposed through diplomatic pressures and in other ways by the British Government, and the case proceeded only because (in contrast to the position in criminal courts, where charges were dropped), the US Government had no power to halt a civil suit. Broadly, anti-predation legislation in the United Kingdom relies on the possibility of complaint to a regulatory agency, the Office of Fair Trading. In the absence of more specific provision, the agency can, in some cases of its own volition and in others with the support of the Monopolies Commission, require that the offending practice cease. The contrast with American legislation, which permits private action for punitive treble damages, could hardly be more marked.

There are other industries in which competition is possible but may be undesirable. The principal cases are those where substantial commercial and non-commercial activities are combined, as in British Rail and the Post Office. Since it may well be cheaper to undertake these together rather than separately, there are respectable arguments for protecting the commercial areas from competition. Again, however, if competition in the market is undesirable, competition for the market through franchising may nevertheless be feasible.

Competition in the activities which have traditionally been undertaken by British nationalised industries is thus a tender plant, requiring considerable nurture and shelter if it is to grow. We now consider why it is that the objective that it *should* grow has not enjoyed particularly high priority.

V. Financial Objectives of Privatisation

It is trite, but important, to observe that monopolies are worth more than competitive industries. A Treasury concerned to maximise the revenue obtained from the sale of public assets could not therefore be expected to support measures of liberalisation. This stress on the revenue effects of privatisation has been increased by the practice of judging public sector performance by reference to the public sector borrowing requirement. This treats the proceeds of asset sales as a revenue receipt, and presents cash transactions without reference to their impact on future incomings and outgoings or reference to any form of balance sheet. It is clearly erroneous to treat these receipts analogously to other items of government revenue (Hills, 1984; Buiter, 1983). Even in the short term, the transaction will only facilitate government financing to the extent that the quasi-equity assets provided by shares in state industries are more acceptable to the market than conventional forms of government borrowing; but that is the limit of the effect of the transaction.

The consequences of this mismatch between private sector accrual accounting and public sector cash accounting extend beyond the treatment of the sale itself. Table 2 shows the effects on the 1985/6 PSBR of the British Telecom flotation. Despite the sale of a half share in BT earnings at a price of £3.9 bn, the net impact of the transaction (excluding proceeds of the second tranche) is to raise the PSBR by only £230 million. Because BT reinvests a

Table 2 The effect of privatising British Telecom on the 1985/6 PSBR

The sale of BT has the following effects on the 1985/6 PSBR	£ million
Proceeds from the sale second tranche, collected June 1985	–1,200
Removal of BT's gross trading surplus from public revenue	+3,000
Removal of BT's capital requirements from public spending accounts	–1,900
Receipt by government of its dividend on 3 billion shares (net)	–200
ACT receipt on all BT dividend pay outs	–170
Interest paid by BT to rest of private sector	–150
Interest paid by BT to government	–350

Note: Gross trading surplus for 1985/6 assumed to be 10% higher than in 1984/5.

Table 3 Offers for sale

Company	*Discount (%)*	*Increase from issue price to current share price (%)*
Amersham International	35	10
Associated British Ports	98	169
British Aerospace	15	66
British Petroleum	6	–130
British Telecom	91	111
Cable and Wireless	15	295
Jaguar	8	45

Notes: The discount is measured by the change in price from the issue price to the closing price after one week's dealings after allowance for market-wide share price movements.

The increase from issue price to current (30 September 1985) price is similarly adjusted for market-wide movements in share prices.

Table 4 Tenders

Company	*Discount (%)*
Associated British Ports	–2
British Petroleum	3
Britoil	–21
Cable and Wireless	–3
Enterprise Oil	2

Note: Discount calculated as in Table 3.

substantial proportion of its profits, the cash flow impact of removing it from the public sector is very much smaller than the stream of earnings forgone.

These accounting conventions should not obscure the basic truth that whether it is a monopoly or a competitive industry that is privatised, the financial gain or loss from a sale depends on whether the price paid is more or less than the present value of prospective earnings from the asset. Thus the critical question is whether the assets concerned have been sold at a discount or a premium to the market's assessment of their value. Table 3 contrasts the fixed prices at which offers for sale were made with the prices which were established in the market immediately after flotation, and with the (market-adjusted) current prices of the shares concerned. The average level of discount appears high by the standards of private sector flotations.

The government has responded to criticism of the low selling prices achieved in these transactions by making a number of offers by tender.

Discounts here have been much narrower, and indeed in a number of cases the minimum tender price has been pitched too high with the result that offers were under-subscribed e.g. Britoil (35% of shares applied for), Cable and Wireless (70%) and Enterprise Oil (73%). Thus the mechanics of privatisation have proved unexpectedly difficult and, in general, the sales proceeds have been less than could have been obtained by tight pricing of the issues concerned and have been less than necessary to maintain the net worth of the public sector. While it remains true that the peculiar accounting conventions of the PSBR give artificial incentives to privatisation, it does not appear that financial objectives have been the primary purposes, or achievements, of privatisation.

VI. The Rolc of Management

We have noted that there have been distinct shifts of emphasis in the policy of privatisation since 1979. An initial concern for liberalisation can be seen in the 1980 Transport Act – which deregulated express coaching – and in the 1981 Telecommunications Act and 1983 Energy Act. Increasingly, however, the primary objective has become the transfer of ownership. A statement of government objectives (Moore, 1983) asserted that competition was still the primary consideration, but these words have not been supported by actions. And indeed in its most recent policy statement the government asserted that it plans to privatise natural monopolies where competition 'does not make business or economic sense' (Moore, 1985).

The clear theme to emerge from the political history of privatisation is that by far the most effective and influential of interest groups is the senior management of the potentially privatised industry. Their positive interest in privatisation is in being rid of what is seen as a burdensome form of Treasury control; their concurrent interests are in ensuring that this is achieved without change to the existing organisational structure and without a move to a more competitive environment. This is the structure which they have supported in every case and, with one area of exception, it is a structure which they have succeeded in persuading the government to adopt. If, as we have argued, the privatisation of large, dominant firms is at best pointless and possibly harmful in the absence of effective competition, the result is that no benefits to economic performance are likely to be achieved. Privatisation of this kind would not, of course, be the first ineffectual restructuring of relationships between government and nationalised industries, which has had a lengthy history. But it is potentially more damaging than the others because privatisation makes it more difficult to introduce competitive incentives in the future. Future liberalisation of airline routes would, for example, devalue shares of the privatised British Airways. Also fragmentation into smaller operating units is harder to impose on a private firm than a public one.

British Telecom was privatised as it stood: the idea of following the American route and creating local operating companies was rejected, as was the separation of the international divisions. American experience has shown that there are three critical elements in the promotion of competition in telecommunications: entry, access and resale. Mercury are licensed to provide competing services, but no further licences are to be issued until the end of the decade. Their effective entry depends on access to BT local networks; this was the subject of litigation as Mercury sought to establish the power of OFTEL to impose effective access terms. Resale of capacity is prohibited till the end of the decade.

The Civil Aviation Authority recommended that the privatisation of British Airways should be preceded by the establishment of a route network sufficient to establish British Caledonian as an effective competitor. After an intensive parliamentary lobbying campaign British Airways persuaded the government to reject these proposals and instead British Caledonian were compensated with exclusive rights as flag carrier on extremely profitable, because tightly regulated, routes to the Persian Gulf.

The majority of commercial activities undertaken at British airports are undertaken by airlines, contractors or franchisees under the oversight of the British Airports Authority. The Authority provides the airport infrastructure and sets prices for aircraft landings and the more important services. It is not a commercial organisation in any familiar sense and the arguments it uses to support the continuation of the existing organisational structure – principally the public interest in a coordinated approach to the expansion of London's airport capacity – are those of a regulatory authority. But it has succeeded – again after an extensive lobbying campaign – in persuading the government to reject the difficult but conceivable course of a competitive market solution to airport development (Starkie and Thompson, 1985). In this the price of landing slots would be determined, as far as possible, by market forces and ownership and operation of London's three principal airports would be entrusted to three different organisations. The government has accepted that BAA should be privatised as a single entity.

And recent reports may be taken to indicate the shape of privatisation to come.

> 'Proposals to privatise the British Gas Corporation as a whole, rather than piecemeal, have been submitted to a Cabinet Committee by Mr Peter Walker, the Energy Secretary, with a view to early legislation. Mr Walker has made no secret of his scepticism about the desire of his predecessor, Mr Nigel Lawson, to break down the present monopoly and to introduce competition into the energy utilities' (*Financial Times*, 29 April 1985).
>
> 'Sir Walter Marshall, chairman of the Central Electricity Generating Board, said last night that he saw the privatisation of the electricity industry as a logical consequence of the proposed sale of the gas industry.... It

would also be "the only logical thing to do" for the Government to sell off the CEGB intact rather than power station by power station. This is what had been done with British Telecom and what was being done with British Gas.' (*Financial Times*, 13 June 1985).

'The Thames Water Authority said it was keen to be privatised. Mr Roy Watts, the Chairman, estimated that the authority might be worth £1 billion on the stockmarket. The Welsh Water Authority, however, has urged the Government not to privatise it. The 10 Authorities are opposed to any suggestion that their function should be divided' (*Financial Times*, 19 June 1985).

The conflict between privatisation and liberalisation – noted by Kay and Silberston (1984) – is no longer a conflict but a rout. There is one important area of exception. We have noted that express coaching services were deregulated in 1980. It was expected that privatisation of the National Bus Company, or at least of its express coaching subsidiary, would follow deregulation. But this has not happened, principally because of disagreement about the future structure of the industry; the Department of Transport wishing to see a number of distinct operating units, the National Bus Company favouring retention of the existing structure. Instead, a bill is now before Parliament extending deregulation to stage carriage services.

VII. Conclusions

Privatisation in the United Kingdom has increasingly come to emphasise the virtues of denationalisation over, and even at the expense of, the promotion of competition. This change of direction is, we have argued, not supported by empirical evidence on the relative performance of public and private enterprise. This stresses the role of competition and supports scepticism about the value of privatisation outside a competitive environment. The promotion of competition in the areas covered by nationalised industries is rarely straightforward, and indeed it is often the problems which would arise in a competitive environment which provided the initial rationale for nationalisation. But we have shown that the range of possibilities is wider than has hitherto usually been assumed. Scope exists for introducing competition (in particular through franchising) to industries traditionally regarded as natural monopolies or where significant external benefits and costs require recognition. The primary obstacles to competition, however, are not technical but result from the opposition of incumbent management to any restructuring of their industries; and it is this opposition which has framed the development of the programme of privatisation.

Acknowledgements

The authors are grateful to Samuel Brittan, Dieter Helm and Colin Mayer for comments on an earlier draft and to Evan Davis and Shirley Meadowcroft for assistance in the research: the usual disclaimer applies.

References

Ashworth, M. H. and Forsyth, P. J. (1984). *British Airways*. IFS Report Series 12. Institute for Fiscal Studies, London.

Audit Commission (1984). *Securing Further Improvements in Refuse Collection.*

Averch, H. and Johnson, L. K. (1962). 'Behaviour of the firm under regulatory constraint.' *American Economic Review*, vol. 52, December.

Baumol, W., Panzar, J. C. and Willig, R. (1982). *Contestable Markets and the Theory of Industry Structure*. New York: Harcourt Brace Jovanovich.

Borcherding, T. E., Pommerehne, W. W. and Schneider, F. (1982). 'Comparing the efficiency of private and public production: the evidence from five countries.' *Zeitschrift für Nationalökonomie*. Journal of Economics, Supplement 2.

Buiter, W. H. (1983). 'Measurement of the public sector deficit and its implications for policy evaluation and design.' *IMF Staff Papers*.

Caves, D. W. and Christensen, L. R. (1978). *The Relative Efficiency of Public and Private Firms in a Competitive Environment: The Case of Canadian Railroads*. Social Systems Research Institute, Workshop Series.

Chadwick, E. (1859). *Research of Different Principles of Legislation and Administration in Europe of Competition for the Field as Compared with Competition within the Field of Service*. Journal of the Royal Statistical Society, Series A, 22.

Civil Aviation Authority (1984). *Airline Competition Policy*.

Crain, W. M. and Zardkodhi, A. (1978). 'A test of the property rights theory of the firm.' *Journal of Law and Economics*.

Davies, D. D. (1971). 'The efficiency of public versus private firms in a competitive environment: The case of Australia's two airlines.' *Journal of Law and Economics*.

Davis, E. H. (1984). 'Express coaching since 1980: Liberalisation in practice.' *Fiscal Studies*.

Demsetz, H. (1968). 'Why regulate utilities.' *Journal of Law and Economics*.

Domberger, S. (1985). 'Economic regulation through franchise contracts.' Paper to IFS Regulation Conference.

Drucker, P. (1974). *Management: Tasks, Responsibilities, Practices*. London: Heinemann.

Fisinger, J. and Pauly, M. V. eds. (1985). *The Economics of Insurance Regulation: A Cross-National Study*. London: Macmillan.

Forsyth, P. J. (1984). 'Airlines and airports: privatisation, competition and regulation.' *Fiscal Studies*.

——— and Hocking, R. D. (1980). *Economic Record*.

Furubotn, E. G. and Pejovich, S. (1972). 'Property rights and economic theory: a survey of recent literature.' *Journal of Economic Literature*, December.

Hills, J. R. (1984). 'Public assets and liabilities and the presentation of budgetary policy.' In (M. H. Ashworth, J. R. Hills and C. N. Morris) *Public Finances in Perspective*. IFS Report Series, no. 8.

Hotelling, H. (1938). 'The general welfare in relation to problems of taxation and of railway and utility rates.' *Econometrica*.

Hunt (1982). *Report of the Inquiry into Cable Expansion and Broadcasting Policy.* Cmnd 8679, London: H.M.S.O.
Kay, J. A. and Silberston, Z. A. (1984). 'The new industrial policy – privatisation and competition.' *Midland Bank Review*, Spring.
Little, I. M. D. (1952). *A Critique of Welfare Economics*. Oxford: Oxford University Press.
Manne, H. G. (1965). 'Mergers and Market for Corporate Control.' *Journal of Political Economics*, vol. 73.
Millward, R. (1982). 'The comparative performance of public and private ownership.' In (ed. E. Roll) *The Mixed Economy*. London: Macmillan.
Moore, J. (1983). Speech by John Moore MP, at the annual conference of City of London Stockbrokers Fielding, Newson Smith: 1 November 1983.
Moore, J. (1985). Speech by John Moore MP at Hoare Govett Ltd dealing rooms: 17 July 1985.
Pescatrice, D. R. and Trapani, J. M. (1980). 'The performance and objectives of public and private utilities operating in the United States.' *Journal of Public Economics*, vol. 13, pp. 259–76.
Primeaux, W. J. (1977). 'An assessment of *X*-efficiency gained through competition.' *Review of Economics and Statistics*.
Pryke, R. (1982). 'The comparative performance of public and private enterprise.' *Fiscal Studies*, vol. 3.
Savas, E. S. (1977). 'An empirical study of competition in municipal service delivery.' *Public Administration Review*.
Schmalensee, R. (1979). *The Control of Natural Monopolies*. Lexington: D. C. Heath & Co.
Sharkey, W. W. (1982). *The Theory of Natural Monopoly*. Cambridge: Cambridge University Press.
Starkie, D. and Thompson, D. (1985). *Privatising London's Airports*. IFS Report Series 16. London: Institute for Fiscal Studies.

79

Privatisation: A Comment on Kay and Thompson

Samuel Brittan

Source: *Economic Journal*, 96(1), 1986, pp. 33–8.

The Kay–Thompson paper interprets privatisation as the sale of public sector industrial assets. It would be best to stick to this interpretation, for the discussion of other aspects of privatisation in the Kay–Thompson paper is not extensive.

The authors list five possible aims in the denationalisation of public sector industry. (1) improvement of the economic performance of the industries concerned, (2) resolving the difficulties of relations between government and nationalised industries, (3) revenue raising, (4) reduction of the power of public sector unions, (5) the promotion of a popular capitalism through wider share ownership.

Some of these aspects are not analysed at all, and others only partially or indirectly. The authors' interest is obviously mainly in the first aim – improved economic performance.

Here they provide an illuminating summary of recent academic literature, which suggests that it is the *interaction* of private ownership and competition which produces efficiency. Competition ensures that low efficiency is penalised by low profits; while private ownership and effective capital markets ensure that low profits are met by eventual withdrawal from the activity concerned.

The main thesis of the paper is that the managements of nationalised industries will oppose more competition, either in the form of breaking up existing structures or introducing a more liberal regulatory regime. But as the co-operation of existing managements is important (or essential? the authors are not clear) to the success of privatisation, they have the power to frustrate the competitive objectives. Hence privatisation has not brought competition, but simply involved the transformation of public into private monopolies. Moreover this tendency has increased as the privatisation exercise has got under way. The result, as I understand the authors, is not merely useless or neutral, but positively harmful, because it is more difficult to unscramble organisations or change the rules of the game after denationalisation.

My first inclination was to agree with the authors about the broad tendency, although to substitute the slogan 'missed opportunity' for their 'worse than useless' conclusion. But on re-reading the paper doubts grew.

Most of the early acts of privatisation did not include public sector monopolies. They were either sales of concerns already operating in highly competitive markets such as Britoil, or Amersham; or they consisted of sales of shares from the Government portfolio such as the successive tranches of BP.

The authors list six examples of asset sales involving public sector monopolies or semi-monopolies. These are British Telecom, British Airways, British Airports Authority, National Bus Company, British Gas and the Regional Water Authorities.

Of these only Telecom has already occurred; and the authors concede that regulatory restrictions have been eased in a number of ways, although far less than would have been desirable.

Of the remaining organisations, the authors see severe technical limits to increased competition for the water authorities. In the case of National Bus, the Secretary of State for Transport has gone very far to secure competition before privatisation in his present Bill, despite backbench as well as management pressure; and the paper is grudging, if not misleading, here.

This leaves the twin cases of British Airways and the British Airports Authority, and British Gas, where the authors' generalisations may hold. There have not yet been any concrete proposals on gas, only general statements of intent. Gas and Telecom are far and away the financially most important examples of privatisation; and one would have liked more information on the technical possibilities of competition in the case of gas.

But all we are given is a quotation from a newspaper story, saying that the previous Energy Secretary intended to privatise the British Gas Corporation wholesale, in place of the desire of his predecessor to 'break down the present monopoly'. What were these earlier trust-busting plans; and would they have been either adequate or effective? The authors might have made a few enquiries.

At any rate, out of five cases where increased competition was a possibility, the Government has partially grasped two, and effectively turned it down in three.

The paper is, however, disappointing because, having pinpointed the main dynamic force against competition – the vested interest of existing managements – it leaves the matter there. Do we have to take a fatalistic view of management obstruction; and is the whole idea of privatisation plus competition a delusion? Or are there ways of circumventing this opposition? And would such circumvention have involved lower realisation prices – lower even than those arising from the introduction of competition itself? And how much would such a shortfall have mattered? A critique of Government policy, which fails to come to grips with such questions, is analytically inadequate.

This brings me to some broader misgivings about the paper, namely the absence of a public choice framework. It is very clear that the promotion of efficiency and competition is far from being the only motive behind the privatisation programme, and that many other causes have contributed to the present preoccupation. *The authors have given the Government a low grade, but in an examination which the Government is not actually taking.* If economists are to have an impact on policy, or even just improve understanding, they must move from the comparison of policies with some ideal of their own devising, to the economic analysis of the political market place.

This paper does so on one point only – management opposition to promoting competition – and I have mentioned why I think this part of the analysis is incomplete. It misses out the main preliminary question, which is why privatisation has become so prominent in the Thatcher Government's programme. Not why Ministers say it has been, but why social scientists observing from outside think that this should have occurred.

The sale of government industrial assets hardly featured in the Conservative manifesto of 1979 and it was not a major issue in the1983 election. Here are a few hypotheses on the increased emphasis.

(1) The stated Conservative desire to reduce public spending and taxation as proportions of GDP has proved impossible to realise. Both these ratios are now higher than in 1979. On the other hand, denationalisation has proved technically easier and politically more acceptable than originally supposed. Hence it has been promoted as a partial ideological substitute for the earlier goal of reducing the role of public spending. It has also been promoted as a 'success story' in the crude sense of lists of industries and companies sold off – when there has been a scarcity of success in other fields of policy.

(2) Inside Whitehall, privatisation received an impetus from the sheer difficulty of devising criteria for regulating the borrowing of nationalised industries. The beguiling suggestion of 'taking the nationalised industries out of the PSBR' and for allowing them to borrow on the capital markets proved a delusion. A state concern, which has the Government behind its debts, cannot help borrowing on privileged terms compared with privately owned companies. The Treasury insisted that any loans raised outside the PSBR must contain a genuine element of risk, a point on which it was not easily convinced. The most traumatic single event was the failure to devise a 'Buzby bond' which would enable British Telecom to borrow on the private market.

The inference drawn from these protracted controversies was that an arm's-length relationship with nationalised industries was impracticable; and that if they really wanted to escape Treasury control the private sector was the best place for them.

(3) A motivation the authors do discuss is revenue raising. But the role of this factor is extraordinarily elusive. It is surely pretty clear to the Treasury that asset sales are a way of *financing* Government borrowing, alternative to gilt-edged sales, rather than reducing it. The fact that Treasury ministers and officials are understandably reluctant to embark on a grand exercise to revise the definition of the PSBR, does not mean that they are misled by PSBR conventions. Extreme stupidity is as unlikely a motivation for public officials as disinterested concern for the abstract public good. No Chancellor and no economic adviser supposes that if another tranche of £500m. of BP is sold, taxes can be reduced one-for-one. If more BP is sold, the appropriate PSBR target is also reduced, whether you are a Keynesian, a monetarist, or a believer in the new classical economies.

On the whole it has been the departments sponsoring the privatised industries that have put most emphasis on the revenue from asset disposal, while such impetus as there has been for promoting competition, and thus reducing realisation prices, has come from sections of the Treasury.

One reason for this may be that the sponsoring departments are closer to the nationalised industries; and consciously or unconsciously realise the connection between monopoly power and sales proceeds.

There is also a more institutional reason. Treasury or any other financial control must work through numerical objectives which contain an arbitrary element, but which spending departments have to respect. If control is to be maintained, it is only the central financial department that can authorise either changes in the financial objective or its definition or authorise overshoots. To a non-Treasury minister, especially to a not-so-closet reflationist, some £2bn. off the PSBR will look like a way to tax cuts or expenditure increases. But the Treasury, which sets the PSBR objective, is more likely to see the need for an offsetting change in target.

We are still left, however, with a cosmetic question. If a Government wishes to reduce taxes or increase public spending, either because of a genuine macroeconomic judgement, or because it wants to take a political risk, does a cosmetic reduction in the PSBR due to privatisation help?

The most one can say is that, as the PSBR has come to occupy a place in public mythology, which it was never intended to do in the MTFS (partly because of the breakdown of the monetary aggregates as effective indicators), if a PSBR overshoot is likely or desirable in any case, a moderate bringing forward of asset sales, which were going to take place in any case, might slightly bolster government credibility. Successful asset disposal might mean a Budget judgement nearer the upper end of the range, but that is all.

(4) Kay and Thompson are right to point out that asset sales techniques are not designed to maximise revenue. Technical improvements, such as selling

shares a little at a time, as the paper suggests, can be made. But realisation will always fall short of the maximum, while the Government has the further objective of 'wider share ownership'.

'Wider share ownership' in the eyes of the present Government does not mean shares for all citizens. It is an enlargement of the shareholder class by means of concessionary terms for small shareholders and workers in the privatised concerns. There are no comprehensive figures of numbers involved; but there are known to be 1¾ million shareholders in Telecom; and over 300,000 employees have shares in privatised companies in which they work. Thus the total number of shareholders is certainly above the 1979 low point of 1¾ million; and it is likely that the proportion of United Kingdom shares owned by individuals, which was down to 28% by the end of 1981, has begun to recover.

These new shareholders are a strong constituency against a future Government renationalising the industry at less than fair market price; and they provide some discouragement to renationalisation altogether. Although possession of a small number of Telecom shares is unlikely to be a major factor in a person's vote, any impact it has favours the Conservatives (short of a market disaster with privatised stock).

These measures do not however create 'citizen ownership'. On the most optimistic assumptions, over 90% of the British public remain without shares; and the relatively cheap disposal price is a regressive subsidy from the general body of taxpayers to those on the fringes of the existing shareholder class.

If the Government were really interested in a 'people's capitalism', it would not sell privatised shares on concessionary terms but hand them over 'free' pro rata to every citizen. This would create a much greater, if more thinly spread, opposition to renationalisation. Much more important, every citizen would for the first time have an opportunity to participate in equity profits.

The give-away option is not, of course, costless. If the government hands over £1 bn. of assets it might otherwise have sold, then for a given financial deficit, it will have to sell £1 bn. more of gilt-edged securities and meet the interest burden on this extra £1 bn. for ever afterwards.

So a handover of state assets would reduce the scope for future tax cuts or increase any need for future tax increases, compared with conventional privatisation. Instead of lower taxes, citizens would receive dividend payments on the denationalised stock.

These dividend payments would have the following advantages over tax reductions:

(*a*) *Distribution.* Nationalised industry stock would initially be distributed equally to all citizens. Tax cuts inevitably benefit those who pay most taxes.

(*b*) *Capitalisation.* Even more important: holders of the new stock would be able to realise their assets in the markets, or borrow on their strength, and thus have the benefits of wealth ownership. There is not, on the other hand, and could hardly be, a market in rights to hypothetical future tax cuts.

It was a pity that Kay and Thompson did not explore the implications of alternative methods of assets disposals, and I shall myself have to be brief on the implications of the give-away method.

There is an obvious effect of any give-away of assets in making the ownership of capital assets less concentrated. The wider spread of capital ownership and investment income would be a small but worthwhile step in bringing the undoubted benefits of a private investment income – what used to be called a 'modest competence' – to citizens whose sole assets have hitherto been houses and pension rights.

Wider capital ownership could also make an indirect contribution to reducing unemployment. One aspect, at least, of high unemployment is wages above market-clearing rates. It is likely that market-clearing factor prices have moved against unskilled labour and in favour of capital. A shift towards market-clearing wages would have less objectionable distributional effects if capital were more widely held and workers could recoup some at least of the losses from lower wages in investment income.

Popular ownership of shares in the formerly nationalised industries would be only a start. Measures to secure a broader spread of ownership of other capital assets outside the state industry sector would be necessary too. But the give-away form of denationalisation would at least point the way to a widespread popular ownership of capital. Thus with more imagination than has so far been shown, privatisation could both be given a more radical thrust and at the very same time contribute towards the policy combination required if we are to return to anything approaching full employment.

But I must stop chasing this hare – not only because of lack of time, but because I would have, in the spirit of my own criticism of the paper, to suggest how governments could be given incentives to hand over rather than sell state assets, and this is unfinished business.

Conclusion

While I share most of the authors' objections to recent methods of privatisation, my own verdict would be 'Slightly better than nothing' rather than 'Slightly worse than nothing'.

Some of the reasons for this difference have been given *ambulando*. But the main reason is a different view of the political dialectics. The present revival of interest in competition and anti-monopoly policy, and the economics of regulation, owes much of its impetus to the privatisation debate. Faced with the charge of simply creating private monopolies, the Government is impelled to introduce some competitive elements, despite the undesirable influence of existing management, described in the paper. Some moves to promote competition are better than none at all. The debate on whether the newly privatised enterprises are abusing their market power would hardly have taken off in an earlier period when it was taken for granted that these were boring public utilities, reserved for state monopoly.

The most accurate conclusion is the rather vague one that privatisation has stirred up many corners of British industry – much less effectively than truly radical policies such as unilateral free trade – but more effectively than anything else on the political horizon.

An Analysis of the Privatization of Japan National Railway Corporation

Tetsuzo Yamamoto

Source: *The Political Economy of Privatization*, eds T. Clarke and C. Pitelis (London: Routledge, 1993), Chap. 15, pp. 337–59.

Introduction

The period from 1981 to 1987 could be defined as the age of administrative reform in Japan. This period began with the creation of the second *ad hoc* Council on Administrative Reform (Rincho) and ended with the privatization of Japan National Railways (JNR).

Rincho, chaired by Toshiwo Doko, raised two basic ideas of reform – namely, building a revitalized welfare society, and contributing positively to the well-being of the world. It aimed at drastic reforms concerning: the replacement of a paternal and protective administration by a new one which would require the people to be more independent and self-supportive; the promotion of deregulation and privatization instead of an increase in government control; a readjustment of relationships between the central and local governments, especially with respect to the transfer of power or jurisdiction to the local self-autonomies.

Rincho submitted five reports during 1981–3. The Third Report in July 1982 was very important: it recommended that the so-called three public corporations (JNR, NTT – the Nippon Telegraph and Telephone Public Corporation, JTSPC – the Japan Tobacco and Salt Public Corporation) should be privatized and opened up to competition. In particular the privatization of JNR was the most controversial and symbolic of the range of regulatory reforms in respect of its scale and overall significance for the Japanese economy.

In this chapter, we will first of all consider the background and factors which acted as a catalyst to privatizations in Japan, especially that of JNR; second, the various opinions which advocated or opposed JNR's privatization; third, the process of the privatization; fourth, its managerial effects; and, finally, the influence of JNR's privatization on the land transportation markets. The purpose of this chapter is to estimate the effects in the short term, to clarify the problems which Japan Railways (JR) faces now, and to conclude provisionally as to whether JNR's privatization was successful or not.

The Background

We will first define Japanese-style privatization. The word 'privatization', which reminds Japanese people of the transfer of government companies to the private sector in the Meiji era, means basically the selling off or the transfer of public corporations or government enterprises to private companies within the framework of the Commercial Code. In contrast to Britain's privatization, which includes three concepts – denationalization, liberalization or deregulation, and contracting out – it can be said that Japanese-style privatization is much narrower in scope. Privatization in Japan can be compatible with regulation as seen in the case of NTT. It is also different from contracting out, which is expressed in Japan by the word *minkatsu* (the injection of private sector competitiveness or vitality into the public sector).

Now to the question of what significance the privatization measure holds in the wide range of administrative reforms of the mid-1980s. It could be evaluated as the representative policy among many measures suggested by Rincho. In fact privatization of the three public corporations became a key problem in terms of inefficiency, the impediments of monopolies, and diseconomies of scale. The proposal of JNR's privatization was especially seen as the focus of Rincho/Doko because of its huge financial deficits and fierce objections against the privatization.

Next, we examine the background and the factors which acted as a catalyst to privatization. Japan has previously experienced booms of privatization twice in modern history. The first wave of privatizations occurred during the early 1880s – the so-called *Kangyo Haraisage* in the Meiji era. At that time the government, urged to reconstruct fiscal conditions, found itself forced to sell off a number of infant enterprises to the private sector. As a result of *Shokusan Kogyo* (policy for promoting industry and increasing production), the government had owned and managed many enterprises in the major industries. The second wave was realized as part of the American Occupation policies which compelled the Japanese government to scrap or sell off most of the state-owned enterprises, and as part of the Dodge Line shift from 1949–52 which aimed to make the Japanese economy more efficient and to reduce the continuing costs of supporting Japan. For example, the Japan Electric Power Company, owned by the state, was divided and privatized in this period.

The boom in the mid-1980s can be seen as the third wave of privatization in Japan. We can pick out the following factors as the background of recent privatizations:

1 *Socioeconomic change.* Rapid technological changes in the field of hi-tech industries and their diffusion into nearly all industries, not only brought about environmental changes in market conditions and structures where government's monopolistic services were hitherto deemed indispensable, but also required the improvement of efficiency and service in the fields of industrial infrastructure.
2 *Fiscal crisis and rising financial costs of the public corporations.* Between 1974 and 1979, Japan's national deficit rose from 1.6 to 6.1 per cent of GNP, with the national debt service burden also increasing from 5.3 per cent of general account expenditures in 1975 to 11 per cent in 1979. Without tax reform, including a reduction in corporate tax, the government could not increase military spending as it was compelled to do by the Reagan administration. The government examined the fiscal conditions to reduce expenditures and was inclined to sell off the government-affiliated enterprises. In particular JNR's financial losses, non-profitability and inefficiency, which tended to eat up public money, were regarded as one reason for the national fiscal deficits.
3 *Maturity of conditions.* The government failed to improve the performance of the public sector in the 1960s. The Ikeda Cabinet advocated public sector retrenchment as a means of unshackling the private sector and established the first *ad hoc* Council on Administrative Reform in 1960. But the Japan Socialist Party (JSP) and the Sohyo (the largest federation of trade unions at that time) objected to the government's proposals; the bureaucracy resisted the reforms too. The conditions for privatization were not mature yet. But through the 1970s the surroundings were altered. Rincho's chairman Doko, who put forward the reforms, and Prime Minister Nakasone, who orchestrated the process of privatization, took the initiative and people who made complaints against the inefficiency of the public sector supported their activities. With regard to the circumstances, various factors such as socioeconomic changes, the rapid progress of new technologies, and fiscal crisis, all required administrative reforms. It should be noted that the decline of the JSP and trade unions in the 1980s facilitated the reforms.

These factors, however, were not sufficient to realize the privatizations. There also existed other catalysts which stimulated the process of privatization:

1 *Foreign pressure.* In determining the profile of privatization in the 1980s, the role of foreign pressure should not be underestimated. The US in particular felt that privatization could open new opportunities by increasing competition and accelerating market growth – this in turn increasing demand for imports. Japan had to concede to America's pressure in order to alleviate escalating trade friction.
2 *Boom in the capital markets.* In the mid-1980s Japanese capital markets

developed rapidly and sales of public assets promised to be highly profitable to the state, as well as to the financial intermediaries involved in underwriting them. In fact, the proceeds to the government by selling off 12.5 per cent of NTT shares came to more than 11 per cent of the total fiscal 1987 national revenue.

Opinions For and Against the Privatization of JNR

In the Third Report of Rincho, the special panel chaired by Hiroshi Kato, pointed out that public corporations had difficulties in certain areas of operation. First there was the special principal-agent relationship, the Diet and government interventions, the ambiguity of managerial responsibility, and a lack of ability to deal with labour problems, etc. Second, there existed a lack of self-awareness on the part of labour as to their role as public servants. Third, there were the excessive demands from the people made on the public corporations and, finally, the difficulty of managerial control due to the large scale of the organization.

The Report insisted that the public corporations could not control themselves or promote the reforms within the existing framework, further suggesting that the public corporations should be privatized and effective competition be introduced in this field. It highlighted JNR's problems, which were identified as external interference; uniform management which disregarded different regional conditions concerning transport demands and regional economy; and the unstable relationship between management and labour, etc. To remedy the faults, the report suggested that the Diet intervention should be abolished and that government regulations be decreased to the same level as those affecting the private sector, concluding that JNR should be divided into seven special corporations and privatized completely through a selling off of its shares to the public after five years.

With regard to the clearance of the huge liabilities, the Report suggested that Japan Railways (JR) should inherit a level of debts consistent with being able to repay the amount with interest included, subject to the implementation of rationalization and cost reduction. It also suggested that the remaining debts should be kept in the JNR Settlement Corporation and subsidized by the government. Following these suggestions, the JNR Reconstruction Supervision Commission was set up in 1983 and it considered privatization measures to solve the problems of the debts and inefficiency.

Opinions against the Privatization

After the announcement of the Third Report, an anti-privatization campaign was promoted by the JSP and the Kokuro (the largest trade union in JNR which played an important role in the Sohyo labour movement) and many critical opinions were expressed. In 1986, when the drafts of JNR's privatization laws were submitted to the Diet, the controversies reached their height. A number of different opinions were voiced.

1 The possibility of impeding the 'public interest'. If the abolition of unprofitable rural lines was permitted it would enlarge the gap among regional economies. Accordingly, privatization would be likely to destroy 'equity'.
2 The influence on labour problems. Privatization would bring about mass unemployment and worsen the labour conditions, thus threatening passenger safety.
3 Division into regional companies would not only make it impossible to supply a universal service, but would also induce managerial inequality in the six regional passenger companies. It would give advantages to one or two companies (JR Higashi and JR Tokai) and drive the other companies into a hopeless condition.

Despite these opinions, the proposal for privatization was supported by most of the people and the mass media in the hope that train fares would be stabilized and bad service eradicated.

Opinions for Privatization

In Japan there were no academic groups or research institutes which influenced policy formation like the Chicago School in the US or IEA in Britain. However, some academics, who believe in neo-liberalism and public choice theory, participated in Rincho as commissioners; others, who imported the contestability theory and principal-agent relation theory, were drawn to the ministries for policy formation (*seisaku chosei kancho*) such as the Economic Planning Agency.

Although they played a role in enlightening the people, it is doubtful whether the government applied the theories of these academics to the mechanics of Japanese privatization. For example, in the case of JNR, the theory of contestability may have been ineffectual because JNR competed with the private railway companies and underground railroads in the urban areas and had lost its monopolistic position: the market structure was more competitive than the contestability theory had supposed. Though the regional monopoly would be maintained in the countryside, the hypothesis of 'sunk cost = zero' would not be developed here. A lease or second-hand market had not developed because of the nature of the industry (the difficulty of separating the base structure from the superstructure) and the decreasing number of passengers, many of whom had abandoned the railway and made use of cars. The 'hit and run' strategy of the new entrants does not work in the railway industry.

It is wrong, however, to say that there was no place for theory in the privatizing of the public corporations. Several previous failures to reconstruct JNR required consideration of the following problems: government failure;

comparison of performance between the public corporations and private enterprises; principal-agent relationships; management accountability; and the relationship between management and labour. These factors were studied pragmatically. Thus, privatization in Japan was implemented on the basis of analyses obtained from domestic experiences rather than from imported theories.

The Process of the Privatization

Japan's first railway line, between Tokyo and Yokohama, was opened under government auspices in 1872. But the state did not suppress the construction of private railways. Its model was the mixed public-private railway system of Prussia. At the turn of the century, the private companies became much larger than the national railway in terms of the length of track lines and the volume of passenger transport. In 1906, the government nationalized the Japanese railway industry by acquiring seventeen private companies under the National Ownership of Railways Law. It was mainly motivated by military objectives (the efficient operation of a nation-wide transport system). After that it established a monopolistic position in land transportation and its management developed favourably till 1944, when the air raids of the US Army disrupted its operations.

In 1949, JNR was created in order to improve organizational efficiency in response to the demands of industry and to weaken the nascent labour movement, General Douglas MacArthur's design being to strengthen Japan as a bulwark against Communism and to disrupt the power of the militant public sector unions. JNR became a *kohsha*, or public corporation, whose model was based on the Anglo-American public corporation.

JNR maintained its monopolistic power in the 1950s and in 1955 accounted for 55 per cent of the passenger transport market and 52 per cent in the freight market. But its share began to decrease gradually in the 1960s because of the rapid development of motorization and urbanism. When automobiles and aircraft became the most efficient means of transportation, the railways lost their dominant position. In competition with private railways, JNR could not maintain the advantage, either. In 1964 JNR recorded operating losses of ¥30 billion and faced financial problems in the late 1960s. Its conditions became worse in the 1970s and its deficit reached ¥100 billion in 1980 alone. The company's share of transportation decreased to 24.7 per cent (passenger) and 8.4 per cent (freight) in the same year.

In order to revive JNR's share of the market, a kind of 'equal-footing' policy such as Kennedy's transport policy which aimed to equalize the base structure and secure a fair competition between railways and automobiles was examined. But such a policy was not adopted. One reason was that the 'equal-footing' policy had not stopped the decline of railways in the US and West

Germany; another was that JNR's failure was thought to exist in management itself rather than in the disadvantageous position that railways found themselves in when competing against automobiles.

The causes of JNR's decline were:

1 *External intervention.* JNR was subjected to excessive government intervention, particularly by politicians with various 'local' concerns. Faced with these pressures, it was forced to engage in large-scale investment for which tariffs and fares were to be set by the government to cross-subsidize one line by another. The result was that JNR was compelled to operate a number of deficit rural lines.
2 *Organizational inefficiency.* Management's accountability was not as firmly established as in the private sector. Management's concern with efficiency was lessened by its expectation that whatever financial loss it made was likely to be made up for by the government. Management failed to meet the socioeconomic changes and to control its relationship with labour (overmanning, wage scale).
3 *Lack of the market principle of the survival of the fittest.* In spite of monopolistic rights ceasing, JNR relied upon them and tried to be free from the competitive pressures of market forces.

The sixth (final) draft for reconstructuring JNR, suggested the downsizing of management and an increase in efficiency by means of a reduction of employees (420 to 350 thousand); a revision of tariffs and fares; the abolition of deficit rural lines; and subsidies by the government to pay for the interests. This reconstruction attempt resulted in failure owing to the poor relations between management and labour. Indeed, JNR's financial deficits increased year by year. Though JNR had more than 358,000 employees and revenues exceeding ¥3 trillion in 1984, it also had huge operating deficits which required subsidies of ¥648.8 billion. In the same year, JNR borrowed ¥836 billion and the government issued public bonds of ¥620 billion for JNR.

Throughout the early 1980s, JNR was known as one of the '3K's (Kome – rice, Kokutetsu – JNR, Kenpo – National Health Service)' – one of the largest contributors to national budgetary deficits. In 1986 the pure operating loss approximated to ¥1,800 billion. The company's debt exceeded ¥25 trillion and pension fund deficits of the mutual aid association were ¥4.9 trillion, making a total debt of about ¥30 trillion in all.

Faced with the financial crisis, the JNR Reconstruction Supervision Commission submitted a 'report of JNR's reconstruction' to the Prime Minister after two years of investigation. Following this proposal, the government presented the drafts relating to JNR's reform to the Diet in 1986. The bills were passed and became law in 1987. JNR was dissolved and split into seven successor firms.

In privatizing JNR, the following steps were adopted as transitory measures: the establishment of rules in the workshop (abolition of implicit

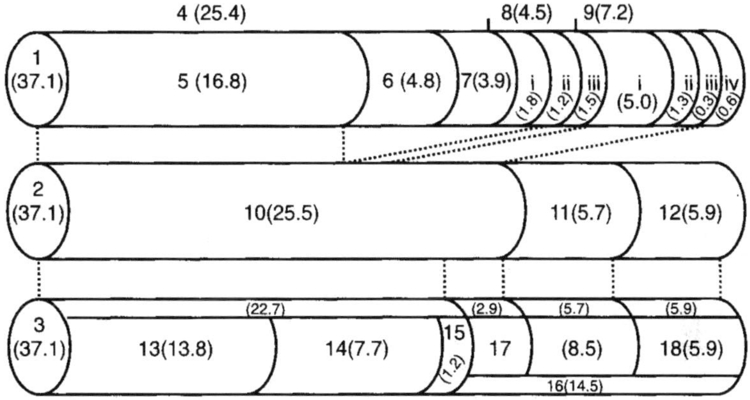

Figure 1 Disposal of Japan National Railways' long-term liabilities and other debts (in ¥ trillion)
Source: JNR Settlement Corporation 1990.
Notes: 1 Long-term liabilities total; 2 Transferred liabilities total; 3 Resources for repayment total; 4 JNR's long-term liabilities etc.; 5 Others; 6 Transferred to JR (passenger companies in Honshu, the freight company, etc.); 7 Equivalent of Tohoku, Tokaido and Sanyo Shinkansen assets (book price); 8 Railway Construction Public Corporation liabilities: i – for Joetsu Shinkansen facilities, ii – for conventional line facilities in Honshu, iii – for Seikan Tunnel facilities etc.; 9 Other liabilities: i – Pension obligations etc., ii – Financial stabilization funds for JR companies in the three smaller islands, iii – Cost for re-employment promotion, iv – Honshu-Shikoku Bridge Authority's liabilities; 10 Transferred to JNR SC; 11 Transferred to Shinkansen Holding Corporation; 12 Transferred to other JR organizations; 13 Borne by the public; 14 Revenue from land sales; 15 Revenue from stock sales, etc.; 16 Borne by JR organizations; 17 Shinkansen rent; 18 Operating revenue.

agreement); a reduction of employees; the discontinuance of capital investment; rationalization of the freight sector; the adjustment of special rural lines; entrance into profitable businesses; control of wage increases; and the freezing of tariffs and fares.

Thus, JNR was split up and privatized in 1987. The regional division was decided on the following criteria: to realize the appropriate size of management; to respond to the demand of regional economies; to introduce competition; and to guarantee accountability in each region.

With regard to the long-term liabilities, the JNR Settlement Corporation assumed the burden of ¥25.5 trillion of the total debt amount of ¥37.1 trillion (as of April 1987). The seven companies and the Shinkansen Holding Corporation took over ¥5.9 trillion and ¥5.7 trillion respectively (see Figure 1).

As for the problem of overmanning, a measure to suspend recruitment was adopted. Surplus workers were gathered to the JNR Settlement Corporation, which was responsible for promoting re-employment through activities such as job-training. It also held shares of the seven companies (9.19 million shares, the value of each unit share ¥50 thousand, making a total of ¥459.5

Table 1 Japan Railways: stocks owned by JNR SC

Company	*Face value (yen)*	*Number of stocks (thousands)*	*Amount (¥ bn)*
Hokkaido Railway Co.	50,000	180	9
East Japan Railway Co.	50,000	4,000	200
Central Japan Railway Co.	50,000	2,240	112
West Japan Railway Co.	50,000	2,000	100
Shikoku Railway Co.	50,000	70	3.5
Kyushu Railway Co.	50,000	320	16
Japan Freight Railway Co.	50,000	380	19
Total	–	9,190	459.5

Source: JNR Settlement Corporation 1990.

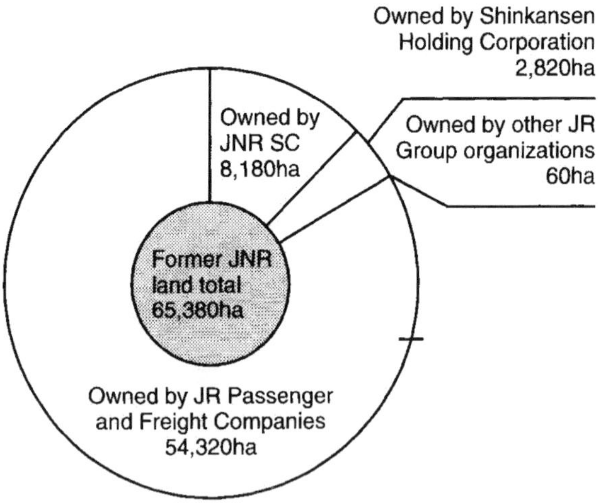

Figure 2 Land taken over by Japan National Railway SC
Source: JNR Settlement Corporation 1990.
Notes: 1 Of the land owned by JNR SC, the area reported to the national Diet as available for sales is 3,350 ha; 2 In addition to the land shown in this figure, JNR SC has about 630 ha of land transferred from the Japan Railway Construction Public Corporation; 3 All figures are as of 1 April 1987.

billion) and a part of the railway lands (see Table 1, Figure 2).

The Shinkansen Holding Corporation was established to deal with the debts related to the Shinkansen. It owned four Shinkansen lines (Tokaido, Sanyo, Joetsu, and Tohoku) and began to lease them to JR. The debts related to the Shinkansen are expected to be made up for by the lease proceeds (see Figure 1).

The privatization of JNR was implemented from the viewpoint of overcoming management problems, because the causes of deficits were seen to exist in the public corporation system itself. But in a wide sense, the factors which deteriorated JNR's management were thought to lie hidden in a series of implicit agreements between the Liberal Democratic Party (LDP) and the JSP – especially concerning JNR's budget in the Diet – and in the failure to separate base-structure from superstructure. The former enabled the employees to increase wage scales above the level of productivity. As for the latter, the creation of the Japan Railway Construction Corporation (1964) did not work well because of the political interventions. For example, JNR's routeing decisions were exposed to greater political influence than before. Throughout the late 1960s and 1970s, JNR continued to increase salaries and benefit packages, and to expand its network of unprofitable rural lines, leading to an accumulation of deficits that attracted growing opposition from the government and the business world.

The Effect of the Privatization on JR's Management

It is said that the industrial behaviour of JR has changed remarkably since 1987. Some economists have analysed these changes by employing the principal–agent theory of Vickers and Yarrow (1988). For example, Okano divided these relationships into two stages (Diet–bureaucracy, bureaucracy–JNR) and analysed the effects of privatization on their management. He argued that privatization could improve the existing principal–agent relationships which inevitably caused inefficiency. The others were critical that JR's profits after privatization were artificially created by the Transport Ministry's plan and that JR's management was inferior to that practised by JNR.

Which opinion is right? Five years have passed since privatization and it is now possible to analyse the performance of JR. According to our observation, the principal–agent relationships have changed to some degree and the financial conditions of the corporation have improved gradually.

As for the volume of passenger transport (person/kilometre), this has been increased by the three inland companies of JR by 1–3 per cent yearly. However, the three island companies of JR have either maintained the same level or volume has fallen by 4 per cent in the Hokkaido company. With regard to freight transport, despite a decrease in the volume transported by freight car the annual growth rate was increased by 3–7 per cent as a result of the increase in cost of container transport.

Reflecting the gradual increase of the volume, the conditions of profit and loss have improved to some extent. Since the privatization, the three inland JR companies have recorded operating profits of ¥100–300 billion. As for the three island companies these have continued to operate in the red. Making up for the losses by the proceeds obtained from the use of the Fund for

Table 2 Japan Railways: revenue and expenditure in 1989 (billion yen)

	JR Hokkaido	*JR East*	*JR Central*	*JR West*	*JR Shikoku*	*JR Kyushu*	*Total (passenger companies)*	*Freight company*	*Overall total*
(A)	Part of ordinary revenue and expenditure								
(A.1)	Section of operating account								
(1.1)	80.9	1672.8	999.5	823.1	41.0	129.7	3747.0	192.1	3939.1
(1.2)	131.7	1395.5	887.1	734.4	51.1	152.9	3352.7	182.2	3534.9
(1.3)	–50.7	277.3	112.4	88.6	–10.0	–23.2	394.4	9.8	404.2
(1.4)	18.9	62.6	3.6	11.2	2.8	14.2	113.3	–	113.3
(1.5)	20.8	58.8	2.3	8.9	4.4	19.7	114.9	–	114.9
(1.6)	–1.9	3.7	1.3	2.2	–1.6	–5.5	–1.8	–	–1.8
(1.7)	–52.7	281.1	113.7	90.9	–11.6	–28.7	392.7	9.8	402.5
(A.2)	Section of non-operating account								
(2.1)	3.4	–177.6	–5.3	–50.6	2.5	4.4	–223.2	–3.4	–226.6
(2.2)	49.5	–	–	–	15.1	28.2	92.8	–	92.8
(A.T.)	0.2	103.4	108.3	40.2	6.1	3.8	262.0	6.4	268.4
(B)	Part of extraordinary revenue and expenditure								
(B.1)	0	1.7	16.6	1.9	0	0.7	20.9	0.1	21.0
(C)	0.3	105.2	124.9	42.1	6.0	4.5	283.0	6.5	289.5
(D)	0.1	47.9	58.2	16.4	2.4	0.7	125.7	3.5	129.2
(E)	0.2	57.2	66.7	25.7	3.6	3.8	157.2	2.9	160.1

Source: The White Paper on Transportation 1990.

Notes:

(1.1) operating revenues of railway business
(1.2) operating expenses of railway business
(1.3) operating revenue and expenditure of railway business
(1.4) operating revenues of the other businesses
(1.5) operating expenses of the other businesses
(1.6) operating revenue and expenditure of the other businesses
(1.7) Total operating revenues and expenditure

(2.1) non-operating revenues and expenditure
(2.2) revenue and expenditure from employing fund for stabilizing management
(A.T.) Total ordinary revenue and expenditure
(B.1) extraordinary revenue and expenditure
(C) income for this term before taxes
(D) corporation tax and like
(E) income for this term

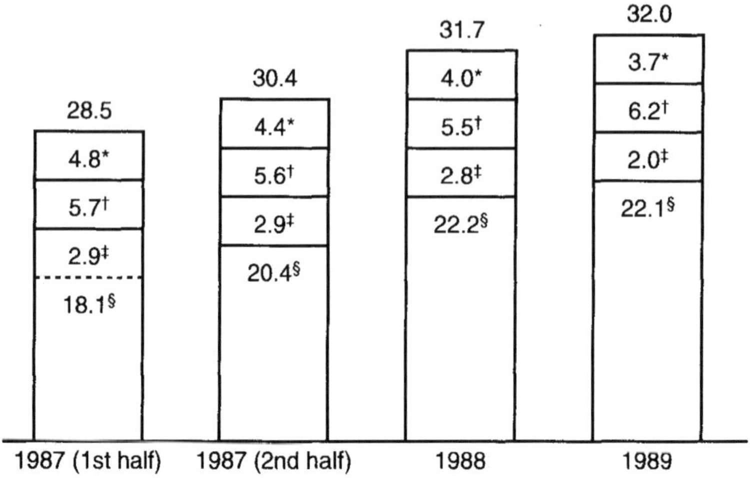

Figure 3 Japan Railways: situation of long-term liabilities, 1987–9 (in ¥ trillion)
Source: The White Paper on Transportation 1990.
Notes: *Liability of JR; †Liability of Shinkansen Holding Corporation; ‡Burden of Shinkansen Holding Corporation; §Liability of JNR Settlement Corporation. Increase of liabilities of JNR Settlement Corporation in 1987 and 1988 was due to taking over the debts of the Seikan Tunnel and the Seto Bridge.

Stabilizing Management, the three island JR companies have barely maintained profits. Overall, the total operating profits of JR reached ¥268.4 billion in 1989, an increase of 26.7 per cent. The Japan Freight Railway Company has also secured ordinary profits through the increase of container transport and rationalization such as cost-cutting and the reduction of employees (see Table 2).

The good performance of JR has been supported by the growth of the land transportation market accompanied by domestic prosperity and the effects of big projects such as the Seikan Tunnel and the Seto Bridge. Much of this is due, however, to the endeavour of JR's management to develop positive profit-earning policies (operation of extra trains, expansion of section operations, speed-up, improvement of train connections, provision of diversified services, introduction of new trains, improvement of stations and facilities), and to the retrenchment policy through rationalization (reduction of operating costs such as adjustment of deficit rural lines, constraint of personnel expenses and management costs).

At the level of JR's management, it can be said that the privatization has been successful. Some serious problems still remain, however. The largest problem is that the primary plan of eliminating the long-term liabilities has not proceeded according to schedule (see Figure 3). The JNR Settlement Corporation had a responsibility to sell the railway lands on a large scale through competitive tendering. But it could not do this because the

Table 3 Japan Railways: disposal of land

	Open competitive bidding		*Free contract*		*Total*	
	Area (ha)	*Price (¥100m)*	*Area (ha)*	*Price (¥100m)*	*Area (ha)*	*Price (¥100m)*
Fiscal 1987	21	213	250	1,116	271	1,329
Fiscal 1988	94	281	872	1,760	966	2,041
Fiscal 1989	71	374	448	2,394	519	2,768
	(1.2)	(24)				

Source: JNR Settlement Corporation 1990.
Notes: 1 Figures in parentheses show the scales in areas under special surveillance, and are included in the upper figures; 2 Prices include those of depreciation assets such as buildings.

government was worried that there might be a sudden rise of land prices, particularly in the metropolitan areas (see Table 3). In addition, it was unable to sell off the shares of JR (the inland companies). The share sale is likely to be postponed for some time owing to the current decline of the Japanese stock-market. Furthermore, the deficit of pension funds became one of the factors that accelerated the financial crisis at JR, though this problem is expected to be solved by integrating this fund into the general pension fund for civil servants.

The second problem is related to the sources from which JR's profits stem. In gaining profits, JR depends on the Shinkansen and the metropolitan transport too heavily. This may cause an imbalance in services to users should rural lines grow worse as a result. The third problem is that JNR's privatization has hardly brought about deregulation. Regulation by the *Tetsudo Kyoku* (railroad office) in the Transport Ministry continues in the field of fares and entry into new businesses as well as in the appointment of managers.

The Effect of Privatization on the Transport Market

First, we will examine the effect of the privatization on the transport market. From 1987–9 the total volume of JR's passenger traffic (person/kilometre) increased by 2–6 per cent year by year (see Figure 4 and Table 4) – a growth rate exceeding that achieved by any private railway company since 1987. It is probable that the introduction of competition resulted in a synergy effect, both on increasing demand and on enlarging the traffic market (see Table 5).

Second, we will analyse the influence of privatization on the transport industry from the view of microeconomics. We don't adopt the SCP

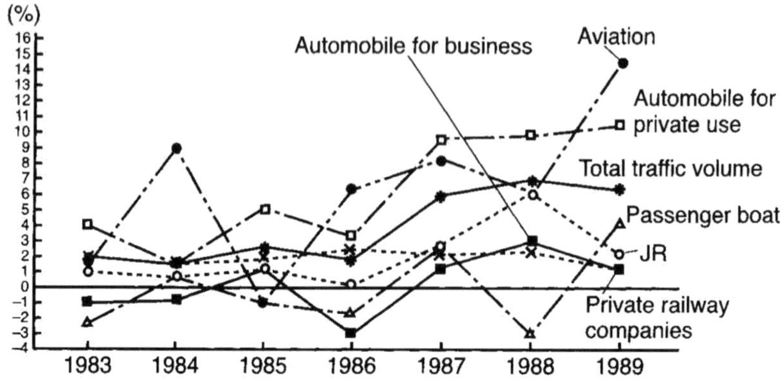

Figure 4 Japan Railways: trend of domestic passenger transport by means of transportation, 1983–9 (person/kilometre)
Source: Kohtsu Nenkan 1991.

(structure, conduct, performance) paradigm of the industrial organization theory. One reason is that I think the paradigm has some theoretical problems; for example, regarding market conduct as a 'black box' on the assumption of concentration-profit, also the mismatch between the spectrum of market structure (measured by concentration) and market performance (measured by efficiency of resource allocation). Another reason is simply that we don't have enough data to complete the work. Therefore, our analysis is based on the following criteria: efficiency; equity; transformation of the system or stability of supply; and safety.

Efficiency

This can be estimated using two criteria: the total productivity and the allocation of resources. With regard to the former it is labour productivity which is the most important factor.

Labour Productivity

JR has achieved a substantial increase in labour productivity. The total number of employees has decreased from about 350,000 in 1984 to below 200,000 in 1989, meaning that half the number of employees are now handling intensified work in comparison with the labour situation in 1980. In general it is said that little labour rationalization was undertaken in Japan prior to privatization. However, this was not so in the case of JNR. As JNR's workers union (Kokuro) and its political party (the JSP) lost their strength and declined rapidly in the 1980s, the labour rationalization proceeded. Furthermore, the relationship between management and labour has been improving for the past few years. The wage scale has been restricted and no labour disputes such as strikes and walk-outs have taken place.

Table 4 Japan Railways: traffic volume

1 Domestic passenger

	Person/kilometre*		Compared with previous year (%)	
Means of transportation	*1988*	*1989*	*88/87*	*89/88*
Total traffic volume	1,190.60	1,267.04	107.5	106.4
Railway	361.80	368.82	105.0	101.9
JR	217.59	222.67	106.3	102.3
Private companies	144.21	146.15	103.0	101.3
Automobile	782.03	845.12	108.8	108.1
Bus	107.22	109.13	104.2	101.8
Bus for business	73.36	74.93	104.7	102.1
Bus for private use	33.86	34.20	103.2	101.0
Car for business	16.06	15.92	100.0	99.2
Car for private use	465.90	519.35	110.5	111.5
Light car	117.20	123.50	110.0	105.4
Freight car	75.65	77.22	106.2	102.1
Aviation	41.10	47.14	106.7	114.7
Passenger boat	5.67	5.96	97.0	105.0

2 Domestic freight

	Ton/kilometre†		Compared with previous year (%)	
	1988	*1989*	*88/87*	*89/88*
Total traffic volume	482.94	513.44	107.6	106.3
Railway	23.48	25.14	114.7	107.1
JR	23.03	24.67	115.0	107.1
Private companies	0.45	0.46	99.7	103.1
Automobile	246.14	262.86	108.7	106.8
for business	170.66	184.26	109.9	108.0
for private use	75.48	78.60	106.5	104.2
Domestic shipping	212.63	224.69	105.6	105.7
Aviation	0.69	0.75	108.9	109.1

Source: Kotsu Nenkan 1991.
Notes: *hundred million passengers per kilometre. †hundred million tons per kilometre.

It should be noted that the reduction of employees did not lead to a problem of unemployment in Japan. The JNR Settlement Corporation, under a special law designed to promote recruitment (1987), took care of the employment of those who had lost their jobs, the shortage of workers in a prosperous Japanese economy greatly assisting this. Though the special law ended in 1990, by that time the number of surplus workers had been reduced from

Table 5 Japan Railways: rural lines planned to be transformed

	*Transformed rural lines**		
	Bus	*Railway*	*Total*
First planned lines	22	18	40
Second planned lines	20	11	31
Third planned lines	3	9	12
Total	45	38	83

Source: The White Paper of Transportation 1990.
Note: *As at 1 April 1990.

about 19,000 in 1987 to about 1,000; these were finally dismissed by the corporation in that year.

Allocation of Resources

The division and reform have enabled JR to secure managerial autonomy to some extent and to reduce operating costs. Allocation of resources has become efficient due to retrenchment policies such as the revision of investment policy and the strategy of revitalizing manpower. Concerning the efficiency of allocation, the most important reform is that the adjustment policy of deficit rural lines, which the JNR was forced to keep on running, has been implemented under a special law designed to accelerate the reconstruction of JNR's management. According to this plan (see Table 5), 83 rural lines have been abolished and replaced by bus services or transferred to the third sector (mixed enterprise). The plan was enforced in 1983 under the special law relating to the reconstruction of JNR management. At the time of privatization 30 rural lines remained and these were not to be transferred. Later, the scheme was accelerated and the plan fully achieved in 1990.

Furthermore, it is important that the super-base structure ('base' means, essentially, the fixed capital such as railway lines, stations and railway lands; 'super' means the operations and services which use the 'base') has been separated clearly as seen in the case of the Shinkansen. The separation of ownership and use would not only make JR's management more efficient, but also avoid the risk of fixing capital for a long time.

The Japan Railway Construction Corporation (JRCC) might face a deterioration in its financial conditions, however, if it is unable to avoid political intervention. The JRCC has constructed new railway lines under various pressures, which were not necessarily viable. Although the deficit of the JRCC (¥4.5 trillion) was taken over by the JNRSC, the JRCC has reviewed its plan and strengthened its market behaviour by means of leasing its lines to the private railway companies. After privatization, the railway business, under the Railway Activity Act 1987, was divided into three kinds of enterprises (Type 1, Type 2,

Type 3) based on the separation of the super-base structure. As a result of this, new management forms (the third sector and so on) have arisen. Allocation of resources has become more efficient as a whole.

Equity

In the case of the railway industry, the equity can be examined in terms of fares and services. As for the former, JR maintains fares which are traditionally based on an equal nation-wide rate system (fare depends on distance travelled). This serves the public interest – a state which the government is determined should continue. Taking into consideration the fact that JR supplies a large number of people with stable and safe traffic services and that its dominant position, especially in the countryside, would allow it to abuse that position, it is natural that the Transport Ministry continues substantially to regulate JR in the field of fares etc. Otherwise, if JR fixed its fares freely in accordance with the fluctuations of demand (business cycle, season, regional conditions), some customers would become losers. Though the system of setting railway fares was changed to the permission system, by which the Department of Transport had to approve JNR fares, in effect the legal system has continued to work. Required to constrain the increase of fares, JR has attempted to gain profits by diversifying its business or by putting on extra trains.

As for the latter, the problem is related to the opportunity of enjoying a universal service. It can be said that universal service, including alternatives supplied by other means of transportation (for example bus), is almost guaranteed: the government subsidized the rural small private railway companies (¥1.0 billion), regional bus companies (¥10.4 billion), and the companies managed by the third sector (¥1.4 billion) in 1989. If the service of the Shinkansen express were included in a 'universal service', however, equity is not satisfied in the three islands. For the purpose of correcting this inequality, the new Shinkansen (the so-called Seibi Shinkansen), which was discontinued for a time, is to be constructed. In this, many politicians of the LDP and JSP have played an important role. None the less it is doubtful that the new Shinkansen will bring about profits to JR.

Generally, speaking, we can evaluate the consumer benefits positively. The services of passenger transport have been diversified in response to the demands of customers and shifted in accordance with the actual needs of the regional economies. The staff attitude towards customers has improved rapidly. The largest benefit for consumers is that JR has not raised train fares since the privatization. This has enabled JR to reduce the price gap in relation to the private railway companies and to recapture customers in urban areas.

Transformation of the System

The privatization did not cause much confusion in the market for land transportation. The transaction cost, which was accompanied by transforming the trade mechanism, has not been great – even if the costs of judicial cases and organizational reforms (managerial cost, retirement funds, etc.) were included.

Safety

With regard to safety, the number of railway accidents, especially those at crossing points which account for almost 90 per cent of all the accidents, has decreased gradually. This is due to the promotion of safety policy (for example, the improvement of railroad crossings) and technological progress.

The effect from the viewpoint of macroeconomics cannot be evaluated at the present time. Nevertheless, it should be noted that a range of rationalizations, especially the tariff policy and cost-reduction tactics, have had a good effect on the Japanese economy if we consider the fact that JR still constitutes one of the main industrial infrastructures.

The Unsolved Problems

The most difficult problem in privatizing the public sector is to harmonize economic efficiency with the public interest. External intervention, often in the name of the public interest, stifles efficiency and creates an irresponsible attitude towards profitability. Contrary to this, market economy, if it is implemented freely and thoroughly, could cause a market failure which damages the public interest.

The JNR's reform has overcome this dilemma to some degree. Under the leadership of Nakasone and Doko, the effort to reconcile the public interest with efficiency was pursued. Though the LDP supported this process, it did not forget to placate the JSP. Judging from the political side, JNR's privatization was a product of compromise between the government, the LDP, the business world (Keidanren), and the JSP.

This was the reason why the privatization did not lead to liberalization or deregulation in Japan. At the same time the problem casts a doubt over the future of JR if it remains unsolved. Competition should be promoted through deregulation. In order to compete with the private railway companies and other transport industries it is required that JR should be transformed into a number of complete private companies which make themselves responsible for their own management. In this respect we must pay attention to the continuous decline of JR's market share in relation to the competition with automobiles and aeroplanes.

JR's share of passenger transport has decreased annually and is likely to fall to under 20 per cent – what is worse, that of freight transport, despite a slight recovery since 1987, has been stagnant at the 4 per cent level (see Figure 5). If the Japanese economy should fall into recession in the near future, it is doubtful that JR could enhance market share by increasing volume.

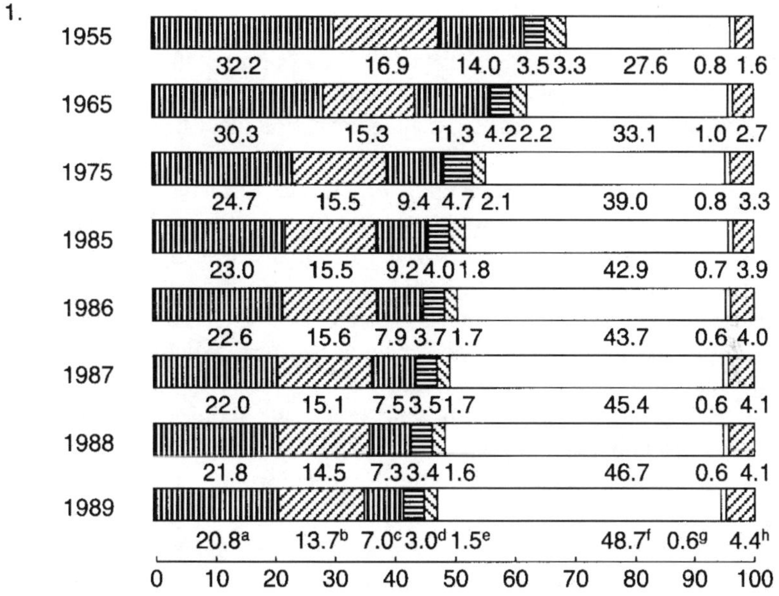

1 Domestic passenger transport (person/kilometre)
Source: Kotsu Nenkan 1991.
Notes: [a]JR; [b]Private railway companies; [c]Bus for business; [d]Bus for private use; [e]Automobile for business; [f]Automobile for private use; [g]Passenger boat; [h]Aviation.

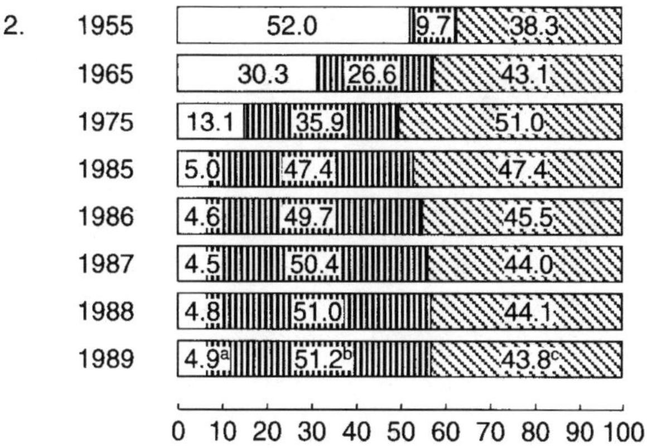

2 Domestic freight transport (ton/kilometre)
Source: Kotsu Nenkan 1991.
Notes: [a]Railway; [b]Automobile; [c]Domestic shipping.

Figure 5 Japan Railways: trend of market shares, 1955–89 (%)

The second remaining problem is related to long-term liabilities, which grow worse and worse. The White Paper on Transportation in 1990 proposed that JR should finalize privatization by tackling its long-term liabilities, as well as endeavouring to modernize management and clear the pension fund deficit.

Following this, the JNR Settlement Corporation reacted by developing various methods of selling railway lands (for example, including the introduction of a land-trust system). But these plans have not yet come to fruition.

The third problem, related to the sale of the state assets, is that the share sale of JR has not been realized on schedule because of the decline of the stock-market. Despite the market trend, however, it is important that the shares of JR Tokai and JR Higashi be sold as fast as possible. If this can't be achieved, the principal–agent relationship would not change in the direction of enhancing efficiency and of promoting deregulation.

Last, we need to understand a style specific to JNR's privatization. The delay of JR's transformation into private companies caused some misunderstandings in this respect. Some economists, who refute the introduction of a 'profitability' concept into the public sector, regard it as not *Mineika* but *Shieika* (complete ownership and control by private capital). Others, who support Thatcher-style privatization, regard it as *Tokushu Kaishaka* (changing to a special company only).

The former group of economists neglect the public character of a network industry such as that of JR. The JR companies would be regulated by the government even if the necessary conditions of the privatization (share sale, control of shareholders) were satisfied completely. The latter group of economists disregarded the fact that the shares of JR will be floated and sold out to the public in the near future, interpreting the meaning of the privatization only in a narrow sense. Certainly the privatization of JNR was not accompanied by selling its shares at once, and lacked some factors (liberalization or deregulation) in comparison with a Thatcher-style privatization. In spite of this difference, JNR's reform should be interpreted as a Japanese-style privatization where the concept of public interest (in particular equity) was thought much of and share sale was decided to be postponed deliberately till after the success of management (see Table 6). The latter school of thought has a fault in that JNR's privatization is attempted to be understood by applying the criteria of Britain directly to it.

This chapter has presented an opinion founded on the basis of several years' observation. If we try to estimate what developments are likely to occur in the long term, the conclusion may be different from this. In fact, two serious problems which may cause some concern about the future of JR happened in autumn 1991. The first is that the Shinkansen Holding Corporation was dissolved and absorbed into a new organization named the Railway Development Fund (*Tetsudo Seibi Kikin*) on 1 October 1991. It is

Table 6 Differences between the old system and the new system of Japan National Railways

Item	*Old system*	*New system*
Management form	Public corporation	• Special companies (six passenger companies, one freight company) • Shinkansen Holding Corporation • The other private successors of JNR's businesses • JNR Settlement Corporation
Investment	All capital invested by the government	As for special companies, the capital of which was invested in kind by JNR Settlement Corporation. However, JR will be transformed into purely private companies through share-sales to the public as soon as the management is stabilized.
Scope of business	• Railway business • Ferry business connected with railway • Oil-pipeline business where JNR made use of its railway lands • Generation and transmission of electric power • Incidental business • Other business	• Passenger (Freight) railway business • Incident business • Transportation by automobile (bus) • Travel agent • Other business Some businesses related to JNR were transferred to the private sector through divestment.
Regulation	• Budget decided through the Diet • President of JNR was nominated by the Prime Minister, and commissioners of JNR–RSC were appointed by the Secretary of the Transport Ministry • Authorization of constructing the new railroad etc. came under JNR Act.	• Approval of business plan • Approval of election of a representative director and inspectors • Approval of the businesses and activities under the Railway Activity Law Regulation for JR is to be at the same level as that of private railway companies.
Fares and tariff	Principle of legal price system (by 1977)	Approval system
Labour relations	Application of National Public Service Law	Application of the so-called Three Labour Laws (the Labour Standard Law, the Trade Union Law, and the Labour Mediation Law)

feared that this reform, motivated by the construction of Seibi Shinkansen, may impede efficiency by destroying the clear-cut separation which is the main feature of the super-base structure. The second problem is that the largest trade union (JR Soren) was disbanded, with a new militant trade union which insisted on strikes in the wage struggle (*shunto*) being created. This factor will also have a negative influence on the performance of JR's management. It can be concluded that the success of the privatization will depend on the extent to which the JR can solve the above difficulties in the early 1990s.

Acknowledgements

This chapter would not have been completed without the co-operation of Ian Smith (visiting researcher of the Institute of Business Research, Daito University) and Etsuo Kozawa (Associate Professor of Waseda University).

Bibliography

Calder, K. E. (1990) 'Public corporations and privatization in modern Japan', in E. N. Suleiman and J. Watebury (eds), *The Political Economy of Public Sector Reform and Privatization*, Boulder, Colo.: Westview Press.

Gow, I. (1989) 'Government–industry relations: Japanese-style public corporations and privatization', *Japan Forum* 1(2).

Hirotaka Yamauchi (1990) 'Kokutetesu Kaikaku to Atarashii Tetsudo Seisaku', in Toshihiko Hayashi (ed.) *Koeki Jigyo to Kiseikanwa*, Tokyo: Keizai Shinposha.

Hurl, B. (1988) *Privatization and the Public Sector*, London: Heinemann.

JNR-SC (1990) *Nihon Kokuyu Tetsudo Seisan Jigyodan* '90, JNR-SC.

Kay, J., Mayer, C. and Thompson, D. (1986) *Privatization and Regulation*, Oxford: Clarendon Press.

Kazuaki Tanaka and Masahiro Horie, *Mineika to Kiseikanwa*, Kokyo Sentaku no Kenkyu, no. 16 (1990), no. 17 (1991).

Kotsu Nenkan, Kotsu Kyoryokukai, 1987, 1988, 1989, 1990, 1991.

Rinji Gyosei Chosakai (1982) *Rincho Kihon Teigen*, Gyosei Kanri Kenkyu Centre.

Seizaburo Sato (1985) *The Experience of Japan's Privatization: Policies, Methods and Procedures*, Manila: Asian Development Bank.

Unyusho, *Unyu Hakusho* (The White Paper on Transportation), 1987, 1988, 1989, 1990.

Veljanovsky, C. (ed.) (1989) *Privatisation and Competition*, London: Institute of Economic Affairs.

Vickers, J. and Yarrow, G. (1988) *Privatisation: An Economic Analysis*, Cambridge, Mass.: MIT Press.

Yataro Fujii (1989) 'Tetsudo', in Masahiro Okuno *et al.* (ed.), *Koutsu Seisaku no Keizai gaku*, Nihon Keizai Shinbunsha.

Yukihide Okano (1989) 'Kisei to Kigyo Katsudo' (Tokyou University), *Keizaigaku Ronshu* 55(2).

Made in the USA
Monee, IL
12 November 2026

c4f4943c-bee4-4967-94d3-43bb60f4cf50R01